Helen Keller

A Timeline of Her Life

Doug Baldwin

ISBN: 978-1-7369953-1-0

Book design by Sarah E. Holroyd
(https://sleepingcatbooks.com)
The cover and interior layout of this book were designed by Sarah Holroyd. Sarah's work is excellent (wonderful), I appreciate her many talents, and I am proud of our longstanding professional relationship. Sarah is the owner of Sleeping Cat Books, an author services company which provides copyediting, proofreading, and print/ebook services to independent authors. Sarah also runs Sleeping Cat Press, which releases bilingual English-French editions and multi-author anthologies.

Cover art & illustrations by Terry LeBarr, Swanton, OH
(gonefishn@yahoo.com)
The great cover illustrations for all my books were designed by my friend Terry LeBarr in Swanton, Ohio. I am delighted by Terry's drawings and I am proud of her important contribution to the Helen Keller story. The cover of this book depicts what Terry calls a Personalized Typography; symbolic images woven into a name. I was delighted when Terry created this design. The first thing I noticed was that the famous water pump was the spine of the H in Helen's name—how appropriate! Here is how Terry explains Helen's "Typography:"

The H
We start where Helen's cognitive enlightenment started, at the famous water pump. The water is overflowing onto the canvas, symbolizing all that water has come to represent for humanity, the life affirming essence that enables all lifeforms to grow. The pump leans against a post with Ivy wrapped around it. This symbolizes Helen's Home, her beginning at the Ivy Green homestead in Tuscumbia, Alabama. The keyhole and key represent Helen's awareness that keys open all kinds of real and metaphorical doors. The key is also an allusion to Helen's playful Humor—she locked her mother in a pantry and sat on the steps at Ivy Green laughing to herself. She also locked Anne Sullivan in a room—an act that holds many layers of symbolism. The dog represents all of Helen's beloved dogs and suggests the loyalty and love human beings share with

their animals, especially with emotionally-attuned dogs. This drawing is of a Great Dane—at one time, Helen had eleven Great Dane puppies.

The E

The E represents Education. Helen Keller's books and all the books written about her are symbolized in this typography. Books were key to Helen's mental development; she loved her braille books; reading was her passion. Helen typed on a regular typewriter as well as brailled using what came to be called the Perkin's Braller. She could also sign her name using standard English. This is represented by the paper, ink well, and pen. I embedded the year the drawing was created, 2021.

The L

The letter L has a double meaning. It symbolizes Language and it stands for Love. Helen is shown as a small girl learning fingerspelling, which will become her portal into the worlds of language and communication. Helen is with her young teacher, Anne Sullivan, a woman who will teach Helen about love and dedication. Teacher and student are touching a youthful tree, while sunlight playfully blesses them from above. The tree and the sunshine represent Helen's love of nature and her subtle connection with the esoteric soul of all living creatures. The tree also stands for textures, smells, and the calming influence of nature. The sunshine symbolizes warmth which brought forth Helen Keller's bright smile. To the right of the tree is a darkness, a black portal through which Helen emerged after she discovered Love and Language. The L is tall and central in the image because Helen Keller's message to humankind was Love and Service. As a Swedenborgian Christian, Helen's mission was to insist that Love stand tall and reside within the heart of the human species.

The E

The second E stands for Eloquence. The podium represents all the speeches that Helen gave; she and Annie were stars on the Vaudeville stage, they participated in Chautauqua lectures all across the United States, and Helen spoke passionately to audiences in many countries. The luggage shows her love of travel. Helen, Annie, and Polly Thomson had a hunger for travel; they were on the road for months every year. In the body of the E is the shield of Harvard's Radcliffe College where Helen graduated cum laude in 1904—she was just 24. Below the Radcliffe shield are the flags of the United States, Alabama, and Japan; Helen had a special relationship with the people of Japan. Helen's love for dogs is again depicted. Shown here are Sir Thomas, a gift from Helen's Radcliffe classmates, and Kamikaze-Go, an Akita, a gift from the Japanese government. Helen's Akita was the first of its breed to come to America. At the top of the E is Helen's graduation cap. Strolling from the E are Helen and Anne with their traveling cloaks and bags. After graduation, Helen and Annie began their years of traveling. I added flowers because Helen loved flowers and plants.

The N

Helen found joy and peace in Nature, so the N represents her love of the outdoors. Helen loved walking along the ancient stone walls of New England, one branch of which meandered behind her house in Wrentham, Massachusetts. She explored the walls with her fingers on her daily walks. Helen liked the thought of fairies and elves among the trees. Celebrating this esoteric side of Helen Keller, I added the elf at the base of the tree and the fairy hovering above. I had read that Helen loved the rain, so flowing off the edge of the tree I drew the rain blessing a stretch of stone wall. The wall contains moss and bugs, which she would find as her fingers danced over the ancient rocks. There are secrets, subtle voices, hidden in the stones, which Helen could detect. She wrote about the famous stone walls of New England in her book The Song of the Stone Wall (1910).

CONTENTS

This Timeline contains commentary about books and articles, indicated with italics.

TIMELINE OF HELEN KELLER'S LIFE

I created this timeline as a companion volume to my book *The Esoteric Helen Keller* (2021). The timeline began as a compilation of research notes, a way to understand Helen Keller's life from a historic perspective. I had originally intended to include the timeline as a chapter at the end of *The Esoteric Helen Keller*, but it quickly grew too large to fit within a single volume. I did not want to abandon all this work, mostly because I enjoyed what I had accomplished. I also thought it might help future researchers see Helen's life from a relative perspective. In a way, the timeline tells Helen's life story again (as others have done) but embeds her story in history.

Deaf-blind Helen Keller was the so-called *miracle* brought about by the devotional work of Anne Sullivan who became known as the *miracle worker*. Their story is a product of the time when they lived. In our era, the Keller/Sullivan saga has become a global treasure, a much-celebrated hero's journey. The lessons for humanity which Helen Keller left us are timeless; her words will echo long into the future.

As I encountered the dates during which Helen published her books and articles, I commented on her ideas and on the contents of her publications. I also reviewed some of the major books about Helen Keller and Anne Sullivan as they were published. Therefore, there are book reviews embedded in the timeline.

I also did not want to lose my original intention: to study Helen Keller's unique mind. The companion book to this text, *The Esoteric Helen Keller*, is essentially an in-depth study of the evolution of a remarkable deaf-blind mind. Where I could in this timeline, I referred to my esoteric theme. In addition, all my books focus—in various ways—on the evolution of human consciousness. The human mind has been steadily evolving in parallel with an exponential explosion of technologies. I commented on the evolution of the human mind and the evolution of technology where it seemed fitting to the dialogue.

The timeline started as a list of events, but then became a compilation of potential research directions, which I slowly attended to as the months passed. So, for example, when I read that John Macy (Anne Sullivan's husband) died in 1932 (age 55), I wondered about his life beyond the years when he lived with Helen and Annie. Then, to my surprise, as I researched John Macy's fascinating life, I found that he had been born not far from where I write these words; he was born in Wayne County in Detroit, Michigan (I am in Saginaw, Michigan). Then I found information on Ancestry.com that John Macy—after he and Sullivan had split up—had a deaf-mute mistress (Myla) and with her he had a child (Margaret Briggs). John Macy even dedicated one of his books to Margaret. There seems to be no trace in genealogical records of the deaf-mute mother and the child that John Macy had to raise after the mother's untimely death.

The little vignette above about John Macy and his deaf-mute mistress is just one of many interesting events that appeared as this timeline was being crafted. The timeline took me down many wonderful side trails (off the main path), often leaving more mysteries than discoveries. Every date below became an opportunity to flesh out the Helen Keller story. I also had a chance to reflect on what was happening historically from year-to-year. Helen Keller lived through two world wars, the Korean War, and through half of the war in Vietnam (1955 to 1975). She saw the great depression, the advent of television, computers, photography, the telephone, antibiotics, and the rise of the information age. Helen Keller weathered the storms of history quite well, often speaking with great eloquence about historical events.

At one point in my research, I drew a rough chart showing the parallel timelines for key figures in history. I did this initially because I knew that Helen lived through—and was influenced by—the Transcendentalist movement in the United States. I wanted to see how the lives of the Transcendentalists (for example, Ralph Waldo Emerson, Henry David Thoreau, and Walt Whitman) overlapped. I was somewhat startled when I viewed this comparative timeline comparing Helen's contemporaries.

For example, I had not realized that Helen Keller (1880), Albert Einstein (1879), and Carl Jung (1875) were born within a few years of each other. Helen outlived both Einstein and Jung. Ralph Waldo Emerson, the Father of American Transcendentalism, died two years after Helen was born, in 1882. Emerson was psychologist William James' godfather. William James (1842–1910) and Rudolf Steiner (1861–1925) also lived during Helen's lifetime and James was her friend. Walt Whitman (1819–1892) was an elder stateman as Helen was entering her teenage years. Fredrich Nietzsche died when Helen was twenty. With the possible exception of Albert Einstein, all these historically significant thinkers were influenced by Emanuel Swedenborg, who begins this timeline, moving the beginning of the Helen Keller saga to the 1600s. Einstein left no comments concerning Swedenborg, although it is hard to accept that he did not cross paths with Emanuel Swedenborg's ideas. Swedenborg was the polymath and mystic whose writings framed Helen Keller's spiritual insights.

~

As I was doing my research, I often found fragments about Helen Keller's life but could not see where they might fit into *The Esoteric Helen Keller*. This timeline turned out to be the perfect place to preserve these tiny (totally random) gems. Here are a few:

- According to her own account, Helen could laugh and cry naturally. She made sounds and "word elements" even after becoming deaf and blind. She told her friend Georgette Leblanc that "I weep as much as the others, but I believe it to be good for the soil, like rain. All my visions are born of love and poetry; and those flowers cannot bloom without tears."
- Helen liked to row a boat and she was a strong swimmer. Near their home in Wrentham, Massachusetts, Helen and Annie often rented a cabin on Lake Wollomonopoag. Helen and Annie also swam in the Atlantic Ocean at Sophia Hopkin's beach house on Cape Cod. After swimming in the Atlantic for the first time, and after being dunked by a big wave, Helen exclaimed "Who put salt in the water!"
- Helen learned to ice skate in New York City.
- Helen also loved to ride a tandem bike because "speed intoxicated

her and put her in high spirits," according to her friend Georgette Leblanc.

- Helen could embroider, knit, and do every kind of needlework.
- Helen would often play cards, checkers, or chess in the evening with Annie, Polly or Herbert (their handyman). Her greatest pleasure, however, was reading her braille books (even in bed).
- The blind Greek poet Homer was one of her favorite authors. She had a medallion of Homer on the wall of her study.
- Helen loved to study philosophy. In her office were books by Shakespeare, Horace, Aeschylus, Virgil, Cicero, Plato, and Pascal. She read the philosophers in their native language: Goethe, Schiller, and Heine in German; Maeterlinck in French; and the classical writers she read in their original Greek and Latin.
- Helen is known for her love of dogs but at one time she had a cat named Topsy and a rabbit whose name is lost to history. When they lived in Wrentham, Massachusetts with John Macy, the household had chickens, horses, and at one point, eleven Great Dane puppies.
- Helen often cleaned up after meals and washed and dried dishes.
- Friends (mostly John Macy) built a thousand-foot-long fence (handrail) that Helen could follow to explore the environment around her house in Wrentham, Massachusetts. Later, in her Connecticut home (Arcan Ridge), her walking trail—complete with rails and ropes—was built by Helen's handyman Herbert Haas.
- Helen was selected to represent Alabama on its 2003 state quarter, and on October 7, 2009, a bronze statue depicting seven-year-old Helen at the water pump replaced that of J. L. M. Curry in Statuary Hall in the U.S. Capitol building.
- Helen used ropes while swimming so she could find the dock. Ropes also led into the woods and between landmarks—for example, ropes went from the cabin to the lake when they were vacationing.
- Helen Keller's first word learned through fingerspelling (according to her) was "doll."
- Helen could dance in harmony with the rhythms she felt through the floor, through the air, and while touching a musical instrument or radio. She could keep time with the music.
- Helen could sing and play the piano—not well, of course, but she

tried everything. She was exposed to singing and the piano when she was studying how to speak at a school for the deaf.

- Helen could touch an instrument while it was being played (a piano or violin, for example) and keep a beat with her hand. She could sometimes even determine what composition was being played.

- The first sentence Helen learned to speak was "It is warm." She started her lessons by first learning to say the word "it."

- Both schools for the blind and schools for the deaf were instrumental in Helen's development. It is a misconception that her training came only from schools for the blind.

- Helen loved stage plays and movies. She says, "People sometimes express surprise that a deaf-blind person can get any pleasure in the cinema. Polly reads me the titles, spells the dialogue, and describes facial expressions and the costumes, which is pretty rapid work."

- Helen, Annie, and Polly got the travel bug (a compulsive need to travel) when Helen was still a young woman. They sailed on luxury liners across the ocean and then took trains and private automobiles to explore different nations. They eventually visited 39 countries, giving speeches, meeting dignitaries, and fundraising for the blind, deaf, and deaf-blind. The trio was on the road for months at a time.

- Polly, Helen, and Herbert Hass traveled to Europe in 1946 on an overseas flight, the first time any of them had been on such a big airliner—the flight typically took over 17 hours. On this trip, Helen met Pope Pius XII and later Queen Elizabeth. Helen also went to Athens and toured the ancient ruins.

- One of Helen's favorite countries was Scotland. Polly Thomson was born in Scotland and had family there—she frequently went home to visit. Helen's home in Connecticut was named after a location in the Scottish Highlands called Arcan Ridge. The American Foundation for the Blind Helen Keller digital archives contains a photograph of the stone house in Rosshire, South Arcan, Scotland where Helen Keller, Annie Sullivan, and Polly Thomson stayed in 1932.

- When asked how she felt about growing old, Helen said: "Never count how many years you have, but how many interests."

If you Google "What did Helen Keller like to eat?" you get the message that she loved hotdogs. This is a reference to a comment made by Helen's nurse Winnie Corbally. Helen was in her eighties at the time. Corbally's comment was recorded In Joseph Lash's *Helen and Teacher* (1980):

> Miss Helen was a rogue. . . . We had oodles of fun. We would go to a hot-dog stand. Polly Thomson would turn in her grave. She would never allow hot dogs in the house. But Miss Helen loved them. "Don't forget the mustard," she would say.

Besides hotdogs, I found many more references to her food preferences. Here are a few from random locations in *Helen Keller's Journal*, published in 1938:

- In her travel journal in 1936, Helen wrote, "Today I had a lunch of frankfurters and sauerkraut—the first meal I have eaten with any relish in many weeks."
- After all that activity we came home very hungry, and I had one of my favorite lunches—a mixed salad and biscuits with Camembert cheese. I eat salads a great deal, not only because I enjoy them, but also to keep my figure. Which alas! It is difficult . . .
- Quoting Shakespeare: "my eyes are still "seeled up" by drowsiness, but a cup of hot coffee has waked me sufficiently to write." . . . [Helen loved a cup of coffee].
- English bacon and eggs for breakfast—the first I have had since arriving in London, and how good they tasted! . . .
- [I am] with Dr. Love alone at breakfast this morning. When I entered, he jumped up, cut my bacon and eggs for me and patted my hand by way of coaxing an appetite. But with him I need no coaxing, the eggs are so good and the fire so warm; and his terse, penetrating comments on the news from the *Glasgow Herald* render breakfast an event in itself . . .
- Enjoyed the delicious melon and toast with Dundee marmalade which I always order in New York. The wonderful coffee . . .
- Haggis for dinner today. What a succulent, tasty, satisfying dish it is! . . .
- When we left Havre, I solemnly declared to Polly, hand on my heart, that I was going to diet, but the dinner tonight—mushroom soup, fish melting in the mouth, meat smothered in juices I had

not dreamed of, and Crepe Suzette—knocked over my good intentions like ninepins!

The following is quoted from the September 1968 special issue of *Outlook for the Blind* about Helen Keller. It is not clear who is traveling with Helen and Polly (and writing this reflection), but probably an American Foundation for the Blind (AFB) board member.

"In 1951 I traveled to Florida by train with Miss Keller and Miss Thomson. We were going to Daytona Beach, where Miss Keller was to receive the Shotwell Award of the American Association of Workers for the Blind. During the day she insisted that the door to her compartment be left open and minded not at all the gazes of other passengers on their way to the dining car. While by no means a heavy drinker, she did on occasion enjoy a beer or highball. And a bottle of scotch, ice bucket, glasses, peanuts, and potato chips were there for all passersby to see. Hypocrites they were not. Neither Helen nor Polly would give in to the pleas of some of us that they be concealed. Lest our concern seem excessive, I add here that at one time a national temperance organization vented strong and public criticism of Miss Keller because a profile of her in a Texas newspaper included a passing reference to the fact that she occasionally took a drink."

~

Here is Helen Keller speaking about friendships:

So long as the memory of certain beloved friends lives in my heart, I shall say that life is good.

As I wrote this book, I felt like Helen was a lifelong friend, and that Anne Sullivan had my back as I struggled to keep my prose clear. Helen died in 1968 when I was just 23; I was studying for my doctorate at the Illinois College of Optometry at the time. Helen was a contemporary of mine—it is too bad that I did not have the foresight to seek her out; just to be in an audience and gaze on her from a distance would have been a powerful and wonderful memory.

I hope that your emotions will be impacted by Helen's story as mine have, and that Helen Keller, Annie Sullivan, Polly Thomson, Sophia Hopkins, Kate Keller, John Hitz, John Macy, Mark Twain, William James and many other special friends of Helen's will change your life for the better as you become intimate with their stories and struggles.

~

I had deliberately ignored "Helen Keller jokes," as I discovered them online. However, I have a feeling that Helen would have been okay with American humor and probably would have laughed heartily (at times) when people poked fun at her. There are many Helen Keller jokes, however, in my opinion, most are tasteless and cruel. Here are a few that I found less offensive:

- If Helen Keller fell in the woods, would she make a sound?
- How do you torture Helen Keller? Glue doorknobs to the walls.
- How did Helen Keller burn her fingers? She was trying to read the waffle iron.
- What do you call a tennis match between Helen Keller and Stevie Wonder? Endless love.

There is a hairbrained movement on social media (Tik Tok) claiming Helen Keller never existed, or could not possibly have existed, or is a virtual reality hoax, just like moon landings and pandemics. People who believe conspiracy "theories," who reject scientific evidence, have (in my opinion) unevolved levels of consciousness, and they often lack empathy—on a kinder note, it could well be that these conspiracy believers are just young individuals with evolving souls who have temporarily veered off course. I wrote about levels of consciousness in *The Esoteric Helen Keller*. Helen was a remarkably evolved soul, *a very real*, down-to earth American; her intellect and spirituality went beyond what many people in her era could comprehend.

EMBEDDED, EXPONENTIAL, ENLIGHTENED

If we stand on the moon and look at our home—a blue dot suspended in space, the third planet from the sun—we can get an overhead view of evolution from the beginning of cellular life. With our moon-scopes and our vast knowledge, we can watch the unfolding of consciousness in minute detail from the moment cells proliferated to our modern time. From our distant, overhead perspective, the miracle of human life can appear to us along a timeline.

Helen Keller lived for almost 88 years. She was born in 1880 and died in 1968. What can we see from our moon perspective that will help us understand the world she experienced? How will we make sense of all the data, all the evidence we have gathered? Let us begin by acknowledging four clearly observable phenomenon.

The first thing we notice from our overhead perspective, is that changes on Earth are *embedded*. Everything is part of a vast network. Everything affects and alters everything else. Every movement has a consequence. Change causes more change. Networks produce more networks. Everything is flowing, nothing ever stands still. This interrelatedness, this flowing inter-dependence, the embedded nature of our reality, is the first phenomenon that becomes obvious as we survey the timeline of life on Earth. What we believe and how we behave, individually and collectively, matters because we are part of the flow of life; we are embedded in our time, surrounded by others.

But the ever-present flow of change on Earth is not chaotic, not random. **There are patterns hidden in the flow**—we can pick out these repeating patterns as we watch consciousness emerge along the timeline. Hermetic (esoteric) wisdom has passed down the mother of all patterns: *As Above So Below*—in other words, as we notice patterns on one scale of observation (microscopic, for example), so, also, we see the same patterns on other scales of observation (macroscopic). Knowing this Hermetic wisdom gives us a tool to guide our research and our thinking; if we find a pattern, we know to look at larger and smaller scales for duplicate patterns. Patterns, trends, and trajectories have been part of the fabric of life as consciousness has unfolded through the ages.

The flow does not feel random. From the moon looking down, there seems to be a plan embedded in the magic of our existence. Consciousness seems to be driving a great migration. This endless march of the human species seems to need each individual's subjective mind to play a part.

The third thing we notice—besides embeddedness and repeating patterns—is that *the speed of change is exponential*. Something is causing an acceleration; the flow of change is unfolding faster and faster. Look at the well-documented speed of acceleration in the universe. As above—the universe expanding—so below, everything on Earth changing, faster and faster. Everything is connected, so acceleration over there causes acceleration over here (as above, so below). Plainly, technology has an exponential trajectory—we have the evidence before us on both cosmic and minute scales.

Parallel to the pace of technological change, *the evolution of the human species* is also flowing with ever greater speed. Consequently, human consciousness is changing at an accelerating pace (my speculation). Helen Keller's lifetime took place as technology had reached a threshold; she died just before we reached what is called *the knee of the curve* (this occurred in the 1990s), when the flatline of "progress" turned sharply upward and headed for the heavens.

The fourth thing we notice is that there is a *balance between destruction and creativity*—the old must die to make room for the ever-arriving new. Dead leaves are the foundation upon which living forests flourish. The human species has always had to choose between acting hatefully, destructively, or acting with love and creativity. What we witness from our moon base is that the potential for mass destruction—powerful enough to end the human species—has been, up until now, balanced by a flow toward *enlightenment*. We have the potential to turn the Earth into Hell, a fiery mass that consumes all life forms, or we can turn the Earth into Nirvana, Paradise, Heaven. Hellish forces ebb and flow with Heavenly forces. This oscillating pattern seems to be a foundational principle of life—God and the Devil validate each other's reality; one cannot exist without the other, or so it seems.

Helen Keller was a crusader for Heaven, for Enlightenment. She was an optimist and she trusted that Love would win the final battle. She directed her energy, for a lifetime, toward kindness and service. Helen emerged into our collective consciousness because of all the events that came before. She is now busy influencing all that comes after her.

Before I continue, I need to confess that this is a shamelessly Western perspective, as if—from our moon view—I was only surveying one hemisphere of the earth. I have focused on European and American perspectives because that is the embedded world that Helen Keller was born into—she was a child of Western history (as am I). The task of previewing the whole planet was too daunting, so I narrowed my focus to what I knew.

Timeline Themes

I could have picked any number of historical themes to follow as I crafted this timeline, but there are a few themes that seemed especially relevant to Helen Keller's life. She was, for example, an extraordinary example of humanity, a spokesperson for the entire human species. Who, we can ask, were a few other great minds who walked through life in parallel with Helen Keller's life (1880–1968)? Who are some other miracle people, extraordinary people, who also spoke for humanity? I explored this question in *Theme One* for the timeline, recording *other historical pathfinders and leaders* who might have influenced (or been influenced by) Helen Keller. Helen was a good friend to several of these great minds, including Mark Twain, William James, and Alexander Graham Bell.

While Helen Keller was alive, a patriarchy was firmly entrenched in the United States. During her life, she would observe this male-dominated mindset (on a global scale) cause two world wars and, consequently murder at least 100 million human beings. As a woman, Helen Keller was also a victim of institutional (political and economic) "slavery;" women had few legal rights during her youth; they could not own land, could not vote, and could not file for divorce. Helen fought alongside her feminist sisters in the battle to overthrow stagnant masculine mindsets. Although she and her fellow suffragettes eventually won the battles, one after another, the patriarchal problem is still with us. The *evolution of freedom* is *Theme Two* in the timeline.

It is hard to track all the times European nations declared war on each other. War has been a cultural constant in the Western world for centuries. This *war culture* was alive and active during Helen Keller's entire lifetime and she opposed the dark side of the Warrior mind with passion. She was an anti-war pacifist, which was not a popular position to take during her lifetime. She could see that soldiers were victims of this primitive mentality, and she visited the wounded warriors after both world wars. There is no reason to trust that our age is any different than Helen's when it comes to hostilities between tribal cultures—just as there are minds that cannot shake prejudice, there are minds that cling to hatred and violence. *War, violence, hatred, and destruction is Theme Three*—it is not hard to find hatred and mayhem arising repeatedly, century after century.

Recent estimates suggest that knowledge is doubling every 12 hours. Therefore, twice a day, our databases swell with new information. The data we use to make decisions is now overflowing the human brain's capacity to process the flood of change. The unceasing march of *knowledge and technology* is *Theme Four* of the timeline.

The evolution of philosophy is Theme Five. Every century was marked by one or more brilliant thinkers who helped to define Western civilization. These are the scholars who had an impact on the future and on Helen Keller's evolving mind. Helen read the original works of the greatest Western philosophers when she was at Radcliffe college. Essentially, philosophers study the evolution and functioning of the human mind, and, therefore, they explore the nature of consciousness. There is a parallel timeline that tracks the evolution of consciousness as the sophistication of philosophy evolved.

350 Unique Years

You can sense something momentous happening from century-to-century, then from decade-to-decade, and now, in our era, massive changes are occurring yearly, even monthly. The media has historically helped identify important people, recording their names and stores. This intense recording and remembering of our collective past began arguably in the 1600s, when the ability to mass produce written material became commonplace. Reading and writing (language in symbol form) changed the way the human mind evolved. The rapid evolution of the human mind accelerated in parallel with accelerating technology and with the easy sharing of knowledge. Consequently, the number of individuals with remarkable minds has dramatically increased as the decades have unfolded.

The evolution of media technologies has resulted in a cataloguing of cultural pioneers in many professions. For example, we venerate scientists like Albert Einstein and Isaac Newton, philosophers like Nietzsche and Goethe, and exemplary psychologists like Carl Jung and Sigmund Freud. However, a time came, in the mid-1900s perhaps, when too many great minds existed simultaneously to be recorded, honored, and placed in the public eye. It has gotten harder and harder to keep track of pioneering breakthroughs in all disciplines—pioneers in all the professions are simply coming onto the scene too fast to be acknowledged. In the 21st century, as I write these words, we have moved beyond the Era of Individual Genius to the Era of Teamwork; *Genius Teams* of experts are driving innovations at lightning speed.

There was a time from about 1600 to 1800 when Renaissance Men could learn all the knowledge that had accumulated in their lifetime. This was a golden era when we could name the greatest scientists, greatest novelists, most esteemed philosophers, most heroic soldiers, most charismatic political leaders, and most influential religious teachers. However, in our era, knowledge is doubling monthly; there is no way we can venerate a select few from the onrush of brilliance that is arising in our time. People like Helen Keller were celebrated and worshipped in the golden era of veneration, but people like Daniel Kish, for example—who are just as remarkable as Helen Keller and Anne Sullivan—are not seen at all by most of the public. Stories about Daniel's accomplishments (for example)—like the accomplishments of so many other remarkable human beings—are buried in an avalanche of ever-increasing knowledge, accumulating in ever proliferating media outlets. Daniel Kish is the subject of the second volume of *Knights for the Blind in the Battle against Darkness.*

What we are witnessing in this timeline, about Helen Keller's remarkable life, is a unique period in history in which it was possible to single out a select few individuals as worthy of veneration. I suggest that this peak of hero-worship lasted from about 1600 to 1950. In our modern world, fame lasts only briefly and not much fuss is made over individual breakthroughs. If the media does notice, the fuss lasts only a few days, or only a few hours, and then we quickly move on to our next media fix; "breaking news" is constant and we filter most of it out as irrelevant to our everyday lives. We are also forgetting at an accelerating pace. Our minds cannot store all that impinges on consciousness. This ubiquitous forgetting has serious side-affects, especially as we forget our emotions and spiritual moments.

We can if we want, make a list of people (experts, leaders) *who influenced our own lives.* Other people would agree or disagree with our list, but, for sure, we would have left out unsung geniuses, dedicated saints, and many Workers of the Undercurrent who made unseen but profound contributions to humanity. These pioneers were not lone wolves remaking the world; they were each surrounded by teams of fellow explorers without whom great contributions could never have manifested. Helen Keller emerged from such a dedicated team of friends and relatives.

1688: THE BIRTH OF EMANUEL SWEDENBORG

Important Pathfinders: 1600 to 1700

As the 1600s were ending, the world saw the birth of Emanuel Swedenborg, an extraordinary spiritual leader whose words and life transformed the heart and mind of Helen Keller. Swedenborg was born January 29, 1688 in Stockholm, Sweden. He became a Renaissance Man, a prolific author, and—like Helen Keller—a Spiritual Prodigy. Over his long life, Swedenborg gained a vast multi-disciplinary base of knowledge in the sciences, in Christian theology, and in philosophy. He was also a mystic who came to be revered by many of the world's greatest artists and thinkers, including William Blake, Carl Jung, Ralph Waldo Emerson, and Helen Keller. His books still influence generations. In her book *My Religion* (1927), Helen wrote this about Swedenborg (referring to his books):

> When I began [reading] *Heaven and Hell*, I was as little aware of the new joy coming into my life as I had been years before when I stood on the piazza steps awaiting my teacher . . . Here was a faith that emphasized what I felt so keenly—the separateness between soul and body, between the realm I could picture as a whole, and the chaos of fragmentary things and irrational contingencies that my limited senses met at every turn. I let myself go, as happy healthy youth will, and tried to puzzle out the long sentences and weighty words of the Swedish sage . . .

The words "Love" and "Wisdom" seemed to caress my fingers from paragraph to paragraph and these two words released in me new forces to stimulate my somewhat indolent nature and urge me forward evermore . . . I was not "religious" in the sense of practicing ritual, but happy, because I saw God altogether lovely, after the shadows cast upon his image by the harsh creeds or warring sects and religions. The Word of God, freed from the blots and stains of barbarous creeds, has been at once the joy and good of my life.

The "barbarous creeds" still exist on our fragile planet, and Love and Wisdom are still being assaulted by warring religious sects. We still need Helen Keller's courage and optimism to guide us through the fearful realities; and we still acknowledge and honor her chosen sage, Emanuel Swedenborg.

On April 23, 1616, the world lost William Shakespeare. Helen Keller and Anne Sullivan admired Shakespeare's work; they were influenced by the great man, especially by his remarkable wizardry with the English language. Scientists Galileo Galilei (1564–1642) and Johannes Kepler (1571–1630) also died in this century.

Leaders in the 1600s (Thomas Hobbes, for example) championed Democracy and the importance of individual liberties alongside the right of governments to decide laws and policies. Sir Francis Bacon popularized the scientific method, emphasizing reason and empirical evidence. Political thinkers, such as John Locke developed the foundational ideals of Democracy. Art and music had a Golden Age at the beginning of the Baroque period (1600–1750) in Europe.

From our overhead view, we can see that the 1600s brought us the scientific method (the dawn of science), the first glimmers of the Industrial Revolution, the rise of Democratic values (the seed of future Democracies), and a Golden Age in music and art. All these revolutions were occurring despite 100 years of constant warfare.

Freedom: 1600 to 1700

About a month after Swedenborg's birth, on February 18, 1688, in Germantown, Pennsylvania, The Religious Society of Friends, (the Quakers) conducted the first formal (recorded) protest of slavery. This was almost two hundred years before the Civil War put a legal end to slavery in America. The battle for freedom and equality has been long and bloody.

The practice of enslaving Africans began vigorously in the 1600s. England, Portugal, Spain, and France established the slave trade to bring workers to labor on sugar and tobacco plantations, and, later, on cotton plantations in the southern states of America.

What kind of a human mind existed (and still exists) that thought it was okay to denigrate and enslave other humans? It was, I think, a primitive mind, an unevolved mind, a mind that did not have empathy. Empathy and higher-order reasoning skills are found in advanced forms of consciousness (I wrote about levels of consciousness in *The Esoteric Helen Keller*), but not in the less evolved minds of the 1600s.

War: 1600 to 1700

The decades of the 1600s are known as the *Age of the Religious Wars*. Religion often walks through history arm-in-arm with the Devil—the Devil learned early on to dress in holy robes.

On September 24, 1688, France declared war on Germany; no one was surprised that another war had been declared; the human timeline is smeared with blood. Patriarchal males with low levels of consciousness went to war again, just as they had been doing for thousands of years, except now the weapons of war were more horrific with each renewed conflict and the consequences were getting more and more severe.

The Thirty Years War raged from 1618 to 1648, and the English Civil War lasted from 1642 to 1649. Wikipedia lists 159 wars that took place during the 1600s. This is mostly a Western perspective and does not include lesser conflicts. But the point is well made: the human species (in the Western nations), is constantly fighting. This is a patriarchal, historically-derived fact; males are constantly fighting with other males—it was true in the 1600s and it is still true.

Philosophy: 1600 to 1700

In 1637, French philosopher René Descartes (in his *Discourse on Method*) declared "Cogito, ergo sum," which is Latin for "I think, therefore I am." Perhaps that is the beginning of Western philosophy's obsession with consciousness, a time when our species turned attention inward toward the mind and a time when the seeds of emerging self-consciousness sprouted.

Both René Descartes and Emanuel Swedenborg wrote that they were being helped by spirit guides. Both men spoke about their out-of-body experiences, strange paranormal events which influenced their cognitive evolution, as if unseen esoteric forces worked behind appearances to inform humanity of hidden spiritual domains. Like René Descartes and Emanuel Swedenborg, Helen Keller also seemed aware of energy and subtle messages that arise from below visual and auditory perception, although there is little in her history to suggest she had out-of-body experiences.

The *Age of Enlightenment* began in the late 1600s. This European intellectual movement emphasized intellect and individualism rather than tradition or collectivism. The Age of Enlightenment set the stage for the advent of the scientific method and the rise of Modern levels of consciousness. The Enlightenment was heavily influenced by philosophers such as René Descartes and by scientists like Isaac Newton.

English philosopher John Locke (1632–1704) laid the foundation for the Enlightenment and made contributions to the development of liberalism. Isaac Newton (1642–1727) invented the calculus in the 1660s and formulated the theory of universal gravity. Newton was also an Alchemist, a student of esotericism.

Locke's contemporary G.W. Leibniz developed a theory of mind in his *Discourse on Metaphysics* (1686) that identified *degrees* of wakeful consciousness as well as unconscious thoughts, which he called "petites perceptions." Leibniz distinguished between perception (awareness) and apperception (self-awareness); he is one of a long line of philosophers to identify a cognitive duality inherent in the human mind.

Technology: 1600 to 1700

Here is a partial list of technologies that were invented in the 1600s: the telescope, the adding machine, the barometer, the air pump, hand grenades, the micrometer, the pendulum clock, the pressure cooker, and the steam engine. The simple technologies that emerged in the 1600s were the foundational inventions upon which the miracles of the Industrial Age would be built.

1772: THE DEATH OF EMANUEL SWEDENBORG

Emanuel Swedenborg died on March 29, 1772 in London, England. He had asked that his teachings not be turned into a church and that he not be turned into a person to be worshipped. However, his wishes were ignored by those who felt his works and his spiritual energy should not be lost to history. Therefore, on May 7, 1787, in England, *The New Church* was created in Swedenborg's honor; his ideas and revelations are now followed and admired across the world.

Science is still trying to figure out how out-of-body experiences occur, how psychic phenomenon might be explained, and how subtle vibrations could contain information that people like Swedenborg, Descartes, and Helen Keller could perceive. Historically, science has lumped all esoteric studies under the heading of superstition and ignorance, although this is changing as Modern thinkers review the concept of esotericism.

Swedenborg was popular because he believed the Bible to be allegorical and mythological—it did not have to be taken literally. From Swedenborg's perspective, the Bible might be full of insights and compelling stories, but it was, above all, a book about the evolution (a history) of consciousness. In the Bible, Jesus showed humanity what a spiritual mind should look like. Loving-kindness and concern (empathy) for others came into being when a mind was transformed into Christ-like consciousness.

There is an image which shows Jesus pointing toward *The Way* while his followers, who did not understand that he was showing them a spiritual pathway, sucked on his finger. *The Way* forward is a pathway toward ever more tolerant, accepting, loving expression, not toward the idolization of Jesus, or Swedenborg, or Helen Keller.

The human mind is not a static entity, it is dynamic. Human cognition has become more sophisticated as the centuries have rolled forward because the brain can be changed through experiences. The Neolithic mind was not the same as the mind in the Middle Ages. The human mind of the 14th century was not like the mind of the 21st century. The mind in our time is still changing, very rapidly. We now have a variety of minds (levels of consciousness) living side by side. I gave examples of levels of consciousness in the companion book to this timeline (*The Esoteric Helen Keller*). The minds—levels of consciousness—described below are taken from a more extensive discussion in *The Esoteric Helen Keller*.

Narcissistic minds, operating at an exceptionally low level of consciousness, are not capable of loving-kindness, empathy, or tolerance. Ethnocentric minds, one step more-evolved than Narcissistic minds, are not capable of expanding love and service beyond the confines of their tribes. Traditional minds, one evolutionary step higher than Ethnocentric minds, take the Bible (any religious text) literally and often miss the messages of love, service, and the evolution of consciousness. More evolved Modern minds embrace science, the intellect, and technology but dismiss spirituality (as an equal partner with the intellect). Post-modern minds, having evolved beyond Modern minds, and having compassion for those struggling, reach down to help other minds evolve further. Integral and Post-Integral Minds are where modern cultures should draw leadership (my opinion) since they are currently the most evolved levels of cognition. Given a choice between Mussolini and the Dalai Lama, Narcissistic, Ethnocentric (Tribal), and Traditional minds would vote for Mussolini. If civilization is to continue to evolve, we cannot continue to allow primitive minds to make decisions for modern societies.

Emanuel Swedenborg and Helen Keller had highly evolved minds that were tolerant, loving, and dedicated to service. Swedenborg may have died in 1772, but his legacy lives on, as does Helen Keller's legacy. They both speak for the mystical heart of Christianity, for the expansion of Love.

Important Pathfinders: 1700 to 1800

America leaders declared independence from England and fought in the Revolutionary War that created the United States in 1776. General George Washington (1732–1799) became the first president of the new nation. The laws of the new country were based on Democratic values, which were championed by leaders like John Adams (1735–1826), Thomas Jefferson (1743–1826) and Alexander Hamilton (1755–1804).

The Industrial Revolution rapidly evolved as did the scientific method that made the revolution possible. Scottish engineer James Watt (1736–1819) improved primitive versions of steam engines, creating more efficient and reliable steam-generated machines; these new inventions became the backbone of the Industrial Revolution.

The Golden age of music occurred in the 1700s with the birth of Western civilization's pioneering composers, including Johann Sebastian Bach (1685–1750), George Frederick Handel (1685–1759), Joseph Haydn (1732–1809), Wolfgang Amadeus Mozart (1756–1791), and Ludwig van Beethoven (1770–1827).

Freedom: 1700 to 1800

Democracy and freedom evolved together as the 1700s unfolded. Revolutions in America and France established the basic rights of individuals, breaking with the old feudal idea that royalty should rule over human subjects. Older forms of government did not recognize or honor individual rights. Therefore, the revolutions in America and France established a system of laws that set limits on the power of governments. The principles of liberty and freedom were written down and set into the laws of newly forming Democratic governments.

When Helen Keller was born, the revolutions in science, in technology, and in governing, were still being challenged. An exceptionally large portion of the world's population either knew nothing about these rising revolutions or were fearful of them. Most of humanity still had minds that were Narcissistic, Tribal, or Traditional. There were very few Modern minds and almost no (if any) Post-Modern minds. Only a Modern mind would have grasped the essence of the revolutions in science and technology, and only a Modern mind would have understood that economics and governing would be impacted by these revolutions.

When Helen Keller was born in 1880, there were very few Modern minds; most of humanity still had Feudal (tribal) minds, with an inability to transmute their worldview. Freedom (in the Western world) was a concept that did not yet give non-whites and females any rights or any power. Tribal and Traditional Minds were dominant during Helen's youth; Democracy was still fragile, science was still in its infancy, and the Industrial Revolution was moving so fast that men were being injured and demoralized in primitive factories—dangerous machines and Feudal administrative practices maimed or ruined the health of industrial laborers. As a young woman, Helen Keller became a socialist, in part because of the flaws inherent in the early Industrial Revolution.

War: 1700 to 1800

The wars in Europe (in Western civilization) continued as they had for centuries. Because of ever more sophisticated technologies of war, the results were bloodier with each passing decade. The focus of wars shifted to America in the 1700s, most notably with the American War for Independence. But there is another theme that emerges as the 1700s ended. The European settlers that had arrived to colonize North and South America pushed the native populations aside as if they were irrelevant. Indian wars began as the native populations fought back; these wars continued until the middle of the 1800s.

Technology: 1700 to 1800

The Eighteenth Century (1700–1800) was a period marked by the emergence of science, the beginning of a technological revolution that still rages in our era. The Modern level of consciousness emerged in parallel with science and technology during the 1700s—the scientific method shocked previous levels of cognition. Traditional, Ethnocentric, and Traditional minds rebelled against the heresy they saw emerging from the Modern level of consciousness (from the Age of Reason).

Political upheaval, the new political ideas of the Enlightenment, and the rise of science and technology culminated in the American and French Revolutions and, toward the end of the 1700s, caused the acceleration of the Industrial Revolution, which saw machines begin to replace human labor. New technologies were now arriving at a pace that frightened and awed the lay population.

Here are a few technological breakthroughs that occurred in this century: Scottish scientist Daniel Rutherford discovered nitrogen gas, isolating it from air; Bartolomeo Cristofori invented the modern piano; John Shore invented the tuning fork; French C. Hopffer patented the fire extinguisher; Gabriel Fahrenheit invented the mercury thermometer; Benjamin Franklin invented the lightening rod and bifocal glasses; Alexander Cummings invented the flush toilet; John Barber invented the gas turbine; Early bicycles were invented in Scotland; Eli Whitney patented the cotton gin; Edward Jenner created a means to vaccinate against smallpox; and Alessandro Volta invented the battery. The modern age of weaponry was also dawning in the 1700s. Muskets and pistols replaced bows and arrows; cannons replaced catapults.

Philosophy: 1700 to 1800

Established churches faced increasing challenges from philosophy and from the new scientific method. English poet and philosopher Samuel Taylor Coleridge (1772–1834) could see the duality of mind and he tried to explain this human cognitive conundrum to his followers. Coleridge was instrumental in forming my own worldview.

French philosopher and social critic, Voltaire (1694–1778) was instrumental in promoting the Democratic ideals that led to the French Revolution. Voltaire was a staunch critic of absolute monarchy. Benjamin Franklin (1706–1790), one of the American Founding Fathers, was a diplomat, a scientist, an inventor, and a highly respected statesman. Immanuel Kant (1724–1804) was a remarkably influential German philosopher who sought to unite the intellect with experience. Johann Wolfgang von Goethe (1749–1832) was a German poet, playwright, and popular author. Goethe's play *Faust* also attempted to unite intellect with experience. The prominent philosophers of the 1700s could sense the duality of mind—their ideas are the philosophical foundation of modern dual-process theory.

William Blake (1757–1827) was an English poet, painter, and (in some esoteric camps) a mystic. Robert Burns (1759–1796) was a Scottish romantic poet who wrote in both English and Scottish; he became the national poet of Scotland. Jane Austen (1775–1817) wrote *Pride and Prejudice, Emma,* and *Northanger Abbey.* Her novels are about the struggles of women in the 1700s in England. Jane Austen was a pioneering female author who set the foundation for later demands of women for civil and human rights. Philosophy and creative energy were merging in the 1700s, creating a new kind of human mind.

1801: THE BIRTH OF SAMUEL GRIDLEY HOWE

Samuel Gridley Howe was born November 10, 1801 in Boston, Massachusetts. He was an American physician, an abolitionist, and an advocate for the education of the blind. Howe established and was the first director of the Perkins School for the Blind in Watertown, Massachusetts where both Anne Sullivan and Helen Keller attended school (Helen only attended informally, as a short term "guest"). Howe died January 9, 1876, four years before Helen Keller was born.

Howe married Julia Ward in 1843. Julia (1819–1910) became celebrated herself. She was a poet, an author, and she became famous for writing "The Battle Hymn of the Republic." Julia Ward Howe was also an abolitionist, a social activist, and a suffragette. Samuel and Julia were a formidable couple, both made significant contributions to American culture.

Samuel Gridley Howe attended Harvard University, Brown University, and Harvard Medical School. He later became world famous for his work with deaf-blind Laura Bridgman, whom Howe taught to communicate using fingerspelling, long before Anne Sullivan taught Helen Keller. Sullivan studied Howe's methods for teaching the deaf-blind and, living in the same cottage at Perkins with Laura Bridgman, Annie learned to communicate using fingerspelling.

～

In the biographies of Helen Keller and Anne Sullivan there are references to a falling-out between Sullivan and the administration at the Perkins

School for the Blind, particularly with Perkin's new director Michael Anagnos. Anagnos, Samuel Gridley Howe's son-in-law, became director after Howe died. This controversy may have been due (in part) to the perception that Helen Keller's star status and Sullivan's achievements eclipsed that of Howe and Bridgman. The Perkins institution was loyal to the monumental accomplishments of Howe, especially his groundbreaking and world-famous work with Laura Bridgman. Anne Sullivan had branched out from Howe's curriculum, forging her own pioneering ideas for teaching the deaf-blind. Some of Sullivan's new ideas conflicted with Howe's pedagogy and with the beliefs of a few teachers at Perkins.

Undoubtably, there were personality clashes and genuine debates around the issue of deaf-blind education that affected the key people at this time in history, including Helen Keller, Annie Sullivan, and Michael Anagnos. Looking back, we can forgive the conflicts and understandable emotions of all concerned. These people were *all* giants in the field, they *all* left their mark in history; our modern world is a better place because of their dedication.

Sullivan and Keller acknowledged that they stood on the shoulders of giants like Howe, Bridgman, and Anagnos. There was great love and respect for Michael Anagnos, especially coming from Anne Sullivan who had been nurtured by Anagnos when she came to Perkins as a feisty, streetwise teenager. Anagnos had selected Anne Sullivan (after her graduation from Perkins) to work with Helen Keller; he was fond of Sullivan's feistiness and sharp intellect, even though the two strong egos occasionally clashed. Without Michael Anagnos, and Samuel Gridley Howe before him, there never could have been a Keller/Sullivan miracle; Helen and Annie knew this and honored the memory of those who came before them.

Important Pathfinders: 1800 to 1900

Newspapers and books became powerful influences during the 1800s. The result was that print media could decide—depending on where authors directed their attention—who was to become famous and who was to slip into oblivion. Even with this narrow focus, the names selected by the media and historians is too long to mention everyone who gained national notoriety.

Here are a few names, as examples from the 1800s, which most people in our modern era would recognize: Albert Einstein (1879–1955), Mark Twain (1835–1910), William James (1842–1918), Abraham Lincoln (1809–1865), Napoleon Bonaparte (1769–1821), Thomas Jefferson (1743–1826), Charles Dickens (1812–1870), Karl Marx (1818–1883), Ralph Waldo Emerson (1803–1882), Harriet Beecher Stowe (1811–1896), Walt Whitman (1819–1892), Emily Dickinson (1830–1886), Florence Nightingale (1820–1910), and Vincent Van Gogh (1853–1890).

The list goes on and on because most of the legendary people we study in school and venerate today came of age during this nineteenth-century revolution in print publishing. When we began to be overwhelmed with other forms of media and ways of recording after the 1800s, we were unable to continue this practice of veneration. Helen Keller was born during the Age of Veneration; she and Anne Sullivan became legendary icons because of the attention and adoration they received.

Freedom: 1800 to 1900

If our goal as a global community is to free people from slavery and to free people from injustice and poverty, then the worldviews of individual human beings (especially those in power with a low level of consciousness) will have to be altered; this is not an easy task. The struggle to alter worldviews, to evolve the human mind, requires an actual rewiring of the anatomy of the neocortex—it is exceedingly difficult to "change a mind." The human brain is neuronally hard-wired by the environment, genetics, and by experiences.

The brain is also malleable, it *can* change. However, to alter a worldview (the neocortical wiring) requires extensive evolution. There is evidence that the human brain (the mind and consciousness) has been continually evolving due to natural selection. Theories have postulated several historical stages that minds naturally go through as they mature. I reviewed some of these theories in my earlier textbooks and recently in *The Esoteric Helen Keller*. When we look from century to century, we can discern patterns and from these patterns we can postulate stages of cognitive evolution.

Most minds in the 1600s and 1700s were Tribal, an Ethnocentric level of consciousness. By the 1800s, minds were either Tribal or Traditional, but a few minds were becoming Modern as they were exposed to the scientific method and to the insights coming from proponents of the Enlightenment. To convince a Tribal (Ethnocentric) mind to grant justice, economic prosperity, and equality of opportunity to members of another tribe was not part of tribal neocortical hardwiring—Freedom was not going to be granted to other tribes without mind-altering rites-of-passage forcing neuronal rewiring.

Similarly, for a Traditional mind to become a Modern mind requires extreme experiences to shock the Traditional brain into reorganizing. A Traditional mind could not convince a Tribal mind to be more tolerant or spiritual just by talking—an extreme experience is usually needed to cause neuronal rewiring. The same reasoning holds when we wish to alter the neocortex of a Traditional mind so that it becomes a science-embracing Modern mind. Given the anatomy of the human brain, it is no wonder that it is so hard to *change a mind*.

The problem humanitarians and spiritual leaders face when they try to increase toleration and foster loving kindness, is tribalism, which is deeply embedded in the anatomy and physiology of the human body. We are a tribal species, a clan-based animal; we have our family and friend groups, and we are fiercely loyal to the self-reinforcing worldview of our tribes. The only way around this cortical hardwiring is the development of higher-order thinking skills. Once we know about our tribal genetics, once we cultivate an internal witness (an inner psychologist), only then can we override our intolerance and knee-jerk hatefulness.

The 1800s, like previous centuries, was rocked by an endless succession of wars. From a philosophical perspective, some of these wars, like the American Civil War, were battles to (essentially) decide how a human mind should evolve. These wars were battles between those who believed in freedom, justice, and kindness *for all humanity*, regardless of skin color, gender, or ethnic origins, and those who were opposed to giving freedom to others who were not white, male, or European. Tribal loyalty overrode reason, tolerance, sharing, and kindness.

After the American Civil War, there was a civil rights movement (1865–1896) aimed at eliminating racial discrimination against African Americans. The period from 1865 to 1895 saw a tremendous positive change in the fortunes of the American black community, but, of course, from a historical perspective, the battle for equality and respect had just begun.

Immediately after the Civil War, the federal government launched a program to rebuild the southern states. This federal Reconstruction period also provided help to former slaves. African Americans gained political power during this era, and many were able to avoid stark poverty. Unfortunately, the war and new laws did not change Tribal and Traditional minds in the South. Ethnocentric whites (primarily males) started a campaign of violence that still endures to this day, despite further laws and protests.

To this day, many minds in the United States are just as locked-in to Tribalism and Traditionalism as they were in the 1800s. Helen Keller's mind was close to Post-Modern in her final years; she was so far ahead of her culture it is no wonder she received such violent, vitriolic hatred for her political and spiritual views (primarily from Tribal minds).

Belief in the sanctity of human life has ancient precedents but the acceptance of this perspective has been slow in coming. The foundations of modern human rights began (arguably, in the Western cultures) in the 1500s and slowly evolved and flowered into the 1800s. The philosophy of liberalism and the belief in natural rights became a central focus of European intellectuals during the Enlightenment. These ideals were at the core of the American and French Revolutions.

The evolution of human rights and civil rights throughout the 1800s also paved the way for the advent of universal suffrage in the twentieth century. When Helen Keller was born in 1880, there was a strong undercurrent in American culture that advocated for greater spirituality, more tolerance, and less injustice. Helen got caught up in this wave and became an outspoken advocate for love and service.

War: 1800 to 1900

The United States was only a few decades old as the 1800s began; there were only 16 states in the Union. Places like Michigan, Ohio, and Indiana were still U.S. Territories with very few European settlers west of New York State. War with the indigenous Indian tribes was constant until after 1850.

Besides conflicts with the Indians, the United States engaged in four major wars during the 1800s. The War of 1812 was a spill-over conflict caused by the constant battles between England and France, most notably the Napoleonic War that started in 1803 and ended in 1815.

The Mexican-American War lasted two years, from 1846 to 1848. The United States won the war and received from Mexico what is now

California, Nevada, Utah, New Mexico, Arizona, and parts of other states.

The American Civil War was fought from 1861 to 1865. Anne Sullivan was born in 1866 in impoverished conditions in Feeding Hills, Massachusetts; her childhood was spent in the destructive aftermath of the Civil War.

The Spanish-American War was short, lasting from April 21, 1898 to December 10, 1898. Anne Sullivan had impulsively wanted to enlist in the war effort. She pondered whether to move on from her teaching years. Helen Keller was getting ready to go to Radcliffe College in 1900, leaving Sullivan without her mentoring role (so it seemed to her). Poor vision and poor health undermined Sullivan's impulsive decision to join the armed forces; fortunately, Helen needed Annie's help at Radcliffe.

During most of the 1800s, Spain was battling to keep its empire in South America, fighting in Mexico, Argentina, Bolivia, Ecuador, Peru, Chili, and in the Caribbean. All these nations eventually became free of colonial rule, although Spanish aristocracy still influences these nations.

Technology: 1800 to 1900

Technology was making weapons of war ever more horrible. When Helen Keller was born in 1880, armies were still using cannons, rudimentary grenades, primitive landmines, swords, bayonets, muskets, crude machine guns (invented in 1884), and knives. Soon, in the 1900s, weapons of mass destruction would be invented, and humanity would stumble into the age when the whole human species could potentially be annihilated.

The list that follows is an incomplete record of inventions and technologies that were developed during the 1800s. So much of what we take for granted, from toilet paper to paper clips had to be invented. There was an explosion of inventions in the 1800s that set the stage for an even more shocking acceleration of innovation in the 1900s. That acceleration in new technologies continues as I write these words in 2021. Innovations in the 1800s were in place when Helen Keller turned 20 in the year 1900. She was born into an age of noticeably exponential increases in knowledge and tool creation. She would live to see the industrial age give way to the information age.

Here is a partial list of technologies that Helen encountered as a young adult: Wooden matches, the stethoscope, the battery, microphone, typewriter, sewing machine, dish washer, bicycle, mechanical calculator, telegraph, postage stamp, gyroscope, gliders, gramophone, traffic lights, telephone, motorcycle, escalator, roller coaster, diesel engine, automobile, barbed wire, stapler, cement, tin cans, American braille, refrigerator, cameras, antiseptics, dynamite, moving pictures, Coca Cola, electric lights, the zipper, cotton gin, cupcakes, suspension bridges, fire hydrants, dental floss, graham crackers, the doorbell, combine harvester, circuit breaker, gas mask, safety pin, potato chips, clothespin, breast pump, egg beater, condensed milk, toilet paper, mason jars, ironing board, electric stove, vacuum cleaners, jelly beans, breakfast cereal, cowboy hats, urinals, paperclips, paper bags, American football and baseball, clothes hangers, the pipe wrench, can opener, earmuffs, grain silo, dental drill, metal detector, electric fan, solar cell, thermostat, the screen door—and a great deal more.

Technology extends human longevity. Average life expectancy in Europe in the 1600s through the 1800s was about 40 years of age. In the United States, life expectancy rose from 40 in 1900 to almost 80 in 2020. Scientists predict that this rapid increase in quality years of life will continue at a steady pace—some researchers even suggest that with gene surgery and advances in technology, people might eventually live forever. Certainly, if this steep curve continues, the twenty first century will see average life spans well beyond 80 years of age.

Philosophy: 1800 to 1900

The 1800s was a Golden Age for Philosophy and several of Western civilization's greatest thinkers came out of this decade, including Søren Kierkegaard, Friedrich Nietzsche, Karl Marx, Friedrich Engels, Charles Sanders Peirce, William James, Ralph Waldo Emerson, Henry David Thoreau and Walt Whitman. Their philosophies often overlapped. As I discussed in earlier books, almost all the philosophers in history discovered a version of dual-process theory, even though they assigned different names to the duality. Philosophies of the 1800s include this partial list: Positivism, Transcendentalism, Social Darwinism, Pragmatism, Existentialism, Marxism, Phenomenology, Utilitarianism, and German Idealism. Helen Keller would become familiar with these philosophers and their proclamations because she read many of the original works of the philosophers—in their native languages—while at Radcliffe.

1829: The Birth of Laura Dewey Lynn Bridgman

Laura Dewey Lynn Bridgman was born December 21, 1829 in Hanover, New Hampshire. She died on May 24, 1889 at the Perkins School for the Blind in Watertown, Massachusetts. Laura Bridgman lays claim as the most famous deaf-blind individual in American history having been born 50 years before Helen Keller and having mastered language through fingerspelling long before Anne Sullivan taught Helen Keller the same skill.

Laura Bridgman and Anne Sullivan were friends; Sullivan learned to fingerspell proficiently so that she could converse with Laura when they were housed in the same dorm at Perkins. Helen Keller also met Laura Bridgman at Perkins. In a way, Laura Bridgman handed the baton to Sullivan/Keller just as her time on earth was coming to an end. She died shortly after meeting Helen.

What Else Happened in 1829?

Johann Wolfgang von Goethe's *Faust, Part 1* premiered in January 1829. *Faust* is one of the most powerful Western works of art portraying humanity's cognitive duality. *Faust* is the story of the battle between the Egoic mind (the Ego) and the Self (the Soul). *Faust* is a mirror that Goethe holds up to us (the audience) so that we might confront our dual minds. See *The Esoteric Helen Keller* (2021) for more information about dual-process theory.

Here are some random events that happened in 1829: Britain, France and Russia established the borders of modern-day Greece . . . William Austin Burt patented America's first typewriter . . . President Jackson made an offer to buy Texas, but the Mexican government refused . . . A patent for the accordion was applied for by Cyrill Demian and was officially approved . . . Pope Leo XII died . . . Andrew Jackson was inaugurated as the seventh president of the United States . . . Scotland Yard was founded in London.

1835: The Birth of Mark Twain

Mark Twain was born on November 30, 1835, in Florida, Missouri. He died on April 21, 1910 in Redding, Connecticut. Called the "greatest humorist this country has produced," Samuel Clemens, known by his pen name *Mark Twain*, was a good friend of Helen Keller from the time she was fourteen. William Faulkner called Clemens "the father of American literature."

Helen wrote of Mark Twain: "He treated me not as a freak, but as a handicapped woman seeking a way to circumvent extraordinary difficulties."[1] Twain was surprised by Helen's quickness and intelligence. It was as if they could read each other's auras. It was said that they gravitated to each other; they seemed to find comfort, a peacefulness in each other's presence.

Mark Twain became convinced of Helen's potential and determined that she be given financial support, especially for her education. Right after their first meeting, Twain wrote to his own benefactor Henry H. Rogers, asking Rogers to help fund Keller's college education. Rogers agreed and took charge of Helen Keller's educational future (as did others). Over the ensuing years, other financial backers pitched in to ensure that Helen could reach her full potential. To say the least, the decision to invest in Helen Keller was a world class investment that continues to pay handsome returns.

What Else Happened in 1835?

I was amazed, as I assembled this timeline, to watch the United States emerge as a nation. One-by-one States were added to the union as Helen's life unfolded. Texas, for example, was not a state until 1845. Neither was my home State of Michigan (1837) part of the United States in 1835. Indeed, there were only 24 States in the union when Mark Twain was born. Wars against the indigenous Indians raged throughout much of Mark Twain's life as colonization marched relentlessly across the country.

Following are a few other random events that occurred in 1835: The Toledo War began between the State of Ohio and the Michigan Territory over the city of Toledo and the Toledo Strip. This was a bloodless boundary dispute. The U.S. Congress intervened and granted Toledo to Ohio. Michigan got three quarters of the Upper Peninsula as part of the deal. . . . P.T. Barnum's circus began its first tour of the U.S. in 1835. . . . The Texas Declaration of Independence was signed. . . . The Second Seminole War began in central Florida. . . . The Treaty of New Echota ceded all Cherokee territory east of the Mississippi to the United States.

1836: The Birth of Transcendentalism

Around the year 1836, the philosophical system called *Transcendentalism* started in the United States, in New England. Transcendentalism is an esoteric belief system. The ideas underpinning Transcendentalism were not unique to the Americas; they were imported from Europe.

Hermetic ideas, which are the foundation of Transcendentalism, go back thousands of years. Western philosophers, especially Kant and the Romantic Age philosophers rephrased the principles of esotericism and built entire philosophical systems around the six principles I outlined in *The Esoteric Helen Keller*.

In the middle to late 1800s, a group of Transcendentals made an impact on American literature; these giants helped forge the American identity. Not only did they impact philosophy, they also were active in religion and politics.

As we look at a list of Transcendental philosophers, we see two crosscurrents relevant to this book and to the companion book *The Esoteric Helen Keller*: All the Transcendentals knew about and debated the merits of Emanuel Swedenborg, and all of them deeply influenced the personality and belief structure of Helen Keller. The American Transcendentals included: Ralph Waldo Emerson (who was the center of the movement), Henry David Thoreau, Henry James Sr., and Walt Whitman. Famous American thinkers like William and Henry James (Jr.), and Helen Keller were profoundly influenced by Transcendentalism. The Transcendentals were liberal and spiritual; they opposed slavery and they were in favor of women's rights.

~

Helen Keller's father, Arthur H. Keller, was born on February 5, 1836 in Tuscumbia, Alabama. He died on August 29, 1896 also in Tuscumbia. He first married Sarah E. Simpson (1839–1877) on November 20, 1867 in Tuscumbia; they had three kids in a marriage that lasted 15 years: James Keller (1869–1906), William Simpson Keller (1874–1925), and a daughter, Fannie Keller, who died before she turned two (1871–1872).

Sarah (Simpson) Keller died at age 37 on February 18, 1877. Not long after the death of his young wife, Arthur married Katherine (Kate) Everett Adams on July 1, 1878. He had two young boys to care for from his first marriage and this surely was a factor in his marriage to Kate. Helen Keller was born to Kate and Arthur June 1, 1880.

In her 1998 biography *Helen Keller A Life*, author Dorothy Hermann states that Captain Keller's first wife was Sarah E. Rosser of Memphis Tennessee. Most references record Sarah's surname as Simpson. A quick search brought up this from Alabama Genealogical Trails, Colbert County, Alabama Biographies:

> Captain Keller was married November 12, 1867, to Mrs. Sarah E. Rosser, daughter of William Simpson, a well-known commission merchant at Memphis. She died in March, 1877, leaving two sons.

Mysteries remain, but at least we know that Sarah Rosser and Sarah Simpson refer to the same person. Sarah's exact date of death is also not clear.

What Else Happened in 1836?

The Colt revolver emerged as a multi-shot weapon in 1836. The Colt was part of a long history of weaponry, dating back to when Stone Age people threw rocks at each other. Once the Colt was made available to the public, massive firepower fell into the hands of the common man. War and weaponry were on Helen's list of atrocities; she did not shy away from stating her disgust at the evolution of violence . . . In 1836, Darwin returned from his voyage of discovery to announce a new theory proclaiming that species evolve in a patterned and logical manner;

the world of religion was about to be unexpectedly assailed. Helen Keller would hold her own against biological explanations for human life. She was highly spiritual and maintained that humanity should evolve toward loving kindness and service . . . The Texas Declaration of Independence and the Constitution of the Republic of Texas was written and passed in 1836. Sam Houston was named commander-in-chief of the military forces of the Texas Republic. . . . On April 20, 1936, the Wisconsin Territory was created, and on June 15, 1936, Arkansas became the 25th state admitted into the United States Union.

1837: THE BIRTH OF MICHAEL ANAGNOS

Michael Anagnos, the director of the Perkins Institute for the Blind during the time when Anne Sullivan and Helen Keller attended that famous school, was born in 1837 in Greece. There is a comprehensive summary of his life online at: "Orthodox History; the Society for Orthodox Christian History in the Americas," The following is copied from that site:

> Anagnos (shortened from Anagnostopoulos) was born in a mountain village in Epirus in 1837. The son of a peasant, he grew up tending his father's flocks and studying in the village school. He eventually earned a scholarship to a better school, and ultimately was admitted to the University of Athens. There, he was so poor that he couldn't afford textbooks, and had to copy the required readings by hand. He worked his way through college, graduated, and then studied law.
>
> After law school, Anagnos began a career, not in law, but in journalism. In his mid-20s, he became editor of an Athens newspaper, Ethnophylax (The National Guard). From that post, Anagnos opposed the government of King Otho, which led to his arrest and imprisonment. In 1866, he supported the cause of revolutionaries in Crete. As it turned out, a certain American, Dr. Samuel Howe, was also a supporter of the Cretan revolutionaries, and had come to the region to engage in relief efforts. Howe hired Anagnos to be his assistant, and when Howe returned to the US, Anagnos joined him.

Dr. Howe happened to be the founder of the Perkins Institute for the Blind, in Boston, and he gave Anagnos a position as teacher of Greek and Latin, and also the job of private tutor to the Howe family. Before long, Anagnos and Howe's daughter Julia [Romana Howe] had fallen in love, and they were married in 1870. As Dr. Howe's health declined, he gave Anagnos more and more authority at the Perkins Institute, and after Howe's death, Anagnos became the Institute's head. [2]

Michael Anagnos died in 1906 during a visit to Romania. By the time of his death, he was one of the most famous and loved Greek Americans. He had not only been a central figure in the lives of Anne Sullivan and Helen Keller, but he had also worked tirelessly for the betterment of Greek Americans. This was taken from the Orthodox History website mentioned above:

> Besides his role at the Perkins Institute, Anagnos was a towering figure in Boston's Greek community. He also served as president of the National Union of Greeks in the United States and may well have been the most famous Greek person in America in his day. He made many trips back to Europe, where he donated tens of thousands of dollars to fund schools in Greece, Turkey, Serbia, and Romania.

I had written the name *Michael Anagnos* many times in *The Esoteric Helen Keller* before I decided to have a closer look at his life. When I did, I was stunned. He was a remarkable man, worthy of his own laudatory book. I then began to wonder about all the names I had so easily slipped into my sentences without diving deeper into the story behind their names. I am troubled that I could not honor every name with appreciation and kindness. It is so easy to simply list the names of people (like Michael Anagnos) who stepped onto the stage of history for a brief appearance and then disappeared.

What Else Happened in 1837?

By 1837, America had elected only eight presidents since the Union was formed. The United States was still a set of colonial states and territories.

Andrew Jackson was the president of the United States (the eighth president) as the year began. He was replaced by Martin Van Buren.

There was an economic crisis in 1837 that led to widespread unemployment, depression, devaluing of money, and bank failures. The economy went up and down like a roller coaster as the decades unfolded. President Van Buren blamed the crisis on the easy availability of credit and rampant speculation.

Victoria (1819–1901) became Queen of England in 1837. The Victorian Era was named in her honor (the age of the Victorians). . . . Samuel F.B. Morse demonstrated a crude version of the telegraph. . . . Michigan became the 26th state admitted to the union on January 26, 1837. . . . 15,000 Cherokee Indians were marched from their homelands in the East to the new Indian territory (Oklahoma) in accordance with the Indian Removal Act of 1830. During the forced march, 4,000 of the Cherokee Indians died.

1842: The Birth of William James

American psychologist, philosopher, and eventual friend of Helen Keller, William James was born on January 11, 1842 in New York City. James was educated at Harvard's Medical School (1864–1869) and is now considered to be the *Father of American Psychology*. James died August 26, 1910, in Chocorua, New Hampshire.

When James meet Helen Keller, she was just eleven years old; this was in 1891. He corresponded with Helen the remainder of his life. James was there for Helen when she published her first books and when she graduated from Radcliffe. Here are a few favorite William James quotes found online:

- Act as if what you do makes a difference. It does.
- If you can change your mind, you can change your life.
- Believe that life is worth living, and your belief will help create the fact.
- The deepest principle in human nature is the craving to be appreciated.
- We are like islands in the sea, separate on the surface but connected in the deep.
- A great many people think they are thinking when they are merely rearranging their prejudices.
- The greatest discovery of any generation is that a human can alter his life by altering his attitude.

To change your mind is to change your level of consciousness, your worldview. James knew this in the 1800s. I like best his statement that "The deepest principle in human nature is the craving to be appreciated." I see this need everywhere I look. Human beings need others to care about them but also to appreciate their essence and innate worth. We need our existence to be regularly validated.

What Else Happened in 1842?

The Industrial Age arose in Great Britain and rapidly spread across the globe, eventually impacting policy in the United States. By the mid-1800s, the effects of the industrial revolution were severely impacting individuals everywhere in the world. Great good and great evil were arising from run-away-technologies—the beginning of a trend that rages today.

In March 1842, in Commonwealth vs. Hunt, the Massachusetts Supreme Court made strikes and unions legal in the United States. . . . On June 13, 1842, Queen Victoria became the first British monarch to travel by train (on the Great Western Railway between Slough and London Paddington Station). . . . On October 5, 1842, Josef Groll brewed the first Pilsner beer in the city of Pilsen, Bohemia.

1856: The Birth of Kate Keller

Helen Keller's mother, Katherine Everett Adams, was born October 12, 1856 in Arkansas City, Desha County, Arkansas. Kate died on November 15, 1921 at age 65 in Tuscumbia, Alabama. She is buried in Montgomery, Alabama. The following was taken from genealogy websites—there are often many errors on these databases because amateur genealogists freely add to the records. However, I did try to verify what I found online and in other government records, mostly birth, death, and marriage documents.

Katherine Adams (also spelled Catherine; although, she was called Kate) was the daughter of Brigadier General Charles William Adams (from Memphis, Tennessee) and Lucy Helen Everett. Kate's sister was Gertrude Adams.

Kate Adams married Captain Arthur Henley Keller in 1878. She was Arthur Keller's second wife and twenty years younger. Kate and Arthur had two daughters together, Helen Adams Keller and Mildred Campbell Keller. In 1891, Kate and Arthur had a son Phillips Brooks Keller (who Helen Keller named after her friend, the minister Phillips Brooks). Kate was the half-sister of Evelina Adams (called Ev by the family).

This is from the genealogy website Geni (I did minimal editing for clarity):

> Before her marriage to the captain, Kate had been a Memphis belle who had been pampered and protected by her father, Charles W. Adams, who was a brigadier general in the Confederate Army. But Kate, unlike her husband, was not a

dyed-in-the-wool Southerner. Although she seldom mentioned them in the provincial postbellum society of Tuscumbia, she had illustrious northern roots. Her father had been born in Massachusetts and was related to the famous Adams family of New England. Later he moved to Arkansas and fought on the side of the South when the Civil War broke out. Her mother, Lucy Helen Everett, was related to the celebrated New England clergyman and orator Edward Everett, who had spoken on the same platform at Gettysburg with Abraham Lincoln, as well as Edward Everett Hale, the famous author of "The Man Without a Country," which strengthened the Union cause, and to General William Tecumseh Sherman. When the Civil War ended, Kate and her family moved to Memphis, Tennessee.

Marriage at age twenty-two to the forty-two-year-old captain ended Kate's luxurious existence. No longer did she live the carefree life of a pampered southern lady. Instead, this once indulged beauty was plunged into a rugged and primitive existence that was not unlike a pioneer woman's. As she discovered to her dismay, her jovial husband, like most of the southern gentility, during the tumultuous postbellum period, was struggling to make ends meet.

Although a member of a distinguished southern family, Captain Keller, a former lawyer, was forced to earn a living both as a cotton plantation owner and as the editor of a weekly local newspaper, the North Alabamian. In 1885 his fortunes had taken an upturn when President Grover Cleveland appointed him U.S. Marshal for the Northern District of Alabama. Still money was scarce, and Kate had to raise her own vegetables, fruit, and livestock.

There were black servants to help run the plantation, but she did most of her own work, starting at dawn. To further cut down on expenses, she made her own butter, lard, bacon, and ham. She never complained publicly about her husband's shortcomings, attempting to sublimate her regrets about the marriage by becoming an ardent woman suffragist and finding refuge in books and other intellectual pursuits. She also found the time to cook and tend her flower garden, of which she was intensely proud. It was said that she raised the most beautiful roses that people had ever seen outside of a greenhouse. It was also said that she went for days without speaking to her husband.

I do not know where the author got the source for these observations, so I suggest caution. Kate and the Captain's relationship is sealed in history and how pampered she was prior to her marriage is a subjective observation. However, one thing is clear from many accounts: Helen Keller's mother was a sophisticated, well-educated, and strong-willed woman, just as her daughter Helen turned out to be, no doubt seeing her mother as a role model. I was also surprised when I discovered that the southern belle Kate Keller was a suffragette, a strong advocate for women's rights.

"Helen" was a family name. Perhaps, Helen Keller was named after her maternal grandmother Lucy Helen Everett.

What Else Happened in 1856?

Here are some events that took place the year that Kate Keller came into the world: On November 4th, 1856, James Buchanan was elected 15th president of the United States . . . In May 1856, followers of abolitionist John Brown killed five pro-slavery supporters in Franklin County, Kansas . . . On June 9, 1856, 500 Mormons left Iowa City, Iowa and headed west for Salt Lake City, Utah . . . Sigmund Freud was born May 6, 1856 in the Moravian town of Příbor, in the Austrian Empire (now the Czech Republic) . . . Nikola Tesla was born in the village of Smiljan, in the Austrian Empire (now Croatia) . . . Thomas Woodrow Wilson was born on December 28, 1856 in Staunton, Virginia. He would become the twenty-eighth president of the United States.

1859: THE BIRTH OF JOHN DEWEY

John Dewey, American philosopher of education and democracy, was born in Burlington, Vermont in October 1859, just before the American Civil war broke out. Dewey was a champion of *direct experience* as the greatest teacher. Years later his ideas would be effectively used by Anne Sullivan to teach Helen Keller, even though Sullivan did not know she was a student of Dewey's insights. As a young adult, Helen became a social activist in parallel with John Dewey's career; like Helen, Dewey was a social activist, a radical thinker, an international traveler, and a prolific author. In the same year that Dewey was born, in November 1859, Charles Darwin published *On the Origin of Species*.

I included John Dewey in this timeline because his ideas were so important to me as a young educator in the field of special education. Dewey was also a champion of what I called the Allocentric mind, so I referred to his work in my own writing. I also compared Dewey with my colleague and friend Daniel Kish, the subject of volume two in this series on Knights for the Blind—both men understood that carefully crafted experience was the greatest teacher.

What Else Happened in 1859?

The United States was busy this century adding state after state. Minnesota was added in 1858, Oregon was added in 1859, Arizona, the last of the 48 states to enter the union, did not become a state until February 4, 1912, when Helen was 32 years old.

Here are some random events that happened in 1859: Big Ben on Westminster Palace in London rang for the first time on May 31, 1859. . . . The Pike's Peak Gold Rush began in the Colorado Territory. . . . The University of Michigan Law School was founded . . . *A Tale of Two Cities* by Charles Dickens was published in England . . . Karl Marx published *A Contribution to the Critique of Political Economy* . . . John Stuart Mill published *On Liberty*.

1866: The Birth of Anne Sullivan

Anne Sullivan was born on April 14, 1866 in Feeding Hills, Massachusetts to Irish immigrant parents Thomas Sullivan and Alice Chloesy (or some surname variation). At her baptism, on April 22, 1866, Anne was listed as Johanna Sullivan. Feeding Hills is a section of the city of Agawam, within Hampden County in Massachusetts, bordering Connecticut.

The American Civil War raged from April 12, 1861 until April 9, 1865. A year after the war ended, Anne Sullivan came into the world. The nation was devastated by the Civil War, the South especially lay in ruins, and the North was in shock from all the death and carnage. Stark poverty and little hope greeted Anne Sullivan as she entered the planet.

What Else Happened in 1866?

Like all wars, the American Civil War murdered thousands of innocent young men on both sides of the conflict. Like all wars, from a soldier's point of view, it was senseless and brutal, and it left the country in ruins. Helen Keller fought against such violent stupidity her whole life. She had no patience with historic viewpoints that justified inhumanity. From Helen's vantage point, too many men were spiritually unevolved, going decade-to-decade repeating the same senseless hostility. Helen later witnessed two World Wars, the Korean War, and the first half of the Vietnamese conflict. The remarkable thing is that she never gave up her ideals; she never stopped fighting for love, equality, and justice. Anne Sullivan was much less confrontational; she kept her views on politics and religion pretty much to herself. However, Anne Sullivan shared Helen's revulsion to war, injustice, and poverty.

Here are some random events that occurred in 1866: The United States Congress passed the Civil Rights Act of 1866, the first federal legislation to protect the rights of African-Americans. However, President Andrew Johnson vetoed the bill on March 27. Congress then overrode the veto on April 9. Andrew Johnson was the 17th president of the United States. He came to power after the assassination of President Abraham Lincoln.

Jesse James and his brother Frank James, who were Confederate guerrillas during the Civil War, created the James-Younger Gang and turned their war skills to domestic crime. Their first robbery took place at the Clay County Savings Association in Liberty, Missouri, on February 13, 1866.

The Indian Wars continued in the West all through the year 1866. Sioux Chief Red Cloud battled white settlers in Montana and Wyoming, and the Paiute Tribe attacked settlers in Oregon and Idaho. The battle raged for the next two years before the Indians were forced back onto government reservations.

Alfred Nobel, a Swedish chemist, discovered what came to be known as Dynamite. When he died in 1896, Alfred Nobel set aside nine million dollars to establish the highly respected Nobel Prizes for accomplishments in science.

1874: THE DEATH OF ALICE SULLIVAN

Anne Sullivan's mother Alice died in 1874 of tuberculous. Annie was just eight years old. This quote is from Professor Kim Nielsen's book about Anne Sullivan's life *Beyond the Miracle Worker* (2009):

> Alice Sullivan's life had not been easy, but nor was it substantially different from the lives of many women in the United States at that time. She had been born in the midst of the Irish famine, survived emigration to North America, lived in poverty with a man who apparently drank substantially, and had lost two of her five children to death. In her last years, she likely knew the imminence of her own death.

Professor Nielsen captures the painful weight that hung over our ancestors, especially America's early pioneers; they were victims of poverty, starvation, cruelty, neglect, and despair. Alice was trying to find a better life for her children and herself, but the forces around her crushed her spirit and took her life when she was still young. Unfortunately, Alice did not get to witness her daughter Annie become a globally admired miracle worker.

During Helen's lifetime, immigrants flooded into the United States. They came because of war, epidemics, inequality, lack of opportunity, and for adventure. It was rarely smooth sailing when they arrived. The Irish and Scottish were fleeing from famine and disease. In our time, waves of people suffering from the consequences of war, climate change, inequality, and poverty are still on the move, looking for a better life.

What Else Happened in 1874?

Here are some random events that happened in 1874: The United States Greenback Party was established in 1874; it was composed primarily of farmers who had been financially hurt by the Panic of 1873. . . . John D. Rockefeller Jr. was born in 1874 (he died 1960) . . . American poet Robert Frost was born in 1874; he died in 1963 . . . J. R. Green's social history *A Short History of the English People* was published . . . Thomas Hardy's novel *Far from the Madding Crowd* was published.

1875: The Birth of Carl Jung

Swiss psychiatrist Carl Jung was born July 26, 1875 in Kesswil, Switzerland. Jung straddled the fence between the esoteric world and the material world, giving psychology groundbreaking concepts such as synchronicity, archetype theory, and the collective unconscious. Jung was a medical doctor and a founder (with Freud and others) of psychoanalytical theory. He was careful to avoid association with mysticism, but he was also an expert in alchemy and hermeticism. Jung was not afraid to dance on the fringes of accepted knowledge; he knew that science had just begun to unlock the secrets of the mind and the physical universe. He was a contemporary of other fearless thinkers, including Helen Keller, Albert Einstein, William James, Sigmund Freud, and Fredrick Nietzsche; many great minds overlapped in Jung's lifetime. I tied Jung's ideas into my narrative in *The Esoteric Helen Keller* because he was not afraid of esoteric insights, using them to craft his own unique worldview.

What Else Happened in 1875?

Several major themes run through Helen's life. One theme, which expands as she matures, is the evolution of music and art in the United States. Great composers wrote and performed, great sculptors exhibited their creations, artists painted, novelists emerged with powerful images and emotions. It was as if silence and darkness were being penetrated by the innovations of ever more emerging creative spirits. Helen Keller was maturing during this renaissance; her art was spiritual and linguistic.

Here are some random events from 1875: Georges Bizet's opera "Carmen" premiered in Paris . . . An earthquake in Venezuela and Colombia killed 16,000 people . . . The first Kentucky Derby was run 1875 year: jockey Oliver Lewis rode Aristides to the win . . . Alexander Graham Bell made the first electronic transmission of sound . . . Brigham Young University was founded in Provo, Utah.

1876: The Tewksbury Almshouse

Anne Sullivan and her younger brother Jimmy were dropped off (by their father) at the Tewksbury Almshouse (in Massachusetts) on February 22, 1876. Three months after being admitted, Jimmy died from tuberculous; he was Anne Sullivan's last connection to any family. Annie was totally alone after Jimmy's death—her father had gone to Chicago to find work after dropping his kids at the poorhouse.

Abandoning his children was not necessarily a cruel act by their father. Tewksbury might have seemed like a place of shelter and food where there was none outside the institution. Anne's mother was dead, her father was penniless and without work, there was no family willing to look after Annie and her little brother; it probably seemed to her father as if Tewksbury was the only option. It was a gut-wrenching decision for Annie's father. Many years later, when she was an elderly woman, Anne Sullivan learned from relatives that her father had committed suicide not long after abandoning his children.

Tewksbury opened in May 1854. This is from Wikipedia:

> The original Tewksbury campus consisted of "large wooden buildings [which] were badly designed, poorly constructed firetraps". Upon opening, paupers from across the state were sent to Tewksbury and its two companion facilities, rapidly overwhelming the facilities. Within three weeks, Tewksbury had a population of over 800, well over its intended capacity of 500. By the end of 1854, a total of 2,193 people had been admitted.

By the mid-1860s formal record-keeping had begun at Tewksbury, a series of intake records known as "inmate biographies." Based on these documents, historian and sociologist David Wagner estimates that one-third of the original population were children, and of the remaining adult population, 64% were male. The overwhelming majority of inmates were immigrants, mostly from Ireland.

Anne Sullivan was born in America; her relatives, however, came from Ireland where they were faced with a potato famine and diseases like Cholera, Smallpox, and Typhus. The Irish were also forced off their farmland by The Clearances, where sheep were deemed more valuable to landlords than human tenants. Our Irish-American pioneers were poor and of ill-health when they escaped to North America in the latter half of the 1800s. Anne Sullivan's ancestors were part of this desperate migration.

~

Meanwhile, on a brighter note, Alexander Graham Bell—an eventual friend of Anne Sullivan and Helen Keller—was busy revolutionizing communication. On March 7, 1876, Alexander Graham Bell was granted a patent for the telephone (patent #174,466). On March 10, he made the first successful phone call, saying to his colleague, "Mr. Watson, come here, I want to see you."

Samuel Gridley Howe died on January 9, 1876. He had been born in Boston on November 10, 1801. Dr Howe was a physician and an abolitionist, as well as one of the most famous activists on behalf of blind and deaf-blind individuals. Howe created the Perkins School for the Blind and was the first director. This quote captures his contribution:

Perkins shone as one of Boston's premier educational institutions—the most well-known school for blind students in the United States and perhaps the world. For almost fifty years its larger-than-life director, Samuel Gridley Howe, had dominated the institution and its reputation. Through perseverance, masterful publicity, and the education of the deaf-blind Laura Bridgman, he built a venerable institution before he died in 1876. [3]

Another future best friend of Helen Keller, Mark Twain, was also busy in 1876. On June 24, Mark Twain published a review of his book *The Adventures of Tom Sawyer* in a British magazine; the book's first edition had appeared earlier in June in England. The book was later published in the United States in December 1876.

What Else Happened in 1876?

Indian Wars continued in the Western United States. The Battle of the Rosebud was fought June 24, 1876. Led by the Sioux Chief Crazy Horse, Sioux and Cheyenne warriors beat back General George Crook's forces at Rosebud Creek in the Montana Territory. On June 25, 1876, the Battle of the Little Bighorn was fought. Lieutenant Colonel George Armstrong Custer's forces were defeated by Lakota, Cheyenne, and Arapaho tribes led by Sitting Bull and Crazy Horse.

Other notable events in 1876 included: The United States centennial was celebrated. . . . Colorado was admitted as the 38th state of the union. . . . Wild Bill Hickok died at a poker game in Deadwood, South Dakota. . . . Thomas Edison patented the mimeograph.

1877: The Birth of John Macy

Author and literary critic, John Macy, was born in 1877 in Detroit, Michigan. Macy taught at Harvard University in Boston and it was there that he met Helen Keller and Anne Sullivan. Macy later married Sullivan—he was only three years older than Helen Keller. I will discuss Macy's important role in the Keller/Sullivan legacy later in the timeline.

What Else Happened in 1877?

Significant events happened in 1877. The Civil War had ended but the Indian wars continued. . . . Racial and gender battles for civil and human rights were just getting started. . . . Science was inching forward as the Industrial Age began to replace horsepower and manpower with machine power. . . . The media was gaining attention and influence as newspaper empires were forming.

Here are a few more random events for 1877: Lakota warrior Crazy Horse and his soldiers fought a final battle against the United States Cavalry at Wolf Mountain in the Montana Territory. . . . Henry Ossian Flipper became the first African American to graduate from West Point Military Academy. . . . Kate Edger became New Zealand's first female college graduate and first woman in the British Empire to earn a Bachelor of Arts degree. . . . Thomas Edison completed the first prototype of the phonograph. . . . The Washington Post published its first edition.

1880: The Birth of Helen Keller

Helen Keller was born to Kate Adams Keller and Captain Arthur Henley Keller at Ivy Green in Tuscumbia, Alabama. Helen was born healthy; she was normal in every way. This is significant because for almost two years her physical development was routine. Then, in February 1882 came her illness, sudden, short, and devastating. However, those early healthy months laid down many of her brain's essential neural networks.

Helen Keller's home (Ivy Green) is listed on the National Register of Historic Places and resides within the Tuscumbia Historic District. You can get a good idea of the house and yard using the internet, as I did. I traveled to Tuscumbia with my childhood friend Ron Waxell in 2018. Ron and I explored the town and had lunch there after our visit to the Keller homestead. This quote is from the Ivy Green website:

> In 1954, through the efforts of the Helen Keller Property Board of Tuscumbia and the State of Alabama, Ivy Green was made a permanent shrine and placed on the National Register of Historic Places. Ivy Green is located two miles off Highways 72 and 43 in Colbert County, Tuscumbia, Alabama.

Located on a 640-acre tract in historic Tuscumbia, Ivy Green was built in 1820 by David and Mary Fairfax Moore Keller, grandparents of Helen Keller. The address is 300 North Commons Street, West, Tuscumbia, Alabama, zip code 35674. The house sits on 10 acres and the grounds (and house) are open to visitors year-round. This lovely description is from the Ivy Green website (helenkellerbirthplace.org):

The old "whistle path" carries the visitor to the outdoor kitchen from the main home. Sprinkled around the estate are the Lion's Club's International Memorial Fountain, the "Clearing" and herb gardens, the Carriage House and Gift Shop.

Helen Keller's birthplace cottage is situated east of the main house and consists of a large room with a lovely bay window and playroom. Originally, the small "annex" was an office for keeping the plantation's books.

When Captain Arthur H. Keller brought his bride, Kate Adams (the bride of his second marriage), home to Ivy Green the office was daintily re-furnished and fitted for them as a bridal suite. Later, the cottage would serve as living quarters for Helen and her teacher, Anne Sullivan.

The home and museum room are decorated with much of the original furniture of the Keller family. Each is highlighted by hundreds of Miss Keller's personal mementos, books and gifts from her lifetime of travel and lectures in 25 countries for the betterment of the world's blind and deaf-blind. Of particular note is her complete library of Braille books and her original Braille typewriter.

The entire estate is nestled under a cooling canopy of English boxwoods (over 150 years old), magnolia, mimosa, and other trees, accented by roses, honeysuckle, smilax, and an abundance of English Ivy (for which the estate receives its name).

I will just add that there is an abundance of bird song if you come when the weather is warm. The grounds are lush, and the feeling is exhilarating as you walk from the carpark to the homestead. Be sure to walk around the grounds and chat with the friendly staff. Take lots of pictures and buy something from the small gift shop.

On October 7, 1880, Anne Sullivan left the Tewksbury Almshouse and was admitted as a student to the Perkins School for the Blind.

In 1880, she made a direct plea to a state official who was inspecting the almshouse; the official helped enroll Sullivan at the Perkins School for the Blind in Boston, where she learned to read and write. Additionally, the school paid for several eye operations.[4]

Here is another perspective:

> Anne, against all odds, managed to obtain a scholarship to attend the Perkins Institution for the Blind in Boston after four years at Tewksbury. Though she was an avid student, her enduring anger surrounding her sense of abandonment and the death of her brother helped shape an intransigent personality that antagonized many at the school. Moreover, Sullivan felt intensely and often was made to feel the difference in social class between herself and the other Perkins students. But with the help of teachers like Mary Moore and Fanny Marrett, the friendship of housemother Sophia Hopkins, and the support of Perkin's director Michael Anagnos, Sullivan excelled academically, especially in the study of literature, and graduated valedictorian in 1886.[5]

I love that this quote above mentions two of Sullivan's teachers Mary Moore and Fanny Marrett (Helen's French teacher). Teachers almost always disappear from history without the praise they deserve for the everyday work it takes to forge miracles.

Compared to Anne Sullivan, Helen Keller was born into privilege. She was attended by former slaves who had stayed on at the homestead after the Civil War ended. These former slaves were now called *servants*; however, they still represented an underclass stuck in poverty and ignorance—a situation that Helen Keller would later abhor and challenge.

What Else Happened in 1880?

The United States still did not stretch from sea-to-shining-sea and indigenous Indian tribes still fought again the European invaders west of where Helen was born. In 1880, women did not have the right to vote or own property; they could not sue abusive husbands, or divorce them, or publish books under their own name. There were no special education facilities in the public schools. There were no flush toilets, no telephones, no electricity. The Edison Electric Illuminating Company of New York brought electric light to parts of Manhattan when Helen was two, but progress was slow after that. Most Americans lit their homes with gas light and candles for the next fifty years. It was 1925 (when Helen was 35) before most homes in the U.S. had electric power.

Here are some random events that occurred in 1880: The Panama Canal began construction. . . . Wabash, Indiana laid claim as the first town to be completely illuminated by electric lighting. . . . The first pay telephone service in the United States was installed in New Haven, Connecticut. . . . The Salvation Army was established in London. . . . Dr. Emily Stowe become the first woman licensed to practice medicine in Canada. . . . The first commercial hydroelectric power plant in the world began generating electricity in Grand Rapids, Michigan. . . . The University of California was founded in Los Angeles. . . . Cologne Cathedral in Germany was completed, 633 years after construction had begun. . . . The First Boer War began between the British Empire and the Boer South African Republic.

1882: HELEN KELLER'S ILLNESS

At 19 months of age, in the winter of 1882, Helen Keller contracted an unknown illness described by doctors as "an acute congestion of the stomach and the brain." For over a hundred years, people have speculated about the medical condition that caused Helen Keller's loss of both eyesight and hearing. Most often, the cause was attributed to scarlet fever or rubella. These early observations are both incorrect. I based the following discussion on information I got from an online journal called *Live Science.* The following seems like a more plausible explanation for Helen's deaf-blindness.

In 2018, Dr. Janet Gilsdorf, professor emerita at the University of Michigan Medical School and a pediatric infectious-disease expert, concluded that a likely explanation for Helen Keller's deaf-blindness was an infection caused by either the bacterium Neisseria Meningitides or Haemophilus Influenzae, both of which can cause meningitis, a swelling of the linings that cover the brain and spinal cord. The explanation of bacterial meningitis is "where reasonable deduction would take you," according to Dr. Gilsdorf's analysis.

Dr. Gilsdorf used a digital database to review the literature on what was known in the late 1800s about infectious diseases. Her analysis was published online in the May 5, 2018 issue of the journal *Clinical Infectious Diseases.*

According to Dr. Gilsdorf, historical accounts often attribute Helen Keller's deaf-blindness to scarlet fever, but this disease *does not cause* deafness and blindness. "It's hard to know where this thinking comes from," Gilsdorf said. It is true, she said, that the bacteria which causes scarlet fever can also cause meningitis. However, even in the 1800s, meningitis as a complication of scarlet fever happened rarely, and when it did happen, symptoms of meningitis were usually delayed, occurring more than three weeks after scarlet fever symptoms appeared. Scarlet fever was a known illness in the 1800s; "Helen Keller's physician very likely would have recognized scarlet fever if it preceded meningitis," Gilsdorf wrote.

Some historians attributed Keller's illness to rubella, which can cause deafness and blindness if babies are infected in the womb. If this happens, babies are born with these complications, but Keller was healthy before her illness.

There is speculation that Helen Keller might have had a disease that caused encephalitis, or inflammation of the brain, but this would have caused severe brain damage and led to intellectual disability, which certainly did not happen in Keller's case.

After an extensive literature review, and after considering alternative explanations, Gilsdorf concluded that an infection with the bacteria Neisseria Meningitidis was the probable cause of meningococcal meningitis in Helen Keller's brain. People with this illness can recover suddenly, which fits with what we know about Helen's illness. A report in 1913 on 1,300 patients with this infection found that about a third of the patients survived, and that among survivors, 45 lost their hearing, three lost their vision, and two lost both hearing and vision. This evidence suggests, Gilsdorf wrote in her report, that meningococcal meningitis is "a credible cause of the illness that left Keller deaf and blind."

What Else Happened in 1882?

Here are a few notable events that happened in 1882: Standard Oil of New Jersey was established. . . . The Married Women's Property Act of 1882 was enacted in Great Britain enabling women to buy, own, and sell property, and to keep their own earnings. . . . Tchaikovsky's 1812 Overture debuted in Moscow. . . . Thomas Edison's first commercial electrical power plant in the United States lit one square mile of lower Manhattan; this was the beginning of the Age of Electricity.

1886: Meeting Alexander Graham Bell

The Keller family met with Dr. Alexander Graham Bell for the first time in 1886. Both Alexander Graham Bell and Helen Keller were profoundly affected by this initial meeting as subsequent documents attest; they were quite impressed and delighted by each other. Bell took an immediate interest in Helen's future and recommended contacting Michael Anagnos, director of the Perkins Institution for the Blind in Boston. Captain Keller then wrote to Anagnos, requesting a teacher for Helen.

Anagnos contacted his star pupil and recent valedictorian, Annie Mansfield[6] Sullivan urging her to take a position teaching Helen in her Tuscumbia, Alabama home. Sullivan had no relatives, nowhere to go after graduation, no opportunities had arisen until Anagnos approached her. It must have been a no-brainer for Sullivan—a huge door had just opened, and she must have been quite ready to accept this blessing. I wish we had a rearview camera so we could look in at the moment Anagnos called Sullivan into his office and told her about Helen Keller.

I wonder when it dawned on Anne Sullivan that history was about to be made in which she would play the role of miracle worker. From poverty and hopelessness to global fame and (fleeting, never consistent) financial security in just a few decades—what an amazing journey for the people who had a hand in the miracle.

Alexander Graham Bell's family papers (1862–1939) are housed at the Library of Congress. A search for Helen Keller turns up a few letters between these two friends. The American Foundation for the Blind Helen Keller Digital Archives also contains letters between Helen Keller and Alexander Graham Bell.

~

Anne Sullivan graduated from Perkins in 1886 as valedictorian of her class. Below are some excerpts from her speech. The full address is available online at the American Foundation for the Blind Helen Keller Digital Archives:

> God has placed us here to grow, to expand, to progress. To a certain extent our growth is unconscious. We receive impressions and arrive at conclusions without any effort on our part; but we also have the power of controlling the course of our lives. We can educate ourselves; we can, by thought and perseverance, develop all the powers and capacities entrusted to us, and build for ourselves true and noble characters. Because we can, we must. It is a duty we owe to ourselves, to our country and to God.
>
> All the wondrous physical, intellectual and moral endowments, with which man is blessed, will, by inevitable law, become useless, unless he uses and improves them. The muscles must be used, or they become unserviceable. The memory, understanding and judgment must be used, or they become feeble and inactive. If a love for truth and beauty and goodness is not cultivated, the mind loses the strength which comes from truth, the refinement which comes from beauty, and the happiness which comes from goodness.
>
> Self-culture is a benefit, not only to the individual, but also to mankind. Every man who improves himself is aiding the progress of society, and every man who stands still, holds it back. The advancement of society always has its commencement in the individual soul. It is by battling with the circumstances, temptations and failures of the world, that the individual reaches his highest possibilities.

This is a remarkable document. Anne Sullivan was obviously very brilliant and very dedicated at a young age. Her sentiments and convictions resonate with Helen Keller's worldview, which gives us a taste of the two powerhouse minds soon to blend. According to both Sullivan and Keller, our job on earth is to serve. We are to develop our personal characters, refine our personalities, build our intellect, cultivate love, truth, beauty, and goodness. Sullivan says, almost prophetically: *It is by battling with the circumstances, temptations and failures of the world, that the individual reaches his highest possibilities.* Wow. In a few months from the time this address was delivered to her classmates and teachers, Sullivan would find herself on a porch in Tuscumbia, Alabama facing the challenge of a lifetime.

What Else Happened in 1886?

When I wrote my textbooks on the evolution of consciousness, I saw a pattern playing out decade-after-decade, century-after-century. The pattern showed that there was a cognitive duality built-in to the human species. Published in 1886, Robert Louis Stevenson's *The Strange Case of Dr Jekyll and Mr. Hyde* is a superb example of this duality. Stevenson showed humanity their cognitive dilemma, the dual conundrum of consciousness. Psychologists, scientists in many fields, psychoanalysts, historians, and many others would also show humanity the same duality as the decades rolled forward.

Here are a few notable events that also happened in 1886: Tchaikovsky's premiered his Manfred Symphony. . . . Sigmund Freud opened his medical practice in Vienna. . . . Karl Benz drove the world's first automobile in Germany. . . . The first major earthquake was recorded in the Eastern United States, at Charleston, South Carolina (over 100 people died). . . . The last major Indian war ended when Apache Chief Geronimo surrendered to federal troops. . . . Spain abolished slavery in Cuba. . . . President Grover Cleveland dedicated the Statue of Liberty. . . . Sherlock Holmes' first story "A Study in Scarlet" was accepted for publication.

1887: Anne Sullivan Meets Helen Keller

On March 3, 1887, Anne Sullivan arrived in Tuscumbia, Alabama and began teaching Helen Keller manual sign language (fingerspelling). Helen was just six and a half years old when her lessons began:

> Miss Sullivan began to teach Helen Keller on March 3rd, 1887. Three months and a half after the first word was spelled into her hand, she wrote in pencil this letter (to her Aunt Anna; Mrs. George T. Turner). The letter is dated June 17, 1887 [I added all periods and my spell checker added capitalization]:

> Helen write Anna. George will give Helen apple. Simpson will shoot bird. Jack will give Helen stick of candy. Doctor will give Mildred medicine. Mother will make Mildred new dress. [7]

I knew that Anne Sullivan taught Helen manual fingerspelling and to write and read braille, but I had no idea that Helen could write with a pencil until I came upon the passage above. Learning to print letters requires a whole different set of abstractions to master, plus extensive manual dexterity.

Also, in 1887, Annie made the miracle breakthrough at the water fountain, teaching Helen that "everything had a name." Helen says that she read her first story in May 1887 when she was seven years old. From that day, she devoured everything written—in one form or another—that came within reach.

What Else Happened in 1887?

In the late 1800s, the United States slowly built a military that increased in size and sophistication year-by-year. Meanwhile, cities were growing exceedingly complex and urban populations were growing exponentially. Here are a few notable events that happened in 1887: The United States Senate approved a naval base lease at Pearl Harbor. . . . Work began on the Eiffel Tower in Paris. . . . The first Groundhog Day was observed in Punxsutawney, Pennsylvania. . . . Sherlock Holmes first appeared in the *Study in Scarlet*, by Arthur Conan Doyle.

1888: Moving to Boston

Anne Sullivan, Helen Keller, and Kate Keller traveled north to Boston in 1888, visiting Alexander Graham Bell, President Grover Cleveland at the White House, and Michael Anagnos, director of the Perkins School for the Blind in Boston. Helen turned eight on June 27th.

What Else Happened in 1888?

Art genres began to form in the late 1800s that were much more sophisticated than anything which had come before in history. The American culture came to appreciate writers, especially novelists who would become famous. Photography was emerging as a hobby and as a necessity for reporters. National magazines, many still in business today, came on the scene in the late 1800s.

Here are a few notable events that happened in 1888: Vincent van Gogh cut off his left ear with a razor, after arguing with fellow painter Paul Gauguin; he sent the ear to a prostitute. . . . Writers T.S. Eliot and T. E. Lawrence were born in 1888. . . . The National Geographic Society was founded in Washington, D.C. The first publication of National Geographic Magazine was published later in the year. . . . Frederick Douglass was nominated for United States President. . . . George Eastman patented the first roll-film camera and registered the tradename *Kodak*. . . . On his 44th birthday, German philosopher Friedrich Nietzsche began to write his autobiography *Ecce Homo*.

1889: THE DEATH OF LAURA BRIDGMAN

Anne and Helen traveled to Perkins, where Helen was considered a "guest" of the school. Helen took classes without being a formal student. In 1889, Michael Anagnos was given a leave of absence to travel through Europe for a year. Anagnos visited schools for the blind where he talked of the accomplishments of Helen and Annie. While travelling, he sent back letters to Helen (and she responded); many of these letters are preserved in the AFB Helen Keller Digital Archives.

1889 is the year that deaf-blind Laura Bridgman died. This is copied from Encyclopedia Britannica online:

> Bridgman had been keenly interested in religion since childhood. After the death of one of her sisters in the early 1860s, she experienced a conversion and became an ardent evangelical Baptist. Often, she expressed her new faith in the evangelical clichés of the period, but at other times her religious ideas were more her own, giving voice to her unique experience of the world. For example, in a poem that was published and widely admired near the end of her life, Bridgman spoke of heaven as a "holy home" where her senses would be restored:

> I pass this dark home toward light home.
> Earthly home shall perish,
> But holy home shall endure forever.
> Earthly home is wintery.
> Hard it is for us to appreciate the radiance of holy home

because of the blindness of our minds.
How glorious holy home is, and still more than a beam of sun!

On June 25, 2001, Louis Menand, a Harvard Professor and writer for *The New Yorker Magazine* wrote an article about Laura Bridgman's life. The article was called "Laura's World: What a deaf-blind girl taught the nineteenth century." This is a brilliant piece of writing that tells us much about Laura Bridgman, a remarkable woman who was overshadowed by the accomplishments of Helen Keller. Helen and Laura met shortly before Bridgman's death at age fifty-nine, when Helen was nine. Louis Menand's article serves as a fine obituary for Laura Bridgman, so I have quoted liberally from the article:

> During the course of her lifetime, many people claimed to have discovered the meaning of the Laura Bridgman story. The principal figure among these was the man who (in his own rendering of events) rescued her from her remote farmhouse and her parents' fundamentalism, carried her off to enlightened, Unitarian Boston, and restored her to humanity by conferring on her the gift of language.
>
> This was Samuel Gridley Howe, a veteran of the Greek Revolution (in which Byron, his hero, had died), a Christian reformer, and, later on, a financial backer of the abolitionist kamikaze John Brown and the husband of the author of "The Battle Hymn of the Republic." In 1837, when he went to New Hampshire to find Bridgman and bring her back to Boston, Howe had just been appointed director of the new Perkins Institution for the Blind. He had been on the lookout for a student who was both blind and deaf, and when he heard about Laura, through a professor at the Dartmouth Medical School, he was quick to recruit her. Her parents, unable to educate her, were happy to see their daughter taken off to Boston under the care of the dashing and high-minded Dr. Howe. For six years, Howe made Bridgman the poster child of his efforts to reform the education of blind children in the United States, and she proved an exceptional student. No deaf and blind person had ever been taught to read and to "speak" before, and she was regularly exhibited to audiences of potential donors to Perkins, before whom she displayed her remarkable accomplishments,

among them the ability to recognize, by the touch of the hand, people she had not "seen" in many months. By 1842, after Charles Dickens devoted a long chapter to her acquirements in "American Notes" (he ranked her, with Niagara Falls, as one of the two most impressive phenomena he had witnessed on his trip to the United States), Bridgman was an international celebrity. Little girls poked out the eyes of their dolls and named them Laura. Howe was a celebrity, too. Their names, like those of Helen Keller and Annie Sullivan sixty years later, became inextricably joined. [8]

The coincidences and synchronicities here are amazing. Famous English author Charles Dickens goes on vacation to the United States in 1842. He is a writer by instinct, so he takes meticulous notes as he travels. He then publishes his observations and musings as soon as he gets back to England. Almost 50 years later, Kate Adams Keller is struggling to find a way to help her deaf-blind daughter, Helen. Kate was a prolific reader. When she read Dicken's book about America and saw Dicken's rich and detailed comments about Laura Bridgman, she knew that an avenue had opened in which Helen might get help. Here are the paragraphs from Dickens that gave Kate hope:

> There she was, before me; built up, as it were, in a marble cell, impervious to any ray of light, or particle of sound; with her poor white hand peeping through a chink in the wall, beckoning to some good man for help, that an Immortal soul might be awakened.
>
> Long before I looked upon her, the help had come. Her face was radiant with intelligence and pleasure. Her hair, braided by her own hands, was bound about a head, whose intellectual capacity and development were beautifully expressed in its graceful outline, and its broad open brow; her dress, arranged by herself, was a pattern of neatness and simplicity; the work she had knitted, lay beside her; her writing-book was on the desk she leaned upon. From the mournful ruin of such bereavement, there had slowly risen up this gentle, tender, guileless, grateful-hearted being. [9]

After reading *American Notes*, Kate did not know if Laura Bridgman was still alive, or if her school, the Perkins Institute, was still a viable institution. All she knew was that a deaf-blind child could be educated and cared for; Laura Bridgman was proof of that. Kate's emotions soared as she followed her instincts. She discussed *American Notes* with her husband, and after careful thought, Kate Keller and Captain Keller decided to go through the door that had opened for them. Here is more from Dicken's meeting with Laura:

> Her name is Laura Bridgman. She was born in Hanover, New Hampshire, on the twenty-first of December 1829. She is described as having been a very sprightly and pretty infant, with bright blue eyes. She was, however, so puny and feeble until she was a year and a half old, that her parents hardly hoped to rear her. She was subject to severe fits, which seemed to rack her frame almost beyond her power of endurance: and life was held by the feeblest tenure: but when a year and a half old, she seemed to rally; the dangerous symptoms subsided; and at twenty months old, she was perfectly well.
>
> Then her mental powers, hitherto stinted in their growth, rapidly developed themselves; and during the four months of health which she enjoyed, she appears (making do allowance for a fond mother's account) to have displayed a considerable degree of intelligence.
>
> But suddenly she sickened again; her disease raged with great violence during five weeks, when her eyes and ears were inflamed, suppurated, and their contents were discharged. But though sight and hearing were gone forever, the poor child's sufferings were not ended. The fever raged during seven weeks; for five months she was kept in bed in a darkened room; it was a year before she could walk unsupported, and two years before she could sit up all day. It was now observed that her sense of smell was almost entirely destroyed; and, consequently, that her taste was much blunted. [9]

It was only when I read Dicken's account of Laura's life that I realized Laura's sense of smell and sense of taste had also been lost or severely depleted. Laura's sensory damages were worse than Helen Keller's and, perhaps, her accomplishments were even more profound because she overcame so much to carve out a life. The message for us seems to be that language is available to human beings even when the most severe sensory depravations are present. Dicken's continues:

> It was not until four years of age that the poor child's bodily health seemed restored, and she was able to enter upon her apprenticeship of life and the world.
>
> But what a situation was hers! The darkness and the silence of the tomb were around her: no mother's smile called forth her answering smile, no father's voice taught her to imitate his sounds: they, brothers and sisters, were but forms of matter which resisted her touch, but which differed not from the furniture of the house, save in warmth, and in the power of locomotion; and not even in these respects from the dog and the cat.
>
> But the immortal spirit which had been implanted within her could not die, nor be maimed nor mutilated; and though most of its avenues of communication with the world were cut off, it began to manifest itself through the others. As soon as she could walk, she began to explore the room, and then the house; she became familiar with the form, density, weight, and heat, of every article she could lay her hands upon. She followed her mother, and felt her hands and arms, as she was occupied about the house; and her disposition to imitate, led her to repeat everything herself. She even learned to sew a little, and to knit.
>
> The reader will scarcely need to be told, however, that the opportunities of communicating with her, were very, very limited; and that the moral effects of her wretched state soon began to appear. Those who cannot be enlightened by reason, can only be controlled by force; and this, coupled with her great privations, must soon have reduced her to a worse condition than that of the beasts that perish, but for timely and unhoped-for aid. [9]

We can see why Charles Dickens became a much-loved writer. His powers of observation and his choice of words and topic are splendid. As a mobility specialist, I am taken by his description of Laura exploring her environment and mimicking what she could. Her activities reinforce my observation that navigation is primal in the human being and the sense of proprioception (of being an animated, alive creature) is not lost (or is the last to go) in even the direst collection of impairments. Laura Bridgman could walk straight-ahead; she could use her hands to gather information, her whole skin surface became hypersensitive.

Laura Bridgman also had an aha! moment, just like Helen Keller at the water fountain:

> In reports that Howe wrote later, there was a eureka moment. At first, he wrote, it was as though she were under water, and we [her teachers] on the surface over her, unable to see her, but dropping a line, and moving it about here and there, hoping it might touch her hand, so that she would grasp it instinctively. Then, after months of fishing, Laura bit. She suddenly got language:
> Her countenance lighted up with human expression; it was no longer a dog or parrot; it was an immortal spirit, eagerly seizing upon a new link of union with other spirits! I could almost fix upon the moment when this truth dawned upon her mind and spread its light to her countenance. I saw that the great obstacle was overcome. [10]

What Else Happened in 1889?

Here are a few notable events that also happened in 1889, the year that Laura Bridgman died: The Canadian Pacific Railway was completed from coast to coast. . . . The Great Fire in Seattle destroyed 25 blocks in the downtown area. . . . Cable Cars began operating in Los Angeles. . . . Friedrich Nietzsche suffered a mental breakdown. . . . Benjamin Harrison was inaugurated as 23rd president. . . . The Eiffel Tower opened in Paris. The Tower held the record for the tallest building in the world for 41 years. . . . Thomas Edison showed his first motion picture.

1890: Helen Keller Learns to Speak

In the spring of 1890, Helen started oral speech lessons. Chapter thirteen of her autobiography, *The Story of My Life* (1903), is about this unfolding miracle. Here are a few selections from that chapter:

> It was in the spring of 1890 that I learned to speak. The impulse to utter sounds had always been strong in me . . . in 1890, Mrs. Lamson, who had been one of Laura Bridgman's teachers, and who had just returned from a visit to Norway and Sweden, came to see me, and told me about Ragnhild Kaata [1873–1947], a deaf and blind girl in Norway who had actually been taught to speak. Mrs. Lamson had scarcely finished telling me about this girl's success before I was on fire with eagerness. I resolved that I, too, would learn to speak . . . But it must not be supposed that I could really talk in this short time. I had learned only the elements of speech. Miss Fuller [principal of the Horace Mann School for the Deaf in Boston] and Miss Sullivan could understand me, but most people would not have understood one word in a hundred . . . it astonished me to find how much easier it is to talk than to spell with the fingers, and I discarded the manual alphabet as a medium of communication on my part, but Miss Sullivan and a few friends still use it in speaking to me, for it is more convenient and more rapid than lip-reading. [11]

She was quite young when she began to learn the techniques for producing speech. Helen was born in 1880, so we are talking about a ten-year-old girl. Her autobiography was published when she was only 23. It was her intention at age ten to communicate primarily through speech (because, as she says above, speaking was so much easier than fingerspelling), but this did not happen as she had hoped. For most of her life, Helen used the manual alphabet. She has called this failure to speak intelligibly one of the most disappointing events in her life.

In this same chapter, Helen explains how fingerspelling works:

> Just here, perhaps, I had better explain our use of the manual alphabet, which seems to puzzle people who do not know us. One who reads or talks to me spells with his hand, using the single-handed manual alphabet generally employed by the deaf. I place my hand on the hand of the speaker so lightly as not to impede its movements. The position of the hands is as easy to feel as it is to see. I do not feel each letter any more than you see each letter separately when you read. Constant practice makes the fingers very flexible, and some of my friends spell rapidly—about as fast as an expert writes on a typewriter. The mere spelling is, of course, no more a conscious act than it is in writing. [11]

The internet is full of information about tactile fingerspelling. A good place to start is the American Association of the Deaf-blind: http://www.aadb.org/factsheets/db_communications.html

What Else Happened in 1890?

Here are a few notable events that happened in 1890: Vincent Van Gogh (age 37) died in France after shooting himself two days earlier. . . . At the urging of John Muir, Congress designated Yosemite a National Park. . . . Legendary Sioux leader Sitting Bull was murdered (age 59) in South Dakota. He was killed while being arrested by federal authorities. . . . The Wounded Knee Massacre took place in South Dakota. U.S. troops fired on Lakota Sioux, killing hundreds of unarmed men, women, and children. . . . Congress established the Oklahoma Territory on Indian land, breaking a 60-year-old pledge to preserve this area exclusively for Native Americans. . . . Wyoming entered the Union. . . . The Jukebox was invented in the United States.

1891: The Birth of Phillips Brooks Keller

Helen's brother Phillips Brooks Keller was born July 4, 1891, in Tuscumbia, Alabama at the Ivy Green homestead. Phillips died a few years after Helen passed (1968), on March 26, 1971 (age 79) in the City of Dallas, Texas. He is named after a favorite minister and friend of Helen's, Phillips Brooks. Adding the "s" to Phillip was confusing, but it was Helen's call to name her brother.

The following excerpt written by John S.C. Kemp was taken (and edited) from the AFB Helen Keller archives dated September 1970 under the title: "Transcription for an Article about Phillips Brooks Keller with a photo of Helen Keller and a dog named Kamikaze-Go" [The dog was a gift from the people of Japan]:

> Helen Keller, age 11, was in Boston at the Perkins Institute when she met the great preacher, Bishop Phillips Brooks of Trinity Episcopal Church. Though Brooks never had a family of his own he possessed a boundless love for children. The prodigious, though handicapped, young Helen became the object of his love and concern. His goal was to teach her about God. How do you teach a deaf and blind girl about a spiritual thing which she could not touch and feel? Finally, Mrs. Brooks, who was also deaf, explained to Helen about God's love and, the child was overwhelmed and excited by her latest discovery and her new Christian friends. It was at this time that she received word from home in Alabama of the birth of a brother. Helen Keller immediately requested that they name him for her wonderful friend Phillips Brooks.

We sat and chatted with Phillips Brooks Keller [Helen's brother] . . . and his wife in the comfortable family room of their attractive home. Walls were filled with amazing photos of his famous sister and "Teacher" with Mark Twain, Alexander Graham Bell, and many others. Some prize photos in an album included one of Helen Keller with her sensitive fingers on the lips of tenor Caruso as they conversed. The photo of Dr. Bell with Miss Keller and "Teacher" was inscribed by Helen to her brother, "To Phillips I send a cherished souvenir from my life friendships."

On Helen Keller's last visit to her brother's home in 1961 she delighted in teaching her grandniece and the neighbor children some hand spelling so they could tell her "I love you, Aunt Helen." It was during that visit that Mrs. Keller [Phillips wife] instructed the maid to peep in occasionally at Helen during her afternoon nap to be sure that she was all right. When Mrs. Keller returned the maid reported that Helen Keller must be sick because she noticed her rubbing her stomach so much in bed.

"P.B.'s" wife laughed because she knew what had happened. As was her custom, Helen had taken a Braille book to bed, opened it over her stomach and was reading it with her hands under the covers. Even in old age Helen continued to thirst for knowledge. Her hands always felt for a new experience or hunted for a book in Braille. Helen and I talked as we drove away—how exciting and different the visit had been. P.B. and Mrs. Keller are both tall and vital people, in their late 70's. Their quick response to questions about sister Helen and their fascinating family stories spoke of her character and theirs too.

Such a sensitive, keen, talented, courageous, and determined woman as Helen Keller required the assistance of companions who also possessed some fire and determination, understanding, and love. "Only God could have provided such companions," Phillips said.

P.B. was a road contractor and (though retired for the past 50 years, he still keeps his contact with his company. He is down to earth, quick, and firm. A complaint of his had to do with his name: "People forget the 's' and call me Phillip instead of Phillips." Perhaps that's why he encouraged friends to call him "P.B."

Another complaint was concerning the play of Helen Keller's childhood, "The Miracle Worker." After seeing it in New York he went backstage to say that his older half-brother didn't get a fair deal in the play. The actors laughed and said that it did make a good story, and he agreed. (P.B. was not in the play—the events took place before he was born). Mrs. Keller [Phillips' wife] was a musician and still plays piano on occasion for such groups as her church school class. She was first to respond to my final question, "What do you feel was Helen Keller's greatest contribution to the world?"

"Her happiness which just overflowed! She was able to stimulate other people to action," she said. P.B. followed with, "Her great courage! She gave courage to others." Then he told of his sister's visit to a soldier's hospital during or after World War II. One fellow had been dreadfully shot up and she talked with him. When she left, he turned to a buddy and said, "I'll be d——if I'm going to let this get me down after seeing the courage of that woman!" Phillips Brooks Keller mentioned his sister's great gift of hope to the deaf and blind children. I had to comment that she belonged to all of us—she gave courage and motivation to all people of the world. Helen Keller loved people and was concerned for children. It seemed significant that the children's choir from the Perkins Institute in Boston was flown down to Washington Cathedral to sing for the funeral services of Helen Keller. [12]

I agree that Helen's courage, faith, and dedication are attributes we should admire and remember, but I am also pleased that Phillips' wife, Ravia Belle Walker, honored Helen's jubilant nature. To be deaf-blind but also animated is remarkable. We would expect a statue-like physical response to be the norm in individuals without sight and sound (and it often *is* how deaf-blind people seem—very still), so Helen's animation and exuberance were unusual and joyful to witness.

Here is a quick genealogical sketch for Helen's immediate family (so quick that I urge serious genealogists to simply use this as a starting point):

Arthur Henley Keller; 1836–1896 had two wives:
- Sarah E. Simpson (1839–1877)
- Catherine Everett Adams (Kate) Keller (1856–1921)

Here are Helen Keller's half siblings from the first marriage of Arthur and Sarah:

- James McDonald Keller (1867–1906)
- Fannie S. Keller (1871–1872)
- William Simpson Keller (1874–1925) (married in 1913)

Helen had two full siblings:

- Mildred Campbell Keller Tyson (1886–1969)
- Phillips Brooks Keller (1991–1971)

Helen's younger sister Mildred married Laban Tyson; they lived in Montgomery, Alabama. The 1920 U.S. census shows Mildred and Laban with three kids. It also shows Kate Keller, age 50, living with the family. This means Kate must have moved from Ivy Green after her husband died. Mildred's kids were:

- Katharine K. Tyson
- Patty Tyson
- Mildred Tyson

Phillips married Ravia (Rovia) Belle Walker. The couple lived in Dallas, Texas. They had two children (that I could find):

- Brooks Keller Jr. (died in 1986)
- Katharine Elise Keller Ewin (1924–1988)

∽

1891 is also the year that Helen sent Perkin's director Anagnos the story "The Frost King" as a birthday present. After it was discovered that Helen's story was almost an exact reproduction of a children's book published earlier called the *Frost Fairies*, by Margaret Canby, Helen was accused of plagiarism by the Perkins School Board of Directors. A trial held by Perkin's staff eventually acquitted Helen of wrongdoing, but the impact on Helen was devastating. Professor Kim Nielsen has a detailed account of this drama in her book *Beyond the Miracle Worker* (2009).

∽

Here is a news article from 1892 that I thought worthy of preserving:

> Helen is now a little more than 11 years of age, and during the past three years has grown amazingly fast in body and mind. She advanced toward full stature and maturity with astounding rapidity. She is now five feet and two inches in height, and of symmetrical figure, and she weighs 122 pounds. Her physique is good, and her active brain and heart are sustained by an adequate material frame. Her head is finely formed, with luxuriant curls of brown hair, and her countenance beams with animation and intelligence. She enjoys excellent health. She seldom complains of common ailments, and she eats heartily and sleeps soundly.
>
> This queen of precocious children has made elementary studies in natural history, cosmography, mythology, biography, and English literature, and by the exercise of her faculties she has acquired a capacity for viewing, assorting and arranging the facts within her knowledge. Geography is her favorite study. Foreign countries and their histories and romantic traditions are peculiarly fascinating to her and her dream is to travel abroad when she reaches her thirteenth year. That pleasure has been promised to her. Greece and Italy supply ample material for thought. [13]

What Else Happened in 1891?

Here are a few notable events that happened in 1891: Oscar Wilde's "Duchess of Padua" premiered in New York City. . . . French painter Paul Gauguin left Marseille for Tahiti. . . . Work began on the trans-Siberian railway. . . . The U.S. National Forest Service was organized. . . . The world's 1st traveler's cheques were issued by the American Express company. . . . Thomas Edison patented the motion picture camera. . . . The first game of basketball was played by 18 students in Springfield, Massachusetts.

1893: The Frost King Controversy

The aftermath of the Frost King trial left the young Helen Keller in shock. She felt very timid about writing anything more in fear that her memory might conjure something she had heard as a young child. Writing in the magazine *Youth's Companion*, Helen reflected on her traumatic experience:

The summer and winter following the "Frost King" incident I spent with my family in Alabama. I recall with delight that home-going. Everything had budded and blossomed. I was happy. "The Frost King" was forgotten.

When the ground was strewn with the crimson and golden leaves of autumn, and the musk-scented grapes that covered the arbour at the end of the garden were turning golden brown in the sunshine, I began to write a sketch of my life—a year after I had written "The Frost King."

I was still excessively scrupulous about everything I wrote. The thought that what I wrote might not be absolutely my own tormented me. No one knew of these fears except my teacher. A strange sensitiveness prevented me from referring to the "Frost King"; and often when an idea flashed out in the course of conversation, I would spell softly to her, "I am not sure it is mine." At other times, in the midst of a paragraph I was writing, I said to myself, "Suppose it should be found that all this was written by someone long ago!" An impish fear clutched my hand, so that I could not write any more that day. And even now I sometimes feel the same uneasiness and disquietude. Miss Sullivan consoled and helped me in every way she could think of; but the terrible experience I had passed through left a lasting impression on my mind, the significance of which I am only just beginning to understand. It was with the hope of restoring my self-confidence that she persuaded me to write for the *Youth's Companion* a brief account of my life. I was then twelve years old. As I look back on my struggle to write that little story, it seems to me that I must have had a prophetic vision of the good that would come of the undertaking, or I should surely have failed.

I wrote timidly, fearfully, but resolutely, urged on by my teacher, who knew that if I persevered, I should find my mental foothold again and get a grip on my faculties. Up to the time of the "Frost King" episode, I had lived the unconscious life of a little child; now my thoughts were turned inward, and I beheld things invisible. Gradually I emerged from the penumbra of that experience with a mind made clearer by trial and with a truer knowledge of life.

Helen had no idea that her memory skills far outperformed most of the population. She was a language prodigy with a prodigious and unusual memory.

It was not all bad news for Helen and Annie in 1893. They attended the inauguration of President Grover Cleveland, visited the World Fair in Chicago with Alexander Graham Bell, and stood beside Niagara Falls (on the American side).

What Else Happened in 1893?

As I tracked the years in this timeline, I found that Mahatma Gandhi came up quite often in parallel to the events in Helen Keller's life. I began to see that Gandhi represented anti-colonial forces—he was fighting for India's independence and he was trying to convince the population to embrace tolerance and equality. I knew that Gandhi was a pacifist, just like Helen Keller; he was also the voice of kindness and spirituality, as was Helen. I was quite sad when his story and struggles suddenly were silenced.

I also saw from my overhead view that economies cyclically rose and fell during Helen's life. Crash and fortune went up and down like a roller coaster. This cyclical swinging is still going on in our era. The battle for civil and human rights also went on all the while that Helen lived; the struggle for kindness and tolerance is with us still.

Here are a few notable events that happened in 1893: The panic of 1893 occurred on May 5th, causing stocks to crash. . . . On June 7th, Gandhi performed his first act of civil disobedience. . . . Lizzie Borden was acquitted of the 1892 axe murders of her father and stepmother in Fall River, Massachusetts. . . . The first Ferris Wheel premiered at Chicago's Columbian Exposition. . . . A Tornado hit the eastern coastlines of Savannah and Charleston, killing about 1,000 people. . . . English author Beatrix Potter wrote the story of Peter Rabbit (for a 5-year-old boy). . . . New Zealand became the first country to grant all women the right to vote.

1894: THE WRIGHT-HUMASON SCHOOL FOR THE DEAF

In October 1894, Helen and Anne traveled to New York City where Helen attended the Wright-Humason School for the Deaf—this was a preparatory school where Helen's skills and knowledge would be improved enough to pass college entrance exams. Helen studied German, French, math, and geography.

It was at the Wright-Humason School that Helen refined her ability to use her voice. She was never completely happy with the result, although she did learn to verbally express herself to a considerable degree. She also refined her ability to decode what people were saying: the index finger of her left hand was placed perpendicular to the speaker's lips; the thumb was placed on the speaker's throat. The right hand was free to receive finger-spelled messages.

Helen turned fourteen in 1894; she was already becoming legendary, and many good-hearted individuals began discussing possible futures for her and her teacher. A group of philanthropists began this year to discuss ways to provide financial support so that Helen could get a college education. Here is a short list of the people who initially were inclined to help financially: George Goodhue, John Spaulding, Alexander Graham Bell, John Hitz, William Wade, Sophia Hopkins, Annie Pratt, and Lucy Derby.

I am sure that Michael Anagnos also helped at times, and Mark Twain sent money over several years; Andrew Carnegie eventually set up regular monthly contributions. William Wade's name comes up numerous times over the years as a financial supporter of Helen and

Annie. Sophia Hopkins provided in-kind contributions—lodging, food, educational and emotional support—as well as direct funding. John Spaulding paid eight hundred dollars—a considerable sum in 1894, to kick off the educational campaign. Hopkins and Spaulding joined with Annie Pratt to form the *Helen Keller Club*, which was initially established to raise funds for Helen's education.

Annie Pratt, like John Hitz, worked with Alexander Graham Bell's Volta Bureau. Spaulding died in 1896; a serious loss for Helen and Annie because his philanthropy had been exceedingly generous; his heirs declined further support for Helen after Spaulding's death.

I fear that I have left out names of others who were moved to financially contribute to the welfare of Helen, Annie, and Polly—the above list was made as I did research; I could very well have missed key people. I also regret that I do not have a biographical record of the people who provided financial support. I am quite sure that these were remarkable and interesting people who deserve to be remembered for their kindness.

What Else Happened in 1894?

As I created this timeline, there were ongoing themes, such as the struggle for women's rights, for racial equality, and, of course, war kept popping up as mankind's major tool for settling conflicts. As science moved along at an ever-quickening pace, the ability to extend the human senses was another trend. Microscopes and telescopes were parallel technologies that became refined decade after decade. Medicine also vastly improved at a rapid pace, including ophthalmic procedures. Every time Anne Sullivan had an eye operation the procedures improved, year after year.

Here are a few notable events that happened in 1894: The Columbus World's Fair in Chicago was destroyed by fire in January. . . . The first college basketball game occurred between the University of Chicago and the Chicago YMCA. . . . Coca-Cola was sold in bottles for the first time (in a candy store in Vicksburg, Mississippi). . . . George Bernard Shaw's "Candida" premiered at the Theatre Royal in England. . . . The Lowell Observatory in Arizona recorded canals on Mars.

1895: HELEN KELLER MEETS MARK TWAIN

1895 is the year that Helen Keller met Mark Twain at a party given by Laurence and Eleanor Hutton in New York City. Helen was 14 and Mark Twain was 60. The following quote (edited) is from Wikipedia:

> [Laurence] Hutton was born in New York City in 1843. He spent his summers abroad for about 20 years. Hutton was the drama critic for the *New York Evening Mail* from 1872 to 1874. From 1886 to 1898 he was the literary editor of *Harper's Magazine*. In 1892 he received a degree from Yale University and an honorary Master of Art degree from Princeton University in 1897. From 1901 until his death in 1904, he was a lecturer of English at Princeton University.
>
> Hutton donated his literacy papers (Laurence Hutton Papers) to the Princeton University Library, as well as 801 rare books, and a collection of death masks.

Laurence Hutton and his wife Eleanor became lifelong friends of Helen and Annie. Parties at the Hutton's home in New York gave Helen and Anne the opportunity to meet leading literary figures, including William Dean Howells and Mark Twain. When Keller attended Radcliffe College, she exchanged letters with Eleanor Hutton, who had introduced Keller to the cosmopolitan scene in New York City. The Hutton's also provided emotional and financial support when Keller was at Radcliffe:

Eleanor Hutton . . . had set up a Helen Keller Trust fund to ensure that Sullivan and Keller would have sufficient income to carry on their important work. Hutton recruited donors to maintain the fund. Helen had hoped to get substantial income from her books, articles, and speeches, but financial worries were always present—the Trust Fund was a major factor in their ability to stay afloat. [14]

William Dean Howells was called "The Dean of American Letters." He was an American novelist, literary critic, and playwright. Like, Helen, Howells was a friend of William James and Mark Twain. Howells was born on March 1, 1837 in Martins Ferry, Ohio, and he died on May 11, 1920 in Manhattan, New York City.

I will discuss Helen's relationship with Mark Twain in the section dedicated to her book *Midstream*, published in 1929.

What Else Happened in 1895?

Despite wars and economic hardships, artists continued to paint, sculpt, and write their books and plays; great composers and musicians continued to create symphonies, operas, and folk songs regardless of the political turmoil that seemed never to let up.

Here are a few events that happened in 1895: Tchaikovsky's ballet "Swan Lake" premiered in St. Petersburg, Russia. . . . The moving picture projector was patented. . . . The first commercial movie performance took place on Broadway in New York City. . . . Oscar Wilde was sentenced to two years imprisonment for gross indecency. . . . The first female PhD was granted to Caroline Willard Baldwin (in Science) at Cornell University. . . . Katherine Lee Bates published "America the Beautiful." . . . German physicist Wilhelm Röntgen produced X-rays for the first time. . . . Swedish chemist Alfred Nobel established the Nobel Prize (in his will).

1896: THE DEATH OF HELEN'S FATHER CAPTAIN ARTHUR KELLER

Helen's father, Captain Arthur Keller died in 1896. Below is a copy of a letter Helen sent to her friend Alexander Graham Bell shortly after the death of her father. The original letter can be viewed online at the American Foundation for the Blind Helen Keller Digital Archives. I removed punctuation and spelling errors:

Brewster, Mass.
September 1896

Dear Dr. Bell:

Mr. Warner has forwarded your check for four hundred dollars to Teacher, and I am going to acknowledge it myself because I want to thank you for your great kindness to me. I would like to write you a nice, long letter, and tell you all about our vacation by the seaside, and our plans for next year; but my heart is too full of sadness to dwell upon the happiness the summer has brought me, or upon the bright prospects which await me in Cambridge. My father is dead. He died last Saturday at my home in Tuscumbia, and I was not there. My own dear, loving father! Oh, dear friend, how shall I ever bear it! It seems as if a great, dark cloud had-fallen upon my life that would always keep out the brightness of everything. How strange it is! I never knew how dearly I loved my father until I realized that I had lost him. I think we do not know the depth of love in our hearts until some dreadful sorrow reveals it to us, and then we realize a little of what God's love must be like. Please give my dear love to Mrs. Bell, and Elsie and Daisy. Teacher sends her love to you all. Lovingly your friend, (signed) Helen.

In Helen's autobiography, *The Story of my Life*, she wrote:

My father was most loving and indulgent, devoted to his home, seldom leaving us, except in the hunting season. He was a great hunter, I have been told, and a celebrated shot. Next to his family he loved his dogs and his gun. His hospitality was great, almost to a fault, and he seldom came home without bringing a guest. His special pride was the big garden where, it was said, he raised the finest watermelons and strawberries in the county; and to me he brought the first ripe grapes and the choicest berries. I remember his caressing touch as he led me from tree to tree, from vine to vine, and his eager delight in whatever pleased me.

He was a famous storyteller; after I had acquired language, he used to spell clumsily into my hand his cleverest anecdotes, and nothing pleased him more than to have me repeat them at an opportune moment.

I was in the North, enjoying the last beautiful days of summer of 1896, when I heard the news of my father's death. He had had a short illness, there had been a brief time of acute suffering, then all was over. This was my first great sorrow—my first personal experience of death.

∿

1896 is also the year in which Helen became a devout Swedenborgian— she was just 16 years old. She did not know it at the time, but many of the most beloved sages of our era were followers of Swedenborg—she joined an elite company.

Also, in 1896, Helen was accepted as a pupil at the *Cambridge School for Young Ladies* in preparation for study at Harvard's Radcliffe College for women. Originally known as The Gilman School, the primary mission of the *Cambridge School for Young Ladies* was to prepare females for higher education. In 1918, the Cambridge School merged with the Boston-based Haskell School, and became *The Cambridge-Haskell School.*

There was initial resistance to Helen going to Radcliffe. The complex story is told in Kim Nielsen's book *Beyond the Miracle Worker* (2009). While Radcliffe was debating the challenges of educating a deaf-blind woman, both Cornell University and the University of Chicago offered to admit her. Competition might have been one factor in Radcliffe's final decision to take on the challenge of educating Helen Keller.

What Else Happened in 1896?

Historical events in 1896 include the following: Utah became a state in 1896. . . . The first auto-mobile (the first horseless carriage) was road-tested in Detroit, Michigan. . . . Gold was discovered in the Yukon. . . . The United States Supreme court affirmed racial separation in Plessy vs. Ferguson. . . . The Dow Jones began with twelve industrial stocks. . . . The City of Miami was incorporated. . . . Harvey Hubbell patented an electric light bulb socket with a pull chain. . . . The dial telephone was patented. . . . Bare-breasted women appeared for the first time in National Geographic Magazine. . . ."Stars & Stripes Forever" was written by John Philip Sousa.

1897: Helen and Annie Move to Wrentham Massachusetts

In 1897, Helen and Annie left the *Cambridge School for Young Ladies* and moved to Wrentham, Massachusetts. Helen continued her college preparatory studies with the assistance of a private tutor, Mr. Keith.

Wrentham, now a suburb of Boston, was first settled by the English in 1661 and officially incorporated in 1673. For a short time, Wrentham was the residence of the educational reformer Horace Mann. Anne Sullivan, John Macy, and Helen Keller lived in Wrentham after Helen's graduation from Radcliffe College.

The Wrentham Lions Club is proud of the town's association with Helen Keller. They note on their website that Helen Keller lived in Wrentham from 1904 through 1917. During that time, she published *The World I Live In*, revealing for the first time her thoughts on her isolated world. This sentiment was written in a letter Helen wrote:

> Always I look back to Wrentham as the place where I lived most serenely, where I did my work quietly, and enjoyed undisturbed the treasures of books and of nature.[15]

It is fitting that Helen Keller's last public speech was to Lions International. The Wrentham Lions Club website has this nice commentary:

> Helen Keller made her last major public appearance in 1961 at a Washington, DC, Lions Clubs Meeting. At that meeting she received the *Lions Humanitarian Award* for her lifetime of

service to humanity and for providing the inspiration for the adoption by Lions International of their sight conservation and aid to blind programs. During that visit to Washington, she also called on President Kennedy at the White House. After that White House visit, a reporter asked her how many of our presidents she had met. She replied that she did not know how many, but that she had met all of them since Grover Cleveland! [16]

What Else Happened in 1897?

Historical events in 1897 also included the following: William McKinley was inaugurated as the 25th president of the United States. . . . English physicist J. J. Thomson announced the discovery of the electron. . . . "Dracula" was published by Irish author Bram Stoker. . . . Herbert Henry Dow founded Dow Chemical in Midland, Michigan. . . . German chemist Felix Hoffman synthesized acetylsalicylic acid, later patented by Bayer under the brand name "aspirin." . . . Thomas Edison patented the kinetographic camera, the forerunner to modern motion picture projectors. . . . George Bernard Shaw's play "Devil's Disciple" premiered in New York City. . . . The pencil sharpener was patented by J. L. Love.

1898: THE SPANISH AMERICAN WAR BEGINS

The United States declared war on Spain on April 25, 1898 following the sinking of the Battleship Maine in Havana Harbor on February 15, 1898. The war ended seven months later with the signing of the Treaty of Paris on December 10, 1898. Upon hearing that war was declared, Anne Sullivan applied to be an army nurse. She was under a great deal of stress at the time and entering the armed services must have seemed like an escape, a new future. This decision was wildly off the mark, of course. Sullivan desperately needed another eye surgery at this time and would never have been accepted in the military. Helen was a young adult, about to enter college and Sullivan must have been struggling with her own future. Was she to stay with Helen Keller beyond the adult years—what would be her role, if not teacher? How would she financially survive going forward? There was even concern among her friends that Sullivan was staring at suicide as an answer to the dead-end that seemed to loom ahead. As Kim Nielsen says in her book *Beyond the Miracle Worker*:

> Despite having escaped Tewksbury . . . she still felt herself lacking a definition, a reason. Ever vulnerable despite her pragmatism, she feared that Helen would either leave or be taken from her. [17]

What Else Happened in 1898?

War is a constant in any human timeline. If the United States was not embroiled in conflict, then somewhere else on the planet males were fighting each other. Technology was constantly improving and soon millions would die in worldwide conflicts because of new tools of war. Helen opposed war because of her Christian faith. Love and service to others were not hallmarks of warfare; for Helen, a person could not be a true Christian and support war.

Here are a few events that happened in 1898: The first installment of William Dean Howell's "Life & Letters" appeared. . . . Hawaii was formally annexed to the U.S. . . . Edwin Prescott patented the roller coaster. . . . The machine gun was used in battle for the first time.

1899: Helen Prepares to Enter Radcliffe College

Helen Keller passed her final entrance exams for Radcliffe College in June of 1899 and was admitted to the university. Anne Sullivan would be at her side from this moment forward. There are two facts that seldom are acknowledged about the Radcliffe years and Anne Sullivan. First, Sullivan had to listen to and translate all the lectures. She had to read all the material Helen had to read. She had to help Helen get ready for examinations. When Helen graduated, with great fanfare and accolades, Sullivan stood to the side and applauded. But essentially, Anne Sullivan had also gone to Radcliffe and took all the classes. In my opinion, Sullivan also deserved a college degree. It is a bitter tragedy of sorts that history has failed to acknowledge Sullivan's educational triumph. Second, Anne Sullivan pulled off this incredible feat with eyes so sore, ocular pain so great, that a lesser person would have fled the scene. I worked my whole career with kids who had vision anomalies. In many ways, low vision is worse than blindness, especially when almost unbearable pain is present every day. We should erect a statue of Anne Sullivan that is bigger than the Statue of Liberty and lean it up against Radcliffe.

Representatives from Radcliffe were well aware of Sullivan's sacrifice and achievements. In June 1960, when Helen Keller turned 80, she returned to Radcliffe for the dedication of The Anne Sullivan Macy Fountain. It was tearfully fitting that a fountain was constructed as Sullivan's memorial. In a poetically powerful moment Helen Keller stood before the people assembled and spoke only one word of dedication; Helen said "water."

As for Helen's accomplishments, this account published in 1899 by John Hitz in the *Souvenir* sums it up nicely:

> She was successful in every subject and took "honors" in English and German. I think I may say that no candidate in Harvard or Radcliffe was graded higher than Helen in English. The result is remarkable, especially when we consider that Helen had been studying on strictly college preparatory lines for one year only. She had had long and careful instruction, it is true, and she had had always the loving ministrations of Miss Sullivan, in addition to the inestimable advantage of a concentration that the rest of us never know. No man or woman has ever in my experience got ready for these examinations in so brief a time. How has it been accomplished? By a union of patience, determination, and affection, with the foundation of an uncommon brain.
>
> Here is a sampling of the questions she was asked: "Where are the following: Arbela, Coryere, Dacia, Lade, Rubicon, Trasmene; and with what famous events is each connected?" "Explain the following terms: Comitia, Tributa, Delator, Deme, Pontifex, Trireme." And in English: "Write a paragraph or two on Silas Marner. On the coming of Eppie. On the death of Gabriel. Tell the story of the Merchant of Venice, showing how many and what stories are interwoven in it." [18]

I felt rather dumb after I read the paragraph above. I suppose Helen Keller made many people uncomfortable when they compared their own minds to hers. A deaf-blind woman who is smarter than most of us has much to teach humanity about darkness and silence—she is still teaching, and we are still listening.

What Else Happened in 1899?

Despite continual wars and ongoing denial of civil and human rights, there is a constant counter-force enduring throughout history, a spiritual current wherein year-after-year humanitarians go about their business. The creation of the National Park system in the United States is an example of this thread of goodness—a statement that the earth should be protected and cherished. Acts of kindness, individual and collective, happen every day, everywhere on the planet. Something fine and good will not stop pushing humanity toward love and service. Wars resolve and humanity tries again to be civil as evolution crawls forward.

Here are a few events that happened in 1899: President McKinley signed a bill creating Mt. Rainier National Park (the 5th Federal park). . . . The Treaty of Paris was signed, ending the Spanish-American War. The U.S. acquired the Philippines, Puerto Rico, and Guam. . . . Ernest Rutherford discovered two different kinds of radiation (Alpha and Beta Particles). . . . The first auto repair shop opened (in Boston). . . . On June 2, 1899, black Americans observed a day of fasting in protest against lynchings. . . . Scott Joplin was granted a copyright for his ragtime composition "Maple Leaf Rag." . . . South African Boers declared war on Great Britain. Morning Post reporter Winston Churchill was captured by Boers in Natal. He later escaped.

1900: Helen Keller, College Freshman

Helen became a member of the freshman class at Radcliffe College in 1900. She wanted to go to Harvard, but Harvard did not accept women. The Harvard Graduate School of Education did not admit females until 1920. Harvard Medical School accepted its first female enrollees in 1945. Harvard Law School opened its doors to women in 1950. Because there were no alternatives in the year 1900, Helen Keller choose Radcliffe College (for women), which was affiliated with Harvard and had an outstanding reputation. The quality of education at Radcliffe was considered exemplary, even on par with Harvard (many Harvard professors, like William James, also taught at Radcliffe).

Radcliffe officially became a college for women in 1894, just six years before Helen Keller came calling. Over a hundred years after Helen was admitted to the college, Radcliffe was fully absorbed into Harvard University (on October 1, 1999); female undergraduates were henceforth members of Harvard. Radcliffe College later evolved into the Radcliffe Institute for Advanced Study.

Radcliffe educated women by contracting with individual Harvard faculty to provide instruction. The college offered its own diplomas, countersigned by Harvard's president. In other words, there was an intimate connection between Radcliffe and Harvard; in a round-about way, Helen got the challenging and excellent education she desired.

Helen Keller's good friend, Alexander Graham Bell, was thrilled when Helen insisted on attending one of the most challenging educational institutions in the United States. However, many people in the prevailing patriarchal culture did not think it was a good idea for a deaf-blind woman to seek higher education. People said to her, "'No deaf-blind person has ever taken a college course. Why do you attempt what no one else has ventured? Even if you succeed in passing the entrance examinations, you cannot go on after you get into college. You have no books. You cannot hear lectures. You cannot make notes. You are most foolhardy to attempt something in which you are sure to fail." [19]

It was also believed that women were too physically weak and too intellectually ill-equipped to handle the rigors of advanced education. The language used to characterize women in the late 1800s was not unlike the verbiage used to describe black slaves. However, there were enlightened men who did not agree with this patriarchal, (and in retrospect) ignorant and cruel perspective; there were enough good people in power to enable Helen Keller to enter Radcliffe.

Of course, Helen was used to such negative autocratic pronouncements and as usual, she followed her faith-based energy. A nice irony is that Harvard University eventually gave Helen a well-deserved honorary doctorate in 1955—she was the first woman to ever get an honorary doctorate from Harvard.

The article segment below is from the *Ashville, North Carolina Citizens-Times,* dated Friday, October 19, 1900. This article is a gem, filled with details rarely encountered about Helen's experience at The Cambridge School for Young Ladies where she had prepared for the Radcliffe entrance exams. Here is an excerpt from that article:

It was under the instruction of Arthur Gilman, for many years the treasurer of Radcliffe College, that the bulk of Miss Keller's preparation was accomplished. When Mr. Gilman was approached . . . by Miss Sullivan in regard to the education of her young charge, he felt a natural hesitation in undertaking what seemed to be an almost hopeless task, but Miss Sullivan urged the matter strenuously and successfully and the work was begun.

After becoming familiar with what his pupil had already done, Mr. Gilman saw his way clear to all the examinations except in experimental physics. And this obstacle was got over by the substitution of its alternatives, textbook physics and astronomy . . . As for astronomy, when provided with a planetarium upon which she could feel the positions of the heavenly bodies this presented almost no difficulties.

Geometry and algebra were naturally rather hard for a girl who had only her sense of touch to help her, but by patience and the employment of several ingenious instruments these subjects, too, were mastered. In the manner of foreign languages, Helen was quite at home. She possesses a wonderful memory as well as the philosophical kind of mind. All languages are a joy for her and since she learned to speak English by placing her fingers upon the lips of her instructors she could, of course, learn the oral part of any other language in precisely the same way. For the rest, grammar, composition, and so on, the raised letter books and her wonderful memory supplied everything needed . . .

All her study does not in the least impair the health of this remarkable girl and she is today a fine specimen of a well-developed young woman. She wheels, using a tandem which she shares with a gentleman of her acquaintance and she is extremely fond of pedestrian exercise. Nor is she lacking in womanly accomplishments. She sews, crochets, and she embroiders quite like an old-fashioned girl. And most marvelous of all, she plays a capital game of Chess! All in all, Helen Keller is without doubt the most wonderful college girl the world has yet seen. [20]

One wonders who the gentleman was with whom she wheeled about town, perhaps John Macy, although we will never know. That Helen was a beautiful young woman in her prime as she entered college is clearly seen in the pictures of her taken at the turn of the century.

Anne Sullivan and Arthur Gilman did not always agree on key issues and eventually a conflict resulted in Helen (and her sister Mildred) leaving Gilman's school. The details are in Helen's autobiography *The Story of My Life*.

In 1899, just after her 19th birthday, Helen took the entrance exams for Radcliffe. She passed all of them, receiving honors in German and English. Her dream of going to college was coming true; she was academically and mentally ready when she entered the college in 1900. When she graduated from Radcliffe in 1904, she had earned a cum laude degree and was the first person in the world with deaf-blindness to earn a Bachelor of Arts degree.

Anne Sullivan assisted Helen on every leg of this challenging journey, from Gilman's *The Cambridge School for Young Ladies* all the way through Radcliffe. As I said earlier, Sullivan did not get a parallel degree for her stupendous contributions, nor did she get the recognition she deserved for her dedication and steadfastness—alongside Helen, Sullivan got the knowledge and wisdom that comes from a top-notch college education.

Helen paid special tribute to one of her professors at Radcliffe. He must have been inspirational, and he must have believed in Helen. Here she says *thank you* to him:

> [At Radcliffe] I discovered that darkness and silence might be rich in possibilities, which I might discover to the world. In other words, I found the treasures of my own island. For that I am largely indebted to Professor Charles T. Copeland, my instructor in English composition. [21]

Helen Keller became a miracle because of all the people who befriended and stood by her during her lifetime, like the wonderful Charles Copeland. Helen was part of a benevolent network of intelligent and kind-hearted people who decided they would help her. Miracles do not happen in a vacuum.

Below is a paragraph from Helen's autobiography. We get a sense of the complexity and depth of her education from this quick look are her first year:

> My studies the first year were French, German, history, English composition and English literature. In the French course I read some of the works of Corneille, Molière, Racine, Alfred de Musset and Sainte-Beuve, and in German those of Goethe and Schiller. I reviewed rapidly the whole period of history from the fall of the Roman Empire to the eighteenth century, and in English literature studied critically Milton's poems and "Areopagitica." [22]

For most of us, who do not know our Schiller from our Areopagitica, this list of classes is astoundingly impressive.

What Else Happened in 1900?

Helen's socialist views began to form during her college years. With each passing year, her Christian creed, her faith, and her intense studies forged a remarkable and combative mind. She became a Justice Warrior in the early 1900s and she would spend the rest of her life as a spokesperson for loving-kindness and for service to others. One of her most revered heroes in the early 1900s was socialist leader Eugene Debs, who shared Helen's dedication to love and service.

Here are a few events that happened in 1900: The Social Democrat Party of America (Eugene Debs' party) held its first convention. . . . Helen Keller turned 20 years old. . . . Giacomo Puccini's opera "Tosca" premiered in Rome. . . . The U.S. currency went on the gold standard; Congress passed the Currency Act. . . . The Firestone Tire and Rubber Company was founded.

Important Pathfinders: 1900 to 2000

Mass media in the 1800s created the idea of fame, of being famous. However, during the 1900s the number of people who were singled out for veneration grew exponentially and the whole idea that a few individuals were somehow more exemplary than others began to lose its charm. There were simply too many brilliant minds, too many creative geniuses, too many superstars to keep track of as the decades rolled forward. Furthermore, when mass marketing arrived, we began to *deliberately create* "famous" people. As the 1900s ended, it seemed as if the whole idea of fame was an Egoic obsession that had passed its prime.

Anyway, as a child of the 1900s, here are a few of *my* "favorite superstars (feel free to make your own list):" Helen Keller, Anne Sullivan, Albert Einstein, William James, James Schrodinger, Eleanor and Franklin Roosevelt, Max Planck, Niels Bohr, Richard Feynman, Winston Churchill, Bob Dylan, Pete Seeger, Joan Baez, Martin Luther King, Mahatma Gandhi, Nelson Mandela, Rosa Parks, Nikola Tesla, Tim Berners-Lee, Stephen Hawking, Salvador Dali, George Orwell, J. R. R. Tolkien, Babe Ruth, Muhammed Ali, Bill Gates, Walt Disney, Neil Armstrong, Dwight Eisenhower, The 14th Dalai Lama, Alvin and Heidi Toffler, and Werner Heisenberg. I could fill ten more pages, but those names came first to mind.

Freedom: 1900 to 2000

Looking back at the first ten years of the twentieth century in the Western hemisphere, from 1900 to 1910, we see a world in which minority groups and women had few or no rights. Civil and human rights were not assumed to include anyone who was not a powerful, financially secure white male (in the Western world). But revolt was beginning, fuming in the collective unconsciousness, as the twentieth century dawned. That fuming unconscious gained power as the twentieth century raced forward, although at no time did the struggle end. Right up to the year 2000, humanitarians were still at war with the forces that would deny equal rights and equal opportunity; poverty, ignorance, and violence were still defining characteristics of the human species. The global climate was changing for the worst, our water, our oceans were still being polluted, and the very air we breathe was still being poisoned as the century ended. Still, hope was not abandoned, and tremendous progress was made, year after year, month after month as life-affirming forces pressed forward.

Helen Keller came of age as the collective unconscious was beginning to fight against injustice and inequality of opportunity. To the old white guard, Helen Keller spoke with a bewildering and infuriating voice, silent and dark, a voice that the agents of darkness and cruelty had never confronted before. That did not stop these ugly forces from attacking Helen Keller, but they were still off balance and unsure as she pressed ahead with complete confidence that Love and Service-to-Others were correct worldviews.

The media, the old power structure in the United States, branded Helen with every creepy, tired old abstraction they could dig up; Helen was called unpatriotic, communist, anti-America, naively utopian, pollyannish, misguided, dangerous—whatever bullet-laden language they could fire in her direction was emptied toward her uncompromising Soul. But they could not read her body language, they did not know where her creative power could be coming from, they were bewildered by her popularity, and they could not counter her power. Their nasty proclamations went unheard by her ears, their hateful body language was unseen by her eyes, their threatening gestures evaporated before they reached Helen's serene, quiet, peaceful, gentle body standing in their way.

Helen Keller was a gift from the loving-unknown, and she knew it. That is why she called her deaf-blindness a gift from God. She had been assigned a role on Planet Earth, to be a spokesperson for freedom, to move the human species in the direction of kindness. Helen Keller became legendary, almost mythological; her life was a hero's journey. She showed us the path we were to follow as our species moved toward the future.

War: 1900 to 2000

The twentieth century was the bloodiest, most violent, most savagely stupid hundred years in all human history. Male-dominated conflict, now equipped with horrendous weaponry, murdered over 100 million human beings, men, women, children, grandparents, infants, any creature that breathed was indiscriminately decimated. The Gods stood on distant mountains looking down with horror at the unbelievably insane creatures they had unleashed.

That paragraph above was channeled from Helen Keller's soul—or so it feels to my heart. Helen got in the face of this male-inspired insanity. She called it what it was: cruel, sadistic, insane. The twentieth century exposed a stark, blatant failure of the world's religions to stand up for Love and Service-to-Others. The heartbeat of male-dominated religion was exposed as robotic, powerless, shallow, insipid. And Helen Keller knew this. That is why she became a Swedenborgian Christian. Religion had tossed out the Soul as it de-evolved into route tradition and dumb dogma. Helen Keller was reinventing spirituality as she matured. She is today a voice that says, over and over, *build the world on the foundation of loving-kindness*; it is that simple.

Technology: 1900 to 2000

If the twentieth century was the most insanely savage of all centuries, it was also the most inventive, miraculous, and awe-inspiring. Technology rocketed forward at an exponential pace. Month by month new inventions shook the human establishment, sending theories and old habits spinning and reeling. The floor fell out from beneath natural selection as unnatural selection dropped into the hands of the human species. As the twentieth century came to an end, humanity was being overrun by its own cleverness. And still, the technologies raced exponentially forward, like a driverless cement mixer plunging toward a sleepy village. The twentieth century ended not with a whimper but with a horrific gasp.

Philosophy: 1900 to 2000

Somehow, we have lost contact with the great thinkers of the nineteenth century. We venerated them, knew vaguely what they had said—and knew, without reading their works, that they had left us important insights. But now, modern humanity is moving too fast, incapable of slowing down the pace of life to a comprehensible speed. From my perspective, the great philosophers of the 1800s each gave us *the same answers* to the operation of the human mind. Using different terminology, philosophers declared that humanity had a dual consciousness, now called dual-process theory—the awareness that humanity was genetically hardwired to have two minds, which, unfortunately, are deaf and blind to each other. I will not go over this conclusion again since the concepts are covered in *The Esoteric Helen Keller* and in my other books.

However, there is one overarching philosophical question that now faces humanity, and which will determine our collective future. Here is the question: *What should a human mind be like?*

This fundamental question is now relevant because of unnatural selection. We have the technology and soon will have the knowledge to change the anatomy and physiology of the brain. This means that we will be able to craft worldviews through biological manipulation. Will we craft conspiracy-believing minds, libertarian minds, Narcissistic minds, lovingly kind minds, wise minds, mathematically clever minds, sex-craving minds, musical-genius minds, sadistic minds, hybrid minds, or Rube-Goldberg minds?

Who is kind enough, wise enough, intelligent enough, and sane enough to decide this all-important question? As the twentieth century ended, we had not even formulated the question—*what should a human mind be like*? The question was still not a matter of public concern or public dialogue.

Who will decide how the human mind should evolve in the future? We left that question for the citizens of the twenty-first century . . . so, here we are . . . time to decide.

Meanwhile (I have gotten a century ahead of myself), the 1900s had just bloomed. Helen had started college with Anne Sullivan by her side. Helen's Traditional mind was about to be transformed at the university level as old mental habits were challenged; her young mind was evolving—she was quickly becoming a fervently religious Justice Warrior.

1901: Helen Keller Proclaims: I am an Optimist

Anne Sullivan and John Macy encouraged Helen to write about her personal life for the magazine *The Youth's Companion*. Macy and Sullivan were concerned with the emotional scars that Helen received after the Frost King debacle, so they encouraged her to continue writing.

Helen had been afraid to write for fear that her astounding memory would reproduce something read to her when she was a younger child. Writing in *The Youth's Companion* was meant to be cathartic for Helen. As it turned out, her contributions to the magazine would culminate in her youthful autobiography.

In 1901, Helen published an article on the prevention of disabilities in *Ladies Home Journal*. Here is the conclusion to the article, in typical Helen Keller prose (her confidence in writing was returning):

> My countrywomen, this is not faultfinding. I am not a pessimist, but an optimist, by temperament and conviction. I am making a plea for American women and their children. I plead that the blind may see, the deaf may hear, and the idiot may have a mind. In a word, I plead that the American woman may be the mother of a great race.
>
> Throw aside, I beseech you, false modesty—the shame that shelters evil—and hasten the day when there shall be no preventable disease among mankind. [23]

Helen Keller would be awe-struck by the progress being made in science and medicine in our modern world. We have a long way to go but there is hope for a cure for diseases and genetic disorders. A famous quote of Helen's proclaims that *The Battle has Gone for Humanity*. Let us hope that this winning streak continues.

Helen Keller stood for the middle ground, for balance in human affairs. She was not okay with violent extremes on either end of the political spectrum. Yet history is full of events in which crazy men on the right wing or crazy men on the left wing assassinated a world leader or religious figure for ideological emotions. Nothing ever came of such extremes except more violence. Through it all, Helen Keller remained optimistic about the fate of the human species.

John Macy joined the staff of *The Youth's Companion* in 1901 and remained with the magazine as an associate editor until 1909. Macy was instrumental in getting Helen Keller's books and articles published. This is from Wikipedia:

> *The Youth's Companion* (1827–1929), known in later years as simply *The Companion—For All the Family*, was an American children's magazine that existed for over one hundred years until it finally merged with *The American Boy* in 1929 . . . From 1892 to 1915 it was based in the Youth's Companion Building, which is now on the National Register of Historic Places.
>
> In the 1890s its content was re-centered on entertainment, and it began to target adults as well as children with pieces contributed by writers such as Harriet Beecher Stowe, Mark Twain, Emily Dickinson, Booker T. Washington, and Jack London.

What Else Happened in 1901?

Here are a few random events that happened in 1901: Chekhov's play *Three Sisters* opened in Moscow. . . . U.S. Steel Corporation was founded by J. P. Morgan, Sr. . . . The College Board introduced the first standardized test, a forerunner to the SAT. . . . The first exhibition by Pablo Picasso, age 19, opened in Paris. . . . Butch Cassidy and the Sundance Kid robbed a train of $40,000 at Wagner, Montana. . . . The Cadillac Motor Company was founded. . . . Theodore Roosevelt advised

Americans to "Speak softly & carry a big stick." . . . U.S. President William McKinley was shot and killed by Leon Czolgosz, an anarchist, while visiting the Pan-American Exposition in New York. Theodore Roosevelt was sworn in as the youngest man to serve as U.S. President.

1903: THE STORY OF MY LIFE AND OPTIMISM ARE PUBLISHED

With the help of editor John Macy and Anne Sullivan, Helen Keller wrote *The Story of My Life*. She did this amazing feat at the same time she was attending Radcliffe College. The book is dedicated to her friend and mentor Alexander Graham Bell:

> To Alexander Graham Bell who taught the deaf to speak and enabled the listening ear to hear speech from the Atlantic to the Rockies, I dedicate this *Story of My Life*. [24]

At Radcliffe, Helen was not only studying academics, but she was also reflecting on spirituality. She was getting guidance from the Swedenborgians, the Protestants, and was also exploring Catholicism though her association with Sister Mary Joseph. Here is a letter Helen wrote to Sister Mary:

> Cambridge, February 4, 1903.
> Dear Sister Mary,
>
> Can you forgive me for not writing to you all these weeks? The thought that I have neglected you thus lies heavy on my heart, especially when I remember how many of your kindnesses I have failed to acknowledge. But I know your loving understanding, so I will let this letter explain itself. The past two months have been very full indeed. I am taking four

courses this year, Shakespeare, Philosophy, (unreadable), and Elizabethan Literature, and they require careful and detailed reading. Many times, there is so much of it, we cannot easily finish the day's work, and if we relax our efforts, there it goes accumulating at an astonishing rate! This happened soon after Christmas. I thought I would spend two days with a dear friend to get a little rest; but soon I found it was better to punish the desires of the flesh than to be punished by them. My teacher's eyes were so unmanageable, we went away to consult the oculist who restored her sight, and who lives up in New Hampshire. He said she must wear glasses and use her eyes less. The trip took two more precious days, and on our return, I found my work piled up so that it seemed impossible to catch up. In three weeks, I had to do the regular reading, prepare to write a long thesis and get ready for the Mid-Year Examinations which came all in six days. I was never so hurried in my life.

I finished the examinations a week ago yesterday, and the next day my teacher had a serious operation on her feet. They had given her so much trouble, she could scarcely walk. She suffered terribly at first, and she will not leave her room for two or three weeks. But she is doing well, and her nurse left us last night, and I am seeing how I can help her. I know a nurse must not do too much; but as it is, I fear the time seems very long to her. It is fortunate we have so many kind friends coming to see us.

Now about the books. You were very kind to send me what Cardinal Gibbons said about the Church and the Bible. I understand better than I did before why all Catholics are not provided with Bibles. I found the very facts he has set forth about the way the Bible came to be what it is in the course, English 35, I took last year. But, since you spoke of it, I think I had better tell you that in the re-vision of my story I did not take back all I had said about the Bible. I softened it down, however, as much as I could. You see, there are many things I cannot admit, and so long as I do not admit them, I must say what I really think when I am asked.

I thank you for offering to make it possible for me to meet someone who might be able to satisfy me with regard to the objectionable passages of the Bible. But I do not feel like entering into argument. Certain fundamental questions would come up to which I can find no satisfactory answer, except in experience. One of them—the vital one, is whether people must suffer eternally for refusing to accept what the Church gives. I find this treated in "What Christ Revealed." Dr. Jouin is very strong and clear in his explanations. Still, I have an unconquerable faith in the sincerity and goodness of many friends who hold opinions quite different from mine or yours, and if they are found to be wicked, as Cardinal Gibbons declares people to be who will not listen to the Church, let me share their fate rather than be false and unloving. I beg and beseech you, let us drop this subject, on which all else depends.

I am much interested in the fair for the benefit of the library, and it would make me very happy to do something to help forward the beautiful work; but I must perforce deny myself this pleasure, as the burden of college work is already too great. Next term I shall not have time even to knit or crochet. I can only send heartfelt wishes for success.

I will return Elizabeth Robin's letter, which I have enjoyed very much, and send you the long-promised picture, which did not come in time for Christmas, or I should have sent it sooner. With love and a kiss, I am, Affectionately your friend,

Helen Keller [25]

This is a sweet rejection letter. Helen had long ago decided to be a Swedenborgian and she was at a stage in her life when her tolerance for the concept of Hell and sin was untenable. Helen would rather *go to* Hell than believe in a God that created a Hell. "Let me share their fate rather than be false and unloving," she said. Helen had also just finished an academic course about the Bible that would have challenged certain avenues of unquestioning belief.

We cannot say that Helen never had a choice about religion. She encountered most of the Western religions and came to know the tenets of Zen Buddhism. Through all her education, her dialogues, and her experiences she stayed with Swedenborgianism, as did so many of the sophisticated minds of her age.

Helen could not foresee how miraculous and horrendous the next ten decades would prove to be for humanity: constant and awful wars that would slaughter more people than had been killed in all of history; technological innovations coming so fast on the heels of previous inventions that humanity would become bewildered; the too slow evolution of the human mind; and the ill-equipped primitive souls leading nation states—all this would result in the marvelous madness we call the twentieth century. And the exponential pace of change had just begun in the first decade of the 1900s—more horrendous bewilderment lay dead-ahead.

What Else Happened in 1903?

Here are a few random events that happened in 1903: The first regular transatlantic radio broadcast was established between the United States and England. . . . The bicycle race called the "Tour de France" was planned. . . . The first Teddy Bear was introduced in America, made by Morris & Rose Michtom. . . . Due to drought, the United States side of Niagara Falls ran short of water. . . . North Carolina became the first state to require the registration of nurses. . . . Ford Motor Company was incorporated under the direction of Henry Ford. . . . The Pepsi Cola Company was established. . . . Franklin Roosevelt and Eleanor Roosevelt became engaged. . . . The Nobel Prize for physics was awarded to Pierre and Marie Curie. . . . The Wright brothers made the first aircraft capable of sustained flight; at Kitty Hawk, North Carolina. . . . 1903 was also the year that Helen's essay *Optimism* appeared (published in book form).

Optimism

Optimism was written when Helen was a senior at Radcliffe College, with the encouragement of her English professor Charles Copeland. The book is comprised of three short essays:

- Part One: Optimism Within.
- Part Two: Optimism Without.
- Part Three: The Practice of Optimism.

In Part One, Helen discusses the necessity of evil; an optimist must have something to be optimistic about. Things are not right in the world, that is a given. We can be in despair about this unfortunate situation, or we can be determined to right the wrong. If we set out to make evil go away, if that is our intention, we might as well have faith that we will overcome that evil. To be optimistic is to confront evil, to work against evil, and to believe in our ability to defeat evil. One of Helen's most famous quotes is found in *Optimism*: "Although the world is full of suffering, it is full also of the overcoming of it." She ends Part One by saying, "Optimism is my religion."

In my experience, pain and suffering not only cause emotional crises, they also (often) result in the evolution of individual consciousness (transmutation). Cognitive, emotional, and spiritual sophistication can emerge and evolve from *sacred wounds*, wounds that transform. During a hero's quest, the would-be hero always experiences what it is like to be wounded—heroes do not sail through their adventures unscathed; they are always damaged by their trials, they always must overcome the blows that strike them down as they move from challenge to challenge.

The root of the word *innocent* means *not yet wounded*. Dying, death, sudden tragedy, long term illness, hurricanes and dictators lash out at us as we live day by day—none of us escape injury or insult. Some are destroyed by life's inevitable disasters; but those who choose to survive, are forced to evolve—their wounds become *sacred wounds*.

Helen's innocence was destroyed before she was two years old. She was severely wounded by an illness; she was made deaf, blind, and mute in a flash of fever. Helen was struck down, almost killed by this illness, but, as an adult reflecting on her life, she saw those wounds as sacred and transforming. It was a long struggle to regain her connection to humanity, to find her voice, to find a mission in life, to set out on a hero's journey. Helen's optimism confronted necessary evils, which she encountered on her life-journey, and optimism gave her a life worth living.

Part Two begins with a discussion about Western philosophers who Helen perceives to be isolated men who sat alone and dwelled long hours within their own minds, trying to figure out the world around and the world within. They were, Helen speculates, rather like her, deaf-blind to the tumult of the everyday world, and yet fascinated by human thought. Helen describes the philosophical life as "happy isolation." Within this happy isolation, the optimist perceives evil as "a halt on the way to the good." In other words, Evil is just a distraction as evolution works tirelessly to bring about greater and greater compassion. Helen looks back at the history of cultures and compares the dreadful conditions of long ago with the much better world she finds herself living within. She strongly contends that there is an incessant flow of goodness, a constant force, that brings ever more goodness into the world. She feels that this force for good will prevail. Toward the end of Part Two, Helen says, "To be an American is to be an optimist."

Part Three begins with the proclamation that optimism propels the world forward, while, to the contrary, pessimism retards progress and development. Those who believe that pain outweighs joy, only add to the world's pain, she tells us. Men and women are robbed of their will to fight if they have a pessimistic worldview. Optimism gives mankind the fuel to resist, to strive, to create a better world for humanity. Most of the philosophers, in Helen's opinion, were optimistic—they had to be.

As she got older, Helen saw this small book as too simple, the product of her idealistic youth. Anne Sullivan, in her biography, says of *Optimism*:

> It was immature, as one might expect of a college girl, and full of the "cocksureness" for which she still chides herself when she finds that she has written in a way which seems to imply that she has the last word of knowledge on the subject, but it was bursting with vigor and defiance. She was tired of being pitied. She was proving and ready to prove again that she could make something out of the broken pieces of her life.

I rather enjoyed Helen's cocksureness in this book. What I find in *Optimism* is Helen Keller's basic personality defining itself. This belief in optimism is Helen's core conviction. This is the attitude that will carry her through her entire life. She simply knows in her heart that goodness will prevail over evil, no matter what happens; Helen believes that there is an unrelenting march toward a better world. She ends *Optimism* with her creed:

> I believe in God, I believe in Man, I believe in the power of the spirit. I believe it is a sacred duty to encourage ourselves and others; to hold the tongue from any unhappy word against God's world, because no man has any right to complain of a universe which God made good, and which thousands of men have striven to keep good.

The Story of My Life

The Story of My Life is Helen's autobiography (up to age 22). There is an abridged version credited to Helen, which is only 75 pages, and there is an unabridged version co-authored by John Macy, Anne Sullivan, and Helen Keller that contains the fascinating letters and reports written by Sullivan, as well as delightful letters that Helen wrote in her youth and emerging adulthood. The unabridged volume is called The Story of My Life (1887–1901) and a supplementary account of her education, including passages from the reports and letters of her teacher Anne Sullivan.

In 1901, Anne Sullivan's letters were edited and organized by Sullivan and her future husband, Harvard Professor John Macy. Anne Sullivan and John Macy were both brilliant writers, which is one reason the language in the book flows so delightfully. I suggest you read the unabridged version so that you do not miss Sullivan's and Macy's important perspectives. After John Macy married Anne Sullivan in 1905, and while he lived with Sullivan and Keller (until his separation from Sullivan in 1914), he edited Helen's publications, including her books The World That I live in (1908), and The Song of the Stone Wall (1910).

I read the unabridged edition compiled by Professor Roger Shattuck. Shattuck's version divides the book into four sections and adds an appendix. Included are notes by Helen Keller's biographer Dorothy Hermann, with an afterword by Shattuck.

- Part One is called Helen Keller's Account.
- Part Two is called Anne Sullivan's Account.
- Part Three is called John Macy's Account.
- Part Four is called Helen Keller's Letters.
- The Appendix contains excerpts from books published during Helen's lifetime.
- Dorothy Hermann's section contains short biographical sketches of Anne Sullivan, John Macy, Dr. Samuel Gridley Howe, Laura Bridgman, Michael Anagnos, Dr. Alexander Graham Bell, and William Gibson.
- The book concludes with editor Roger Shattuck's afterword.

Part One: Helen Keller's Account

The Story of My Life had its origin in a magazine piece Helen wrote in 1893 for *The Youth's Companion* entitled "My Life." A revised and expanded version of the original article eventually appeared in *The Ladies Home Journal* in 1902, published as a six-part series, after which it was published as a book in 1903. This well-written, detailed, and fascinating book, thanks greatly to the serialized format and the additions from Sullivan and Macy, catapulted Helen Keller onto the national stage. The media took over from there and Helen Keller eventually became a national icon.

The Story of My Life begins as an easy-to-read personal narrative, filled with stories about Helen's childhood. Helen's writing skills improved in college under the tutorage of her English composition professor Charles Copeland, who helped Helen with style and editing. Professor Copeland had contacted *The Ladies Home Journal* and introduced Helen to the editor Edward Bok, who agreed to pay Helen three thousand dollars for the six-part series. *The Story of My Life* gives the reader a warm sense of Helen's evolution, especially after Anne Sullivan arrived at her home in Alabama.

Interestingly, Helen typed *The Story of My Life* on a regular (not a braille) Hammond typewriter. This became a common practice for her, especially when she wrote letters to her sighted friends. Anne Sullivan would read back (fingerspell) what Helen had typed so that corrections could be made.

In 1996, the New York Public Library called *The Story of My Life* "one of the hundred most important books of the 20th century." There have been several variations of the book. After looking over a few of these, I recommend the version edited by Roger Shattuck (with commentary by Helen's biographer Dorothy Herrmann), from a series called Restored Classics (2003). I came across Shattuck's writing during my research and was quite impressed with his interest in Helen Keller, his in-depth understanding of her life, and his powerful writing style.

Helen's good friend Mark Twain wrote to congratulate her after the book came out and to praise their long-standing affection for each other. This is copied from the Perkins School for the Blind Helen Keller Digital Archives:

Riverdale-on-the Hudson,
St. Patrick's Day, 1903

Dear Helen:

I must steal half a moment from my work to say how glad I am to have your book and how highly I value it, both for its own sake and as a remembrance of an affectionate friendship which has subsisted between us for nine years without a break and without a single act of violence that I can call to mind. I suppose there is nothing like it in heaven; and not likely to be, until we get there and show off. I often think of it with longing, and how they'll say, "there they come—sit down in front!" I am practicing with a tin halo.

The Father of American Psychology, Harvard Professor William James also sent his congratulations:

I won't praise your power over language, or your clearness of discrimination or your genius for psychological insight, for I don't want to add to the spoiling process to which you have been subjected so long! The sum of it is that you are a blessing. ~ Perkins Helen Keller archives.

It is remarkable that two of Helen's good friends were Mark Twain and William James. Three of the most articulate minds in American history were friends. I find this level of serendipity to be wonderful and amazing.

In the beginning of *The Story of My Life*, Helen tells us that she "was born on June 27, 1880 in Tuscumbia, a little town of northern Alabama." She also gives the reader a sense of her genealogy, starting with her paternal grandfather Caspar Keller who was born in Switzerland and then moved to Maryland to settle. We learn that Caspar Keller's wife, Helen's grandmother, was a second cousin to Robert E. Lee. Helen's father, Arthur H. Keller was a Captain in the Confederate Army, which is why he was often called Captain Keller long after the war had ended.

The pressure of writing *The Story of My Life* and keeping up with classroom expectations at Radcliffe was overwhelming, so Harvard professor John Macy was asked to help with the Journal articles and book editing. Macy is described by Nella Braddy, Sullivan's biographer, as a man of "fine intelligence, a critical sense, and a gift for writing." His entrance into the lives of Sullivan and Keller was monumental. He eventually married Anne Sullivan. Although this marriage lasted only a few years, John Macy's impact on Sullivan and Keller was profound and transformative. John Macy guided Helen's crafting of this first chapter, although the memories and expressions are purely Helen's.

Part Two: Anne Sullivan's Account

In Part Two, Anne Sullivan comes across as a brilliant and perceptive writer; her notes about Helen's amazing transformation are poignant, profound, and at times funny. Reading Anne Sullivan's early letters to her friend Sophia Hopkins is also a joy.

I feel that no one can understand the brilliance of Helen Keller who has not read these letters. The letters show that the young Helen Keller was a whirlwind of activity. She races all over the house and knows where she is and where things are in the rooms relative to each other. She dresses and undresses herself—often more than twice a day—and does the same to her dolls, dressing and undressing them. She sews, knits, and makes bead necklaces. Sullivan's letters to Mrs. Hopkins reveal Helen Keller to be a continually active, curious, and highly intelligent young girl.

Mrs. Hopkins faithfully preserved all the letters to her in a shoe box. When *The Story of My Life* was being written, John Macy borrowed the letters and he and Annie chose a few to highlight in the book. They then stored the shoe box in the attic of their house where a leaky roof eventually destroyed *all* the letters. Circumstances erased a historical treasure.

Once the miracle of language was revealed to her, Helen's natural curiosity became an insatiable appetite for knowledge about the world. For a while, Helen became obsessed with counting, and then, on other days, she became fascinated with learning action words (verbs), adverbs, and adjectives. Always she was eager to share what she had learned. She taught the children of the servants (and, unsuccessfully, one of the dogs) to fingerspell. She told her mother or father everything that happened after an outing. Her mind was moving so fast every day that family and friends worried that she was being overtaxed—her poor little mind was overheating, they insisted, which Anne Sullivan proclaimed as nonsense.

Here is a portion of a delightful letter to Sophia Hopkins dated March 4, 1888, written a year after Sullivan had arrived at the Keller homestead in the town of Tuscumbia; Sullivan is reflecting on her initial impressions after she stepped off the train onto the soil of Alabama. This is copied from the American Foundation for the Blind Helen Keller Digital Archives, "The Cape Cod Campus," Summer-Fall 1987:

> I thought, as we drove to my new home through the little town of Tuscumbia, which was more like a New England village than a town; for the roads–there were no streets–were lined with blossoming fruit-trees, and the ploughed fields smelt good, (I think the earthy smell is the best of all spring odors) "Certainly this is a good time and a pleasant place to begin my life-work." When Mrs. Keller pointed out her house at the end of a long, narrow lane, I became so excited and eager to see my little pupil that I could scarcely sit still in my seat. I felt like getting out and pushing the horse along faster. I wondered that Mrs. Keller could endure such a slow beast. I have discovered since that all things move slowly in the South. When at last we reached the house, I ran up the porch-steps, and there stood Helen by the porch-door, one hand stretched out, as if she expected someone to come in. Her little face wore an eager expression, and I noticed that her body was well formed and sturdy. For this I was most thankful. I did not mind the tumbled hair, the soiled pinafore, the shoes tied with white strings—all that could be remedied in time; but if she had been deformed or had acquired any of those nervous habits that so often accompany blindness, and which make an assemblage of blind people such a pitiful sight, how much harder it would have been for me! As it was, I knew the task I had set myself would be difficult enough.

We can picture a pretty, fresh looking Anne Sullivan stepping from the train to greet a smiling Kate Keller, but that image would be wrong. The train ride from Massachusetts to Alabama had taken a grueling four days, and Sullivan had had eye surgery a week (or so) before she stepped onto the train. Her right eye throbbed and was inflamed during the whole trip. And her shoes were too small causing her feet to swell—she had to wear slippers most of the trip. Sullivan had never been out of Massachusetts; this was culture shock for the young woman. She was an exhausted mess as she stepped from the train to greet Kate Keller, who had a four-month-old baby girl (Helen's sister, Mildred) and a wild-child deaf, blind, mute kid waiting back at the homestead.

The correspondence between Anne Sullivan and Sophia Hopkins is a marvelous record of the early months when Sullivan worked with Helen Keller. In a letter to Sullivan, written in 1903, her friend Alexander Graham Bell wrote:

> These letters to Mrs. Hopkins will become a standard, the principles that guided you in the early education of Helen are of the greatest importance to all teachers. They are TRUE and the way in which you carried them out shows—what I have all along recognized—that Helen's progress was as much due to her teacher as to herself, and that your personality and the admirable methods you pursued were integral ingredients of Helen's progress. ~ AFB digital archives

I agree with Dr. Bell, Anne Sullivan's teaching methods were brilliant. As you read these early letters, not only do you witness Helen's marvelous explosion of energy, but you also see how carefully and intuitively the young teacher figured out how to motivate and direct the attention of her young pupil.

There are references in the commentary below to Anne Sullivan's difficult youth. Biographies of Helen Keller and Anne Sullivan discuss Sullivan's childhood in detail. Simply stated, Anne Sullivan had a dreadful childhood; it is a miracle she survived to become the legendary teacher that we now venerate.

Sophia Hopkins was Annie Sullivan's housemother in a cottage at the Perkins Institute for the Blind, where Annie had been schooled. This housemother job was evidently a charitable and devotional undertaking for Mrs. Hopkins since she is described in the Helen Keller archives as a wealthy patron of Anne Sullivan and eventually of Helen Keller. Anne Sullivan was 14 when she came under the charge of Mrs. Hopkins. This must have been a powerful bonding experience for both women. Sullivan was, by all accounts, a feisty, sharp-tongued, streetwise teenager who had no problem with confrontation. Sophia Hopkins was, we imagine, a refined lady with a stable life; she evidently had enough time on her hands to nurture wild-child blind kids.

In an article called the "Cape Cod Campus," referring to Sophia Hopkin's home, we see the first of many powerful friendships that nurtured and encouraged the unfolding of Anne Sullivan's genius and Helen Keller's accomplishments. Sophia Hopkins was a widow who had lost her only child, a daughter who died at a young age:

> . . . having lost her husband and—16 years later—her daughter, the lonely woman sought solace in the expanse of nearby sea and shore, and she wondered what she might do for the rest of her life. Walking the sands, to which a pair of paths led from her house, she paused one day to observe a group of blind children playing there. Learning they came from Boston's Perkin's Institution for the Blind, she applied for work at the school and in 1883 was taken on as a matron in one of the cottage residences.
>
> Among her earliest charges was a fiery-tempered little waif named Annie Sullivan who had arrived at Perkins from a Tewksbury, Massachusetts almshouse only two years before the widow Hopkins and was now living in the dormitory to which the new housemother had been assigned. The youngster was alone in the world: motherless, deserted by a ne'er-do-well father, grieving and furious at the neglectful death of a little brother who had been with her at the almshouse. ~ AFB digital archives

So, a grieving mother, Sophia Hopkins, met a motherless child, Anne Sullivan, in an improbable place and the world slowly improved for both women. They needed each other and they found each other, and now our world is a better place because of this lovely serendipity.

Mrs. Hopkins came to Perkins two years after Anne Sullivan had arrived. Sophia was given charge of the cottage where Anne Sullivan and deaf-blind Laura Bridgman resided. This put Hopkins in direct contact with two people—Anne Sullivan and Laura Bridgman—both of whom would become legendary figures in history.

The Perkins School for the Blind ran their academic program like any other public school in America; so, when the summer months arrived, the students were expected to go home to their families, only to return as the fall months signaled another academic year of study. When the last bell rang, students scattered to their homes across the country. However, Anne Sullivan had no place to go—she had no family and no home. Sending her back to Tewksbury (the state almshouse in Massachusetts) may have been considered an option, but it was certainly a dreadful alternative. After Sophia Hopkins arrived, she took Annie to her cottage in Cape Cod where they spend wonderful summers together between school breaks. Sullivan had never seen the ocean, or felt the warm sand beach, or smelled the sea—Cape Cod was exhilarating for Annie and life-affirming. Her experiences at the Cape Cod Campus are sweetly documented in Kim Nielsen's book *Beyond the Miracle Worker* (2009).

Sullivan not only wrote to Sophia Hopkins on a regular basis, but she also had Helen writing letters to Sophia as soon as Helen was able to use symbolic language. A bond quickly developed between Mrs. Hopkins and Helen Keller. In the "Cape Cod Campus" article, author Philip Jenkin is clear about Sophia's relationship with Anne Sullivan and Helen Keller: the three women were good friends:

> Sophia Hopkins was in no way a surrogate mother to Annie and Helen, nor a kind of self-appointed "auntie." The bonding of the three was a very special kind of chemistry. Annie wrote once, to and of the Brewster widow: "To have a friend is to have one of the sweetest gifts that life can bring, and my heart sings for joy now; for I have found a real friend—one who will never get away from me, or try to, or want to." It was a reciprocated friendship that included Helen as its special beneficiary. ~ AFB digital archives

We do not know the extent of the mother-daughter bonding that might have occurred between Annie and Sophia, but we do know that Mrs. Hopkins had a professional role to play. She was a mentor and a friend alongside any other powerful emotions that might have played out. Mrs. Hopkins is part of the team that created the miracle and the miracle worker—we appreciate and applaud such a genuine and critical contribution. In a way, Mrs. Hopkins represents all human beings who provide support and love behind the scenes of historical events, just off stage, hidden from public view. Without such external support and love, great stories could not unfold.

Sophia Hopkins was a welcome guest at the Keller home in Alabama and at the house Helen and Annie would later come to occupy in Wrentham, Massachusetts. Time and again, Sophia Hopkins was on hand to stay with Helen when Annie or members of the family were not available. Sophia was a member of the wedding when Annie exchanged vows with author and teacher John Macy. When that short-lived marriage eventually dissolved, Sophia Hopkins remained a steadfast presence in the disrupted lives of her two young friends.

Here is a copy of a letter from Anne Sullivan to Sophia Hopkins, dated May 16, 1887. This gives a nice sense of a typical teaching day in Tuscumbia:

We have begun to take long walks every morning, immediately after breakfast. The weather is fine, and the air is full of the scent of strawberries. Our objective point is Keller's Landing, on the Tennessee [River], about two miles distant. We never know how we get there, or where we are at a given moment; but that only adds to our enjoyment, especially when everything is new and strange. Indeed, I feel as if I had never seen anything until now, Helen finds so much to ask about along the way. We chase butterflies, and sometimes catch one. Then we sit down under a tree, or in the shade of a bush, and talk about it. Afterwards, if it has survived the lesson, we let it go; but usually its life and beauty are sacrificed on the altar of learning, though in another sense it lives forever; for has it not been transformed into living thoughts? It is wonderful how words generate ideas! Every new word Helen learns seems to carry with it necessity for many more. Her mind grows through its ceaseless activity.

Keller's Landing was used during the war to land troops, but has long since gone to pieces, and is overgrown with moss and weeds. The solitude of the place sets one dreaming. Near the landing there is a beautiful little spring, which Helen calls "squirrel-cup," because I told her the squirrels came there to drink. She has felt dead squirrels and rabbits and other wild animals and is anxious to see a "walk-squirrel," which interpreted, means, I think, a "live squirrel." We go home about dinnertime usually, and Helen is eager to tell her mother everything she has seen. This desire to repeat what has been told her shows a marked advance in the development of her intellect and is an invaluable stimulus to the acquisition of language. I ask all her friends to encourage her to tell them of her doings, and to manifest as much curiosity and pleasure in her little adventures as they possibly can. This gratifies the child's love of approbation and keeps up her interest in things. This is the basis of real intercourse. She makes many mistakes, of course, twists words and phrases, puts the cart before the horse, and gets herself into hopeless tangles of nouns and verbs; but so does the hearing child. I am sure these difficulties will take care of themselves. The impulse to tell is the important thing. I supply a word here and there, sometimes a sentence, and suggest something which she has omitted or forgotten. Thus, her vocabulary grows apace, and the new words germinate and bring forth new ideas; and they are the stuff out of which heaven and earth are made. ~ AFB digital archives

Anne Sullivan is so articulate and so genuine that we stare in amazement at her eloquence; what a blessing to have these letters preserved. The letters give us an inside look at the strategy that allowed Helen's language to blossom. Many of Sullivan's lectures are also available online at the American Foundation for the Blind Helen Keller Digital Archives.

Part Three: John Macy's Account

Part Three, written and edited by John Macy, has several divisions, including a short section about Helen's personality, a short summary of Anne Sullivan's teaching methodology, a section about Helen's ability to speak, a discussion of Helen's literary style, including commentary about the *Frost King* controversy, and a collection of letters that Helen wrote from age seven until she was a college girl at Radcliffe.

There are many gems in John Macy's part of the book. He describes Helen as animated and expressive. He says she is whimsical, has an adventuresome spirit, and she likes the company of others. Macy tells us that Helen laughs at jokes and responds to the moods of others. Her view of life is full of poetic exaggeration, according to Macy, and no doubt, he says, the universe she perceives is better than the reality the rest of us confront.

Macy observes that Helen's sense of touch is extraordinary but not as acute as other blind individuals, like Laura Bridgman. Macy tells us that Helen seems to have little sense of direction and gropes her way around even familiar spaces. Her sense of smell was highly refined as a child, and she used it to navigate and to identify people and things, but she became less attuned to olfactory information in her adult years. I discussed Helen Keller's sixth sense in Chapter Four of *The Esoteric Helen Keller*, but I like this paragraph from John Macy's perspective:

> The question of a special "sixth sense," such as people have ascribed to Miss Keller, is a delicate one. This much is certain, she cannot have any sense that other people may not have, and the existence of a special sense is not evident to her or to anyone who knows her. Miss Keller is distinctly not a singular proof of occult and mysterious theories, and any attempt to explain her in that way fails to reckon with her normality. She is no more mysterious and complex than any other person. All that she is, all that she has done, can be explained directly, except such things in every human being as never can be explained. She does not, it would seem, prove the existence of spirit without matter, or of innate ideas, or of immortality, or anything else that any other human beings does not prove.

This description is extraordinarily clear and powerful. Macy states unequivocally that Helen is not a prodigy, not a wonder woman, not proof of anything esoteric. She is as ordinary as the rest of us, even if she cannot see or hear. On the everyday level of reality, I agree with John Macy. However, I also think that in his genuine and kind way he is reading Helen's abilities and the world she inhabits from (understandably) a Traditional worldview (on the Cook-Greuter's scale, discussed in *The Esoteric Helen Keller*). Helen herself understood her esoteric powers, even if they were ill-defined. Helen knew, as she told her friend Nevile Wilkinson, that the fairies need to be conjured back to the boardrooms and classrooms. Helen was talking about our intuitive (Allocentric) mind. We miss something precious within Helen Keller if we fail to look below the surface of her everyday world.

Anne Sullivan expressed the same opinion of Helen's normality, agreeing with John Macy—and just as emphatically. Helen also agreed, but she was much more open to mysteries and miracles than her teacher and good friend John Macy. Science has pushed forward since 1903, when John Macy wrote those important words, and we now know that brains rewire in unusual ways. The idea of a sixth sense becomes more plausible when we define our terms clearly, especially when we understand what Eastern scholars said centuries ago: the sixth sense is the mind itself. Just as the blind traveler learns to be more Egocentrically attentive and Allocentrically aware of the domain, so, too, does the mind compensate for sensory loss by becoming more expertly attentive and aware. As I emphasized in *The Esoteric Helen Keller*, Helen evolved a remarkable mind because it compensated for the loss of vision and hearing.

In the section about Sullivan's teaching methods, Macy identifies two key principles that define Sullivan's philosophy:

- Sullivan spelled whole sentences into Helen's hand, right from the beginning. She used the same model we do with young children when we talk to them. When we speak to a child, it is with an adult flow; we do not speak in simple sentences with an overemphasis on nouns and verbs. We do not even hesitate to speak to a child using words that they have yet to assimilate. Sullivan did the same with fingerspelling; she used pronouns, adverbs, adjectives, and did not shy away from talking over Helen's head. In effect, Sullivan proved that this approach was highly effective.
- Sullivan let Helen decide each day what she wanted to learn. Formal lessons were tried but were quickly abandoned. Helen's curiosity was inexhaustible; consequently, her enthusiasm directed the lessons. There was no problem with motivation, because Helen was doing what she wished to do—all day, every day—Anne Sullivan simply flowed with Helen's passion to learn.

I know from thirty years of teaching blind children that finding a child bursting with curiosity, driving their own lessons forward, is not a common occurrence. Motivation is a huge problem that teachers face. Younger children want to play; "lessons" are deadly boring to little children. The educational setting itself (confined to classrooms, desks, time schedules) is often a deadening experience for enthusiastic, curious children. Motivating kids who feel confined and quieted is a challenge. Sullivan's open-ended teaching environment was a key reason for Helen's success, but Helen brought a voracious curiosity to all her challenges, which made Sullivan's tasks easier.

John Macy knew that Anne Sullivan had a philosophy, an overarching principle that she applied from the moment of her arrival in Tuscumbia. In the afterword, Roger Shattuck summarized Sullivan's philosophy. Shattuck said that Sullivan "used discipline plus affection, strictness plus encouragement." Love was at the core of Sullivan's teaching, but love had to come with rules and acceptable behaviors; Helen had to be accepting of love; she also had to learn to receive information, which her initial wild-child reactiveness dampened.

As a young special education consultant, I went from classroom to classroom in different schools. The best teachers had classroom management well established—students followed rules that set up an atmosphere where learning could easily happen. Sullivan was doing what all good teachers do, discipline and teach with love—blend the two artfully.

Many years after the publication of *The Story of My Life*, both Helen and Annie expressed concern about their personal contributions to the book. They were both quite young when the book came out and, from a more mature perspective, were critical of their own contributions. Here is one of Helen's comments:

> In *The Story of My Life*, which I wrote with the carelessness of a happy, positive young girl, I failed to stress sufficiently the obstacles and hardships which confronted Teacher—and there were other defects in the book which my mature sense of her sacrifice will not permit to go uncorrected. ~ Afterword to *The Story of My Life* in the 2003 Restored Classic edition

Sullivan wrote:

> Exceedingly, I regret that in *The Story of My Life* I was careless in what I wrote about the progress Helen made in language and in learning to speak. The narrative was so telescoped that it seemed to ordinary readers as if Helen in a single moment had "grasped the whole mystery of language." What misunderstandings I must have created by my artless account of what I am sure a critical, mature person would have presented with a proper sense of perspective. ~ Afterword to *The Story of My Life* in the 2003 Restored Classic edition

Having written a few books myself, I know how vulnerable (and at times dumb) an author feels when he or she holds their creation in hand. All the flaws, all the unfortunate phrasing, all the typos (despite extensive editing), and all the "facts" that turned out later to be (embarrassingly) wrong are frozen in time. Our contributions are an offering at a time and place in the evolution of humanity. Regrets are inevitable and ultimately okay—there is no need to beat ourselves up. Helen wrote *Teacher* in 1955 to set things straight from her perspective, and Sullivan's biography is also an exercise in bringing greater clarity to history—I will review *Teacher* and Sullivan's biography later in this timeline.

1904: HELEN GRADUATES FROM REDCLIFFE COLLEGE

In 1904, Helen Keller became the first deaf-blind individual in the world to receive a Bachelor of Arts degree, graduating cum laude from Radcliffe College. Helen was 24 and Annie was 38.

Over the four-year period of her education, Helen took seventeen and a half college courses. She had no classes in science, mathematics, drawing, or music, not only because these were prohibitive for a deaf-blind student, but perhaps more relevantly, Helen preferred languages and history. She studied English, German, French, Government, Economics, History, Shakespeare, the English Bible, the History of Philosophy, Elizabethan Literature, and Milton.

∾

Many have asked why Anne Sullivan did not move on after Radcliffe, because she had options. And Helen was now an educated and world-famous adult woman; she no longer needed a teacher by her side. Here is Sullivan's biographer Kim Nielsen on the subject:

> I believe that Annie was afraid to leave Helen—and did not want to leave her. Though publicly her status alongside Helen remained vague, Helen loved her. No one else in her tumultuous life ever provided love and support, or tolerated her moods, as Helen did. [26]

It seems that the two women had no intention whatsoever of abandoning each other. They needed each other, and despite occasional friction, they cherished each other. They were also like two energy fields that poured fire and oxygen into each other's soul. Thank God they did not go their separate ways.

In 1904, Helen and Anne bought a home (a farm) on seven acres of land in Wrentham, Massachusetts, a suburb of Boston. They paid $3,000 for the house, which was on the trolley line so they could easily journey to and from Boston. Helen and Annie bought the house jointly, so that put an end to suggestions that they go their separate ways.

This is copied from the Wrentham Lions Club webpage:

> Ms. Keller had been a resident [in Wrentham] from 1904 through 1917. During that time, she published *The World I Live In* (1908), revealing for the first time her thoughts on her world.

This following sentiment was written in a letter she wrote about her experience at Wrentham:

> "Always I look back to Wrentham as the place where I lived most serenely, where I did my work quietly, and enjoyed undisturbed the treasures of books and of nature." [27]

In the dedication to *The Esoteric Helen Keller*, I paid tribute to Lions Clubs in America and across the world. The Lions organization played a key behind-the-scenes role that paralleled the lives of Helen Keller, Anne Sullivan, and Polly Thomson (who took over when Sullivan died in 1936). It would be nice to see the archives of Lions International and especially the transcripts of meetings of important groups like the Wrentham Lions. I requested these but was unable to establish a dialogue with Lions Clubs in Wrentham or internationally.

The famous stone walls of New England meandered through the seven acres of the Wrentham property. Helen would visit these walls and walk along them as part of her daily routine. She eventually wrote the long poem (in book form) called *The Song of the Stone Wall* (1910).

In October 1904, the World's Fair in St. Louis celebrated *Helen Keller Day*. John Macy joined Helen and Annie for the event.

What Else Happened in 1904?

Wars continued, comedies came and went, natural disasters mingled with manmade disasters, and ice cream cones were invented.

Here are a few random events that happened in 1904: Pope Pius X banned low cut dresses in the presence of churchmen. . . . Baltimore, Maryland caught fire, destroying 1500 buildings. . . . Much of Toronto, Canada was also destroyed by fire in 1904. . . . Japan and Russia declared war on each other. . . . Giacomo Puccini's opera *Madam Butterfly* premiered in Milan, Italy. . . . The United States acquired control of the Panama Canal Zone for $10 million. . . . Cy Young pitched the first perfect game in baseball for the Boston Americans against the Philadelphia Athletics (3–0). . . . George Bernard Shaw's comedy *John Bull's Other Island* premiered in London.

1905: Anne Sullivan Marries John Macy

Anne Mansfield Sullivan married John Albert Macy at the Wrentham house in Massachusetts on May 3, 1905. Anne was 39, John was 28. Although they never divorced, they separated in 1915. Macy is quoted as saying that he felt like he had married an institution, which is exactly the case. Sullivan burned her diary, so the details of the ten years together are lost to history. Here is a blog post from the Helen Keller Archives at The American Foundation for the Blind:

> Sometime after she married John Albert Macy in 1905, the young wife burned her private journals for fear of what her husband might think of her if he should read them. Similarly, she did not want her correspondence to be kept after her death. But for historical purposes, materials were retained, and the Helen Keller Archives at the American Foundation for the Blind contain some of her letters, prose, and verse. Other materials about Anne are located at the Perkins School for the Blind in Watertown, Massachusetts and the American Antiquarian Society in Worcester, Massachusetts. [28]

We are entitled to our secrets, even if we are world famous, like Anne Sullivan was. I suspect that what Annie burned were honest emotions that had no relevance for history. She had documented enough about Helen Keller's life; the world did not need to know her guilty secrets or how she struggled with the emotions of her painful past. Burning old painful notes in a diary probably seemed like a good idea as she was embarking on a positive new direction.

What Else Happened in 1905?

Here are a few random events that happened in 1905: The Russian Revolution was ignited in St. Petersburg when demonstrators marched to the Winter Palace to petition the Tsar; troops fired on protesters in what became known as *Bloody Sunday*. . . . Arthur Conan Doyle published *The Return of Sherlock Holmes* in London. . . . Albert Einstein finished his Quantum Theory of Light. . . . Las Vegas was founded in Nevada. . . . Norway dissolved its union with Sweden, which had been in effect since 1814. . . . Black intellectuals and activists lead by W. E. B. Du Bois organized the civil rights Niagara Movement.

A Chat About the Hand

The essay, "A Chat About the Hand," by Helen Keller, was printed in *Century Magazine* in 1905. This short piece is one of the best explanations for how Helen gathered information about the world using her hands and fingers. The essay was the basis for the beginning chapters in Helen's 1908 publication *The World That I Live In*. Helen also commented about her hands in several of her other books.

Although most of the information below was taken from "A Chat About the Hand," what follows is a compilation of perspectives. Helen suggests that we begin our appreciation of our own hands and fingers by doing a thought experiment:

> Do a thought experiment: imagine you have no hands. No opposable thumbs. What can you not do now: pet the cat, transmit sensual, healing, encouraging, threatening vibrations; use tools, play instruments, read braille, explore with the fingers, swim, shake hands, write or paint, feed ourselves, fistfight, arm wrestle, play catch, play sports, point, gesture, use sign language, disconnect eye-hand coordination, brace yourself, support yourself.

That is, of course, just a partial list of disabilities that arise when the hands and fingers are immobilized. A friend of mine fell forward and broke both her wrists as she caught her fall. Both wrists were put in a cast and she was told not to use her fingers for several weeks. My friend soon found out what the hands do for us: she couldn't prepare meals or feed herself, couldn't wash her body or face, couldn't dress or undress herself, couldn't shake hands, couldn't open and close drawers, couldn't write, hold a book, drive a car, brush her teeth, play her guitar, point in a direction, brace herself against further falls, push herself up out of a chair, apply makeup, tie her shoes, hold her phone, sew a button, type on her computer, pull the covers back before going to bed, hammer a nail, get the mail from the mailbox, get money from her wallet, take her pills, or scratch an itch—to name just a few of the hardships she endured. It does not take long to realize how much we take our hands and fingers for granted.

If such an injury had happened to Helen Keller, especially if her fingers were damaged, she would not have been able to communicate using fingerspelling or read her braille books; she would have been unable to explore a friend's face or read lips, and she would not have been able to examine objects or explore the layout of a room. Her isolation would have been profound had both her hands been damaged.

Therefore, it should come as no surprise that Helen Keller was deeply concerned about her hands. In the quote below, she ruminates on her wonderful hands during a difficult emotional time in her life:

> Sometimes I am uneasy about my hands; I use them constantly, writing, reading, listening to conversation, and reading people's lips; but work is the only sure bulwark against despair. ~ *Helen Keller's Journal* by Helen Keller, 1938

The above diary entry was written just after Anne Sullivan had died. The hands that had guided Helen through her youth and gifted language to her, were gone. Helen's hands must have felt their own despair, loneliness, and grief. I suspect that the limbic region of Helen's brain (where emotions are generated) had rich interconnections with the "hand regions" of the neocortex.

However, it is not just our emotions on display as we gesture and create. The way our thoughts become reality is also through our hands; without our hands we lose the ability to control the world around us and we lose the ability to create art and use tools. The hands and mind work intimately together; thoughts are the ingredients the hands use to mold new relationships and new art.

Unlike Helen Keller, most human beings do not assign their hands the complex task of expressing and receiving information embedded in language. Helen's hands were rarely at rest. The following quotes are from *Helen Keller's Journal* (1938):

> Everybody was talking at once, and Polly was interrupting continually trying to tell me things, so that her sentences resembled bits of spaghetti.

On December 17, 1936 she wrote:

> Things have been spelled in my palm until it is almost raw.

And on December 21, 1936, reflecting on the loss of Anne Sullivan, she wrote:

> This is the shortest day of the terrestrial year, but in my soul's calendar it has been the longest. It seems years instead of two months since Teacher left, and I experience a sense of dying daily.
>
> Every hour I long for the thousand bright signals from her vital, beautiful hand. That was life! The hand that with a little word touched the darkness of my mind, and I awoke to happiness and love; a hand swift to answer every need, to disentangle skeins of dark silence for a fairer pattern; a hand radiant with the light it retrieved that I might see, sweet with the music it transmitted to my inner ear.

We can feel Helen's pain and grief through these words. A strange and dreadful void has entered her darkness and silence. Her teacher's guiding, loving, vibrant hands have been stilled—Anne Sullivan's hands are gone, and Helen Keller has lost a direct connection to a soulmate.

Helen Keller was, of course, curious about the miracle of her hands and fingers (as were many others) so she wrote about the mystery in the *Century Magazine* article:

> In all my experiences and thoughts, I am conscious of a hand. Whatever touches me, whatever thrills me, is as a hand that touches me in the dark, and that touch is my reality . . . My

world is built of touch-sensations, devoid of color and sound; but without color and sound it breathes and throbs with life. Every object is associated in my mind with tactual qualities which, combined in countless ways, give me a sense of power, of beauty, or of incongruity: for with my hands I can feel the comic as well as the beautiful in the outward appearance of things.

Helen spoke to the unseen, unheard universe using her ten fingers and her delicate fingertips; the curved surface of the palm was her slate. She played another's hand like a virtuoso musician played a delicate instrument. She listened with the palms of her sensitive hands with acute focal attention while others played the music of language onto her sensitive skin. Her hands were the windows that revealed the world to her:

When eyes are blind, the mind seeks new ways of seeing. My fingers look not with two eyes but with ten eyes, and the whole body is alert to perceive and hears the voice of life. ~ Helen and Teacher, 1980.

Helen is, of course, using the word "see" to mean "perceive." When a sense like vision is lost, the brain compensates and uses other senses for perception. When both the eyes and ears become non-functional, the sense of touch must step up, become more acute, become a main channel for perception of the world around. That is why Helen's hands became so wonderfully perceptive.

I was fascinated by how much information Helen was able to gather from just holding the hands of another person; I sense that she would have been a good fortune teller. When you placed your hand in hers, she could sense your mood, read snippets of your personality, guess your level of consciousness, and analytically project how your future might play out. That set of skills seems impossible to do without getting clues from vision and hearing, but Helen Keller had this ability using just fingers and the palm of the hand. In other words, she could read an individual's personality from the vitality, warmth, and intentionality of their hands. She muses about this skill in "A Chat About the Hand:"

It is interesting to observe the differences in the hands of people. They show all kinds of vitality, energy, stillness, and cordiality . . . The hand I know in life has the fullness of blood in its veins and is elastic with spirit . . . a loving hand I never forget.

I remember in my fingers the large hands of Bishop Brooks, brimful of tenderness and a strong man's joy. If you were deaf and blind, and could hold Mr. [Thomas] Jefferson's hand, you would see in it a face and hear a kind voice unlike any other you have known. Mark Twain's hand is full of whimsies and the drollest humors, and while you hold it the drollery changes to sympathy and championship.

I cannot describe hands under any class or type; there is no democracy of hands. Some hands tell me that they do everything with the maximum of bustle and noise. Other hands are fidgety and unadvised, with nervous, fussy fingers which indicate a nature sensitive to the little pricks of daily life. Sometimes I recognize with foreboding the kindly but stupid hand of one who tells with many words news that is no news. I have met a bishop with a jocose hand, a humorist with a hand of leaden gravity, a man of pretentious valor with a timorous hand, and a quiet, apologetic man with a fist of iron.

All this is my private science of palmistry, and when I tell your fortune it is by no mysterious intuition or Gipsy witchcraft, but by natural, explicable recognition of the embossed character in your hand. Not only is the hand as easy to recognize as the face, but it reveals its secrets more openly and unconsciously. People control their countenances, but the hand is under no such restraint. It relaxes and becomes listless when the spirit is low and dejected; the muscles tighten when the mind is excited or the heart glad; and permanent qualities stand written on it all the time. As there are many beauties of the face, so the beauties of the hand are many. Touch has its ecstasies.

The hands of people of strong individuality and sensitiveness are wonderfully mobile. In a glance of their fingertips, they express many shades of thought. Now and again I touch a fine, graceful, supple-wristed hand which spells with the same beauty and distinction that you must see in the handwriting of some highly cultivated people. I wish you could see how prettily little children spell in my hand. They are wildflowers of humanity, and their finger motions wildflowers of speech.

It seems almost a miracle that Helen Keller can say of Mark Twain, from only holding his hands, feeling their texture and flow: Mark Twain's hand is full of whimsies and the drollest humors, and while you hold it the drollery changes to sympathy and championship. History reads the same thing from Mark Twain's entire essence, but how did Helen Keller get so much accurate information about Mark Twain's character from just his hands? Helen was probably influenced by the style and character of Mark Twain's publications. Her reading of his essence was probably a combination of insights. Still, there is magic here, something we do not yet comprehend about subtle human communication.

There is something electric that can be felt and transmitted through the skin, especially through the fingertips. Anyone who has ever loved and affectionately touched another human being knows about this unique sensory delight. We know a caring touch from a sensual touch. We know a sexual touch from a healing touch. We know Reiki and Qigong touch. It is not a surprise, then, that Helen Keller knew and treasured a loving touch, because such a purely tactual communication reveals a remarkably high level of spiritual wakefulness. I suspect that every level of consciousness is revealed through the fingertips, skin to skin, hand to hand. In other words, laying your fingers in the palm of Helen's hand allowed her to read your depth of spirituality.

I also like her statement in the above quote that "People control their countenances, but the hand is under no such restraint." The face can lie and has a repertoire of potentially misleading expressions, but the hands, unlike the face, are not equipped with delicately controlled muscles; the hands are more open to expressing and revealing raw truth:

> One of my friends is rather aggressive, and his hand always announces the coming of a dispute. By his impatient jerk I know he has argument ready for someone. I have felt him start as a sudden recollection or a new idea shot through his mind. I have felt grief in his hand. I have felt his soul wrap itself in darkness majestically as in a garment.
>
> Another friend has positive, emphatic hands which show great pertinacity of opinion. She is the only person I know who emphasizes her spelled words and accents them as she emphasizes and accents her spoken words when I read her lips. I like this varied emphasis better than the monotonous pound of unmodulated people who hammer their meaning into my

palm. Some hands, when they clasp yours, beam and bubble over with gladness. They throb and expand with life. Strangers have clasped my hand like that of a long-lost sister.

Other people shake hands with me as if with the fear that I may do them mischief. Such persons hold out civil fingertips which they permit you to touch, and in the moment of contact they retreat, and inwardly you hope that you will not be called upon again to take that hand of "dormouse valor." It betokens a prudish mind, ungracious pride, and not seldom mistrust. It is the antipode to the hand of those who have large, lovable natures. The handshake of some people makes you think of accident and sudden death.

Not only would Helen Keller have been a superb fortune teller, but she would also have been a powerful healer. Too bad she did not learn touch-therapies like Reiki. On the other hand, she *probably did* send and receive healing vibrations as a matter of course every day; it was her nature to be optimistic and loving—she must have routinely projected loving-kindness through her fingertips.

I also wonder about sensual and sexual touch. Holding Helen Keller's hand, when she was in her prime years especially, must have shocked a few souls who experienced her intimate finger-to-finger "loving." I am betting that her love affair with Peter Fagan started with hand-to-hand electricity, with touch that suddenly went from information exchange (communication) to sensuality, a lightning strike of lust, sexual playfulness, and climaxing with waves of unexpected, but genuine love:

> In the strength of the human hand, too, there is something divine. I am told that the glance of a beloved eye thrills one from a distance; but there is no distance in the touch of a beloved hand.

∾

A closed hand, a fist, cannot adequately grasp an experience; a closed hand, like a closed mind, cannot communicate and cannot be receptive to flow. Therefore, a closed hand is dead to the world—it cannot be aware. A hand must be open and ready to learn; fingers must move to explore. The doorway to consciousness for Helen Keller was a portal that opened in the palm of her hand and through the motion of her fingers.

As Helen systematically explored the environment, her mind combined all the separate sensations into a whole. If she had not been allowed to explore, she would not have been able to grasp gestalts (whole scenes):

> My fingers cannot, of course, get the impression of a large whole at a glance; but I feel the parts, and *my mind puts them together.* I move around the house, touching object after object in order, before I can form an idea of the entire house. In other people's houses I can touch only what is shown me—the chief objects of interest, carvings on the wall, or a curious architectural feature, exhibited like the family album. Therefore, a house with which I am not familiar has for me, at first, no general effect or harmony of detail. It is not a complete conception, but a collection of object-impressions which, as they come to me, are disconnected and isolated.
>
> But my mind is full of associations, sensations, theories, and with them *it constructs the house.* The process reminds me of the building of Solomon's temple, where was neither saw, nor hammer, nor any tool heard while the stones were being laid one upon another. The silent worker is imagination which decrees reality out of chaos. Without imagination what a poor thing my world would be!

The italics above are mine. Helen is telling us something especially important in the quote above. The brain intrinsically creates gestalts, even without auditory and visual information. In other words, the human brain has a foundational ability to create whole scenes using fragmentary information; the senses work simultaneously to accomplish this perceptual assembly process. Losing a sense, like vision or hearing does not alter basic brain functions, like perceiving scenes, objects, and pathways. Helen shows us that the human brain can get a relatively complete (usable) understanding of spatial layouts using just tactile and proprioceptive information.

I thought it would be fun to feature a poem that has endured through the decades, which highlights the dilemma that human beings have when they debate from limited perspectives. Below is the famous poem, based on an ancient Hindu fable, called "The Blind Men and the Elephant," which uses blindness to highlight the frailty of human observation and judgment. This is from *The Poems of John Godfrey Saxe*, (1872):

THE BLIND MEN AND THE ELEPHANT
a Hindu fable
It was six men of Indostan
To learning much inclined,
Who went to see the Elephant
(Though all of them were blind),
That each by observation
Might satisfy his mind.
The First approached the Elephant,
And happening to fall
Against his broad and sturdy side,
At once began to bawl:
"God bless me!—but the Elephant
Is very like a wall!"
The Second, feeling of the tusk,
Cried: "Ho!—what have we here
So very round and smooth and sharp?
To me 't is mighty clear
This wonder of an Elephant
Is very like a spear!"
The Third approached the animal,
And happening to take
The squirming trunk within his hands,
Thus boldly up and spake:
"I see," quoth he, "the Elephant
Is very like a snake!"
The Fourth reached out his eager hand,
And felt about the knee.
"What most this wondrous beast is like
Is mighty plain," quoth he;
"T'is clear enough the Elephant
Is very like a tree!"
The Fifth, who chanced to touch the ear,
Said: "E'en the blindest man
Can tell what this resembles most;

Deny the fact who can,
This marvel of an Elephant
Is very like a fan!"
The Sixth no sooner had begun
About the beast to grope,
Then, seizing on the swinging tail
That fell within his scope,
"I see," quoth he, "the Elephant
Is very like a rope!"
And so these men of Indostan
Disputed loud and long,
Each in his own opinion
Exceeding stiff and strong,
Though each was partly in the right,
And all were in the wrong!
MORAL
So, oft in theologic wars
The disputants, I ween,
Rail on in utter ignorance
Of what each other mean,
And prate about an Elephant
Not one of them has seen!

This lovely and classic poem demonstrates that attention defines perception—perceptions knitted together define what we call *reality*. The poem is, of course, more about human nature than about blindness. A blind person—even a deaf-blind individual—can envision whole elephants with just a little exploration. Helen Keller would have explored the entire elephant and then her mind would have assembled the parts into a reasonable facsimile of an actual creature. Miniature statues of animals would also have been available to assist her perception. Of course, if she had been restricted in her exploration (as many blind people are) then she would have been restricted perceptually as well.

This poem also suggests what happens when we partially educate our children; it is a powerful statement about what happens to blind children who are not allowed freedom of movement, not allowed to freely explore their entire environment.

≈

Helen Keller is not alone in her insights and concerns about her hands and fingers. Regarding his sense of touch, especially finger sensations, Jacques Lusseyran (the subject of book three in this series) wrote:

> Movement of the fingers was terribly important and had to be uninterrupted because objects do not stand at a given point, fixed there, confined in one form. They are alive, even the stones. What is more, they vibrate and tremble. My fingers felt the pulsation distinctly, and if they failed to answer with a pulsation of their own, the fingers immediately became helpless and lost their sense of touch. But when they went towards things, in sympathetic vibration with them, they recognized them right away. ~ And There Was Light, 1953.

Lusseyran mentions above that even stones vibrate. Helen, of course, would agree, as her poem *The Song of the Stone Wall* (1910) demonstrates. Vibratory awareness led Helen to explore the subtle world, a world that is normally overpowered by visual and auditory sensations. Helen could feel the connection between her proprioceptive system and the spaces that she moved through—a complex mix of dynamic vibrations that could be used to identify objects as well as ascertain spatial position. Helen and Jacques Lusseyran could "feel elephants" in the subtle world where too many sighted people only saw tusks, and tails, and wiggling ropes.

In 1937, Helen Keller was in Paris and had the unique opportunity to lay hands on Rodin's sculpture *The Thinker*. She wrote about this experience in her journal:

> Mr. Borglum led me to where "The Thinker" sat, primal, tense, his chin resting on a toil-worn hand. In every limb I felt the throes of emerging mind. As I said to Mr. Borglum, I recognized the force that shook me when teacher spelled "Water," and I discovered that everything has a name, and that the finger motions were the way to whatever I wanted. Often before had my deliverance caused me to wonder, but not until then had I perceived clearly how *she hewed my life bit by bit out of the formless silent dark as Rodin hewed that mind-genesis out of the rock* . . .
>
> "Few people have understood the elemental meaning of Rodin's symbol as you do," was Mr. Borglum's comment. "You

have seen the struggle for existence in which the body goes as far as it can, and conscious thinking begins."

Helen's above observations are worthy of deep reflection (the italics are mine). She tells us that Anne Sullivan "hewed my life out of the formless silent dark." As her fingers explored *The Thinker*, Helen could feel that Auguste Rodin had hewed consciousness from the rocks. Rodin knew this was the goal, to show life emanating from the material world—we are made from the stuff of rocks, and from the Granite Race our consciousness emerged. What we need, if we are to breathe life into stone, is a sculptor with innate talents, a Rodin, or an Anne Sullivan.

John Gutzon de la Mothe Borglum, the man who showed Helen Keller Rodin's statues, was an American artist and sculptor, famous for his stone creations at the Mount Rushmore National Memorial in Keystone, South Dakota. Gutzon was deeply affected by his encounter with Helen Keller. He wrote an article called "Eyes of the Soul," which can be viewed online at the American Foundation for the Blind Helen Keller Archives. Here is an edited piece from that article:

> She shook her head slowly. "This man," she remarked, "was a doer and a worker. He is trying to think," she said. "Rodin might have named it *Trying to Think*. I was fully conscious of the tremendous awakening that was going on in the soul of Helen Keller . . . When we came to *The Hand of God*, she studied it gently, lingeringly, as if she did not want to leave. We waited here a few moments, for I realized the intense emotional strain she had experienced. She had entered a world that exists everywhere about us but seen by and appreciated only by the great. I shall never forget that hour with Helen Keller, a great woman passing through a great emotional awakening. From it I learned that *the soul, over and above the body, has eyes.*

The soul has eyes, Gutzon Borglum tells us, after witnessing Helen's soul using inner-vision to study Rodin's *The Thinker*. This is not just poetic phrasing, there is something real here, something science will someday observe and begin to explain, although, so far, science is still struggling to comprehend the likes of Helen Keller. [italics in the quote are mine]

There is an emotional impact as Helen touches Rodin's sculpted hand of God. We can imagine Helen's deep Faith mixing with this symbolic encounter. The human hand is sacred to Helen Keller, more so than for those of us who take our hands for granted. Helen pauses so long over God's hand because, we imagine, she is waiting for the Hand of God to move, to spell, to talk directly to her.

After the profound experiences at the Rodin Museum, Helen later encountered another statue that had emotional impact. In the quote below from her Journal (1938), Helen describes her emotions when she examined a model of Anne Sullivan's hand:

> [The sculptor Bonnie MacLeary] made a cast of Teacher's hand, thinking it might comfort me. It was a touching tribute to Teacher wrought by a true artist. I summoned what composure I could to touch the graceful outline of the hand and the thumb and index finger from the letter L suggesting Love. I traced each line in the palm, startlingly distinct and true—a likeness snatched as it were from deaths relentless waves. In spite of myself I succumbed to the old heartbreak; my tears fell; and I could not speak.

Feeling an exact duplicate of Anne Sullivan's hand would, of course, be startling for Helen; we expect that she would be overcome with emotion. I am sure that part of the shock was that Sullivan's sculpted hand was cold, unanimated, and represented eternal death, eternal silence. The still hand of Anne Sullivan was now and forever unable to communicate, never to share again, never to exchange warmth and love in this lifetime. We can each imagine what it would be like to feel the cold sculpted hand of someone we once loved who has now passed.

Bonnie MacLeary also modeled Helen Keller's hand. I was not able to discover where the models of Helen's and Annie's hands are housed; perhaps they are with a private collector. Many of Bonnie MacLeay's sculptures are in Texas, so maybe the pieces are there somewhere. I am bothered that such important pieces of sculpture are not available for public viewing. During the 9/11 attacks, the Helen Keller International archives were destroyed; perhaps the hand sculptures were lost forever in that tragedy.

1907: OUT OF THE DARK IS PUBLISHED

Out of the Dark: Essays, Lectures, and Addresses on Physical and Social Vision was first published in 1907. This book is a collection of early articles and speeches written by Helen Keller. It was reissued in 1910 and 1913. I will review the 1913 revision later in the timeline.

The Matilda Ziegler Magazine for the Blind was also founded in March 1907 through a collaboration between Electa Matilda Ziegler (1841–1932) and journalist Walter G. Holmes (Holmes died February 7, 1946). The publication became a popular general-interest magazine for the blind and visually impaired, printed in New York City; it lasted 107 years before ceasing operations in 2014. The publication was funded solely by the endowment of Electa Matilda Ziegler through the E. Matilda Ziegler Foundation for the Blind, Inc.

Helen Keller knew both Matilda Ziegler and Walter Holmes and she frequently exchanged letters with them. A few of the letters to Walter Holmes are preserved in the book *Helen Keller in Scotland* (1933). Helen refers to him as *Uncle Walter*. Here is an excerpt from one of the letters written March 11, 1932:

> To Walter G. Holmes, Esq.
> Forest Hills
> March 11, 1932
>
>
> Dear Uncle Walter,

I don't know offhand how many letters I owe you, and I haven't the courage to count them. The truth is, the days aren't long enough for the things that must be done. Polly and I are pretty constantly on the jump, going from one meeting to another in Pennsylvania, New Jersey, and New York. Almost every day in February was taken, and March is being filled up rapidly with diverse engagements. I find it impossible to write all the ceremonious letters I should.

I did not write to Mrs. Ziegler as you requested. I have, as you know, sent her a number of notes thanking her for what she has done for the blind. She must realize the happiness and encouragement which the magazine has brought during twenty-five years to the dwellers in Darkland. Thousands upon thousands utter with affection her name, written in letters of light upon many hours that would be dark indeed without her generosity. No one could be more grateful to Mrs. Zeigler than I am. When you see her, will you please give her my love and the blessing that is always in my heart when I think of her? [29]

Helen was a frequent contributor to *The Matilda Ziegler Magazine for the Blind*. The magazine has been digitally archived at: http://www.matildaziegler.com/tag/helen-keller/.

What Else Happened in 1907?

Here are a few random events that happened in 1907: George Bernard Shaw's play "Don Juan in Hell" premiered in London. . . . Maria Montessori opened her first school in Rome, Italy. . . . English suffragettes stormed the British Parliament; sixty of the protestors were arrested. . . . Psychiatrists Carl Jung and Sigmund Freud met for the first time in Vienna, Austria. . . . The Bank of Italy (later called the Bank of America) opened its first branch in San Francisco. . . . Rudyard Kipling received the Nobel Prize for literature.

1908: The World I Live In is Published

Helen wrote and published *The World I Live In* in 1908. Here is a nice summary from *Harvard Magazine* (written by Professor emeritus Roger Shattuck at Boston University in 2004), about Helen's first books:

> While at Radcliffe, she composed a vivid personal account of her own miraculous coming of age . . . A discerning editor of the Ladies' Home Journal commissioned her to produce a series of six personal narratives under the title *The Story of My Life*. Even though she was still struggling with college courses, Keller completed the series in 1902 and brought out a full-length book with the same title in 1903. *The Story of My Life* has become a major classic of American literature and autobiography. Keller was 23.
>
> Five years later, she wrote *The World I Live In*, a book of personal essays, originally published in *Century Magazine*, to answer skeptics and critics of her first book and to refute the claim that she and Sullivan were impostors. Literary critics such as Van Wyck Brooks, Walter Percy, and Cynthia Ozick, and cognitive scientists such as William James, Oliver Sacks, and Gerald Edelman have found in *The Story of My Life* and *The World I Live In* two of the most revealing inside narratives of the formation of what we call human consciousness. The books also offer an exciting case history of an unprecedented feat of individual education against crippling odds and make clear why Alexander Graham Bell, Mark Twain, and Andrew

Carnegie regarded Keller and Sullivan as two of the most remarkable women of their time. [30]

Roger Shattuck was a Junior Fellow at Harvard from 1950 to 1953 and a scholar of comparative literature. He was the author of numerous books, including *The Banquet Years*, *Proust's Way*, and *Forbidden Knowledge*. He was also coeditor, with Helen Keller's biographer Dorothy Herrmann, of an unabridged edition of Keller's *The Story of My Life*, and editor of an unabridged edition of Keller's *The World I Live In*. I became quite impressed with Dr. Shattuck as I read and enjoyed his clear erudite prose, as the above paragraphs attest.

1908 was also the year H. G. Wells published *New Worlds for Old* in which he cautiously suggested that Socialism might be a better economic alternative to Capitalism. Anne Sullivan read H. G. Wells' book and passed it on to Helen. Sullivan was not emotionally moved by Wells' arguments but the impact on Helen was powerful and reinforced her socialist leanings. She was especially sickened by the plight of children caught in the grips of industrialization.

Child labor and child abuse are themes that run throughout history during Helen's lifetime. However, there was also something kind and nurturing that was also trying to arise during her lifespan; Helen Keller was a powerful voice for this new uprising of spirit. The battle for kindness raged underground, person-to-person, moment-by-moment, playing out in the expanding news media as the decades rolled forward. It was not until the end of Helen's life that the long battle for kindness began to show signs of winning against neglect and hatred. Child labor laws and spouse abuse laws were eventually passed, women's liberation movements spread throughout the Western world, and global cooperation began to emerge.

The battle for kindness has not been won, of course, especially in developing nations, in regions where dictators still rule, and in nations where religious fundamentalism reigns, but the battle for kindness is unceasing and, if Helen Keller was correct, will eventually prevail.

What Else Happened in 1908?

Here are a few random events that happened in 1908: On the first of January, for the first time, in Times Square in New York City a ceremonial ball was dropped at midnight to mark the New Year. . . . Cincinnati Mayor Mark Breith said: "Women are not physically fit to operate automobiles." . . . Katie Mulcahey was arrested for lighting a cigarette, violating the "Sullivan Ordinance" banning women from smoking in public. Appearing before the judge Katie said "I've got as much right to smoke as you have. I never heard of this new law, and I don't want to hear about it. No man shall dictate to me." . . . A giant fireball, likely caused by a large meteoroid, flattened 80 million trees near the Stony Tunguska River in Yeniseysk, Russia—this was the largest impact event in recorded history. . . . Robert Peary's arctic expedition sailed from New York City for the North Pole. . . . Ford Motor Company built the first Model T car. . . . The first Gideon Bible was put in a hotel room. . . . Albert Einstein presented his quantum theory of light.

The World That I live In

The World That I live In is the best explanation for how Helen used her remaining senses to build a representation of the world. It is a marvelous book, filled with insights that are amazing to those of us with normal hearing and vision. As she discusses her skills, we become convinced that she could perceive exceptionally subtle patterns that enabled her incredible mind to determine what was happening around her.

As I review the book below, I will add commentary from my own professional experience, especially calling on my esoteric knowledge and my experience as an Orientation and Mobility specialist.

Helen said that in *The World That I live In,* she poured "everything that interested me at one of the happiest periods of my life." She is answering questions that others have asked about her life, such as:

- What is it like to be deaf and blind?
- How do you know what is happening around you?
- Is your sense of touch and smell better than that of others who are not deaf and blind?

The World That I live In is a collection of 15 short essays (based on articles she wrote for *Century Magazine*), ending with a poem called *A Chant of Darkness*. I will discuss *A Chant of Darkness* in conjunction with my discussion below of Helen's book *The Song of the Stone Wall* (1910).

The World That I live In is a short book; the version I have is bundled with *Optimism*—the entire combined book is only 110 pages.

Chapter One is called *The Seeing Hand.*

Helen tells us that "paradise is attained by touch; for in touch is all love and intelligence." This is a great truth for her; life was revealed through her skin. Helen reminds us that sighted individuals share the same books, the same language, and the same culture as the deaf and blind; it does not matter how we attain knowledge because we have multiple ways to share and communicate.

Whereas others may take their hands for granted, Helen is constantly appreciative of her fingers as they explore, and learn, and share with others. Touch allows her to "throb with life." Thoughts enter through her fingers rather than through eyes or ears. This works perfectly fine, she tells us; she does not feel inferior or lessened by her tactile method for interpreting the world.

Helen also says, with deep conviction, that without imagination her world would be baren and shallow. She says that her imagination projects outward to meet the imagination of others. She tells us that "imagination crowns the experience of my hands."

Chapter Two is called *The Hand of Others.*

This is a valuable and important chapter. Helen explores how it is she gains so much information from the hands of others. Critics had insisted she could not have gotten so much insight about another human being just from hand-to-hand contact; she was accused of already knowing about the personalities of others. But it is the animation within a hand that tells her so much and she has a wealth of experience to draw on as she goes from hand to hand. She says that she has little physical recollection of the features of a hand because she is so focused on the personality that is moving the hand.

Interestingly, she says that trying to get a sighted person to understand what she is talking about is like trying to get a blind person to comprehend the description of a face. There is emotion and conviction in the whole of a hand and Helen can sense this animation and can interpret meaning from the flow of the fingers—the pace, the pauses, the intensity, the temperature, and the vibrational sensuousness of animation enable her reading of others.

Chapter Three is called *The Hand of the Race.*

In this chapter, Helen looks at idioms associated with the hand and playfully lists a few favorites. Helen tells us that the dictionary she is using lists eight pages, twenty-four columns of idioms related to "hand," or to the Latin root for hand "manus." She references the works of Shakespeare and then observes how often the Bible mentions *hands.* Everywhere we look, Helen tells us, "we find the hand in time and history, working, building, inventing, bringing civilization out of barbarism."

Chapter Four is called *The Power of Touch.*

In chapter 4, *The Power of Touch*, Helen talks about the sensations she gets from the soles of her feet. I know from my teaching experience that deaf-blind people use the floor as a map; the floor surface can be used quite exactly to determine position in familiar settings. Helen Keller got a wealth of sensations from the bottom of her feet as she moved over a surface or when she sat with her feet (especially her bare feet) resting on the floor. One can imagine floors in the late 1800s: unlike the level concrete, wood-framed, and tiled floors that the modern world presents, floors a century ago creaked, were uneven, and they vibrated as the foot pressed on weakly supported floorboards. Below, Helen speaks of the footsteps of others:

> Footsteps, I discover, vary tactually according to the age, the sex, and the manners of the walker. It is impossible to mistake a child's patter for the tread of a grown person. The step of a young man, strong and free, differs from the heavy, sedate tread of the middle-aged, and from the step of an old man, whose feet drag along the floor, or beat it with slow faltering accents. On a bare floor a girl walks with rapid, elastic rhythm which is quite distinct from the graver step of the elderly woman . . . Often footsteps reveal . . . the character and the mood of the walker. I feel in them firmness and indecision, hurry and deliberation, activity and laziness, fatigue, carelessness, timidity, anger, and sorrow. I am most consciousness of these moods and traits in persons with whom I am familiar . . . Footsteps are frequently interrupted by certain jars and jerks, so that I know when one kneels, kicks, shakes something, sits down, or gets up. Thus, I follow the actions of people . . . and the changes of their postures.

Who among the sighted/hearing population could even consider that so much information could be gleamed from foot falls? We are incredibly lucky that Helen Keller was so brilliant and so articulate. She takes the mystery out of her world and clearly explains how she functions. This eloquence is an amazing gift; it is a wonder that she was so self-perceptive. Helen could surmise the age, energy level, sex, emotional state, decisiveness, personality, and posture of those around her as they strolled about—she analyzed and judged an approaching person before they even reached for her outstretched hand. Here is another quote (from the AFB Helen Keller Digital Archives) that demonstrates her ability to interpret passing footsteps:

> "Listening" with her feet, she says, in a hotel dining room, she knows the moods and characters of people who walk past her, whether they are firm or indecisive, active or lazy, careless, timid, weary, angry or sad.

"Listening with the feet" is a skill few of us have developed. The above quotes illustrate just how sensitive Helen Keller's vibrational-interpretation abilities became. Her ability to sense subtle vibrations includes the skill of differentiating personalities and making wise judgments about people passing by her. It slowly dawns on us, as we gather information about Helen's sensory skills, that she was amazingly aware of her surroundings and in touch with other human beings in ways that (at best) remain dormant in the hearing and sighted population.

For Helen, subtle vibrations moved along the floor to her feet and then flowed through her whole body to her brain. These vibrations held patterns, information packets, that could be received, cataloged, judged, and remembered. The question arises: if she had such intelligent feet, what else could the feet do for her? Quite understandably, her feet helped her navigate.

Most of us pay little attention to the surfaces we walk upon or to floor-based vibrations. We wear shoes everywhere and we walk on surfaces engineered to be level, hard, and smooth. We keep pathways, like hallways, object-free so that our flow is not impeded. However, many surfaces are rich with information. It is easy to detect thresholds, for example, like where a rug ends and a tile floor begins. The floors of older homes creak and are uneven in exact locations and so these irregularities can be used as landmarks. Floors vary in warmth at various specific locations as well. In other words, even in our modern architecture a floor can be an exceptionally valuable ground-map for people who are blind and deaf-blind.

Deaf-blind people with bare feet can navigate quite well in familiar settings with just the ground-map informing their movements—a cane plus bare feet would provide even more mapping data. Blind mobility specialist Daniel Kish wears very thin-soled shoes that keep his feet warm and protected, but also enable ground-based map reading.

Anne Sullivan's biographer Nella Braddy, reflecting on Helen's ability to navigate on her own, wrote:

> So far as tests have been able to determine, her sensory equipment is in no way, except perhaps in the sense of smell, superior to that of the normal person. She seems totally without the sense of direction which is so pronounced in some of the deaf-blind. In her own home, which is not large, she frequently starts toward the opposite wall instead of the door and orients herself by contact with the furniture. When the rugs are taken up, she is completely bewildered and has to learn the whole pattern again. Her sense of distance is also poor. She does not know when she has reached the door until she has run into it, and in winter when the ground is covered with snow and ice her daily walk becomes a mighty adventure. ~ Midstream, 1929.

This statement confirms that Helen Keller navigated, in part, using information from her feet (she probably went without shoes through the house most days). Each room had familiar rugs, familiar furniture, and walls that were unique (had pictures on them, etc.); therefore, Helen knew (potentially) where she was anywhere in a familiar building. Air currents and humidity changes combined with olfactory clues also contributed to navigation.

I was quite amazed to learn that Helen had mastered Morse Code well enough that she and Sullivan could communicate through foot taps. I am quite sure this was a novelty situation and not a regular practice, but it does show these two friends played with various forms of communication, including floor vibrations generated by deliberate foot taps.

We do not often think of our skin as a vast sensory organ. However, Helen Keller knew from experience that every inch of her skin surface was alive to vibrations of every kind, including the impact of light waves and sound waves. Everything the skin can sense was amplified for Helen.

As a thought experiment, think of a human being as a single-cell organism. We are encased in a skin bag. We are one giant cell moving around a domain, like an amoeba moving through pond water. If our skin surface is penetrated—like a pin jabbing a balloon—we bleed, germs enter our body, and we are in danger. Evolution has engineered many strategies for dealing with injury to the skin and most of these adaptations are successful—we survive our cuts and bruises; our skin can go about its business as a vast sensory network even as it protects us from environmental damage.

Like any cell membrane, the skin lets in some "foreign" substances and keeps out everything else. Therefore, the skin surface is a thin and vast sensory system that decides what to detect and what to respond to. Cell membranes have been evolving for billions of years. We know some things about the "skin as a giant cell membrane," but we are still quite ignorant about all the functions of the skin. Could it be that the skin has become specialized for detecting subtle vibrations—beyond what is currently understood (below conscious threshold)? I think the partial answer to this question is "yes." Let us start by exploring what we do know.

The skin has many kinds of sensory cells. Collectively, these cells comprise the somatosensory system. Using different cell types, the somatosensory system can detect temperature variations, texture, pressure, pain, and various kinds of vibrations. There are four types of common receptors: mechanoreceptors, thermoreceptors, pain receptors, and proprioceptors.

- **Mechanoreceptors** perceive pressure, vibration, and texture. There are four subdivisions of mechanoreceptors: Merkel's disks, Meissner's corpuscles, Ruffini's corpuscles, and Pacinian corpuscles. Merkel's disks and Meissner's corpuscles (the most sensitive cell types) reside in the top layers of the dermis and epidermis and are found in non-hairy skin such as on the palms, soles of the feet, fingertips, and on the face.

  Jacques Lusseyran [the subject of book three in this series] wrote that he perceived the world as pressure; he was consciously aware of the signals coming from the Merkel cells on his skin.

Besides sensing pressure variations, Merkel's disks can perceive subtle differences in location, a process known as two-point discrimination. This ability to determine spacing between two points on the skin surface is what enables blind people to read Braille with their fingertips. Perhaps, (we can speculate) blind and deaf-blind people can use two-point discrimination as a navigation tool, for locating and identifying subtle landmarks and for detecting the relationship between two landmarks.

What if mechanoreceptors are more sensitive than we now understand? Perhaps, subtle (unconscious) touch can provide information to the Allocentric mind, which can be used by blind and deaf-blind individuals. Perhaps Helen Keller's mind could discriminate using skin vibrations far more subtlety than the "normal" population.

- **Thermoreceptors** perceive the temperature of objects contacting the skin. Two kinds of measurements are occurring in these cells: they can directly determine the temperature of objects contacting the skin surface; and they can detect infrared variations from the surrounding air.

  The human skin responds to electromagnetic radiation of various types. For example, thermoreceptors are infrared detectors; they use infrared waves (vibrations in the electromagnetic spectrum) to measure/monitor outside-the-skin temperature changes. As we move through rooms in a house (for example), we encounter air currents of different temperatures. The distance we are from heat generating sources determines what the skin is detecting using infrared (heat) waves. Blind and deaf-blind individuals become more sensitive to the information coming from thermoreceptors and they can use such skin-based temperature-information to help them navigate through a domain.

- **Pain receptors** detect stimuli that could potentially damage the skin surface and endanger tissues directly under the skin. Pain receptors are also found in muscles, bones, blood vessels, and in some body organs. Interestingly, the brain does not contain pain receptors.

  Like thermoreceptors, pain receptors detect input directly from objects contacting the skin and from electromagnetic radiation coming in waves—for example ultraviolet waves cause sunburn.

- **Proprioceptors** sense the position of body parts. These receptors also sense the relative location of body parts to each other, to the body, and to the environment. For example, if we put our right hand behind our head, we know where the hand is even though we do not see it. Proprioceptors are also found in tendons, muscles, and joint capsules where they detect changes in muscle length and muscle tension.

In my Navigational Consciousness hypothesis (discussed in *The Esoteric Helen Keller*), I elevated these proprioceptive cells to an exalted status, as the portal for the sense of consciousness. The reasoning behind such a broad hypothesis starts with the understanding that the proprioceptive network animates the body and gives us a sense of being alive. Blindness and deaf-blindness do not alter our sense of animation or our feeling of being a sentient creature; we are creatures who move through and interact with the world.

If all the skin receptors become more sensitive after the loss of vision and hearing, we might even make the case that deaf-blind people like Helen Keller would sense their animation more keenly and might, therefore, have a greater sense of being alive.

The skin is impacted by light rays, sound waves, and by every kind of electromagnetic energy known. What happens when these waves hit the skin? Are there sensors (besides the list above) in the skin that selectively react to light, to sound, to odors, to chemicals in the air? How sensitive can these cellular systems become in the absence of vision and hearing?

Scientists studying the relationship between sound and touch demonstrate that we comprehend spoken language partly because we sense subtle puffs of air striking the face. The voice (the vocal apparatus) sends out air waves as it emits sound; these waves are simultaneous with what the ears hear. Embodiment puts together the sound waves hitting the ears with air patterns hitting the skin. Helen Keller's extremely sensitive skin-perception probably could detect the air patterns arriving as people spoke to her. The impact and the flow of the air patterns gave her information about when an individual was speaking and when they had finished speaking. Also, the rapidity of the air waves would indicate intention, passion, and emotional state.

We also know that our nervous system *transmits* electromagnetic waves *from* our body outward into surrounding spaces. Scientists do not know how these waves might be picked up by others who occupy nearby spaces. We also do not know how far our transmissions can travel before they can no longer be detected. For example, electromagnetic waves emitted by the heart, as it beats, can be detected by instruments strapped to a chest. However, these same heart waves are so powerful they can be detected by instruments across the room. Could these powerful heart-waves be detected by a deaf-blind individual?

Science has no problem using electromagnetic detection-technologies to scan and read the human body. We know, for example, that the brain puts out weak signals that can be picked up by electroencephalographs. We know (determine) if someone has died from the flat-wave reading that brain monitors record. We also know a person's state of wakefulness from brain wave studies: alpha is a relaxed brain state, beta (an awake state) is what you are doing now as you read, delta waves indicate that you are asleep, and high frequency gamma waves indicate higher-order processing. Electroretinography picks up waves coming off retinal tissue. We can determine the health and functional capacity of retinal cells when we record transmissions from these visual cells.

We have all kinds of technologies, unique to various medical specialists, which pick-up waves coming off parts of the human body. The body is constantly "giving off" radiation of one kind or another. We do not see or hear these waves; therefore, we must use extremely sensitive instruments to do the perceiving for us. What happens when a person becomes deaf-blind? Does the sensitivity of the skin and the brain (mind) ramp-up, open-up, tune into subtle radiations that bodies give off? It is not illogical to suppose (speculate, hypothesize) that the human mind can register (send and receive) subtle vibrations.

We enter the esoteric world when we suggest that there are hidden insights (hidden fields of knowledge, patterns of energy) that reside below the level of the Egoic (reasoning) mind. Science has a lovely habit of "catching up" to the esoteric imagination. Indeed, science is no longer held back by religious dogma and human ignorance. Science is no longer afraid or reactionary. Researchers are busy every day, all over the world, measuring the energy waves that the human body emits and receives.

Using the human skin and the whole-body (somatosensory system) as the foundation, I hypothetically explained, in *The Esoteric Helen Keller*, why Helen Keller had such an impact on people she encountered. The hypothesis is that human beings (all life forms) give off subtle vibrations that Helen Keller could detect and project (probably subconsciously). The explanation has to do with auras (layers of "energetic body shells). I will use the perspective of spiritual philosopher Rudolf Steiner in the discussion below to discuss these energy auras.

Chapter Five is called The Finer Vibrations.

In my third book, The Confusion Caused by Being Your Own Twin (2018), I spent several pages (303–313) discussing the ideas of German philosopher Rudolf Steiner; I was especially interested in Steiner's hypotheses about layered body auras (a common perspective in esoteric literature). Steiner was trying to develop a science of esotericism (a science of spirituality); he felt that his theories would eventually be validated by modern science.

It was because of Steiner's perspective on auras (subtle energy) that I turned to Steiner when I was trying to comprehend what people had said about Helen Keller. Most of the laudatory comments about Helen are hyperbole, but I wondered if a case might be made that she did (actually) have an aura and that it affected people when they encountered her.

Here are some quotes that suggest Helen had an aura around her body that some people could perceive:

Oliver Wendell Holmes made this statement about Helen:

It seems as if her soul was flooded with light and filled with music that had found entrance to it through avenues closed to other mortals. ~ Oliver Wendell Holmes Sr., article in the Atlantic Monthly, volume 65.

Less sophisticated eyes cannot penetrate beyond material appearances. It is the aura-readers who have left us such memorable quotes.

In 1938, in the foreword to Helen Keller's Journal, Augustus Muir, Scottish journalist, novelist, and historian wrote:

Helen Keller is one of those rare beings who have this bewitching essence, and before she was out of her teens, she had become a legendary figure.

She has a "bewitching essence." This makes her "a rare human being" and eventually brings her to the attention of people throughout the world. There is a radiance around Helen Keller that astute observers detect and marvel at.

Alexander Graham Bell, the inventor of the telephone, was the person who recommended that Helen receive her education at the Perkins Institute for the Blind. Dr. Bell became a passionate advocate for Helen and, for as long as he lived, he watched over her life like a guardian angel. They were good friends despite the age difference. Dr. Bell made this amazing observation:

> I feel that in this child I have seen more of the Divine than has been manifest in anyone I have ever met. ~ "The World I Would Help," an essay by Helen Keller, 1935.

That is a powerful statement. Helen was only seven when Bell penned this sentiment; clearly, he felt something powerful in Helen Keller's presence. Could Bell have sensed an aura around Helen? Since I called my previous book *The Esoteric Helen Keller*, I feel justified to go to the edges of science and explore Rudolf Steiner's perspective on auras. I will discuss his perspective below using Helen as the model.

Steiner (1861–1925) straddled the fence between science and esotericism, between what was known and what was hidden. I find Steiner's speculations relevant because Helen Keller (and other astute blind individuals) probably used subtle vibrations to send and receive information. These emanations would be available to Helen in such a way that she could use the information to read the personalities of others (the sophistication of their emanations) as well as ascertain her position relative to others in space (i.e., she could use such vibrations— her own and that of others—for navigation).

Steiner wrote that there were seven layers to the human aura. He based the existence of these energy levels surrounding the human being on both what he knew of the science of his day and what he knew from his study of alchemy and hermeticism—Steiner was both a scientist and a mystical thinker. As I discuss each of Steiner's seven energy layers below, I will speculate on how a deaf-blind person might use these alchemical energy fields to find meaning in the environment.

· Steiner was a prolific writer, a Goethe scholar, a futurist, a mystic, an esoteric guru, and he was an educational reformer. There are Steiner scholars today who spend their careers making sense of Steiner's prognostications. What follows is an overly simplistic rendering of an extraordinarily complex subject—others more knowledgeable than I am are available if you want to explore further.

Before I launch into this speculative realm, I need to mention a few caveats. Rudolf Steiner got his knowledge about "layers of energy surrounding the human body" from esoteric sources, mostly from Alchemy. Alchemists were the pioneers responsible for the development of the modern field of chemistry; as such, alchemists played a vital role in the evolution of science. Integrally interwoven with the science of chemistry was an esoteric thread; alchemists were also exploring the evolution of spirituality and the evolution of consciousness.

Many alchemical speculations and insights (especially concerning the evolution of consciousness) were threatening to Christianity, to religious dogma. Therefore, the alchemists hid their esoteric views inside their study of chemistry. For example, the quest to turn lead into gold (a real scientific effort) concealed the quest to turn hatred into kindness, ignorance into reason, and low levels of consciousness (lead) into enlightenment (gold). This is an insight that psychoanalyst Carl Jung also came to understand. Jung became an alchemical scholar because he could see the alchemical quest to further the evolution of consciousness that lay hidden beneath the study of chemistry.

It is also important to understand that Rudolf Steiner, Carl Jung, and the alchemists might very well have been speaking metaphorically when they postulated the existence of energy fields around the human body. As we explore the energy layers below, keep in mind that Steiner is showing us *a theory* for the evolution of cognition; here is Steiner's rendition mixed with my additional perspectives:

1. The lowest stage of consciousness is a mineral state (the consciousness of rocks, atoms, material stuff). The human body, as a physical machine, is at this level.
2. The next level of consciousness is plant-like "awareness." This is Steiner's *Ether Body*, a biological machine.
3. Then, at a higher plane, Animal Cognition appears on the evolutionary stage. Steiner calls this level of consciousness the *Astral* Body.
4. Human beings, moving animal conscious to new heights, developed various degrees of consciousness—these are depicted in developmental scales, like that of Susanne Cook-Greuter (see

The Esoteric Helen Keller). This level is called the *Egoic* Body in Steiner's taxonomy.

5. Beyond modern human development are potential *Ethereal Minds*, which only a few humans have learned to manifest. I have called this Ethereal Mind *Post-Human*, although, in my prognostications, I also postulate that technologies will blend with the human mind to create artificial hybrid-minds (artificial minds that are blended—by design—with natural minds, i.e., *unnatural selection*). Steiner calls the highest three levels of conscious the First, Second, and Third *Spirit Bodies*.

Steiner tells us that the human embryo begins at a mineral stage and then all the levels of consciousness listed above unfold as the embryo exponentially evolves. Indeed, throughout the human lifespan, consciousness never stops evolving. However, few humans arrive at the highest realms before they die. Most of humanity does not naturally cognitively evolve to have Ethereal minds (but maybe Helen Keller did). A great amount of discipline, education, and foresight is needed to inhabit (evolve into) the more sophisticated levels of consciousness.

There is yet another way to view these energy layers: as representative of the evolution of the structure of the brain. In the 1960s, Paul MacLean, a neuroscientist, postulated the evolution of a "Triune Brain," based on the observation that the brain has three hypothetical regions, representing a hierarchy of sophistication. The three regions postulated by MacLean are the Reptilian Brain (in the brain stem and basal ganglia); the Paleo-mammalian Mid-Brain (the Emotional Brain found in the Limbic System); and the Neo-Mammalian Brain (the Rational Brain found in the Neocortex of humans).

McClean's theory was controversial, simplistic, and speculative, but it caught on with the public and the media of his day (and is still popular). For our purposes, the levels Steiner discusses can be understood to represent a biological hierarchy, from a primitive lizard-like (instinctive) mind, to a mammalian brain, to a human brain, to a post-human (still evolving) brain. These levels are projected outward as auras and can be presumably interpreted (read) by sensitive minds (empaths, mystics, poets) as human beings project and mirror energy.

All that aside, there is also a scientific understanding that the human body is, indeed, surrounded by energy fields of various kinds. Scientists from the U.S. National Institute of Health defined such external energy layers as *biofields* (from a 1994 study). Biofields are now part of a subset of medicine called Energy Medicine (EM). This quote is from an article on the online site "Global Advances in Health and Medicine: Energy Medicine:"

> Energy medicine (EM), whether human touch or device-based, is the use of known subtle energy fields to therapeutically assess and treat energetic imbalances, bringing the body's systems back to homeostasis (balance). The future of EM depends on the ability of allopathic medicine to merge physics with biochemistry. *Biophoton emissions as well as signal transduction and cell signaling communication systems are widely accepted in today's medicine.* This technology needs to be expanded to include the existence of the human biofield (or human energy field) to better understand that disturbances in the coherence of energy patterns are indications of disease and aging. Future perspectives include understanding cellular voltage potentials and how they relate to health and wellness, understanding the overlap between the endocrine and chakra systems, and understanding how EM therapeutically enhances psychoneuroimmunology (mind–body) medicine. ~ "Energy Medicine: Current Status and Future Perspectives," Christina L Ross, PhD.

The italics are mine in the above quote. I am highlighting the sentence that says, in effect, that *biofields are real*; energy medicine is a well-respected growing field of study. Rudolf Steiner was right; science has caught up with esoteric thought. For a recent review of biofields see "Biofield Science and Healing: History, Terminology, and Concepts," published in 2015 by Beverly Rubik, David Muehsam, Richard Hammerschlag, and Shamini Jain.

With this background, we are ready to look at Steiner's summary of Alchemical thinking regarding energy auras that encase the human body. This will suggest (speculatively) how Helen Keller might have been getting usable information from subtle energy. Understand that I am not saying that I agree with this perspective, nor am I urging you to adopt Steiner's theories. I find this Alchemical (ancient) perspective fascinating in the same way that I find Susanne Cook-Greuter's developmental comparison of levels of consciousness fascinating. There is useful information in Steiner's work, food for thought. Steiner was a brilliant human being with a humanitarian soul—the more I study Steiner, the more impressed I am that such a man could have been so far ahead of his time (and ours, in many ways).

One, the Physical Human Body

Steiner's first energy body is the one we are familiar with, that which is enclosed within the skin-boundary that separates our essence from the surrounding domain. This skin boundary contains the proprioceptive system that gives humanity a sense of individual animation, the sense of Allocentric consciousness. I suggest that Helen Keller was hyperaware at this energy layer.

According to esoteric thought, realizing that we have a complex physical body is a simplistic first-stage of understanding. It is a purely materialistic, rock-like (mineral) understanding of existence.

Esoteric thinking suggests that there is a language (and a worldview) that manifests for each layer of the seven-tiered human aura. In other words, communication (signaling) is dynamically happening between cells, between organ systems, and between the mind, body, and domain—which includes communication between energy auras. This design, where everything is connected and exchanging information (as above so below), holds true for all the energy layers discussed below. Each layer is networked with the others; there are languages and communication systems linking all seven energy bodies.

Two, the Ether Body

This level of the human aura is also called the *Life Body*, or life force. When psychics mentally explore this level, they say it is about two inches thick and envelopes the physical body. Like Russian dolls, each energy layer encloses the more primitive energy levels that developed earlier. Evidently, we developmentally create energy fields around us as we mature (at least potentially). Plants also have an ether body. The sense of being alive, of wholeness, is contained in this level of the aura. When we say that someone is full of life, when we marvel at a person's joy and animation, we are experiencing their life force, their Ether Body.

Helen must have been able to pick up energy from this level. That is how she could comment on the vitality and mysterious power of people like Mark Twain and Anne Sullivan—she felt their animation, she could detect the élan vital of fellow saints and artists.

Helen's Ether Body was highly developed—she exercised it constantly, she dwelt within this aura and she found meaning in life from the vibrational energy at this basic level. Helen's Ether Body might have been what others sensed when they first met her and why they were stunned, brought to tears, and often exclaimed that they had been in the presence of a religious figure.

Three, the Astral Body

This level of the human force field is an emotional zone—as if we "wear our emotions on our sleeve." The spiritual teacher Eckhart Tolle became famous for his depiction of a "pain body," which surrounded the physical body. We hold our emotional energy within the Astral Body; some people walk about hunched over in emotional pain, their *pain body* clearly visible—you can see it in their faces and in the rigidity of their body movements. Other people seem to carry a love-filled Astral Body, they float through life and emit kindness from their astral aura.

Children, who are loved and who feel secure, dance through spaces with joy-filled Astral Bodies. Animals have Astral Bodies as well; dogs are famously emotional. Instead of a mineral or plant consciousness, the astral plane represents the evolution of animal consciousness—an unburdened awareness that is not weighted down by Egoic energy.

The astral plane gives us an emotional sense of being alive—sensing and emotionally reacting to life moment-by-moment. We hold our emotional state within a bubble that surrounds the Physical and Ether Bodies—others can perceive our emotions quite easily.

Apparently, Helen could sense the astral plane. Her love of dogs suggests that she easily read emotions. She often comments in her writing about the emotional sophistication of people she met. Her own Astral Body was sophisticated and full of loving kindness. Her astral energy field could also strike out at perceived evil in the world like a lightning bolt—her Astral Body was also a defensive shield, a force field around her body that kept negativity away and allowed her to have an optimistic faith.

Four, the Egoic Body

The Egoic plane is unique to humanity since it transcends mineral, plant, and animal consciousness. It is a zone of self-awareness. We feel human, we feel special, we feel powerful because of the evolution of the Egoic aura. Using my Navigational Consciousness hypothesis and dual-process theory, we can say that the first three levels of the human aura represent primitive Allocentric consciousness; however, the Egoic body is the beginning of Egocentric consciousness.

According to Steiner and to esoteric lore, the Egoic Body is where karma is found (where it evolves); this Egoic body is also the layer (the kind of energy) that reincarnates. From an Alchemical (and Hindu) perspective, the Egoic energy field collects experiences and knowledge from which the Akashic Record creates a library—we are born with access to all that came before, and we add our experiences to the exponentially expanding Akashic Library. When trying to explain how it was that Helen was learning so fast and comprehending so quickly everything Sullivan taught her, Annie wrote:

> The child has dormant within him when he comes into the world, all the experiences of the race. These experiences are like photographic negatives, until language develops them and brings out the memory-images. ~ *Teacher and Helen*, 1980, by Joseph Lash.

Helen Keller had a highly intelligent Egoic Body. Because of her own (extremely healthy) cognitive development, Helen could compare herself with others. That is why she could judge character and perceive ignorance and arrogance. Helen did not suffer fools lightly because she could perceive the fools and their shallow (primitive and yet evolving) Egoic layer of consciousness.

Five, the First Spirit-Body

Steiner calls this energy level the Spirit-Self Body. What our two minds (Ego and Self) sense (but cannot verify) at this level is that they are mutually exclusive, and they oscillate. The two minds also sense that they have great power when oscillation is controlled, enhanced, and then projected, like that which occurs as a laser beam is charged up and then is discharged. This is a *felt* vibrational understanding, not an Egoic concept. Great amounts of potential energy can be projected from this level of vibrational resonance. We can create with abandon and we can influence others from within this energy plane. Accomplished artists know (sense) this aura very keenly.

In my Navigational hypothesis, the Spirit-Self Body is the level of high vibrational energy in which the polarity (the gap) between Allocentric and Egocentric can be ignited through sudden contact; positive energy and negative energy momentarily merge—this is the zone of energy in which "sparks can fly." Human beings become aware of their ability to project (direct, control) their energy currents at this level of vibrational awareness. The concept of *projection* (and mirroring) emerges at this level of vibration.

Helen Keller, through her manipulation of language, was able to project her views and passions outward into the biosphere of ideas. Her impact on others around her, through the media, and through direct confrontation with groups in cultures around the globe, was profound and long lasting. Helen could project from the Spirit Self-Body; she wielded tremendous power.

Six, the Second Spirit-Body

This zone is a new kind of emotional evolution. We can think of this plane of energy as a vibrationally energetic combination of the Physical Body and the Ether Body. Within the Second Spirit-Body, we experience a oneness with a universal life-force. Again, this is not cognitive, not conceptual. It is a feeling of being absorbed into a universal infinity, an eternal life-giving energy. There is also a sophisticated (further) emotional transformation within this aura.

Helen Keller knew this energy sphere very well because this is where Faith is found. This energy field is a spiritual zone of knowing, surrender, of total acceptance to the universal will. This is where spirituality is verified and experienced. Helen Keller *felt* this sphere around her, and she could tell whether others knew this esoteric secret.

Seven, the Third Spirit-Body

This is the highest evolution that the Alchemists envisioned. I suppose it is Enlightenment, Heaven, Nirvana, the ultimate energy state that a human consciousness can expect to become. Of course, the people who lived a hundred years ago had no idea how fast technology would evolve. Today, all bets are off concerning how consciousness will evolve as scientists mess with the human genome, edit the life-code, use drugs to enhance and alter brain functioning, and re-engineer God's original plan—and they are just getting started. No telling what new auras are possible as the future explodes forward.

Maybe God (whatever you want to call the "origin of the life-force") is just doing what was originally in the plan: to merge the immaterial with the material; to create . . . what? I certainly do not know. Neither do the scientists. However, this we do know about Helen Keller: she did not trust the patriarchy of her time to get unnatural selection right (the engineering of consciousness). As a woman born in 1880, she was not entitled to vote, to own property, to divorce a husband (if she had one), or to get an education (she had to fight long and hard to be accepted at Radcliffe). Helen and her fellow suffragettes had to fight for decades to get any rights at all. Helen Keller's mind was pushing the envelope; her aura was expanding, and she was evolving towards Enlightenment. The patriarchy of her time had a collectively shallow aural field, far from Enlightenment—they knew how to react but not how to respond; they knew how to discuss but not how to dialogue; they knew about sympathy but not empathy. They lived in their Egoic Bodies but had yet to evolve into any of the higher spiritual bodies.

The Ego judges and the Self accepts. We are both Self and Ego and our task is to evolve *both* our minds. The Alchemists with their auras and theories that postulate cognitive and spiritual evolution have merged with modern developmental psychologists with their comparative scales of cognitive evolution. Helen Keller leaves us with a critically important question: *How should the human mind evolve?*

Should we become wiser, more intelligent, more tolerant and appreciative of others? Will our auras expand and project ever more subtle vibrations? Or will the human species crash and burn and go extinct as levels of consciousness battle each other to the death? Helen voted for kindness, tolerance, and cooperation to prevail, as do I. How should *your* mind (your auras) evolve? Helen Keller is asking this question of you from beyond the grave.

Chapter Six is called *Smell, the Fallen Angel*. If we had any doubt about Helen's ability to use smell to identify people and things and to use smell for navigation—to locate place and determine pathways—this chapter puts all skepticism to rest. Understandably, Helen had an extraordinary sense of smell. From her midlife autobiography *Midstream* (1929), she wrote the following:

> I usually know what part of the city I am in by the odors. There are as many smells as there are philosophies. I have never had time to gather and classify my olfactory impressions of different

cities, but it would be an interesting subject. I find it quite natural to think of places by their characteristic smells.

Fifth Avenue, for example, has a different odor from any other part of New York or elsewhere. Indeed, it is a very odorous street. It may sound like a joke to say that it has an aristocratic smell; but it has, nevertheless. As I walk along its even pavements, I recognize expensive perfumes, powders, creams, choice flowers, and pleasant exhalations from the houses. In the residential section I smell delicate food, silken draperies, and rich tapestries. I know what kind of cosmetics the occupants of the house use. I know if there is an open fire, if they burn wood, or soft coal, if they roast their own coffee, if they use candles, if the house has been shut up for a long time, if it has been painted or newly decorated, and if the cleaners are at work on it. I suggest that if the police really wish to know where stills and "speakeasies" are located, they take me with them. It would not be a bad idea for the United States Government to establish a bureau of aromatic specialists.

I would love to have seen Helen's olfactory categories. Clearly, she could use smells as both landmarks and clues—she could identify a location by the collection of odors, as well as ascertain the activities occurring during her visit. A landmark is a permanent feature of a landscape, while a clue is temporary and circumstantial—most odors are clues. As a mobility specialist, I am curious if Helen was able to orient her body to smells or if odors were too ubiquitous to be of navigational use. Later in *Midstream*, Helen returns to her appreciation of New York City:

> Cut off as I am, it is inevitable that I should sometimes feel like a shadow walking in a shadowy world. When this happens, I ask to be taken to New York City. Always I return home weary, but I have the comforting certainty that mankind is real flesh and I myself am not a dream.

I was emotionally affected by Helen's observation that she worries at times that she might be just a dream, a shadow of a person, rather than a real human being. I suppose we all have moments like that, thinking (these days, especially) that we are virtual reality projections in some alien's rendition of earth-space. Reflect for a moment what it must feel like to have no visual input, no auditory input, just body sensations. There might be some terrifying moments especially when you are alone, perhaps awakening in a bed in a strange location—as Helen often did in her busy life—when suddenly you feel totally isolated from people and things. It is the presence of other sentient creatures going about their business that keeps us sane and grounded.

Helen often commented about the sighted population's failure to appreciate the senses, especially the senses that were overpowered by vision and hearing. Below she is commenting on the common man's neglect of the sense of smell:

> When I consider all the delights the sense of smell brings me, I am amazed that this most intimate sense should be so generally neglected . . . The nose is as complex as the eye or the ear, and as well equipped for the acquisition of knowledge, but to speak of educating the nose provokes only a smile.

Helen's observation that the nose is as complex as the eye and ear feels false to sighted and hearing populations. Our sense of smell has been so overpowered by seeing and hearing that we find it hard to believe that the olfactory sense is an equal member of the sensory family. However, Helen is the proof that olfaction can be reactivated, trained, and put to practical use.

Helen Keller was able to read and analyze others using environmental smells to guide her judgments. In the quote below, she reflects on the subway ride into New York City. She much prefers being pressed up against humanity rather than be isolated in an automobile (edited for clarity):

> I was glad of a subway ride and shall take one as often as possible . . . I like any mode of transit, subway, elevated or the bus that brings me into close contact with people . . . powder, perfume, tobacco, shoe polish [tell me much]. I also sense freshness and good taste in the odors of soap, clean garments, silks and gloves. From exhalations I often know the work they are engaged in because the odors of wood, iron, paint of the office cling to their clothes. In a car I miss these intimate revelations of how my fellow-creatures live.

Helen sounds like Sherlock Holmes deducing the personality and livelihood of people she meets. Without hearing and vision, Helen used her sense of smell to analyze personalities, occupations, and emotional states; she could surmise what a person had been drinking and eating, what soaps or perfumes they had recently used, where they had recently traveled, whether they had pets, whether they were smokers or lived with smokers, maybe even what part of the city they lived in.

Helen could usually smell a friend as they entered a room. It was the collection of odors that hung over a visitor that gave them away. She knew the perfumes, nail polish, and soaps a specific friend customarily used. She knew the smell of their breath. She could smell the sweat on a body, which was characteristic for individuals. She was also probably quite adept at smelling pheromones—she knew who was "in heat" and who was not. We could speculate that she might even have been able to sense the health of an individual through the odors their bodies gave off.

It is important to realize that what Helen perceived at any moment was a gestalt, a big picture. For example, if she was typing a letter at her desk and someone entered a room, it was the total set of sensations that enabled the identification of a person. Helen certainly knew the olfactory characteristics of her intimate friends, Polly Thomson and Annie Sullivan, for example. But she also knew what their vibratory presence felt like—the cadence of their walk, the groan of the floor as they approached. She knew who was probably in the house at eight in the morning. Helen had no doubt who had entered her space. She could also guess what they were doing (bringing her mail, offering her coffee, etc.).

Helen might also have been able to follow a scent as animals do. This ability would have greatly enhanced her navigational ability. Additionally, she might have honed the ability to judge distances based on the density of odors.

Sighted individuals marvel at the creations of painters, sculptors, and street artists while music lovers marvel at the creations of composers and songwriters. We are quite familiar with the aesthetics of sight and sound. However, we seem to lack an appreciation of olfactory art. Helen Keller probably stood alone as a person with a great love and appreciation of environmental odors, which washed over her in symphonic waves. Helen found great joy in the chorus of smells that sang in the spaces around her.

Chapter Seven is called the Relative Value of the Senses.

In the article about her hands, Helen asks the reader to consider what life would be like without the use of hands and fingers. In this chapter, she relates how—probably because of a cold—she temporarily lost her ability to smell and taste. It is a devastating experience for a deaf-blind person to lose the sense of smell. But this experience highlights for Helen how precious is her sense of smell. She tells us that losing her smell left her with an appreciation for people who suddenly lose their vision. She also makes the analogy that the loss of a sense does not mean the loss of intellect or emotion; the inner order is not perverted by sensory loss. Helen says that "smell is a little the ear's inferior, and touch is a great deal the eye's superior."

Chapter Eight is called The Five-Sensed World.

For me, these few pages are perhaps the most powerful in the book. I know these themes from reading her other works, but she restates them here in yet more powerfully perceptive language. Here are Helen's words:

> "The only lightless dark is the night of ignorance and insensibility."

> "I have walked with people whose eyes are full of light, but who see nothing in wood, sea, or sky, nothing in city streets, nothing in books. What a witless masquerade is this seeing!"

> "They have the sunset, the morning skies, the purple of distant hills, yet their souls voyage through this enchanted world with a barren stare."

> "The calamity of the blind is immense, irreparable. But it does not take away our share of the things that count—service, friendship, imagination, wisdom."

For me, what Helen is saying is that the evolution of consciousness goes forward regardless of the state of the senses. People with 20/20 vison can have Narcissistic, Ethnocentric, and Traditional Minds; they can drift through life without paying attention or being aware. They can sleepwalk through this gift of life, and that is tragic (for them). Worse, these same people, with the dampened ears and glazed-over eyes can make policy decisions and lead church services.

Chapter Nine is called Inward Visions.

Helen begins by telling us that Love and Faith are mostly independent of the input of the external senses, like vision and hearing. Inwardly, our imagination can build worlds of perfect form and proportion. From this internal spiritual world, we can feel Love being created and Faith being formed. As she repeats in many of her essays and books, Helen observes that too many people who hear and see do not develop the internal powers of Love, Faith, and Imagination. Ironically, these people are deaf-blind to what makes us most worthy as human beings.

In this chapter, Helen has a paragraph about her friend deaf-blind Bertha Galeron [they corresponded for years]. Berthe was the "Helen Keller" of France. Helen tells us:

> I have a little volume of poems by a deaf-blind lady, Madame Bertha Galeron. Her poetry has versatility of thought. Now it is tender and sweet, now full of tragic passion and the sternness of destiny. Victor Hugo called her "La Grande Yoyante." She has written several plays, two of which have been acted in Paris. The French Academy has crowned her work.

Helen also praises blind poet Clarence Hawkes and includes one of his poems. She introduces Hawkes and Galeron because they are examples of accomplished spiritual voices, sophisticated souls despite their sensory deprivation. Like Helen, Hawkes, and Galeron have powerful imaginations; they know how to create enduring inward visions. There have been, and continue to be, artistic, creative, emotionally powerful individuals who were/are blind, deaf, and deaf-blind. It is just that they have no marketing team to bring them to the attention of the masses. There are many Helen Keller Souls among us.

Chapter Ten is called Analogies in Sense Perception.

The world that Helen Keller perceives is the same world that others perceive. The senses that behold human reality may differ, but the substance of the world is solid and dependable. Loss of vision and/or hearing does not negate the physical universe.

Human beings use analogies all the time; they also use metaphors and similes. It is natural to compare one thing to another. A deaf-blind person has a perfect right to use analogies as that person communicates. Helen says that she can understand the concept of shades of color using her sense of smell. The citrus smell can have different intensities and nuances. Helen can tell one variety of rose from another through smell and texture. She knows freshness and staleness. She knows ripe and unripe. Helen can sense harmony and beauty. She can use her sense of smell and touch to make analogies to phrases the sighted use to describe colors and textures and she can use her remaining senses to understand the auditory phrases her hearing friends use.

Chapter Eleven is called Before the Soul Dawn.

This chapter answers the question, "What was it like (before Anne Sullivan came) to be deaf, blind, and without language?" Helen answers that she had no sense of "I am" before her teacher arrived. It was a time of nothingness for her. She had neither Ego nor Intellect. To feel alive, to be human, means that we possess choice, that we possess the ability to consider alternatives—therefore, we must have an Ego (a sense of seer and seen) before we can sense our separateness.

Helen had instincts and vivid emotions but those around her misread these primitive instincts as a desire to choose, based on a thinking facility—both of which, thinking and choice, only emerged after Anne Sullivan brought language to Helen. "My inner life," Helen says, "was a blank without past, present, or future, without hope or anticipation, without wonder or joy or faith."

When her Ego first appeared at the famous water fountain, she discovered an "I" and felt for the first time that she was something separate from the domain (environment/surroundings). She says, "it was not the sense of touch that brought me knowledge. It was the awakening of my soul that first rendered my senses their value, their cognizance of objects, names, qualities, and properties."

Helen could eventually sense that the physical universe, which was filled with living things, was recreated, represented—essentially constructed—by the human brain. She came to know that each mind was constructed by a unique brain. After the dawn of language, Helen could see that every human being carried a universe within them, a worldview, a sense of reality that was like other minds, although not exactly so. Helen says that people who do not create sophisticated models of reality within themselves, fail to see wonder and value in the external world. Helen's penetrating, astute, brilliant mind shines through in this short chapter.

Chapter Twelve is called The Larger Sanctions.

Helen tells us that a blind, deaf, or deaf-blind child has inherited the mind of seeing and hearing ancestors. The anatomy and physiology within the brain awaits visual and auditory patterns. When these patterns do not arrive, the brain searches for other patterns that most resemble light waves and sound waves.

The deaf-blind child is an anomaly; most of the people of the earth see and hear. The deaf-blind child has no choice except to try to see through the eyes of the sighted, to hear with the ears of the hearing, and to think the thoughts of others who have all their senses intact. Fortunately, brains are anatomically constructed the same; the brain of a deaf-blind person is biologically designed the same as the brain of a sighted, hearing person. The mind that comes from such a brain will be similar no matter what the status of the sensory systems. Imagination also arises from within and is common to both sighted and blind, hearing and deaf. Language capability is also inherent in every person regardless of sensory ability. Therefore, a deaf-blind person can learn and cognitively grow just as a sighted and hearing person, and in an almost identical manner.

It is okay (even expected) for the human mind to use metaphors. Therefore, it is okay for a deaf-blind mind to use metaphors regardless of their origin. Most metaphors are related to vision and audition, but anyone may use these language tools to express their thoughts.

Blindness, Helen says, has no limiting effect upon mental vision. She says her intellectual (internal) horizon is infinitely wide.

Chapter Thirteen is called The Dream World.

Helen wondered why men of science were so curious about her dreams. It took a while, but she eventually realized it was because these well-meaning researchers held the assumption that without visual and auditory images, dreams must be dull and barren. Scientists were searching to discover evidence for their assumptions that Helen's reality was "flat, formless, colorless, without perspective, with little thickness and solidity—a vast solitude of soundless space."

Scientists are uncomfortable with dreaming, or so Helen suggests; she can see that there is a border-line beyond which the tools of science are pitifully inadequate. Common sense is not reliable in the dreamworld; thoughts seem to have no discipline in dreamland. Therefore, reason and quantitative analysis are not up to the task of measuring and cataloging dreams. Helen says that while dreaming "the spirit wrenches itself free from the sinewy arms of reason and like a winged courser spurns the firm green earth and speeds away upon wind and cloud, leaving neither trace nor footprint by which science may track its flight . . ."

Having left science at the threshold, Helen tells us that she believes her dreams to be normal, pretty much like everyone else's experience. Some are coherent, many dreams are not. She says she floats among the clouds, flows with the wind, all the while feeling that this sensation is normal. Helen travels to foreign lands and talks with strangers who have a different language. "Yet" she says, "we understand each other."

The people Helen meets in dreams may behave strangely but she is never shocked by their behaviors. Her soul "takes everything for granted and adapts itself to the wildest phantoms." She is rarely confused or disoriented in her dreams. Everything, she tells us, is clear as day.

Like everyone else, Helen has anxiety dreams, dreams that struggle to get somewhere but never quite arrive. She falls down in her dreams, down and down. She reaches for objects but grasps only air. She dissolves into the atmosphere and disappears.

Helen tosses and turns; she dreams that she cannot fall asleep. She gets up, in her dream, and pulls a book with no title from the shelf. When she opens the book to run her fingers over the braille dots, the pages are smooth—there is no information in the book. She is not so much surprised as she is disappointed. Tears fall on the book, which she quickly closes so that her tears do not damage the pages.

Sometimes she dreams that she is awake, but no one will confirm her sensation of wakefulness. The hands on her clock wiggle, whirl, buzz, and then disappear. It is bewildering, Helen says, because the consciousness of the sham waking feels the same as everyday consciousness.

Helen feels that the history of humanity can be reached through the dream state—a quite esoteric perspective. She can feel events in history: "I have held a little child in my arms in the midst of a riot and spoken vehemently, imploring the Russian soldiers not to massacre the Jews. I have re-lived the agonizing scenes of the Sepoy Rebellion and the French Revolution. Cities have burned before my eyes, and I have fought the flames until I fell exhausted. Holocausts overtake the world, and I struggle to save my friends."

This was written in 1908 before two world wars would bring stark, horrendous meaning to the word *Holocaust*. It is almost as if Helen Keller was looking into the future through her dreams. Another dream foresaw the coming of climate change and the descent of winter over much of the land. Once in a dream a message came speeding over land and sea that winter was descending upon the world from the North Pole . . ."For some time, the trees and flowers grew on, despite the intense cold. Birds flew into houses for safety, and those which winter had overtaken lay on the snow with wings spread in vain flight."

For all those who have asked "Did Helen Keller dream?" this is the detailed, dream-after-dream answer. I will not recount further dreams; I leave it to you to read the full chapter.

Chapter Fourteen is called Dreams and Reality.

Dreaming and imagination are cousins. We dream at night without intention and without reason interfering with our random mixing of sensations. However, when we awake, we continue to dream about the future, or we dream of repairing the past. Dreaming while we are awake seems to be a necessary part of consciousness. We build the future using the elements we perceive in waking moments.

Helen says that before her Teacher came to unlock her consciousness, she lived in a perpetual dream-state. Going to bed and getting up in the morning seemed to be the only borders of reality. Yet she did dream in her pre-Sullivan years. Helen recounts smelling bananas so vividly that she woke up and went in search of bananas, but she found nothing in waking reality.

Helen says she is more fortunate than many others because her dreams, like her personality, are mostly optimistic and gentle. In general, she does not have troubled or disturbing dreams. For Helen, dreaming is primarily a pleasure. Dreams seem to lift her burdens and remove trivial emotions.

What I find most pleasing about this little chapter is Helen's concluding observations. She is addressing levels of consciousness and the evolution of spirituality:

> I like to think that in dreams we catch glimpses of a life larger than our own. We see it as a little child, or as a savage who visits a civilized nation. Thoughts are imparted to us far above our ordinary thinking. Feelings nobler and wiser than any we have

known thrill us between heart-beats. For one fleeting night a princelier nature captures us, and we become as great as our aspirations.

Chapter Fifteen is called A Waking Dream.

Helen begins this chapter by using a technique we now call meditation. She sat very still, quieted her mind, and then observed her thoughts as they came and went. She called the process "a wide-awake dream." She had an essay to write and so she needed a "fresh mind." She wanted her mental house in order and her thoughts obedient. Alas, her mind was "throwing a party, confusion was rampant, there was fiddling and dancing and the babble of many tongues."

I laughed when I read her words because my own mind dances and fiddles when it should be analyzing Helen Keller. Taming the mind is like herding cats. The miracle is not so much that we have a mind, Helen suggests, but rather the miracle is that we are able to use the wild thing. Having a mind is one thing but putting it to good use is quite another challenge.

Since her mind was throwing a party, Helen decided to just sit there and watch the crazy thing go about its feverish babble. Giving up the struggle was relaxing and soon Helen was watching her thoughts at play. She says, "I felt like Alice in Wonderland when she ran at full speed with the red queen and never passed anything or got anywhere." What she experienced was a daydream that was every bit as bizarre and awesome as a dream in deep sleep. She describes the daydream in vivid detail for several pages.

The book ends with a poem called "A Chant of Darkness." When I analyzed this poem, I could see that it belonged with Helen's 1910 book—essentially a long poem—called *The Song of the Stone Wall*, which we will turn to later in the timeline.

"Did Helen Keller Dream," that was the original question she set out to answer in *The World I Live In*. This is from her autobiography:

Before and after my teacher first came to me, [dreams] were devoid of sound, of thought or emotion of any kind, except fear, and only came in the form of sensations. I would often dream that I ran into a still, dark room, and that, while I stood there, I felt something fall heavily without any noise, causing the floor to shake up and down violently; and each time I woke up with a jump. As I learned more and more about the objects around me, this strange dream ceased to haunt me; but I was in a high state of excitement and received impressions very easily. It is not strange then that I dreamed at the time of a wolf, which seemed to rush towards me and put his cruel teeth deep into my body! I could not speak (the fact was, I could only spell with my fingers), and I tried to scream; but no sound escaped from my lips. It is very likely that I had heard the story of Red Riding Hood and was deeply impressed by it. This dream, however, passed away in time, and I began to dream of objects outside myself.

This tells us much about our own dreams. The mind will use what it has on hand in memory networks to construct illusory locations and events. For Helen, all she had was vibratory (proprioceptive) and olfactory information. However, she does not often mention smell as being in dreams and we must ask why that might be. Little research has been done on the question of odors appearing in dreams; what little information we do have suggests that smells are a rare phenomenon in the dream world.

It is also interesting that Helen says emotions were also rare in her dreams, except for instinctual fear. Studies suggest that the most common dream emotions are fear and anxiety, with less frequent feelings of anger and sadness.

Helen also says she had no thoughts in her early dreams. But what are thoughts? Does she mean words or language? Are thoughts, insights, and ideas equivalent concepts? Can thoughts arise from a silent and dark location, appearing as sudden insights? Are thoughts immeasurable? How are thoughts related to problem solving? Are thoughts insights that suddenly materialize from thoughtless backgrounds? Without going too deeply into this philosophical quagmire, I will offer some brief comments.

Neuroscientists call thoughts *neuronal activity patterns*—the collected cooperation of bundled neurons. *Processing information is the thought itself.* A good analogy is to consider the brain to be a world-class symphony orchestra, with each musician representing an instrument. That orchestra, sitting quietly before the performance, before the conductor appears, is just a silent picture—there are no musical patterns arising from this quiet orchestra. If all the musicians suddenly start to tune up, you get a cacophony of disharmonious sounds devoid of patterns, useless to the mind—because the mind only uses what has meaning for the organism. The number of potential musical scores this orchestra can play is infinite, but the orchestra needs a conductor, and it needs a musical score to follow so that all the musicians play the same composition at precisely the same time. Synchronicity is a necessity, otherwise musical "thought" will not emerge.

A thought is not located anywhere. Thought is a function of neurons interacting (following a script). A computer cannot really think because it cannot generate neuronal thoughts. Intelligence means you can follow rules (patterns) quickly, accurately, and efficiently. But the mind generates and changes rules—it is creative. We can generate new activity patterns that have never manifested before. The orchestra can play new scripts, new compositions, new scores.

When Helen says that she had no thoughts in her early dreams she is saying several things; foremost she is saying that she had no verbal language. But the ability for the symphony to play was intact in Helen's brain. She was born with the potential to mentally create, to imagine, to problem solve—just as she was born to walk when she was developmentally ready. Her dreams got richer and more sophisticated as she got older.

If my Navigational Consciousness hypothesis is correct, then dreams are the efforts of the mind to continue to navigate—to get somewhere, to create a location and a time-stamped event (a happening). Dreams are not still-life photos; they are animated shorts. We would also expect dreams to be an oscillation between Self and Ego—a battle to determine whether the background or the foreground will dominate. Presumably, the brain is pulling images, sounds, and emotions from memory silos as it replays the day's activities. In the dream state, Helen could sense her body walking or running straight-ahead, she had memory traces of her posture, tool use, and hand and finger movements; emotions came and went, mixed with movement. Helen's *The World I Live In* and her autobiography leave no doubt that she had rich, complex dreams.

1909: HELEN KELLER JOINS THE SOCIALIST PARTY

Helen Keller and John Macy joined the Socialist Party of Massachusetts in 1909. Helen declared herself a suffragette the same year.

As a pacifist, Helen believed that the First World War (which would break out in all its fury July 28, 1914) was caused by economic and class injustice; she wrote that America should remain neutral in the conflict. The Industrial Workers of the World (I.W.W., a Socialist organization which Helen endorsed) also opposed the war.

In an article published in the Socialist paper *The Liberator*, Helen wrote:

> During the last few months, in Washington State, at Pasco and throughout the Yakima Valley, many I.W.W. members have been arrested without warrants, thrown into bull-pens without access to an attorney, denied bail and trial by jury, and some of them were shot. Did any of the leading newspapers denounce these acts as unlawful, cruel, undemocratic? No. On the contrary, most of them indirectly praised the perpetrators of these crimes for their patriotic service! On August 1st, of 1917, in Butte, Montana, a cripple, Frank Little, a member of the Executive Board of the I.W.W., was forced out of bed at three o'clock in the morning by masked citizens, dragged behind an automobile and hanged on a railroad trestle. Were the offenders punished? [31]

There was something in the heart and soul of white males in America that saw no problem with lynching black men or murdering those of any race or creed who held political or religious views different from their own—Helen Keller faced this evil and named it.

Helen saw the problems facing society as a class struggle between those in power, who were wealthy and indifferent, and those stuck in poverty. The ruling elite of this economic imbalance were white men; the system protected them and enriched them, while the everyday citizen lived in poverty without a legal structure to protect them.

Historically, the patriarchy—masculine minds at narcissistic and ethnocentric levels of consciousness—has used violence to silence the people who spoke out for kindness, tolerance, equality, and peace. There is a special kind of violence that arises when lesser minds encounter greater minds. Lesser minds strike out, often violently against saints and spiritual leaders because unevolved minds cannot comprehend or empathetically relate to minds more sophisticated than their own. America has had its share of such lesser minds; and they are still with us. Helen Keller represents a more evolved mind, and she is a role model for each spiritually emerging generation. It is no mystery why she was so hated for her "socialist worldviews."

This is from an online article (from a socialist publication) about Helen Keller's politics:

> That she was a serious political thinker who made important contributions in the fields of socialist theory and practice, or that she was a pioneer in pointing the way toward a Marxist understanding of disability oppression and liberation—this reality has been overlooked and censored. The mythological Helen Keller that we are familiar with has aptly been described as a sort of "plaster saint;" a hollow, empty vessel who is little more than an apolitical symbol for perseverance and personal triumph.
>
> When the story of Helen Keller is taught in schools today, it is frequently used to convey a number of anodyne "moral lessons" or messages: There is no personal obstacle that cannot be overcome through pluck and hard work; whatever problems one thinks they have pale in comparison to those of Helen Keller; and perhaps the most insidious of such messages, the one aimed primarily at people with disabilities themselves, is

that the task of becoming a full member of society rests upon one's individual efforts to overcome a given impairment and has nothing to do with structural oppression or inequality.

Keller fought her entire life against such bigoted notions and distortions of her life story. She constantly combated attempts to render her a hollow icon. Nonetheless, such images regarding Keller and disability continue to be reinforced everywhere. This can be found in primary school curricula, in the vast majority of children's books on Helen Keller, and in most adult biographies of her. More often than not her radical politics are simply ignored. But even when they are acknowledged, it is usually to discount them. [32]

To remove the story of Helen Keller's passionate fight against class injustice, to remove her distain for cultural prejudices, to overlook her views about women's rights, racial equality, and disability rights, is to remove Helen's soul from her timeline. I am confident that every new generation will reaffirm Helen Keller's soul; her legacy will not be diluted or redefined.

What Else Happened in 1909?

Here are a few random events that happened in 1909: In Great Britain, the Old Age Pension Law was passed, providing pensions for every British subject over 70 with low income. . . . The National Association for the Advancement of Colored People (NAACP) was established. . . . The North Pole was reached by Americans Robert Peary & Matthew Henson. . . . Joan of Arc received beatification by the Roman Catholic Church. . . . The 16th Amendment was passed by the United States Congress, giving the government the right to tax incomes. . . . The first Lincoln head pennies were minted. . . . Swedish writer Selma Lagerlöf became the first woman to win the Nobel Prize for Literature. . . . Colored moving pictures were first demonstrated at Madison Square Garden in New York City.

1910: THE DEATHS OF MARK TWAIN AND WILLIAM JAMES

Helen Keller's good friend Mark Twain died on April 21, 1910. Here are a few memorable Mark Twain quotes:

- Kindness is the language which the deaf can hear and the blind can see.
- Travel is fatal to prejudice, bigotry, and narrow-mindedness.
- Suppose you were an idiot. And suppose you were a member of Congress. But I repeat myself.
- The world owes you nothing. It was here first.
- The more I learn about people, the more I like my dog.
- The two most important days in your life are the day you are born and the day you find out why.

I especially like that first quote; it is a tribute to Helen Keller who could perceive kindness without seeing or hearing. The second quote is also relevant to Helen. She traveled the world gaining experience and wisdom that could never have been attained had she been confined to small spaces and limited in her exploration. The third quote, of course, is a tongue-in-cheek political jab—I like the quote since it highlights the tenuous nature of our Democratic (representative) system, especially as I write these words in 2021.

1910 is also the year that Helen published her poetic book *The Song of the Stone Wall*. The book is metaphorical but also esoteric since it suggests something hidden from vision and hearing. Helen wrote about the idea for the poem in *Teacher*:

Another book, the creation of which was a joy for me, was *The Song of the Stone Wall*. Once, full of the enchantment of a lovely May morning, teacher and I were building up an old stone wall so as to extend my ramble in our green field. As we laid one stone upon another, I kept fingering the various shapes, textures, and sizes, and I became aware of the beauty in them that I had not sensed before. Having lately read a book on geology, I was freshly interested in the stones over which I occasionally stumbled—flat or grooved, big or little, some full of rents and jagged edges, some polished by cold and others crumbled by heat, still others with sharp and curved angles. Despite their rudeness and irregularity there were a peculiar quality that took my fancy very strongly. Through the chinks I could feel small breezes sighing and sunbeams sifting and bringing different odors from the plants surrounding them. "Oh Teacher," I cried, "here's a poem to write on these stone walls, if there is only enough of a poet in me for such a task." [33]

Anne Sullivan was enthusiastic about Helen's desire to celebrate the stone walls and to write a symbolic poem. Annie and Helen's subsequent discussions led to the book—John Macy was, of course, an important editor as well.

∾

In 1910, in a gracious letter, Helen Keller turned down Andrew Carnegie's offer of a regular pension to supplement her income. She and Sullivan needed the income boost, but Carnegie was an extraordinarily rich capitalist and Helen—just a year earlier—had joined the socialist party. It was hypocritical of her to accept the genuinely offered help. Carnegie responded by saying that his offer would remain on the table, should she change her mind.

Three years later, when Anne Sullivan was taken ill and Helen felt vulnerable and despondent, she wrote to Carnegie to accept his offer. Carnegie was, of course, not happy with Helen's socialist passion, but he gave her the pension anyway. There are times when kindness and humbleness trump politics. Andrew Carnegie gained tremendously good karma through his benevolent decisions. He was a kind man who worked hard and was lucky (so he said); he got rich and then he turned his excess cash into acts of kindness, not unlike Bill Gates and Warren Buffet do in our era.

Helen Keller's friend William James died the same year as Mark Twain, 1910. Helen was thirty when these two giants, Mark Twain and William James, passed from the American scene. Helen must have felt a great void in her heart; and she must have felt somewhat alone in the battle for kindness.

~

Helen had both eyes enucleated in 1910; prosthetic eyes were inserted, which greatly improved her appearance. We do not know any details about her operation(s), and we do not know the exact date when her eyes were removed or when ocular prosthetics were created to fit her eye sockets.

Enucleation did not become common practice until the middle of the 1800s. Before Helen was born (1880), there were companies making custom prostheses, usually "eyes" hand-blown (glass) from scratch. During the 1850s, companies started custom-making ocular prostheses in New York City. In the 1920s, several eye companies sent experts to cities in the East to custom-make ocular prosthetics for patients. By the mid-1940s, glass eyes were replaced by plastic eyes—mostly because of the shortage of materials during the Second World War. Helen may have had more than one set of eyes made as technology changed decade to decade.

What Else Happened in 1910?

Here are a few random events that happened in 1910: A (second) revised edition of *Out of the Dark: Essays, Lectures, and Addresses on Physical and Social Vision* was published. . . . John D. Rockefeller Jr. announced his retirement so that he could devote full time to philanthropy. . . . The Zeppelin Deutscheland, the world's first airship, sailed with passengers. . . . The first issue of "Crisis" was published by editor W. E. B. Du Bois. . . . On November 8, 1910, Washington State allowed women to vote. . . . In Baltimore, a city ordinance was passed requiring separate white and black residential areas. . . . Dutch Physicist Johannes van der Waals won the Nobel Prize for physics.

The Song of the Stone Wall

> Oh beautiful, blind stones, inarticulate and dumb!" exclaims
> Miss Keller, with a poignant self-analogy which might be
> painful, but instead is triumphant and sweet. For here is one
> who has annihilated limitation and demonstrated that beauty is
> independent of the senses, and that light and joy are messengers
> who enter by closed doors. ~ New York Times book review,
> December 4, 1910, by Jessie B. Rittenhouse.

In her book, *The Song of the Stone Wall,* Helen cries out: "Oh beautiful,
blind stones, inarticulate and dumb!" She knows that she is like the
historic stone walls of New England, blind and voiceless—yet, of course,
she has learned language and she is brilliant and articulate. She is also a
living being, a lovely woman who can move and explore, learn, and feel.
We can imagine her standing in the shade of nearby trees as she touches
an ancient stone wall with love and fascination. She is living proof that
"light and joy are messengers who enter by closed doors."

The stone walls of New England, which Helen featured in *The Song of
the Stone Wall* (1910), are historic treasures that weave their way through
the hills of New England, alongside rivers, through farmland, passing
randomly through small villages in Maine, Vermont, Massachusetts,
Connecticut, New Hampshire, Delaware, New York, and Rhode Island.
These stone walls are archeological relics from the earliest times of the
American Republic—a time when agricultural civilization flourished
in the new states of the union. Seen through modern eyes, the walls
seem to lead nowhere and enclose nothing; they just meander aimlessly
through the countryside.

Human beings sometimes feel like there is no ultimate purpose to
their lives: we are just meandering, like the stone walls of New England,
wandering deaf-blind through nowhere, wondering what we are supposed
to be doing on this planet. Helen Keller, of course, had a clear purpose
and she did not seem to be wandering or lost. She had a poetic spirit; she
could sense the poetry emanating even from stones. *The Song of the Stone
Wall* is a long poem, a lengthy metaphor, it is Helen's way of sharing subtle
vibrations—only poetry has the strength to pull off such an intention.

Different men and women built New England's stone walls at
different times; the walls are a cultural archeology, a man-by-man,
family-by-family history. In separate stanzas, Helen tells us:

- The men who built the New England stone walls came over conquered sea to the unconquered wilderness.
- The patient sturdy men who piled the stones have vanished.
- Life triumphed over many-weaponed Death. Otherwise, there would be no arisen life.
- The walls stand as symbols of a granite race, the measure and translation of olden time.
- We are shot through and through with hidden color" [hidden vibrations] "A thousand hues are blended in our gray substance.

I love the reference to a *Granite Race*. You can almost see the rock-hard giants at work building a civilization, stone-by-stone. These Granite Peoples are our long-vanished ancestors. All that physically remains of them are these weatherworn monuments.

In the backyard of Helen Keller's home in Wrentham, Massachusetts, a historic stone wall was within walking distance—there was a path Helen could follow that led from her house to a segment of the meandering wall. Helen loved to follow the wall and to explore its tactile and vibratory secrets. These walls spoke to Helen, channeled their wisdom through her fingertips onto the pages of her poetry book.

Helen could feel something intelligent as she played her fingertips over the uneven surfaces of the stones. Here were messages waiting to be deciphered by a mind capable of perceiving delicate and subtle patterns. The vibrations tell the history of the men who made the walls and of the God who made the stones, made the men, and made the insects and plants that seasonally call the walls home. Helen had no doubt that such a God exists, a Granite God that left vibrations (messages) behind, as creation went forth at the speed of light.

For Helen, the stones seemed to outwardly lie silent and unresponsive, yet she could read the stones at vibrational levels. At the level of the molecules, atoms, and quarks she reported that "divine messages lie concealed within:" Helen tells us that "The wall is an Iliad of granite; it chants to me;" . . ."My pulses beat in unison with pulses that are stilled."

We cannot help but wonder where the poetic phrases leave off and the actual reading of vibrational energy begins. I suspect that the poetry and the vibrational energy cannot be dissected out into separateness. Yes, Helen Keller is using metaphor and analogy to speak through the poem, but she is also a witness to sensations that are normally filtered or suppressed in those of us who can see and hear.

As Helen's searching feet followed the winding, undulating wall, she sensed that the stones were not straight; and they led to different domains, to unique environmental niches. The historic walls are a journey that seems never to end as Helen follows a trail from her house to the wall, and then, picking a direction each morning, she goes as far as she dares go before returning home. Always the wall is fresh with news.

Each day is different as the weather changes, the temperature varies, and the seasons unfold. Different plants and insects inhabit different eco-zones; the top surface of the wall tells a different story than the sides of the wall. The stones tell of frost and storm, ice, rain, and sun; there is a different *weather sculpture* at unique places on the wall; there is a mantle of green moss on the top in various places and numerous plants have taken up temporary residence. The information hidden in the stones is "half erased by impartial storms." Each square inch is a new universe to discover.

Using the scented fields that surround the walls, Helen can locate her position. She uses smell variations corresponding to characteristics in the wall. She can identify multi-sensory patterns associated with location. She mentions the various domains associated with her journey along the wall:

- the heaving hill . . .
- by the marsh where the rushes grow . . .
- pine woods fragrant and cool . . .
- rolling acres of rye . . .

She is as sure of her position as a sighted person would be using visual landmarks. Helen's landmarks—heaving hill, pine fragrance, the smell of rye—together define and label the area surrounding where she stands. Just as ants follow a chemical trail as they leave and return to their nests, perhaps Helen also knows how to follow a scent-trail.

The stone walls, Helen muses, are a creation of the labor of men and women (and their children). The walls have a beginning; they are begotten at a time and in a place. However, the stones themselves harbor a greater message: Helen tells us that inside the "gloom" of the stones resides the "gleam" of creation. All stones have the same beginning and, therefore, the stones are brothers and sisters: diamonds, rubies, opals, emeralds, all the gems of existence are related by birth to each other; all are children of mother earth, just as we are. Without the Granite Race, there would be no Human Race. Helen says that we carry the light of creation within us, just as do the New England stones.

Like the wall, human beings are also "fragments of the universe." The wall has a foundation, laid by men, just as God laid the foundation that now holds humanity. Like the wall, we are a strange combination of the animate and inanimate, chaos and order. Helen says, "We are wonderfully mingled of life and death." Like the walls, human beings, through their digestive biome and skin surface, "serve as crypts for innumerable, unnoticed tiny forms."

"The earth is a stir with joy," she writes, as she lays her hands on the stones without moving her fingers; she seems to be giving and receiving energy. Her still fingertips listen to the emotions of the earth. Perhaps, this is an Aha! moment, when she realizes that subtle energy can speak a language that human beings can interpret if they still their eyes and ears and listen with their whole body.

"All the broken tragedy of life and all the yearning mystery of death," she writes "are celebrated in sweet epitaphs of vines and violets." Wherever she stands, she senses the environment around the walls: "Close by the wall, a peristyle of pines sings requiems to all the dead that sleep . . . I am kneeling on the odorous earth . . . Up from the south come the odor-laden winds . . . Hark to the songs that go singing like the wind through the chinks of the wall and thrill the heart. Alluring secrets hide in the wood and hedge, like the first thoughts of love in the breast of a maiden."

"Crows are calling from the Druidical wood," she writes, "the morning mist still haunts the meadows like the ghosts of the wall builders." Like the stones, trees reveal their secrets through touch: "The elm tree's song is wondrous sweet . . . the ancientest language of trees . . . I feel the glad stirrings under her rough bark."

Suddenly, the vibrations shift, and Helen feels more disturbing voices speaking: "In the old walls there are sinister voices:"

> The groans of women charged with witchcraft,
> I see a lone, gray, haggard woman standing at bay;
> helpless against her grim, sin-darkened judges.
> Terror blanches her lips and makes her confess
> bonds with demons that her heart knows not.
> Satan sits by the judgment-seat and laughs.

The gray walls, broken, weatherworn oracles,
sing that she was once a girl of love and laughter.

We just about choke when we read those lines, because we know they are true: There was, indeed, a young woman alive with emotional acuteness who was deliberately drowned or set on fire because she was a poet before her time, or because her menstrual hormones made her momentarily shrill and vividly sensual. Or maybe there was an old and gray woman, her hair knotted and lice-infected, who was done with following orders from nasty priests and said so with vehemence. Tens of thousands of innocent women, one horrible moment at a time, were deliberately, dramatically, hatefully murdered in the name of the Christian God.

Dressed in the robes of the Church, the Devil thought he got away with these murders, but *the stones were watching.* The stones that were birthed by Mother earth, did not forget the women who stood terrified about to be put to death by the Devil's henchmen. The cruelty of men to women and to each other is not the stuff of legend; these murderous memories are true events; the stones have witnessed and preserved the awful truth of the Devil's work.

The Devil's greatest skill is dressing in the robes of the Church as he goes about his atrocities. Helen Keller's poem is as valid today as it was when she wrote it in 1910; the Devil is still wearing his Holy Disguise as he goes about his modern atrocities. Helen Keller's vibratory stones have preserved every one of the Devil's crimes; if you place your fingertips on the stones you will shutter as the subtle vibrations reveal the truth to you.

This segment of Helen Keller's poem—the terrified woman, friendless, about to be murdered—doubles us over in pain. Pious shepherds of God drowned thousands of so-called witches. The savage cruelty of the male of our species, holding aloft the holy books, makes the galaxy shutter:

> It has been estimated that tens of thousands of people were executed for witchcraft in Europe and the American colonies over several hundred years. Although it is not possible to ascertain the exact number, modern scholars estimate around 40,000 to 50,000. Common methods of execution for convicted witches were hanging, drowning and burning. Burning was often favored, particularly in Europe, as it was considered a

more painful way to die. Prosecutors in the American colonies generally preferred hanging in cases of witchcraft. ~ Wikipedia

History makes it abundantly clear that burning, hanging, and drowning—all forms of deliberate violence—are primarily the actions of males. In her poem, Helen is speaking as the Divine Feminine confronting the atrocities of the patriarchy. This patriarchal mindset still haunts the earth; the Devil is still in power in too many places; he is still hiding behind the Bible or the Koran, still masquerading as God. But the stones are still listening and recording—nothing goes unnoticed, and no violence, in the end, is ever condoned by Love.

New York Times Book Review

Below are excerpts from the *New York Times* review of *The Song of the Stone Wall*, December 4, 1910, written by Jessie Rittenhouse. This is a wonderfully perceptive review of Helen Keller's sensory world and deserves to be remembered:

> Modern psychology cannot account for Miss Keller nor explain the psychic sense by which she apprehends the minutest phases of a beauty she has never witnessed. Note, for example, the exactness of impression, the perfect sense of reality, the apparently loving observation in these lines:
>
> • Sunbeams flit and waver in the rifts.
> • Vanish and reappear, linger and sleep.
> • Conquer with radiance the obdurate angles.
> • Filter between the naked rents and wind-bleached jags.
>
> Is not this the report of an exquisite vision? Yet only sentient hands have discovered that "sunbeams flit and waver in the rifts."
> This passage is, however, more directly allied to the physical than many others which leads one into conjecture as to Miss Keller's conception of beauty. How, having seen neither object, and lacking all data for their association, could she embody both in so exquisite an image as a "peristyle of pines"?

The Song of the Stone Wall is conceived and executed in the Whitman spirit and with the Whitman influence apparent in its form. But what more liberating influence to an imprisoned art-sense just seeking its expression? Miss Keller conceives her subject broadly: "The wall is an Iliad of granite; it chants to me," she says, with that fine elation worthy of her master and listening with ears not dulled by mortal sounds. The wall is the symbol of its Puritan builders; stone upon stone it is fashioned of their ideals: it stands firm in their convictions; unyielding in their will. Miss Keller sees the procession of the builders: "One by one, the melancholy phantoms go stepping from me. And I follow them in and out among the stones."

But the pursuit does not depress, it inspires, and as this eager spirit follows with guiding hand upon the stones, they become to her "Embossed books unobliterated by the tears and laughter of Time."

Miss Keller leaves us filled with wonder, rather than in the working out of her poem on the symbolical side. This is done as others might do it, albeit with ideality and often with eloquent music, but the real offering of this little book is the sense that beauty is a spiritual conception, a dream-sphere of the soul, made one with nature and life in a mystical reality.

I quoted from this 1910 review of *The Song of the Stone Wall*, written by Jessie Belle Rittenhouse Scollard, because Jessie Rittenhouse was herself an accomplished and well-respected poet. She was also a literary critic. What better tribute could there be to Helen's writing abilities than to have another astute feminine sensitivity celebrate Keller's poetry.

Jessie Rittenhouse wrote over a hundred years ago that "Modern psychology cannot account for Miss Keller nor explain the psychic sense." I am here to testify that modern psychology still cannot account for the esoteric Helen Keller. We still have not figured out what those subtle vibrational patterns are that she could sense—where, we wonder, are the vibrations coming from and how might we, also, hear the chanting of the stones?

Helen writes metaphorically in this poem and in *A Chant of Darkness* (below), telling humanity that there is a "chanting going on" below the visual and auditory worlds. There exists a harmonic mix of ethereal vibrations that arrive—as chants reach us—to soothe the human body and make all our cells ring together. And there is information embedded in the chanting. A sub-aware messaging system is real, according to Helen Keller.

Helen's vibrational universe put her in direct contact with animals, plants, and with the stones of the earth—she could feel the earth's heartbeat and she could sense the earth's breathing. Helen Keller, the social activist, the eloquent writer, the curious, disciplined, good-humored, feisty spiritual saint, was also an accomplished and inspirational poet.

A Chant of Darkness

> Night-time sharpens, heightens each sensation.
> Darkness wakes and stirs imagination.
> Silently, the senses abandon their defenses,
> Helpless to resist the notes I write.
> For I compose the music of the night.
> ~ "The Music of the Night," from *The Phantom of the Opera*,
> by Andrew Lloyd Webber.

When I was writing this section, I watched a 25th anniversary special performance of Andrew Lloyd Webber's *The Phantom of the Opera*. I marveled at how art overlaps, how recurrent themes penetrate to our core and sing deep within our souls. I could hear the Phantom singing beneath my Egoic consciousness. He was singing about Helen Keller, how night-time (blindness) sharpens and heightens each remaining sensation. Vision and hearing have defenses and when they are dropped, we become helpless to resist the music of the night. That was Helen Keller's fate, she could not block or filter out the Music of the Night. Helen Keller embraced hidden (esoteric) music, and we are the recipients of her singing.

Helen's book *The World I Live In* (1908) ends with a poem called *A Chant of Darkness*. You can hear the poem read on YouTube, which I found helpful and enjoyable. The poem is both about Helen's life, isolated in silence and darkness, and about the human condition, the innate deaf-blindness that defines humanity's sensory imprisonment.

Helen begins her poem with five lines from Percival Shelley's poem *Prometheus Unbound*:

My wings are folded o'er mine ears;
My wings are crossed o'er mine eyes;
Yet through their silver shade appears,
And through their lulling plumes arise,
A Shape, a throng of sounds.

There are multiple ways to interpret Shelley's lines, but for our purposes I suggest that Helen Keller is describing herself, speaking to us about her condition using the words of Shelley. Helen's "wings" cover her ears and her eyes; she is deaf-blind. Yet, there is something out there that she perceives, "a throng of sounds"—many vibrations reach her even though she has no vision and no hearing.

We could also say, as Helen does in her political and religious work, that whole cultures can be ignorant, cruel, deaf-blind, and unresponsive to cries for help. Helen Keller is a champion for Love. She knows that what she perceives (coming from deep within a silent darkness) her fellow compatriots do not perceive. She is not the only one with ears and eyes covered.

We can better understand what Helen is trying to tell us in her poem if we examine what Shelley (1792–1822) was saying in *Prometheus Unbound*. Shelley was a Romantic poet living in the early 1800s; his theme is in harmony with the sentiments of the Romantic Age (roughly 1770 to 1850).

Prometheus is the hero in Shelley's poem. Like Helen Keller, Prometheus opposes injustice and cruelty. As the poem begins, we find that Prometheus has gone against the will of the evil god Jupiter (the Devil). As a result of his courage and defiance, for not giving in to the will of the Dictator, Prometheus is chained to a mountain and tortured. What most enraged Jupiter and unleashed his wrath was that Prometheus had shared hidden esoteric secrets with human beings.

The Supreme Gods, led by the Devil, believed that human beings were too ignorant and too unprepared to handle *The Esoteric Secrets*. Jupiter believed that humanity would destroy itself because human beings were not ready to "play with fire." However, Prometheus disagreed with the council of the Gods. Prometheus believed that human beings *were* ready to learn *The Secrets*; Humanity *could* handle the truth.

Despite being horribly tortured, Prometheus would not relent, nor would he compromise his intentions. Prometheus has the best and noblest motives toward humanity—he is the ultimate good-guy hero.

All cultures have epic mythologies about good guys fighting bad guys. In our culture, we have turned Helen Keller into a mythological-Goddess-for-Good. Like Prometheus, Helen Keller accepts her fate. She goes into battle to face the evils of her time. Helen Keller is a modern-day hero, *our* Prometheus.

Against the will of the Gods, Prometheus has given esoteric knowledge to human beings. Knowledge is not supposed to be given to the ignorant masses—they cannot handle sophisticated knowledge, or so the Gods insist. Knowledge must be hidden from humanity—for their own good. It has been forever forbidden to share secret knowledge with mere mortals. However, Prometheus disagrees with Jupiter, with all dictators, with the Devil. Prometheus defiantly showed mankind how to turn mythological fire (the power of knowledge) into a force for good.

In Shelley's poem, Prometheus is the last hope that love, cooperation, and service to others will prevail on earth; Prometheus is the last chance we have for spirituality to rise and endure. Everything in the world has been metaphorically dead since Jupiter took control; the earth is barren, men are ignorant, and this is how it should be where Evil is King. Prometheus represents hope for humankind, for the end of ignorance and confusion. Prometheus's gifts to humanity are a threat to Jupiter; knowledge will allow human beings *to think for themselves* and (horrors) question authority.

Shelley suggests, like all the Romantics did, that reason (the God of the Enlightenment) cannot answer all of humanity's needs. There are loving vibrations that would speak to us if only we had the sensory apparatus to "hear." The natural world may not look like it is alive to the human senses (vision and hearing especially), but *the natural world is, indeed, alive*, vibrating and subtle. Mysterious hidden realms of nature speak to us with spiritual voices.

In the final act, Jupiter, despite his power and cruelty, cannot subdue Prometheus in his role as humanity's heroic spirit. Human beings now understand that knowledge can generate more knowledge and Love can generate more Love; therefore, humanity will not give up on Love, including Love for Knowledge. Like Prometheus, human beings can be tortured and killed, but they will never, as a species, give up on Love and the right to generate knowledge. Although they lack the power to totally defeat Jupiter, humanity still resists his evil intentions, and humanity still fights on against all odds.

At the end of Shelley's poem, Jupiter falls, Prometheus escapes his chains, and knowledge begins to flow throughout the earth. Human beings discover new arts and new sciences, the Earth turns green again, colorful flowers reappear, the air and waters run clean and fresh, and Love begins to blossom in the hearts of individual human beings and through their cultures.

That is how Helen Keller begins her poem: with Prometheus unbounded, freed from his chains. Helen Keller believes that Love will win in the final scene of humanity's play. Knowledge and compassion will win out over dictators and evil. Helen's Faith is on display through the spirit of Prometheus as she begins her poem and begins to speak in her own poetic voice.

The Chant of Darkness begins with Helen saying that she does not know why her mysterious God, the Great Creator, has given humanity a sense of vision and a world for vision to behold, but then, in her situation, takes sight away and leaves her in darkness. However, she has unwavering Faith, and her faith tells her that God is wise, and He has his reasons—which are mysterious and bewildering to mere humanity. God's reasons are esoteric, they are hidden—most human beings are not ready to know certain kinds of knowledge; the mystery that is God is unknowable. Helen ends the first stanza of her poem with a haunting phrase she will chant throughout her poem, repeating the words and rhythm in different verses:

> Out of the uncharted, unthinkable dark we came,
> And in a little time we shall return again
> Into the vast, unanswering dark.

We all emerge (at birth) from a dark place where everything human is at first hidden, where sensations and perceptions remain only potential— we are blind to that which came before our birth and blind to what lies ahead as we emerge from the womb. Then, after a brief sojourn in the light (our lifetime), we return to our deaf-blindness, back to the completely silent and completely dark Source.

New life arrives from darkness, a lifetime flows by, and then old lives move back into the womb of darkness. That is the cycle, the wheel that we are on. Helen Keller felt that God put her on earth to show humanity that the silent darkness is full (like Helen) of Love, Faith, and wonderful Mystery.

Helen then shouts into the silent, dark void: "O Dark! Thou awful, sweet, and holy Dark!" The Unknown makes us fearful but from the Unknown came the sweet life that is us; we were born into a sea of lifeforms. We feel holy as we face the Dark Creator who crafted essence, souls, and spirits. Out of an infinite formlessness came eternal form.

With each new stanza, Helen sends her voice into the dark, silent void: "O Dark! Thou secret and inscrutable Dark!" We cannot understand or interpret the Dark. Reason is of no use. We cannot dissect the wholeness. We cannot argue with silence. And yet, from the inscrutable Darkness "God wrought the soul of man." Here is the first miracle: from nothing came life. From the seemingly uncaring, unknowing Dark Silence came compassionate souls.

Helen shouts into the silent, dark void again: "O Dark! Wise, vital, thought-quickening Dark!" Helen tells us that within the Dark Mystery there is a vastness where Light is hiding. Something has been hidden from mankind and that something is light itself. Light is the child of the Dark; after the birth of light came Love. Light created Love, Life, and Humanity. Helen repeats what she has said many times in her life: "I am not afraid:"

> I dread no evil;
> though I walk in the valley of the shadow,
> I shall not know the ecstasy of fear.

She refers to Bible Psalm 23:4 "Though I walk through the valley of the shadow of death, I will fear no evil: for you are with me . . ." If we have Faith (rather than mere Belief), fear vanishes.

A Chant of Darkness is divided into three parts, the first part has six stanzas, the second part has five stanzas, and the third part has nine stanzas. Helen's soul is speaking to us from long ago, but her words come from the heartland of esotericism. In Part One, Stanza Five, Helen says:

> The timid soul, fear-driven, shuns the dark;
> But upon the cheeks of him who must abide in shadow
> breathes the wind of rushing angel-wings,
> and round him falls a light from unseen fires.
> Magical beams glow athwart the darkness;
> Paths of beauty wind through his black world

To another world of light,
Where no veil of sense shuts him out from paradise.

Those who are afraid do not turn to gaze into the darkness; they are afraid of mystery; they are not ready to receive esoteric knowledge. But there are some human beings who can feel the beat of angel wings on their skin—these people can sense the presence of subtle vibrations. You must stand in the shadows, on the horizon between darkness and dawn to perceive angel wings beating. Stand long enough inside the shadow-horizon and you will slowly be enveloped by light coming from an unseen rising Source. Then the emerging light will illuminate pathways through the blackness. Follow any of these illuminated paths and you will come to a City of Light, a Paradise, Heaven, Nirvana. No human sense can perceive the City of Light from where we now stand. We can only come to know the Pathways and the City of Light if we are brave enough to enter the veil of darkness.

Helen ends Part One reflecting on who she is. She is a "lone exile" who must dwell within the Darkness. Unlike almost the whole of humanity, she has been exiled from the external sounds and sights of the physical world. But what she finds in the Darkness is kindness and peace. She is protected from the harsh realities that attack the senses of the rest of humanity—she is blessed by that which is Silent and Dark. And because the Darkness is her home, Helen Keller has learned the language embedded in the Silence. She receives and translates the secrets formerly hidden from humanity. She is a messenger sent to earth to inform humanity. She is Prometheus come to share esoteric knowledge; she has come to tell us that there is more than what meets the eye and ear.

As she wanders through the Darkland, which is her life, Love speaks to her: "Hast thou entered into the treasures of darkness? Hast thou entered into the treasures of the night? Search out thy blindness. It holdeth riches past computing."

Ah, yes, the Darkness is filled with Love—and Love can communicate. Love says to us (smiling, I think, as an adult speaks to a child): "You have no idea what is hidden from eyes and ears." There are wonderful, dazzling, mind-boggling treasures hidden from worldly view. Love is like a bright torch held in the hand that illuminates the feet as we walk the Holy Pathways through the pitch Darkness. "Search out thy blindness," Helen says.

When we turn our gaze into the Darkness and are drawn into the blind journey, our spirit is set aflame. We become "shaken with gladness, our limbs tremble with joy; the ecstasy of life is abroad in the world."

"Knowledge," Helen tells us, just as Prometheus showed us, "hath uncurtained heaven." If you perceive correctly, you will see things as they really are, you will see what was formerly hidden from you. I especially liked these few lines in Part Two, Stanza Five:

> In the obscurity gleams the Star of Thought;
> Imagination hath a luminous eye,
> And the mind hath a glorious vision.

The mind and its ability to imagine are born from silence. Out of the rock-of-nothing comes animated thought. It is with our imagination that we most easily penetrate the Darkness. It is with our ability to reason—to use our minds as a search engine—that we come to treasure knowledge. Glorious visions and wonderous discoveries wait for us within the Darkness, patiently waiting for us to use our luminous eyes to behold the Holy Secrets.

"Hast thou seen thought bloom in the blind child's face?" Helen asks us. She is telling us that there is a miracle called *inward sight*. The mind is itself a sensory organ that can see. The mind looks outward by projecting emotion-heavy imagination. The mind's eye can see into the future and can reexamine the past. That look on the blind child's radiant face is the act of seeing.

We can also see the same radiance on Helen Keller's face in photographs and in film clips. She says that she dwells in realms of wonderment, which is what we read as we gaze on her beautiful face. She has daylight in her heart that illuminates an inner world made from imagination blended with compassionate emotions.

Not only does she have a powerful internal vision system, but she also has her blessed hands and fingers. Helen's fingers have opened the book of life for her: "With alert fingers I listen to the showers of sound that the wind shakes from the forest." "My fingers are wise," she says, "they snatch light out of darkness, they thrill to harmonies breathed in silence."

Helen ends her poem chanting in praise of the dark:

O Night, still, Odorous Night, I love thee!
O wide spacious Night, I love thee!
O fathomless, soothing Night!
Thou art a balm to my restless spirit,
I nestle in thy bosom,
Dark, gracious mother!
Like a dove, I rest in thy bosom.
Out of the uncharted, unthinkable dark we came,
And in a little time we shall return again
Into the vast, unanswering dark.

We end where we began; it is a circle. We emerge from the unknown and—after a brief visit to Earth—we return to unknowing. However, some humans have never quite left the Dark and the Silent realms; these Helen Keller-like souls can sense the Unknown. These old souls walk among us, relating their wisdom.

Helen Keller was one such Old Soul, she was a voice arising from a dark, silent mystery. Helen Keller was, and still is, telling us that it is okay for this moment to be as it is: Therefore, be at peace, open your heart, let love and light enter the universe that is your mind.

1912: HELEN KELLER CAMPAIGNS FOR SOCIALIST EUGENE DEBS

Helen Keller campaigned for Eugene Debs in the 1912 Presidential Election. Keller also wrote articles for socialists' publications, including *The New York Call* and *The Masses*. As a member of the Industrial Workers of the World (IWW), a socialist trade union, Helen wrote:

> Surely the demands of the I.W.W. are just. It is right that the creators of wealth should own what they create. When shall we learn that we are related one to the other; that we are members of one body; that injury to one is injury to all? Until the spirit of love for our fellow-workers, regardless of race, color, creed or sex, shall fill the world, until the great mass of the people shall be filled with a sense of responsibility for each other's welfare, social justice cannot be attained, and there can never be lasting peace upon earth. [34]

That first line above contains the definition of socialism: when the workers, the people who produce the goods are also the owners of what they produce. Helen put it better: "the creators of wealth should own what they create." Democratic socialism eventually caught on in the world as a blending of Capitalism and Socialism, especially in the Scandinavian countries. The debate goes on in our era, but underneath the arguments is the struggle between those who favor loving-kindness and a cohesive social web and those who believe that favoring individual rights best serves mankind. Using my Navigational Consciousness theory, in which the Ego and Self are forever separate and yet inter-independent, what we seek is a balance that honors both cohesion and competition.

Labeling someone socialist, capitalist, fascist, communist, or a Nazi has little meaning in our modern world. It is better to call Helen Keller a humanitarian; better to judge politicians based on their spirituality, on their platform, and on their plans for a better future. Modern politicians are dealing with complexities far beyond what the population faced 100 years ago when Helen lived.

What Else Happened in 1912?

On April 10, 1912, the Titanic set sail from Southampton, England for her maiden voyage, heading first to Ireland and then to New York City. On April 14, the Titanic hit an iceberg at 11.40 pm off Newfoundland. The Titanic was the largest ship in the world when it hit the iceberg; it sank on April 15, 1912. There were 2,224 passengers, including wealthy people and poor immigrants. The ship had only enough lifeboats for half the passengers. When the ship sank, 1,000 people were still on board. Most of those who jumped into the water died of cold shock. In all, about 1,500 people died, one of the worst peacetime maritime disasters in history. The ship Carpathia arrived an hour and a half after the sinking and was able to rescue those in lifeboats.

Here are a few random events that happened in 1912: Sun Yat-sen formed the Republic of China. . . . Arizona was admitted to the Union as the 48th state. . . . U.S. Army Captain Albert Berry performed the first parachute jump from an airplane. . . . Mrs. William Howard Taft planted the first cherry tree in Washington, D.C. . . . The District of Alaska became an incorporated territory of the United States.

1913: HELEN AND ANNE ON THE LECTURE CIRCUIT

Helen and Annie began their career on the lecture circuit in 1913. From 1913 to 1920, Helen Keller and Anne Sullivan would travel constantly between speaking engagements; they needed income to survive, and they were much in demand. Keller said that eventually, after traveling so much, she could tell one American city from another by the city's odor.

In 1913, John Macy sailed to Europe. His marriage with Anne Sullivan was faltering and the couple parted company as Helen and Annie set out on the lecture circuit.

In the same year, the third edition of *Out of the Dark: Essays, Lectures, and Addresses on Physical and Social Vision* was published including a collection of Helen's writings on socialism, women, and disability. She began the book with an essay called "How I Became a Socialist." The book had become quite popular within left-wing circles since the first edition appeared in 1907.

Mary Agnes (Polly) Thomson traveled from her birthplace, Glasgow, Scotland to the United States in 1913. Little did she know that she was about to become a legendary figure in history. Most people who admire the Helen/Sullivan legacy have never heard of Polly Thomson and yet she was with Helen Keller longer than Anne Sullivan.

What Else Happened in 1913?

Here are a few random events that happened in 1913: The 16th Amendment to the US Constitution was ratified setting up a federal income tax. . . . The first U.S. law was passed allowing the shooting of migratory birds. . . . Woodrow Wilson was inaugurated as 28th President of the United States. . . . Women suffragettes marched through Washington D.C. demanding women's rights. . . . English suffragette Emily Davison died after throwing herself in front of King George V's horse during the running of the Derby at Epsom, England.

Out of the Dark: Essays, Lectures, and Addresses on Physical and Social Vision

On October 5, 1913, the New York Times did a short review of Helen's book of essays that she called *Out of the Dark*. Here are excerpts from that review called "Miss Keller's Essays:"

> "Out of the Dark" is a collection of various magazine articles, letters and addresses, written by the author in the past few years, and is expressive of the views of a sympathetic, and intelligent young woman on the live questions of the day. Among the various topics discussed are socialism, capital and labor, higher education for women, woman suffrage, and the problem of the blind. Naturally, Miss Keller's opinions as to what should be done for the blind will be of the greatest interest to the reader; her socialistic and economic theories, although well put, contain nothing new or startling to those who keep up with the discussions of these subjects.
>
> The articles on the blind and deaf, however, give prominence to an actual need with what may be regarded as an authoritative statement of how to meet it. "Our Duties to the Blind," "What the Blind Can Do," "Preventable Blindness," "The Education of the Deaf," are some of the titles. Many of these are reprints of addresses delivered by Miss Keller before Massachusetts and New York associations working for the cause of the blind. Other miscellaneous essays, "Christmas in the Dark" and "The Message of Swedenborg," throw light on the personality of the author and her courageous spirit in the face of her misfortune. The book should draw attention both as propaganda and as the work of one in whom a number of people are tremendously interested. [163]

That is a curious and well-done review; it is generous and supportive of Helen and yet unable to suggest her ideas, beyond blindness, are to be taken seriously. Calling her writing "propaganda" and implying that she has nothing new to add to the debate about the economic and social problems of the times is a reaction that Helen expected, having seen it in print frequently. It was also delicate territory in 1913 to explore these political triggers; any discussion of socialism raised eyebrows. The First World War loomed on the horizon, women still did not have a right to vote, and deaf-blind women were tolerated for their emotional opinions, rather than taken seriously.

There are twenty-nine chapters in the book. I will not review each essay but will comment on important insights. The book begins with a few essays about Socialism. After that, Helen's response to the plight women is addressed (the middle third of the book). Most of the rest of the book explores Helen's opinions about blindness. There is a short essay about deafness and a few short essays about her religion at the very end of the book.

The first chapter is about the importance of human hands, a topic she frequently returns to since she is aware of the miracle of hands and fingers—more than most of us. In this chapter, Helen is talking about the people who labor with their hands, who build or maintain the fabric of a society. All around her is the evidence of hands that labored to make (for example) the room where she feels safe as she writes, sheltered from the wind, protected from the bitter cold during the winter months in New England. She reflects on the hands that made the roof over her head, hands that crafted her clothes, hands that manufactured the braille pages she uses to communicate. Helen feels that we seldom reflect on the importance of the hands of laborers, which have done so much for us and received so little appreciation and respect.

When I was re-reading the first chapter of *Out of the Dark*, I felt unease. I had crafted an entire chapter about the evolution of the human mind (Chapter Four in *The Esoteric Helen Keller*), and I had talked with admiration and awe about bilaterality and the bicameral mind; I had also honored language and memory as mind builders. But nowhere in my logic—leading to our dual minds—had I mentioned the evolution of human hands. I see now that this was a serious oversight. Language and great minds are almost useless without hands to carry the tools that build civilizations. Language and hands need each other; they are co-dependent, and they evolved in tandem.

Helen also reminds us that the hands which build and serve also destroy and are too often careless or deliberately cruel, even murderous. Moreover, and ironically, modern hands are hard at work creating machines to replace hands. Helen's concern in *Out of the Dark* is very much a product of her time. Men and women (and children) were operating unsafe machinery in the early years of the Industrial Age. These machines were killing workers or blinding them or causing physical impairments. Her socialist views were forged knowing about machines that maim the innocent bodies of laborers. Helen also realized that all the dirty work, the back-breaking labor of the workforce, was rewarded with pitiful wages, while the Industrialists, the owners of the factories got rich. The unfairness was deeply felt by Helen and by many others at the dawn of the Industrial Age. Helen's Socialist sentiments arise, I think, from her empathy and sense of injustice. This first chapter is a lead-in to the second chapter called "How I became a Socialist."

Helen says her political views came from reading Socialist literature. Her decision to be a Socialist was her own, she insists, based on her personal research (she was especially influenced by author H.G. Wells). Helen maintains that she was not influenced by friends and colleagues; she was not urged by those around her to adopt Socialist views. Anne Sullivan, for example, was not a Socialist. John Macy (who *was* a Socialist) was disinclined (according to Helen) to direct Helen's evolving worldview.

Like everything else she took on, Helen expressed her Socialist views with her characteristic in-your-face rhetoric. She did not back down. After the *New York Times* wrote an anti-Socialist editorial, damning the red flag that symbolized Socialism, Helen wrote:

> I am no worshipper of cloth of any color, but I love the red flag and what it symbolizes to me and other Socialists. I have a red flag hanging in my study, and if I could, I should gladly march with it past the office of the *Times* and let all the reporters and photographers make the most of the spectacle. According to the inclusive condemnation of the Times I have forfeited all right to respect and sympathy, and I am to be regarded with suspicion.

I contend that Helen's Socialism was a form of humanitarianism, a Justice Warrior stance against cruelty and neglect. Helen found it baffling and somewhat humorous that the *New York Times* had asked her to write an article about her views but then, days later, came out with their editorial attacking the Socialist movement.

Personally, I want to be supportive of Helen's passions as I craft this review of *Out of the Dark*, but I have a retrospective view of what happened to the economic worldviews that were clashing prior to the First World War; all the *isms* came off (in retrospect) ill-equipped to govern. It was jarring (to me) when Helen referred to fellow Socialists as "comrades," and when I come across sentences like this one: [regarding socialism] "Our German Comrades are ahead of us in many respects." I know there were many well-meaning humanitarians in 1912 when this essay was printed in the *New York Call* (a Socialist publication). Socialist in the early twentieth century disparaged Capitalism and celebrated Communism and Socialism, but the evolution of all three of the *isms* failed to live up to the rhetoric and hopefulness of their supporters.

After her Socialist views are introduced in the book, Helen takes on the women of the world through three essays. Helen is frank in her judgment of women who do not stand up for what is right and just. I commented on her views and quoted her words about women when I addressed her Justice Warrior years in *The Esoteric Helen Keller*, so will only provide brief comments.

In the first chapter about women, Helen tells us that she receives many delightful (but sometimes appalling) letters from young girls essentially pleading for Helen to: "Tell us what to do." "A sincere request demands a sincere compliance," Helen writes to these young women, even though she feels not up to such a task.

Study where you are, she writes to her young admirers. You have been placed in a time in history and at a location on Planet Earth. That is your beginning place. That is the location you must study. The people around you need your help. That location on the planet where you find yourself is where you can make a difference. Look around you; there is much to do, much suffering:

> I tried to tell them what has been said many times, that the best educated human being is the one who understands most about the life in which he is placed, that the blind man, however poignantly his individual suffering appeals to our hearts, is not a single separate person whose problem can be solved by itself, but a symptom of social maladjustment.

Helen is telling the young women who write to her for guidance that they are to begin where they find themselves, but with this understanding: everything is connected to everything else. There are reasons for the existence of blindness, poverty, and injustice. Look around you, watch what is said, notice how things are organized. In your microcosm, the whole world can be viewed. No man is an island, no man need be alone in their suffering. Human beings are embedded in a domain, surrounded by others; what we do influences others—what they do, impacts us.

Out of the Dark (dedicated to her mother, Kate Keller) contains the clearest statement Helen made about blindness and deafness. Her views are dated, of course, and modern writers—many of them blind or visually impaired—have much higher regard for what blind people can do and should be expected to do in the modern world. In Chapter Six of *The Esoteric Helen Keller*, I contrasted Helen's views about blindness with those of my colleague and friend Daniel Kish.

Helen Keller and her European Sisters

I found this document in the Classic Reprint Series by *Forgotten Books*. The full title is *Man's Miracle: The Story of Helen Keller and her European Sisters* (1913). The author, Frenchman Gerald Harry, was a friend of Georgette Leblanc, who knew Helen Keller. Leblanc later wrote her own book about Helen called *The Girl Who Found the Bluebird* (1914). Leblanc wrote the introduction to Harry's *Helen Keller and her European Sisters*.

Gerald Harry describes the books and articles about Helen Keller as a "wilderness of speculation." He sets out, as I have done in my speculations, to address the miracle of Helen Keller's mind—how could such a complete and extraordinary mind emerge from a deaf, blind, mute body? What does a sophisticated deaf-blind mind tell us about the human mind generally? I find it fascinating that more than a hundred years ago an articulate writer asked the same questions that I posed in *The Esoteric Helen Keller* (2021). I suspect that decades from now a new writer will have another try at comprehending Helen's mental evolution, but this new writer-scientist will have vastly more knowledge than Harry or I had at our disposal.

Gerald Harry asks a leading question, "What is the limit of human perfection, and up to what point may our will correct and overcome hostile nature?" In a sense, Harry is asking the age-old question, how much are we a product of innate development and how much are we molded by experience? He contends that deaf-blind Marie Heurtin (from France), Laura Bridgman, and Helen Keller, and are each evidence that something powerful is born within us, awaiting specific experiences to unlock potential. It is as if experiences are portal-keys that unlock innate behaviors. Harry says, " . . . consciousness exists, a priori, in us, since it can be illuminated and born in the most obtuse of our race."

However, Harry is skeptical with the view that we are born with a spiritual template. He argues that Laura, Helen, and Marie was indoctrinated with Western religious traditions by those who had rigid, if well-meaning beliefs. Each of these deaf-blind girls became Christians, not because they had innate *Kingdoms Within*, but because others told them what they should believe:

> Naturally, these [three] girls, originally so incapable of knowing and judging for themselves, could hardly have done otherwise than impose silence on their own doubts and hesitations, and accept with humble deference the versions of our origin and our end, put before them by their generous benefactors. . . .

Rather than a spiritual template that leads toward a particular religion, Harry suggests that human beings are born instead with a spiritual spark, a hidden, esoteric place within that arrives at birth ready to blossom into a religious creed. He cautions, however, that these three remarkable women, despite their accomplishments, might have been better served outside the trappings of Western religion. Helen seems to have escaped indoctrination when she found the liberal, open-minded Swedenborgian worldview, but Marie and Laura had been steeped in the doctrine that they would be rewarded with a normal body after their death—Helen was also comforted by this doctrine. Harry feels that this "wait until later" approach reduced the efforts (and appreciation) needed in this world, in this life. Humanity is capable of acting in the moment and does not need later rewards to move progress forward.

When Marie, Laura, and Helen were asked whether life was worthwhile despite their afflictions, all three women answered, each in their own way and emphatically, "Yes!" But they also rebelled when they were told about aging, illness, and death. How could the miracle of life have such a horrific unfolding and such a dreadful finale? A child with normal eyesight and hearing slowly figures out and accepts the human condition, but a deaf, blind, mute child often finds out suddenly that aging, illness, and death are inevitable—the shock is severe. It seems like a betrayal of the religious education they have been receiving. They cannot reconcile the image of a God of Love with the cruel reality of His design. Something does not feel right or just. This sudden awareness feels like an unkind betrayal rather than Divine power generating loving kindness.

~

Harry reports some unusual events which I had not come across in other publications. He says, for example, that in her dreams Laura Bridgman claimed to be able to see. There was no way to verify this, so nothing was made of her assertions. Samuel Howe was quoted as saying that Laura had a sixth sense, she moved about as if she could see. For a mobility specialist, this sets off alarm bells. There are a few visual anomalies wherein central vision is lost but peripheral vision is retained, or islands of vision remain after illness—sometimes peripheral vision is sufficient to allow for normal navigation. There are also cases in which people are psychologically blind—these people cannot see objects or faces, but they navigate almost flawlessly. Here is Harry's account:

> Dr. Howe assigned to Laura Bridgman . . . a sixth sense—she was able to guide herself with surprising ease. In spite of her blindness, she would go straight to a window or door, without hesitation or feeling her way, and stop at once at the desired destination without running against any obstacle, and she could also establish the relative position of objects with almost mathematical accuracy.

Laura Bridgman spent her entire life at the Perkins School for the Blind, primarily indoors, in familiar rooms with familiar smells and dependable doors and windows at exact locations. She must have mastered these spaces through continual movement within familiar walls. Air currents certainly contributed to her perceptions, especially when approaching windows and doors. The unevenness of floors, the position of rugs, and thresholds between surfaces all informed her orientation. As I mentioned in *The Esoteric Helen Keller*, it could be that residual pockets of hearing or vision might have gone undetected in the late 1800s and early 1900s, given the state of medical knowledge.

∼

There is a rather startling picture in this book of John Macy, Helen Keller, and Georgette Leblanc. I had never seen the picture before, perhaps because it was taken for Georgette Leblanc and brought to France, where Gerald Harry discovered it. The picture shows a smiling John Macy looking past Helen at a smiling Georgette Leblanc—they are making eye contact and look engaged in a pleasant conversation. Helen looks lovely in the middle of the frame, but she also looks like a statue, her prosthetic eyes fixed, frozen, a shallow smile on her unanimated face. It almost looks like she was cut and pasted from another photo and glued between the two animated new friends. It is an unnerving picture.

The photo does go well, however, with Georgette's description of her visit; she was shocked by Helen's unmoving eyes and by her robotic speech (she spoke French to Leblanc)—Georgette was initially unnerved by her first visit with Helen.

Harry spends the last section of the book reviewing what his friend Georgette Leblanc told him of her two visits to Helen Keller's home in Wrentham, Massachusetts. His reflections go nicely with Georgette's recollections in her own book about Helen.

∼

I was somewhat disappointed that this book had little to say about any deaf-blind *European Sisters*, as the title suggests. Harry is referring mostly to deaf-blind Marie Heurtin, an impoverished French girl who was raised and educated by dedicated nuns. Unlike Helen Keller and Laura Bridgman, Marie *was born* deaf, blind, and mute; she *never* saw light, *never* heard a sound. The task of educating her was much more challenging than for Helen and Laura.

Marie Heurtin's parents were cousins. They had nine children, three of whom were deaf-blind, two were blind, one died in infancy, one was rickety, and only two were normal. The parents are described by Harry as "honest, decent people, but quite ignorant and uneducated." Marie was considered an "idiot" up until the age of ten. Marie was abandoned to the care of nuns as a young girl. Heurtin had her own Anne Sullivan-like savior, Sister Sainte Marguerite (of the order Sueur's de la Sagesse), of Notre-Dame de Larnay, located in west-central France.

The *European Sisters* is a reference to Marie Heurtin and to her younger deaf-blind sister Martha Heurtin, who came to Notre-Dame de Larnay more than a decade after her older sister. Since the girls were considered *idiots*, Harry was expecting dull, inactive children when he visited the girls at their school. He was quite surprised when he met the girls, who had their own classroom and teachers:

> What struck me was the wonderful vitality of their brains. They overflowed with curiosity, and were eager to communicate . . .

This section of the book was the most fascinating for me. Harry describes the behaviors of the two girls and expresses his amazement at their quickness and intelligence. There are two pictures of the girls at desks which show them to be physically normal and attractive youngsters. My professional inclination is to suspect that there was residual vision of some kind, but we can never know.

Some Europeans dismissed the stories about Laura Bridgman and Helen Keller as exaggerations of the American imagination. I do not want to fall into the dismissive category. The accomplishments of the Heurtin sisters and the dedicated nuns—hard working teachers—remain, even if there was severe low vision rather than total blindness.

1914: JOHN MACY AND ANNE SULLIVAN SEPARATE

John Macy left Annie Sullivan in 1914, though they never officially divorced:

> It was a lengthy process of counteraccusations that Helen characterized as Annie's "greatest sorrow." Understandably, no one dealt well with the locked rooms, tears, and innumerable letters, accusations, and counteraccusations flying among the *three* of them. Everything about the situation pained Helen. Annie, Helen wrote, wept "as only women who are no longer cherished weep." [35]

John Macy and Anne Sullivan had lived with Helen in Wrentham, Massachusetts after they were first married. Slowly, partly because they were separated so often due to Helen's public obligations, the marriage bond began to unravel. Sullivan had to accompany Helen to her speeches and civic responsibilities, so she was frequently gone from home. Travel was difficult in the early 1900s and took a long time. Separation evidently strained their relationship:

> Sullivan frequently traveled with Keller on lecture tours to supplement her income from writing; following a 15-month tour in the Northeast, she and Macy separated in 1914. [36]

John Macy's life went up and down after he left the Keller/Sullivan household. Some say he suffered from alcoholism; others say he did quite well on his own:

> He never became rich, but he had friends and he wrote. Beginning in late 1921 he went on to publish a sizable amount of respected literary criticism, both books and articles. In 1922 and 1923 he served as literary editor of the *Nation*. Working with fellow Harvard graduate and composer Frederick Shepherd Converse, he wrote the text to several operas. He met another woman, a purportedly "very beautiful" deaf woman, and dedicated *The Story of the Worlds Literature* (1925) to their daughter. The book earned a favorable full-page New York Times review. Macy [Anne Sullivan] followed his career, as did Keller, and would later read his book *About Women* (1930) with great trepidation. [37]

About Women is John Macy's take on the rebellious women of his era; he comes across as a man still clinging to the 1800s, not able to grasp the feminine wave that is washing over the new century. It is fascinating that John Macy would be compelled to investigate the power of independent and proud women, especially having survived the household of Keller and Sullivan. Fortunately, John Macy's books are still available on Amazon.com.

Polly Thomson joined Helen and Anne's household in October 1914. They called Polly "a spirited Scottish lassie."

Also, in 1914, Helen demonstrated with the Woman's Peace Party, advocating for peace in Europe. Helen gave an anti-war speech after the rally in Carnegie Hall where she advocated for Socialism.

The Girl Who Found the Bluebird

This is a delightful and eloquent little book, published in 1914 by Georgette Leblanc (1869–1941), a French operatic soprano, actress, and author. In the last decades of her life, Leblanc produced two autobiographies, several children's books, and a few travelogues. One of the highlights of her remarkable life was meeting Helen Keller and becoming her friend.

In keeping with my esoteric theme, I will add that Georgette Leblanc was involved with the mystic G. I. Gurdjieff. She was also a good friend of fellow Gurdjieff student Margaret Anderson. Leblanc came into contact with Gurdjieff's experiential teaching methods (dance, choreographed movements), which Gurdjieff had learned in secret esoteric schools in the East. It became clear to me, as I read about her, that Leblanc was no ordinary opera singer; she hung out on the fringes of things and followed esoteric energy flows—it is no wonder that her spirit was drawn to Helen Keller.

Leblanc begins her small book by exploring the mysterious interplay of energy that occurs when one human mind encounters another. Regarding her visits to Helen Keller, Leblanc writes:

> Though I lived for centuries, I should not forget a colour, a shade, a line, nor any single detail of the thousand that form the memory of my visits to Helen Keller . . .

Each individual we meet is a new experience, Leblanc tells us. We can see outward appearances and know names and addresses, but we can discern nothing of the mind and heart of those we encounter. We search for common ground, a mental bridge, that might be the seed for something deeper than surface interaction. "We go on a quest of each other," Leblanc says. She suggests that human beings live under the charming illusion of understanding and being understood. Knowing this about the human conundrum, Leblanc heads off to visit Helen Keller in Wrentham, Massachusetts for a first visit. Leblanc is expecting to be bewildered by an inability to connect with Helen; she tells the reader her expectations:

> I was going to encounter an admirable intelligence, but never hoping to make myself understood; certain of finding myself in the presence of a perfect soul yet imagining no opening through which to reach it.

Helen soon demonstrated to Leblanc that two minds seeking to connect could "pass beyond looks and words and find each other." What Leblanc saw in Helen Keller was extraordinary:

> From the day on which Helen Keller first became a sentient being, her progress was unprecedented and swifter than that of normal

children; her imagination was surprising; and we see shinning in the depths of her darkness the divine spirit of enquiry that will support her all the days of her life. She thinks, she improves her mind, she writes; she is zealous and active; she creates institutions for the welfare of the blind, founds libraries, interests herself in politics, travels, plays games and visits museums.

When Helen entered the room to meet Georgette for the first time, holding Anne Sullivan's arm, she was smiling, holding herself erect and then, suddenly, Helen *spoke*, shocking Leblanc:

But Helen spoke! With an effort, she pronounces a few words of welcome [in French]; and, when I hear that voice which comes from an abyss, that laugh, that ghostly laugh, which echoes through her silence . . . I feel the hateful distance that parts us and I am filled with dread.

Leblanc was struck by a force that she was not expecting, having never encountered such energy. Editor Nella Braddy later wrote that people were often moved to tears when they first met Helen, as if they had suddenly found themselves in the presence of a Saint. Georgette Leblanc found herself in such a moment:

. . . when I first set eyes on Helen Keller, I was excited, anguish-stricken, shuttering, tossed incessantly between enthusiasm and horror, by turns astounded and revolted, incapable of estimating, grasping, or analyzing my impressions; my imagination was distraught, my reason unbalanced, my whole mind was in disorder; and this first visit was wholly dominated by the force and novelty of my sensations. While Helen, with serenity stamped upon her brow, but yet curious about my life, *spoke* and asked me a thousand questions—gathering unwitting answers from my mouth, it was I who was deaf and dumb and blind in the presence of that being who seemed to see me without seeing, to hear me without hearing and to speak to me from the heart of the unknown . . .

Georgette Leblanc was an artist, a creative genius. She may have been stunned by Helen's presence, but all the while she stood in awed silence, she was keenly observing the room, the faces and body language of Helen, Anne, and (later) John Macy; she notes how everyone is dressed and how they move. Here she is describing her first impression of Helen:

> The full, grey-cloth skirt and the blouse of embroidered *ninon* [silk fabric] suggest a well-proportioned and softly rounded figure. She gesticulates freely; and the nervous vigour of her movements is full of interest and significance.

I am struck by observations many people have made regarding Helen's posture. She holds her head and body erect, she is animated, she gestures enthusiastically, she has appropriate facial expressions, and she seems to be facing the person who is speaking. These are *highly* unusual and refined behaviors.

Blindness tends to freeze the body in an unanimated pose that is immediately noticeable by a sighted individual. I worked with blind children for 30 years and I *never* saw a child with "normal" gesturing, normal animation, and normal facial expressions—even though our staff worked on postures and mannerisms. Many congenitally blind individuals hold their head downward and do not make eye contact— they do not hold the head and body erect, facial expressions and gesturing are rare.

I can think of two reasons for Helen's normal animation. First, knowing Anne Sullivan's intensity, I am betting that Helen's animation was trained, quite insistently, over many years—she was taught about body posture, gesturing, and facial expressions. I can hear Sullivan saying sternly, "Stand up straight Helen . . . and smile!" Sullivan taught Helen how to play, how to laugh, and how to express emotions. That is a stunning accomplishment.

The second reason Helen may have developed such "normal" animation is because her deaf-blindness did not affect her proprioception, which was extraordinary. Gestures, body language (posturing), and facial expressions have a genetic component, therefore, if her proprioceptive biology was unimpaired, then she had the innate ability to animate her body. As I discussed in *The Esoteric Helen Keller*, deaf-blindness also caused her proprioceptive system to make profound adaptations, to become hyper-alert and greatly sophisticated. This "otherworldly" proprioception might be what caused people to burst into tears when first meeting Helen Keller—they had never encountered such Saintly serenity mixed with sudden outbursts of hyper-animation.

I found an interesting paragraph in Georgette's little book that speaks directly to my concern with Helen Keller's ability to navigate through space. Intuition tells us that being deaf-blind would make a person hyper-cautious when moving through space. Here is Leblanc's observation:

> I have mentioned Helen's step. It alone is a revelation. All her energy, her tenacity, her pluck, her superhuman courage, all her power is there, in that firm and rapid walk which seems to dart forward under the constant governance of an irresistible law . . . Very few people give so powerful an impression of vitality.

This paragraph reminds me of the image of seven-year-old Helen Keller moving forcefully through her house at Ivy Green, pushing everything aside as she rushes forward—oil lamps, end tables, her baby sister's cradle. One of Anne Sullivan's first tasks, as she saw it, was to discipline her little student, a wild deaf-blind colt. I have mentioned numerous times how amazed I am—given my experience teaching blind kids— that Helen moved about with so little fear and at such a determined pace. Such navigational flow is extremely rare. Leblanc comments later about Helen's pace:

> "Don't be astonished," says Mrs. Macy [Anne Sullivan], laughing. "Helen cannot walk slowly. I no longer try to keep up with her in the country: she used to tire me too much. Now, she goes out with my husband [John Macy]; and they take long walks together in the morning."
>
> "Does she get up early?"
>
> "She is always the first," replies Mrs. Macy. "She is up at six o'clock, dresses and does her hair by herself; and she even likes doing her own room. She must always be active."

Helen marches forward with vigor even though she cannot see pathways and obstacles. She moves quickly even though she hears no echoes and gets no auditory feedback as she changes location. Where does this fearlessness come from? Is there something about total deafness and total blindness that contributes to such determination, some proprioceptive adaptation? My first thought is that Sullivan must have taught Helen about human animation. There are suggestions (hints) that Sullivan taught Helen to run, to wrestle, to animate (to develop proprioceptive skills), to be as fearless about space as she was in her use of language, to move through space as eloquently as language flowed from her mind.

When Helen is "listening" to Georgette speak, there are a series of body reactions that she makes which can be read by a sighted observer. Leblanc's observations are important, they tell us about Helen's cognitive processing:

> At moments of direct communication . . . her grave expression first denotes attention; next a joyous convulsion of her whole body takes us by surprise. It is a movement brilliant as a lightning-flash which tells us that her darkness is suddenly riven. Thus, her erect and formal bearing is constantly broken by shivers which are caused by nothing that is apparent to those who watch her. To her, they correspond with so many vibrations and with a whole world of sensations which we do not perceive. Those faint thrills and violent convulsions, which make her start exactly as though she had received an electric shock, are the revelation of a life that has its own laws and its own conventions.

We are fortunate to have such an observant witness to history. Here are some more of Leblanc's impressions:

> I feel her to be ardent and passionate, full of health and of impatience. This woman whom I am observing with all my powers and who sometimes quivers under my glance as though it reached her mind, this woman assuredly is not one of the meek. Her face is modelled by the cruel and exquisite fingers of an infinite sensitivity; her nostrils seize and savor the slightest breeze and, at such times, tremble with a longing that sets her face rippling like water brushed by a bird's wing.

I realize, as I work my way through Leblanc's book, that I might end up quoting the whole thing if I am not careful. However, before I complete this short review, I will offer a final quote. I am reminded by my colleague Daniel Kish that Helen was great at making adaptations. He suggests that rather than burden Helen with labels like *gifted* or *prodigy*, we simply acknowledge her talented ability to adapt. This is Georgette speaking:

> I no longer care about becoming understood, I wish to understand. I wish to find the solution to the sublime riddle which she presents. For, though Helen was born defective, she has, thanks to her pluck and her strength, become merely "different." She had to create her own relations with the universe; she adapted herself to it in a fashion other than ours; and she moves in a world peculiar to herself.

Helen, of course, was not born defective; her illness occurred at nineteen months of age. Leblanc's comment that Helen was "merely different" resonates with current thinking. Daniel Kish, for example, prefers the term "differently abled," rather than "disabled."

The title of Georgette's book refers to a 1908 stage play by Georgette's husband, Belgian playwright and poet Maurice Maeterlinck. The play reached Broadway in 1910 and has subsequently been adapted for films and TV. Georgette fell in love with Maeterlinck's story and produced a novel based on the adventure—two children, sister and brother, go in search of the Bluebird of Happiness. *The Girl Who Found the Bluebird: A Visit to Helen Keller* implies that Helen found and embraced happiness. Georgette quotes Helen saying: "Men are to be pitied. They do not know how to be happy."

What Else Happened in 1914?

Here are a few random events that happened in 1914: Franz Ferdinand, Archduke of Austria and his wife Sophie were assassinated in Sarajevo, setting the stage for World War One. . . . On August 3, 1914, Germany invaded Belgium and declared war on France, beginning the first World War. . . . On August 4, 1914 Britain declared war on Germany. On the same day, the United States declared neutrality. . . . Henry Ford announced a five-dollar minimum per-day wage, which doubled most worker's pay. . . . The British House of Lords rejected women's suffrage. . . . The United States Congress established Mother's Day. . . . Robert Goddard was granted the first patent for the liquid-fueled rocket engine. . . . A gallon of milk in 1914 was roughly 12 cents, and a loaf of bread in 1914 was 6 cents.

1915: HELEN KELLER CO-FOUNDS HELEN KELLER INTERNATIONAL

Helen Keller co-founded *Helen Keller International* (HKI) in 1915 along with American city planner George Kessler. HKI's mandate was to combat unnecessary blindness, diseases and disorders that could be cured. This is from the Helen Keller International website:

> Helen Keller International was co-founded in 1915 by two extraordinary individuals, Helen Keller and George Kessler, to assist soldiers blinded during their service in World War I. Kessler was a wealthy New York merchant who survived the sinking of the Lusitania in 1915 and vowed, as his lifeboat repeatedly capsized, to help those less fortunate in the world if he survived.
>
> While recovering in London, he resolved to devote his remaining years to helping soldiers blinded in combat. In November 1915, George and his wife, Cora Parsons Kessler, founded the organization and asked Helen Keller, then 35 years old, for her support. She enthusiastically agreed.
>
> Since then, we have committed ourselves to continuing Helen's work. And that work has evolved. Guided by her fierce optimism, we have been working on the front lines of health for more than 100 years. Our programs prioritize preventing and treating vision loss and blindness—as well as addressing major global health problems such as malnutrition and neglected diseases that threaten sight, productivity, and well-being.

In the U.S., Africa, and Asia, Helen Keller International's proven, science-based programs empower people to create opportunities in their own lives and build lasting change. Working in 20 countries, we are ranked among the most effective charities in international development and global health, with a four-star rating from Charity Navigator for several consecutive years. We have more than 107 projects around the world that reach millions of people each year. [38]

Tragically, during the 9/11 attacks on the World Trade Center, the HKI archives were lost:

Our offices in New York City were destroyed during 9/11 terrorist attacks on the World Trade Center; no employees were injured, although Helen Keller's archives are lost. [38]

There are so many awful tragedies associated with the 9/11 attack, so many innocent lives were senselessly lost. However, it is wonderful that no employees of Helen Keller International died in that disaster—the loss of the Helen Keller archives, of course, was devastating.

In January 1915, Helen, Annie, and Polly went on a tour of the American Southwest. While a world war was busy murdering millions of young men, the women in the United States were still fighting for equality. Science was evolving rapidly but would be accelerated in the interests of building war machinery. Poets and saints continued the battle for kindness.

What Else Happened in 1915?

Here are a few random events that happened in 1915: World War One continued to rage. Germany's Kaiser Wilhelm approved the strategic bombing of Britain, but forbid bombing London, fearing his relatives in the royal family might be killed. Four people in Norfolk were killed in the first German Zeppelin air raid on the United Kingdom. . . . On January 12, 1915, the United States House of Representatives rejected a proposal to give women the right to vote. . . . Alexander Graham Bell in New York called Thomas Watson in San Francisco inaugurating transcontinental telephone service. . . . Rocky Mountain National Park in Colorado was established. . . . John McCrae wrote the poem "In Flanders Fields." . . . The Second Battle of Ypres ended with 105,000 casualties. . . . Cecil Chubb bought the prehistoric monument Stonehenge for £6,600. . . . An estimated 25,000 suffragettes marched in New York, led by Dr. Anna Shaw and Carrie Chapman Catt, founder of the League of Women Voters.

1916: Helen Falls in Love

Peter Fagan, John Macy's assistant, fell in love with Helen and the two carried on a private romance. The two lovers knew that their affair might not go over well with family and friends on Helen's side, so they maintained their secrecy. Fagan eventually proposed to Helen Keller and they took out a marriage license in Boston, preparing to elope. However, their intentions were discovered by Anne Sullivan and Kate Keller, both of whom strongly felt that marriage was a wrong decision. Helen's mother forced Helen to publicly renounce her engagement, which Helen did. Helen then went to Montgomery, Alabama to visit family. I will discuss this affair later when I review Helen's memoir *Midstream*.

Meanwhile, Anne and Polly traveled to Lake Placid and later Puerto Rico in hopes of aiding Anne's failing health. On top of the drama caused by Helen's relationship with Peter Fagan was the news that Anne Sullivan had tuberculous, the same disease that killed her mother (Anne's case might have been a misdiagnosis, however). That is the reason Sullivan took a long vacation; she needed rest and time to reflect.

What Else Happened in 1916?

Here are a few random events that happened in 1916: The first bombing of Paris by German Zeppelins occurred. . . . Military conscription began in Great Britain. . . . Suffragette Emma Goldman was arrested for lecturing on birth control. . . . The Battle of Verdun began with a German offensive. An estimated one million casualties resulted after nine months of trench warfare. . . . The Easter Uprising of Irish Republicans against British occupation began in Dublin. . . . The Boeing Company produced its first product, a Seaplane.

1917: THE DEATH OF SOPHIA HOPKINS

Helen and Anne sold their farm in Wrentham in 1917, after having lived there for thirteen years. Helen, Anne, and Polly Thomson then moved to Forest Hills, located in the Borough of Queens in New York City. The Forest Hills home was only minutes from New York City by train.

This is also the year that Anne Sullivan's friend Sophia Hopkins died. Sophia had helped Sullivan through some of the most difficult moments in Annie's life and had become a friend and benefactor for Helen. Sophia Crocker Hopkins was born February 5, 1843 and died at age 74 on November 4, 1917 in Brewster, Barnstable County, Massachusetts. She is buried in Brewster Cemetery.

In 1917, Helen Keller donated money to the NAACP (the National Association for the Advancement of Colored People). Here are excerpts from a letter written by Helen in 1916 and published in the NAACP Journal:

> This great republic of ours is a mockery when citizens in any section are denied the rights which the Constitution guarantees them, when they are openly evicted, terrorized and lynched by prejudiced mobs, and their persecutors and murderers are allowed to walk abroad unpunished. The United States stands ashamed before the world whilst ten million of its people remain victims of a most blind, stupid, inhuman prejudice.
>
> How dare we call ourselves Christians? The outrages against the colored people are a denial of Christ. The central fire of his teaching is equality. His gospel proclaims in unequivocal words that the souls of all men are alike before God. Yet there

are persons calling themselves Christians who profit from the economic degradation of their colored fellow-countrymen.

Ashamed in my very soul, I behold in my own beloved southland the tears of those who are oppressed, those who must bring up their sons and daughters in bondage . . . I feel with those suffering, toiling millions . . . Every attempt to keep them down and crush their spirit is a betrayal of my faith . . .

Let all lovers of justice unite, let us stand together and fight every custom, every law, every institution that breeds, or masks violence and prejudice, and permits one class to prosper at the cost of the well-being and happiness of another class. Let us hurl our strength against the iron gates of prejudice until they fall, and their bars are sundered, and we all advance gladly towards our common heritage of life, liberty and light, undivided by race or color or creed, united by the same human heart that beats in the bosom of all.[39]

If anyone wondered about Helen's position on slavery, which she experienced firsthand in her Alabama community, let the above paragraphs ring forth. Helen Keller had no patience for fake Christians, fake Democracy, injustice, and inequality.

What Else Happened in 1917?

Here are a few random events that happened in 1917: President Wilson called for war against Germany on April 2, 1917. The United States Congress officially declared war four days later, on April 6. . . . The suffragettes (the "Silent Sentinels") protested outside The White House, in Washington D.C. They were led by Alice Paul and the National Woman's Party. . . . United States President Woodrow Wilson was inaugurated for a second term. . . . Jeannette Rankin (R-Montana) began her term as the first woman member of the House of Representatives. . . . The so-called Silent Parade was organized by James Weldon Johnson; 10,000 African Americans marched on 5th Ave in New York City to protest lynching. . . . Suffragette Alice Paul began a 7-month jail sentence for protesting women's rights. . . . The Bolshevik revolution began with the bombardment of the Winter Palace in Petrograd. . . . The 18th Amendment to the US Constitution was authorized prohibiting the sale of alcohol.

1918: DELIVERANCE

Deliverance, a silent film based on Helen's life, was proposed by film maker Francis Trevelyan Miller in January 1918. After several months of negotiation, a contract to make the movie was signed in May. Unfortunately, the film was ultimately not commercially successful and was a financial loss for all the backers.

I had read only disparaging comments about *Deliverance*. It was the age of silent movies and, evidently, the task of portraying deafness, blindness, and muteness in a silent film was (in retrospect) a brave but foolhardy undertaking. Thinking back on the failure of the film, Helen agreed that she was not an ideal actress. She was larger than the usual skinny starlets of Hollywood—not sexy star material—and, besides, her life was not filled with wild adventure and passionate romance. Helen felt there was not much in her life story to hold the attention of the typical audience in 1918.

It also needs to be pointed out that producing a film during one of the worst pandemics in global history was not the wisest decision. People were not rushing to theaters; they were hunkering down at home, hoping death would pass them by. There was also a union strike going on between actors and film producers when the film opened; theaters were being picketed. Helen supported the union and refused to go to the opening of her own film. In 1918, World War One had just ended—people were in shock, millions of young soldiers had died, families were grieving, the nation was grieving—it was not the best time to bring out a film, although *Deliverance* tries to weave the war into the narrative. There was also bickering and powerplays going on that undermined the making, release, and distribution of the movie. There is little wonder that the film was not a commercial success. Not that the critics panned the movie—they did not:

> The reviewers were enthusiastic. *The New York Times* called it "one of the triumphs of the motion picture," with the opening night audience several times breaking into spontaneous applause. In places it was "over-burdened with moralizing and its optimism is sometimes spread too thickly," but in the main it was "compelling . . . and, let it be repeated, the story, as a story, grips and holds the interest as few photo stories do." *The New York Sun* credited the director, George Platt . . . for "a new technique . . . a method approximating that of the speaking stage . . . it is one of the most compact photo plays ever screened, each flash upon the silver sheet being filled with action that has meaning." Another paper could not praise deliverance "too highly." It was an "educational picture in the highest sense." ~ Helen and Teacher, by Joseph Lash, 1980.

Helen had counted on the film bringing in desperately needed income, so the failure of the film was a financial blow. In her book *Beyond the Miracle Worker* (2009), Professor Nielsen reports that the household—Macy, Thomson, and Keller—often lived on credit. Financially, the women were in a bad place in 1918:

> Helen lamented to her mother, "We have been frightfully 'hard up,' mother. I don't remember a time since college days when we were so much 'up against it.'[40]

Financial hardships were instrumental in determining important decisions, including the decision to go on the lecture circuit, to join the Vaudeville Circuit, to make *Deliverance*, and later to work for the American Foundation for the Blind.

~

One Saturday, on a wintry February evening, as I was re-reading the *Deliverance* chapter in Joseph Lash's biography *Helen and Teacher* (1980), I decided to finally watch the film. I had been avoiding the movie while I was writing about Helen. I cannot pin down my emotions, but I guess sitting through 85 minutes of jerky silent footage had not appealed to me. The Library of Congress preserved the movie; it is available for viewing on YouTube. Early in the film we find these words:

> I come from the Kingdom of Darkness.
> The world is my country.
> Humanity is my religion!
> I come in the name of the struggling people
> of all races and nations.

That is quite good, I thought, as I settled into the film; it also looked like they were using the actual homestead at Ivy Green as a site location—how splendid to see it in 1918! My first impression was quite positive and hopeful.

The processing speed of humanity in the twenty-first century is blazingly fast compared to the excruciatingly slow pace of silent movies—or so it seemed to me as I patiently waited for words to get out of the way so I could watch the story unfold. The words also jiggle on the screen in a way that I imagine might cause epileptic seizures. I also confess that the background piano music made me slightly nuts as it droned on incessantly. I am only minutes into the film so maybe I should wait for the bad scenes (which I suppose must be coming) before giving my review—I am enjoying the beginning despite my grumbling about the old days of cinema.

> "I hope you can teach her," Kate Keller says to Annie, shortly after Sullivan has arrived at Ivy Green.
> "Love and patience overcome all obstacles," says Annie, as the lovely young women gaze into each other's eyes.

The dialogue is fine at the beginning, true to Helen's autobiography. After Annie and Helen meet for the first time, the next message appears:

> The Battle Begins
> Within the Walls
> Of Darkness and Silence.
> Patience and Love
> Struggle with Ignorance.

That is still quite good; I wonder if Helen and Annie had a hand in writing these scene-dividing comments. There are some background images that range from awesome to bizarre—for example, there is an ape with a big club as a backdrop to the above quote, for some reason. There is, also, not-so-subtle racism here and there.

It is apparent that at least two of the most dramatic scenes from William Gibson's stage play and movie *The Miracle Worker* were based on early scenes from *Deliverance* (also from Helen's autobiography): the food fight scene, and the stunning moment at the water fountain when Helen discovers that everything has a name.

Unfortunately, the *Deliverance* version of the meal scene does not show the food fight. Instead, we see Helen carefully folding her napkin— we assume a battle has taken place wherein Annie has forced Helen to obey, although both females appear unruffled. Meanwhile, Kate Keller has been anxiously waiting for the battle-of-wills to end.

Whoa! Anne Sullivan bows her head to daydream and suddenly we have a prolonged shot of a wall upon which the shadow of Jesus appears. The screen reads: "Suffer little children to come unto me." Followed by a quick shot of apparently suffering little white kids.

Helen Keller was a devout Christian, so it is okay, I think, for Jesus to have a cameo appearance. Helen deeply believed in the words that next appear on the screen:

Through Him
The blind shall see.
The deaf shall hear.
And the dumb shall speak.

Helen was sure that she had a non-material body that was an exact duplicate of her material body. She was sure that when she got to Heaven, she would be made whole.

The next scene is at the famous water fountain, a scene which Sullivan likened to a religious experience for Helen. This is a special moment in the film as Sullivan, slowly and deliberately, letter-by-letter, spells w-a-t-e-r. We see a close-up of Sullivan's fingers spelling onto the surface of Helen's little hand. Then Helen spells w-a-t-e-r in Sullivan's hand.

Now a servant brings Helen's baby sister to the water fountain and Sullivan spells b-a-b-y into Helen's hand. After learning *water* and *baby*, Helen quickly learns 30 more new words. At this point, the film crashes from sublime to frivolous. After Helen unsuccessfully tries to teach a dog to fingerspell, we see a rapid series of scenes with Helen, three kids, and farm animals. Helen's black playmate Martha Washington has a major role for about five minutes. Martha was Helen's friend when they were little, so it is nice to see the relationship highlighted.

The movie jumps from Helen learning fingerspelling to Helen writing. A quick scene shows her learning braille then we see the actual first letter she ever wrote—in pencil. There are now some historically fabricated little vignettes (mini-story lines) that distract from the movie (for me) and then we leap into Annie and Helen's time in Boston.

The movie sets up a comparison between a fictional girl named Nadja (who is about Helen's age) and Helen. A lot of the film (way too much) sets up the less intellectually-driven Nadja as a contrast to the virtuous, hardworking Helen. Part One (of the three-part movie) ends as Nadja faces the death of her father and brother in an accident. Part Two looks at the two women ten years later (in their late teens); Part Three is called Womanhood.

The scene where Helen learns to speak (with Sarah Fuller at the Horace Mann School for the Deaf) is dramatized with equal power to the scene at the water fountain, which is fascinating to see. We do not often glorify the miracle of Helen learning to speak. I suppose this is partly due to her not mastering the skill of speaking, although she made herself understood often when giving speeches and in everyday conversations with Sullivan and Polly Thomson.

We now see Helen and Anne at the Cambridge School for Young Girls where Helen is preparing to take the entrance exams for Radcliffe College. Quick switch back to Nadja—I am beginning to think that this is the Helen and Nadja story.

Nadja's worldview seems to be "Life ain't no use, life is tragic, and book-learning is also useless." Suddenly, Nadja seems to be discovering romance and music, but the scene quickly cuts back to Annie and Helen studying.

Helen passes the Radcliffe exam with distinction. Cut back to Nadja learning to play piano with her budding boyfriend—they hug, and life ahead seems happy and tolerable for Nadja. Cut back to Helen and Annie.

Now the caption says, "distinguished people come to pay homage to Helen." First in is Mark Twain. Then we watch Helen and Annie meet Joseph Jefferson getting ready for his role as Rip Van Winkle. Cut to Nadja who's lover seems to be having a heart attack and, yes, he has died.

Fate keeps hammering Nadja's soul into a sorrowful heap, while Helen's soul is soaring. We start to feel that Nadja is right, "Life really ain't no use."

Cut back to Annie and Helen at an outdoor party. We are told that Helen pines for the love that has been denied her by her deaf-blindness—now she stands alone in a darkened room. Helen decides that if she cannot have real love, she can at least dream of love. Her fingers run over the brailled words of the blind poet Homer as she says to herself, "I shall be a sorceress like Circe and summon Ulysses."

And there she is as Circe, who then becomes a siren and lures Ulysses to her shores (so to speak). She summons Ulysses to dream with her and he consents; they are suddenly together. Ulysses is a tall dashing lad and Helen as Circe is radiant. I have to say that the costumes in this movie should have won an award, especially the women's dresses and hats (it would be fun to colorize this film).

Helen obviously has regained her sight, hearing, and voice in the dream-state. She instructs everyone to leave so that she and the dashing hero can be alone. Now there is a wonderful scene by the ocean, beautifully set up and photographed. Helen bids Ulysses to sit while an all-girl siren band plays alluring music to charm the handsome hero. Then the sirens break out in dance—which is also splendid. Ulysses is wooing Helen and she is loving the moment. They almost kiss but . . . Cut to the long-legged toga-clad sirens prancing about. Cut back to Helen and Ulysses almost . . . almost, almost kissing, but not quite.

Okay, Ulysses has had enough of almost-kissing, so he seizes Helen and passionately presses his hungry mouth against Helen's starving-for-love lips. Cut to dancers for two seconds, then Cut to the ocean scene again. The sirens, sensing the seriousness of the situation back out of the scene. But then, suddenly, Ulysses decides to head back out to sea. I guess he has adventures to pursue. Helen is sad as the scene goes dark. When we see Helen again, she is awakening from her daydream. She feels happy and content; dreaming is cathartic for her. Part three: Womanhood begins.

What is so splendid about Part Three is that Helen, Annie, Kate Keller, and Helen's brother Phillips Keller play themselves. But first, before we see actual footage of the Keller family in 1919, we check in on Nadja. She appears to be doing piece work at a clothing factory, surrounded by many other unfortunate young women sitting before sewing machines.

We discover that she has a son—grownup now. The women at the sweat shop rebel (I cannot tell why) and call her son a slacker (he works there, too). Anyway, the boy is encouraged to enlist and fight for his country—the women all cheer. Cut to Helen and Annie.

Helen has just graduated from Radcliffe. There are shots of Helen with her cap and gown. These brief moments are worth the whole film for me. What a magnificent treasure, what a joy to see these images. Now we see Helen and Annie together, an image I have never seen before. The next scene is of Helen about to ride a horse. The animation in Helen's face is amazing. Facial expressions must be innately tied to emotional state—Helen did not learn these socially appropriate facial movement by mirroring others. I am puzzled by her animation because I do not recall ever seeing such facial expressions on anyone who is deaf-blind—did Sullivan teach her gesturing, I wonder?

Now here is another puzzling moment. The words on the screen say, "One of the mysteries of Helen's life. Science cannot explain how she can distinguish colors by the touch." But that is all, we are left with the mystery! I have seen evidence of this phenomenon, so it should not be written off as impossible.

Part Three of this film makes it a treasure for all ages. Here we see the animated Helen Keller, we see the real woman, not imagined from a book, even more wonderful than rare photographs of her. As Helen dances gracefully, waltzing with a partner, the scene suddenly cuts to Nadja alone in a room thinking of her son. Then there is a rapid edit back to Helen smelling flowers she has just picked.

In a rare moment captured on film, we see Helen walking with her mother Kate Keller. Mother and daughter walk together before greeting Helen's soldier brother Phillips as if he has just returned from the front lines and as if they are seeing him for the first time after years of separation. Suddenly, we cut to Nadja who hears a knock on the door. It is her son returning from the war . . . blind!

Nadja hugs and kisses her blind son and then exclaims, "It is the price of liberty!"

"There is hope," Nadja tells her son. "We will go to Helen."

Cut to Helen about to get into a biplane. It looks like Polly Thomson and Anne Sullivan are helping Helen get into her flying gear. The helmet is dashing. These are brilliant shots.

As we approach the end of the film, Helen is fixing her hair in the bedroom while Annie is reading in a family room. In comes Polly

Thomson, leading Nadja and her son, and a comrade of her sons from the war (the friend has lost an arm). Sullivan greets them warmly.

Polly goes to the bedroom to tell Helen that a friend has come to see her. Helen greets the visitors and then stands between the two young soldiers; she takes the hand of each young man and says, "Humanity owes a tremendous debt to you, my boys. Ten million human sacrifices . . . can it ever repay?" She then says to the blind son, "I once dwelt in darkness without hope. Then came love bearing this message! Though blind, you can follow the bright path of the sun. Why fear the night? It only leads to day."

Helen continues talking to the blind young man, "They have taken, we will give . . . I have been over every step of the road you are starting upon. Come, we are soldiers of the new freedom that shall sweep all tyrannies from the earth! We are solders in a battle that shall free the minds and hearts of the unfortunate . . . we shall inspire them with confidence in themselves!"

The last minute of the film is meant to be a triumphant cinematic spectacle. Helen proclaims, "I must join hands with my fellowmen. I send out my spirit, like a bugle call, to lead humanity joyously to the height."

Now we see Helen charge in on a white stallion, blow on a bugle, and exclaim, "Only those are blind who do not see the truth. Only those are deaf who do not hear the oracle of their better selves." For the finale, Helen, bugle to her lips, leads thousands across a bridge to the land of freedom . . . The End.

I am certainly glad that I decided to watch this masterpiece. It is one of history's most important silent treasures. We would not have these images of Helen, Annie, Kate, Polly, and Phillips without the filming of this movie. As the years roll on, these images become ever more historically important.

∾

Humanity has battled pandemics and serious illnesses for centuries. In our time (I write this in February 2021), we are battling climate change, the Covid-19 pandemic, and political unrest. These same trends played out over Helen Keller's life; she was, for example, alive when the Spanish flu killed 50 to 100 million people worldwide, starting in 1918, while World War One still raged in Europe.

As I write these words, Covid-19 is still a raging pandemic; 110 million people have had the virus and 2,500,000 of them have died globally. Scientists are working around the clock to build defenses against viruses, but thousands of people are still dying every day. Hopefully, by the time these words reach your consciousness, humanity will have beaten back the virus and normality will have returned. Pandemics have plagued the world off and on throughout history but then they have subsided as herd immunity eventually occurred.

What interests me is that Helen Keller never mentions the 1918 pandemic or the great depression in the 1930s. World events raged around her but, somehow, she was sheltered from global catastrophe— or her mind filtered out the everyday news as she went about her mission.

What Else Happened in 1918?

Here are a few random events that happened in 1918: The first case of Spanish flu (Funston Army Camp, in Kansas) was recorded in the United States. The Spanish flu killed 21,000 people in the U.S. in a single week. . . . The United States Congress authorized time zones & approved daylight savings time. . . . The Romanov royal family were executed by a Bolshevik firing squad. . . . During World War One, Adolf Hitler received the Iron Cross first class for bravery on the recommendation of his Jewish superior, Lieutenant Hugo Gutmann. . . . The last German air raid on England occurred; four Zeppelin airships dropped bombs in the Midlands and North East England. . . . Cecil Chubb gifted the prehistoric monument Stonehenge to the British nation. . . . After killing about eleven million soldiers, the first world war ended on November 11, 1918.

1920: Vaudeville

Helen and Anne began their vaudeville career in 1920. They remained on the vaudeville circuit until the spring of 1924. Helen very much enjoyed this experience, but Anne Sullivan did not. Sullivan was sick much of the time and at one session fell and injured herself. She also got the flu and was quite sick for a while—maybe the Spanish flu, although we will never know. A rare film clip exists on YouTube showing one of the Vaudeville sessions. Typically, Sullivan would start with Helen off stage. Then Helen would enter, and they would demonstrate how Helen could lip-read with her fingers; she would also demonstrate her voice. They would then take questions, many of which delighted Helen. In his wonderful autobiography of Helen Keller, Joseph Lash listed some of the questions and answers that were written down. Here are a few:

Can you feel moonshine?
  No, but I can smell it.

Who are the three greatest men of our time?
  Lenin, Edison, and Charlie Chaplin.

Who are the most unhappy people?
  People who have nothing to do.

What do you think of ex-president Wilson?
  I think he is the greatest individual disappointment the world has ever known.

What did America gain by the war (WWl)?
The American Legion and a bunch of other troubles.

Who is your favorite hero in real life?
Eugene V. Debs. He dared to do what other men were afraid to do.

What is the greatest obstacle to universal peace?
The human race.

What is the slowest thing in the world?
Congress.

Do you think women are men's intellectual equal?
I think God made foolish women so they might be a suitable companion to men.

Do you desire your sight more than anything else in the world?
No! No! I would rather walk with a friend in the dark than walk alone in the light.

Which quality do you admire most in your teacher?
Her sense of humor; her many-sided sympathy; her passion for service.

These answers reflect many of Helen religious and political views. She did not hold back her opinions. That she and Sullivan enjoyed a good sense of humor and were quite witty themselves comes across clearly.

～

On August 18, 1920, the 19th Amendment was ratified; American women won the right to vote. A lot of women had to be humiliated, beaten, denigrated, and their self-worth attacked before this day arrived. The battle had raged for decades, not only in the United States but across the Western world. Helen Keller had been a vocal suffragette and champion for women's rights; this must have been a day of celebration for her even though she knew that a cultural paradigm shift had to occur before the reality of feminine equality would finally emerge. We are still experiencing the battle for gender dignity and equality a hundred years after the Amendment. Also, the 19th amendment did not help minority women much and many suffragettes refused to stop fighting for their black and brown sisters—that battle is still with us,

1920 was also the year that Helen Keller helped form the American Civil Liberties Union (ACLU). The ACLU was founded by a committee including Helen Keller, Roger Baldwin, Elizabeth Gurley Flynn, Jane Addams, Felix Frankfurter, Crystal Eastman, Walter Nelles, Morris Ernst, Albert DeSilver, Arthur Garfield Hays, and Rose Schneiderman. The ACLUs initial focus was on freedom of speech, primarily for anti-war protesters. As I write this in 2021, the American Civil Liberties Union (of which I am a member) is still at the forefront of the battle for kindness and justice.

What Else Happened in 1920?

Here are a few random events that happened in 1920: Helen Keller turned forty this year. The National Negro Baseball League was organized. . . . The inauguration of the League of Nations was held in Paris. . . . The League of Women Voters was formed in Chicago. . . . President Woodrow Wilson declared the Communist Labor Party illegal in the United States. . . . Joan of Arc (Jeanne D'arc) was canonized a saint by the Catholic church. . . . The U.S. Post Office established that children could not be sent by parcel post (after various instances of children being mailed). . . . Belgium started paying old age pensions. . . . The "Wall Street bombing" occurred; a horse-drawn wagon exploded on Wall Street killing 38 people and injuring 143.

1921: THE DEATH OF KATE KELLER

Helen's mother, Kate Keller (1856–1921), died in 1921. Helen and Anne were about to go on stage in Los Angeles when the news arrived of her mother's death. In shock and grief, Helen went ahead with her obligation. "Every fiber of my being cried out at the thought of facing the audience, but it had to be done," she wrote.

Later in 1921, while performing in Toronto, Anne Sullivan collapsed from a severe case of the flu. [41] For Helen, the sudden incapacitation of her friend and teacher, followed so closely by the death of her mother, caused a severe sense of panic and dread. Anne Sullivan eventually got better, but her heath never stabilized—she was sick with numerous ailments until her death in 1936. [42]

1921 is also the year that the American Foundation for the Blind was established to address blindness on a national scale. Helen organized a concert at the Metropolitan Opera House that provided seed funds for establishing the American Foundation for the Blind.[43]

Helen had opposed the national sentiment that had led to the First World War; she was a reluctant pacifist. Her socialist worldview was based on a sense that the common man was a victim and that the Egoic minds of aggressive men were the enemy of people like her who espoused kindness and service to others. The following was taken from an interview in 1921. Helen is reflecting on the results of World War One:

> The socialists failed the world. Alas, they are human, all too human. Like millions of Christians, they preach a glorious doctrine but lack the religious zeal to suffer for their faith."

She read Hunters "Poverty." Then Karl Marx's "Capital." She knows the "Communist Manifesto" almost by heart. She diligently read the opponents of socialism and the replies by Kautsky, Hillquit, and Frankfurter. She then made a more thorough investigation of the industrial problem and discovered, as she believed, the root of the evil. The captains of industry were concerned in producing wealth, not for social service, but for profit. Whether they produced booze or bibles was determined by the amount of profit. Labor was regarded by them as a mere commodity, like coal or crude material, and the cheaper they could purchase it, quality considered, the better they liked it; whereas labor when selling itself, desired to get as much for its efforts as possible. Therein lay the cause of the inevitable class struggle, the conflict between the purchasing employer and the selling employee. She accepted as the solution the socialization of production and distribution of commodities.

"My heart goes out to all oppressed people," she said. "I am strongly for disarmament, for it is by brute force that people are enslaved. Ireland must have industrial and political freedom. Any nation that does not recognize the equal right of other nations to liberty is itself unworthy of having liberty." [44]

Helen Keller felt that wars come about because of inequality, injustice, unfairness and because too many minds were not spiritually evolved. Ireland was struggling for independence from Great Britain when Helen was interviewed, so she offered her opinion. Colonial nations had no right to plant flags and declare whole populations subjects of a foreign power. Colonialism, from Helen's perspective, was a patriarchal plan to conquer foreign lands and harvest the material riches of those lands.

What Else Happened in 1921?

Here are a few random events that happened in 1921: The Republic of Turkey was established out of the remnants of the Ottoman Empire. . . . The British crime writer Agatha Christie published her first novel *The Mysterious Affair at Styles*. . . . Warren G. Harding became the 29th President of the United States. . . . Albert Einstein lectured in New York City on his Theory of Relativity. . . . Sweden abolished capital punishment.... Adolf Hitler became the leader of the National Socialist German Workers Party.... Franklin Roosevelt got polio at his summer home on Canadian island of Campobello..... John Edgar Hoover became Assistant Director of the FBI.... Partito Nazionalista Fascista was formed in Italy by Benito Mussolini.

1922: THE DEATH OF ALEXANDER GRAHAM BELL

Helen Keller's mentor and lifelong friend Alexander Graham Bell died at age 75 on August 2, 1922 in Nova Scotia, Canada. Every phone in North America was silenced during his funeral in his honor. Bell was born March 3, 1847 in Edinburgh, Scotland.

From Scotland, Bell's father had moved the family to Brantford, Ontario. In Brantford, young Alexander learned the Mohawk language and put it in writing. The Mohawk people made him an Honorary Chief.

When he was 25, Bell opened *The School of Vocal Physiology and Mechanics of Speech* in Boston, where he taught deaf people to speak. At age 26, he became Professor of Vocal Physiology and Elocution at the Boston University School of Oratory.

Bell was one of the founders of the National Geographic Society; in 1897, he became its second president.

What Else Happened in 1922?

Here are a few random events that happened in 1922: James Joyce's *Ulysses* was first published in Paris. . . . U.S. Commerce Secretary Herbert Hoover convened the first National Radio Conference. Radios were placed in the White House. . . . The United States Supreme Court unanimously upheld the 19th amendment to the Constitution—women's right to vote. . . . The first vampire movie *Nosferatu* premiered in Germany (an adaptation of Bram Stoker's Dracula). . . . British magistrates in India sentenced Mahatma Gandhi to six years in prison for disobedience. . . . President Warren G. Harding signed a joint resolution of approval to establish a Jewish homeland in Palestine. . . . The Italian government resigned under pressure from fascists led by Benito Mussolini. . . . Howard Carter discovered the tomb of Tutankhamun in Egypt. . . . Adolf Hitler addressed 50,000 national-socialists in Munich, Germany. . . . Danish physicist Niels Bohr was awarded the Nobel Prize for Physics in Copenhagen. . . . The USSR was formally established in Moscow.

1924: American Foundation for the Blind

Helen and Anne began their work with the American Foundation for the Blind in 1924. This event would turn Helen Keller's attention toward global blindness; for the rest of her life, it was her work with the blind that took center stage, rather than her deafness, or deaf-blindness, or politics. Had she gone to work for an organization serving deaf people, which could very well have happened, her story would have been much different. Helen was ambivalent about this concentration on blindness, as she expressed in this letter to her Scottish friend Dr. James Kerr, who was a medical doctor with a professional interest in deafness:

> As you say, most of my little work has been done for the blind. But it is largely an accident. Workers for the sightless have asked me to help them and have given me many opportunities to say a word in their behalf. Perhaps the reason that I have done little or nothing for the deaf is, I am not competent. I hardly know where to take hold of their work. But I am deeply interested in them. I am just as deaf as I am blind. The problems of deafness are deeper and more complex, if not more important, than those of blindness. Deafness is a much worse misfortune. For it means the loss of the most vital stimulus—the sound of the voice that brings language, sets thought astir and keeps us in the intellectual company of man. [45]

In *Beyond the Miracle Worker* (2009), Professor Kim Nielsen wrote:

AFB's first president M. C. Migel, a wealthy businessman and chair of the New York State Commission for the Blind, eventually became a reliable friend to both Macy and Keller. The AFB provided Macy respectability, professional recognition, a salary, and structure for the last years of her life. She and Keller provided the AFB legitimacy and incredible star power. [46]

The *Helen Keller Campaign*, as marketing called the effort, began in October of 1924 with the goal of raising two million dollars to establish an AFB endowment fund. They soon surpassed this ambitious goal and set up the AFB financially for the next few decades.

What Else Happened in 1924?

Here are a few random events that happened in 1924: The Republic of Greece was established. . . . The first Winter Olympic Games opened in Chamonix, France. . . . George Gershwin's "Rhapsody in Blue" premiered at a concert called "Experiment in Modern Music." . . . Thomas Watson renamed the Computing-Tabulating-Recording Company (CTR) International Business Machines (IBM). . . . The British released Mahatma Gandhi from jail. . . . J. Edgar Hoover was appointed head of the FBI. . . . The Pulitzer Prize was awarded to American poet Robert Frost. . . . Calvin Coolidge declared the Statue of Liberty a national monument. . . . Astronomer Edwin Hubble announced the existence of other galaxies beyond the Milky Way at a meeting of the American Astronomical Society.

1925: LIONS INTERNATIONAL

In 1925, Helen made a famous appeal during a speech to the International Convention of Lions Clubs. She asked that all Lions Club members become "Knights of the blind in this crusade against darkness." She was referring to the *Helen Keller Campaign* sponsored by her employer the American Foundation for the Blind. She had become an official spokesperson for blindness. Asking the Lions members for help was a moment of genius because the Lions Organization—since her appeal—has donated millions of dollars to the cause of blindness (and directly to blind individuals) since 1925; that is almost a hundred years of service and dedication to blindness. Here is the short speech she gave that has resulted in almost a century of dedication by Lions Club members across the globe:

Dear Lions and Ladies:

I suppose you have heard the legend that represents opportunity as a capricious lady, who knocks at every door but once, and if the door isn't opened quickly, she passes on, never to return. And that is as it should be. Lovely, desirable ladies won't wait. You have to go out and grab 'em.

I am your opportunity. I am knocking at your door. I want to be adopted. The legend doesn't say what you are to do when several beautiful opportunities present themselves at the same door. I guess you have to choose the one you love best. I hope you will adopt me. I am the youngest here, and what I offer you is full of splendid opportunities for service.

The American Foundation for the Blind is only four years old. It grew out of the imperative needs of the blind and was called into existence by the sightless themselves. It is national and international in scope and in importance. It represents the best and most enlightened thought on our subject that has been reached so far. Its object is to make the lives of the blind more worthwhile everywhere by increasing their economic value and giving them the joy of normal activity.

Try to imagine how you would feel if you were suddenly stricken blind today. Picture yourself stumbling and groping at noonday as in the night; your work, your independence, gone. In that dark world wouldn't you be glad if a friend took you by the hand and said, "Come with me and I will teach you how to do some of the things you used to do when you could see?" That is just the kind of friend the American Foundation is going to be to all the blind in this country if seeing people will give it the support it must have.

You have heard how through a little word dropped from the fingers of another, a ray of light from another soul touched the darkness of my mind and I found myself, found the world, found God. It is because my teacher learned about me and broke through the dark, silent imprisonment which held me that I am able to work for myself and for others. It is the caring we want more than money. The gift without the sympathy and interest of the giver is empty. If you care, if we can make the people of this great country care, the blind will indeed triumph over blindness.

The opportunity I bring to you, Lions, is this: To foster and sponsor the work of the American Foundation for the Blind. Will you not help me hasten the day when there shall be no preventable blindness; no little deaf, blind child untaught; no blind man or woman unaided? I appeal to you Lions, you who have your sight, your hearing, you who are strong and brave and kind. Will you not constitute yourselves Knights of the Blind in this crusade against darkness?

I thank you. [47]

As I write this in the year 2021, there are 48,000 Lions Clubs in the world, 1.4 million members, women and men. This book is dedicated to all the millions of people, from all corners of the planet, who have served as Lions Club members from the founding of the service organization in 1917 to the present day.

What Else Happened in 1925?

Here are a few random events that happened in 1925: Benito Mussolini dissolved the Italian parliament and proclaimed himself dictator of Italy, taking the title "Il Duce." . . . The first issue of the *New Yorker* Magazine was published. . . . The *Great Gatsby* was published by F. Scott Fitzgerald. . . . The World's Fair opened in Chicago. . . . Walter Chrysler founded automobile manufacturer Chrysler Corporation. . . . Anthropologist Margaret Mead arrived in Samoa. . . . Irish playwright George Bernard Shaw was awarded the Nobel Prize for Literature.

1927: HELEN PUBLISHES MY RELIGION

My Religion, Helen's account of her Swedenborgian beliefs was published in 1927. Swedenborg appealed to Helen for at least three reasons. Swedenborg wrote that:

1. There existed a universal spiritual afterlife, a bother/sisterhood that was beyond the physical reality of the corporeal world.
2. God was a purely loving force. There was nothing vindictive or hateful in the Supreme Being.
3. In the afterlife, there are no limitations, no physical or mental impairments. Humans are made whole again after they pass from earth-bound life.

All debates aside, we can see why this theocratic perspective appealed to Helen Keller; to be made whole again is a powerful promise. We might as well believe such a powerful proclamation; it is more hopeful and comforting than the scientific worldview, which holds that humanity is a superior kind of bug with one trip through life (I personally remain undecided between God and the Bugs of Science—but Helen voted for God).

1927 was also the year that editor Nella Braddy Henney joined with the Keller-Sullivan-Thomson household to assist with editing Sullivan's biography. Helen seemed to be always surrounded by talented writers; if she did not have John Macy looking over her early work, she had Nella Braddy assisting with later books. When Nella was not available, Anne Sullivan was there ready with her mastery of the English language. Of course, Helen became a marvelously eloquent writer herself, probably (in part) because of her contact with so many other accomplished authors.

~

Helen was examined at Columbia University to determine if her sensory organs were more developed than in other people. The examinations were conducted by Dr. Frederick Tilney, Professor of Neurology at Columbia. Dr. Tilney concluded that Helen's remaining sensory systems were completely normal. Dr. Tilney saw no anatomical or physiological changes in Helen's sensory systems. He also observed that Helen did no better than others on functional tests.

These findings were exceedingly disconcerting for Helen and for others who had marveled at her sensory discrimination—Helen sensed that something was amiss. I have no doubts about Dr. Tilney's findings. In a way, they cause us to look elsewhere for Helen's skills. Dr. Tilney realized this and explained that Helen's behaviors had more to do with her mind and her adaptation skills than with any alteration in the physiology of her sense of touch and smell. Using my own dual-process theory, Helen's body did not rebuild the end organs of touch and olfaction; instead, her mind honed the ability to attend using her Egocentric *attention system* and her Allocentric *awareness system*.

There are two additional observations we can make in an age more scientifically advanced than Dr. Tilney's era. First, Dr. Tilney (as far as I know) did not measure the activity of the proprioceptive system—the set of internal sensory systems responsible for animation and space analysis. As I discussed in *The Esoteric Helen Keller*, it was the proprioceptive system that evolved after deaf-blindness occurred. Second, it is plausible that Helen developed synesthesia—maybe even more than one variety. Dr. Tilney knew nothing of this recent development in brain science. I discussed the possibility of Helen having synesthesia in *The Esoteric Helen Keller*.

What Else Happened in 1927?

Here are a few random events that happened in 1927: The Tennessee Supreme Court overturned (on a technicality) John T. Scopes' guilty verdict for teaching evolution; the law against teaching evolution remained. . . . Actress Mae West was found guilty of "obscenity and corrupting the morals of youth" in a New York court. . . . Charles Lindbergh took off from New York, flying the Spirit of St. Louis on a flight path across the Atlantic for Paris. . . . Leon Trotsky was expelled from the Soviet Communist Party; Joseph Stalin assumed leadership.

My Religion

Helen's original publication of *My Religion* (1927) was accomplished with little help. With her previous books, she had editors like John Macy and Nella Braddy Henney to fuss over her sentences and ideas. However, there were no allies in her effort to explain why she had chosen Swedenborgianism to be her religion; her friends were puzzled by this choice and they did not understand why artists like Blake and Whitman, and thinkers like Carl Jung and William James would give credence to this mystic's proclamations.

Swedenborg claimed to have visited Heaven and Hell—that was enough to turn most rational people off the trail. Presumably because Helen got so little editing help, this book was flawed at publication, with many typos, spelling errors, and incorrect punctuation; the book did not have chapter headings and subsections. A Wiki article states that "the original publication was loosely put together and hastily printed." Consequently, decades later, a Swedenborgian minister, professor emeritus, Dr. Raymond Silverman thoroughly revised Helen's book to make it more readable. Silverman called the revised edition *Light in My Darkness* (2000). I will speak further of Helen's religious writings when I review Dr. Silverman's book below.

1929: Helen Publishes Midstream

Midstream, an autobiographical account of Helen's first half century of life, was published in 1929. The book is divided into sections celebrating friends who influenced her life. I will discuss her relationship with some of these friends in the following pages.

This is also the year, in June of 1929, that severe eye problems returned for Anne Sullivan. This time, the complications were so severe that her right eye had to be enucleated. She was also told that her left eye needed surgery to remove a cataract. Annie refused to go to the eye doctor for surgery on her remaining eye even though the cataract had made it impossible for her to read. I suspect that Annie was highly skeptical of medical practices—her eyes had been operated on numerous times since she was a teenager without ever gaining any long-term betterment. My guess is that scar tissue had made her situation worse as the years went by. The state of eye surgery in the 1930s was primitive compared to the present day—Annie's dread and lack of trust were probably well-founded.

Dr. Conrad Berens (1889–1963) was Annie's ophthalmologist. His office was at the New York Eye and Ear Infirmary in New York City. Dr. Berens had authored several textbooks about diseases of the eye; he was well-regarded as a skilled surgeon. Dr. Berens was not only an ocular surgeon for Anne Sullivan, but he was also a close friend of Anne and Helen. He had written about Helen and Annie in the Matilda Ziegler Magazine. This is from an online article:

> In 1929, Annie's right eye, which had developed a cataract, became so painful that her eye had to be removed. Her left eye then developed a cataract, and her vision became very dim. By

1934, her sight had almost completely failed. Against the wishes of Dr. Conrad Berens, a New York eye surgeon, Annie had an operation on her left eye in May 1935 that left her only able to distinguish light and color. At the end of her life, she could perceive only gray shadows. [48]

By the time of her death in 1936, Anne Sullivan had become completely blind, and Helen Keller had become her caregiver and her main avenue for communicating with others.

What Else Happened in 1929?

Here are a few random events that happened in 1929: Mother Teresa arrived in Calcutta, India to begin her work amongst India's poorest people. . . . Tarzan and Buck Rogers appeared for the first time. . . . Herbert Hoover was inaugurated as the 31st U.S. President. . . . The German airship Graf Zeppelin began a round-the-world flight which ended in disaster when the ship exploded and burned. . . ."Black Thursday" started the stock market crash of 1929; the Dow Jones dropped 12.8%. . . . August 1929 is officially designated as the beginning of the Great Depression, which ended March 1933.

Midstream

Helen's book *Midstream* is a major work that covers the first half of her life. She called *Midstream* an extension of *The Story of My Life*. Helen turned 50 the year *Midstream* was published.

Midstream mostly pays tribute to the people who influenced her emerging adulthood. There is a wonderful tribute to Mark Twain, for example—a few lovely vignettes that capture his humor and sincerity—stories about Alexander Graham Bell, a loving and fatherly force in the lives of both Helen and Annie, and a chapter on Andrew Carnegie, a kind man who saw the beauty of Helen and Annie's journey and who eventually became a financial supporter. There is also a chapter on Kate Keller, Helen's wonderful mother.

Kate Keller is so important that she deserves a book of her own. It is ironic and unfortunate that the miracle and the miracle worker overshadowed the remarkable young mother who gave birth to Helen Keller and then nurtured and loved her for a lifetime. Kate Keller was smart, steadfast, and well-read; she was remarkable in her own right.

I will use this section to highlight Helen's relationships with key people in her life, including her mother Kate Keller, her close friend Mark Twain, her first and only love Peter Fagan, her favorite authors Walt Whitman, Henry David Thoreau, and Ralph Waldo Emerson, her psychologist friend William James, the literary genius and Anne Sullivan's husband John Macy, Polly Thomson, the woman who replaced Anne Sullivan after Sullivan died, Helen's live-in editor and close friend Nella Braddy Henney, Laura Bridgman, the deaf blind trailblazer who came before Helen, and Berthe Galeron, the celebrated and accomplished deaf-blind phenomenon from France who corresponded with Helen for many years. All quotes are from Midstream unless otherwise indicated.

Mark Twain

Helen Keller met Mark Twain at a party given for her in New York City when she was just fourteen. Mark Twain was an elder stateman at the time, already an American icon:

> The long friendship of Keller and Clemens began at a party at Laurence Hutton's New York home on 31 March, 1895. Keller was fourteen, the same age as [Mark Twain's daughter] Jean Clemens. She [Helen] was introduced to both Twain and William Dean Howells, a meeting recalled and discussed many times after with great warmth and affection by all three.
> ~ The Mark Twain Encyclopedia by J. R. LeMaster. Garland Publishing, Literary Criticism and Collections, 1993.

Laurence Hutton and his wife Eleanor were lifelong friends of Helen and Annie. They provided social, emotion, and substantial financial support for the two women.

Below is a portion of a letter that Helen wrote regarding Mark Twain. In her passionate style, Helen salutes her friend and celebrates him as a champion of noble causes. I edited this version to remove spelling and punctuation irregularities (the content was not affected):

How I loved Mark Twain when I, a girl of fourteen, met him in New York! It was a joy to me simply to be in the same room with him, he was so beautiful. His presence shone with the light of his spirit, and he had the unconscious grace and majesty of a Greek god. As I grew older, I realized more and more that he was a great American, a great human being, I marveled when he talked, and I felt the power of his mind—broad, splendid, exuberant as the Mississippi he loved. Like thousands of others, I saw his unfailing sympathy shown wherever there was suffering or misfortune. I honored him even more when I knew that no man ever had greater contempt for injustice, hypocrisy, and tyranny than Mark Twain. From my heart I thank him for all the brave words he uttered, for all the shams he held up to ridicule, for the wrath poured upon cruelty and tyrants. I thank him for the joy and laughter he has given to thousands of his fellowmen.

Change is shaking America and the rest of the world to the foundations. Tradition is being challenged, and every idea questioned, all problems are being discussed from every side, and the desire for truth is seeping like a slow, yet mighty flood through the barriers of a conventional, stultified mode of thought . . . Liberty and justice will not come to the world through "watchful waiting" and prayer. Mark Twain knew that ignorance is the only darkness we need to fear, and he strove unceasingly to dispel it. ~ Helen Keller Digital Archives, American Foundation for the Blind.

Two things jumped out at me as I read this letter. Helen says of Mark Twain that "His presence shone with the light of his spirit, and he had the unconscious grace and majesty of a Greek god." She also says that "she felt the power of his mind." I wonder how she felt grace and majesty. And I wonder how she was able to sense the power of another mind. I do not doubt that she was being honest, sincere, and accurate when she wrote those words, but how did she gage such grace and power without eyes and ears? There must be some other sensory apparatus—besides seeing and hearing—operating in all of us that allows for the reading of vibrational essence. Somehow, we can perceive souls (essence) without eyes or ears. That is the heart of esoteric theory: that such vibrational energy is real and can be received and transmitted between living beings.

Second, I was struck by how relevant Helen's words are even today—that last paragraph seems timeless. "Change is shaking America," she said. "Tradition is being challenged." It helps us cope with current trauma when we realize that similar bewilderment and emotional pain occurred in earlier generations—there is nothing new about chaos, shock, uncertainty, angst, and fear. History shows us that every era must grapple with changing and unsettling paradigm shifts, especially as humanity gradually awakens. Consciousness, individually and collectively, is always evolving.

Mark Twain and Helen Keller were kindred spirits with the same ability to detect and react against hostile vibratory energy. Helen Keller loved Mark Twain, I believe, because he was so much like herself. She could describe his grace and empathy because she was also describing her own grace and empathy.

The quote below shows how Mark Twain and Heller Keller were comrades in the effort to bring loving-kindness to humanity, while at the same time facing down stupidity and hatred. This is from a letter Helen wrote to Mark Twain on his seventieth birthday:

My dear Mr. Clemens, I have just finished reading a most interesting account of the Thanksgiving dinner that was given in honor of your seventieth birthday more than a week ago in New York. Although I am somewhat in the rear of the great procession which brought you its tribute of love and admiration, yet you will accept my little handful of flowers gathered in the garden of my heart, will you not? They are not intended so much for the great author whom the world has crowned with its choicest blossoms as for the kind, sympathetic, noble man, the best of friends and champions with the heart of Santa Claus, who makes others good and happy.

Your birthday shall always be a Thanksgiving Day to me. Indeed, I have thanked you a thousand times for the bright laugh that is like a drop of honey in things bitter that we must all taste, before we learn to know good from evil, and distil sweetness and peace from deprivation and sorrow. I thank you, too, for the flash and tingle along the veins when your fiery words smite the wrong with the lightning of just anger.

Again, I thank you for the tears that soften the heart and make it compassionate and full of kindness. Your message to the world has been one of courage and brightness and tenderness, and your fellowmen make a feast on your anniversary, and give thanks for the many days that you have lived among them.

And you are seventy years old? Or is the report exaggerated like that of your death? I remember, when I saw you last, at the house of our dear Mr. Hutton in Princeton, you said, "If a man is a pessimist before he is forty-eight, he knows too much. If he is an optimist after he is forty-eight, he knows too little." Now we know you are an optimist, and nobody would dare to accuse one on the "seven-terraced summit" of knowing little.

Mrs. Macy and her husband join me in sending you sincere love and admiration.

Your friend, from Wrentham [Massachusetts], December eighth, 1905. ~ Helen Keller Digital Archives, American Foundation for the Blind.

No doubt, as her letters clearly show, Helen had an intellectual and emotional kinship with Mark Twain that was deep and genuine. What she says of him could be said of her. Helen was as fierce an optimist as Mark Twain and just as powerful a spokesperson for love and justice. They made a fascinating pair, a unique blending of the Divine Feminine with the Divine Masculine.

Peter Fagan

Midstream also contains a short but powerful look back at the only romance Helen ever had with a young man. Too many forces opposed her passion, and the romance was not allowed to flower. Helen's desire to be a wife and a mother, to live a "normal" life, ended as the young suitor was excluded from her life by circumstances and by the people around her. The domestic Helen Keller seemed to have died with that failed escapade, but the woman crusader emerged with a clearer understanding that she belonged to the world as a leader and a role model. Still, there is a sadness that lingers over this poignant time for Helen.

The young suiter, Peter Fagan, and Helen planned to elope and get married, but their plans became public when the newspaper published their marriage application. Peter was subsequently expelled from Helen's life. Below, Helen reflects on the first moments when she realized that a man had fallen in love with her:

> I was sitting alone in my study one evening, utterly despondent. The young man who was still acting as my secretary in the absence of Miss Thomson, came in and sat down beside me. For a long time, he held my hand in silence, then he began talking to me tenderly. I was surprised that he cared so much about me. There was sweet comfort in his loving words. I listened all a-tremble. He was full of plans for happiness. He said if I would marry him, he would always be near to help me in the difficulties of life. He would be there to read to me, look up material for my books and do as much as he could of the work my teacher had done for me. . . . His love was a bright sun that shone upon my helplessness and isolation. The sweetness of being loved enchanted me, and I yielded to an impervious longing to be part of a man's life . . . ~ Helen and Teacher, 1980.

Keep in mind that Helen was thirty-six when this moment happened (Peter was 29). She was a well-respected author, lecturer, socialist, fervent suffragette, and a national role model. She had every right to live her life as she pleased. But the people closest to her, Anne Sullivan and Kate Keller, saw her disability as an overpowering and defining reality. A husband, and maybe a future baby, would cause so many disruptions and challenges that Annie and, especially, Helen's mother reacted with swift anger. Kate Keller had not liked Peter Fagan (so he said) from the moment she met him, and this certainly affected how she reacted when she heard the shocking news from Anne Sullivan, who had found out through the family cook:

> Ian, the Russian boy whom Teacher had trained to cook and look after the house, came to say goodbye [Sullivan was going away because of her health]. He always called Teacher "My Madam." "My Madam," he said that morning, "my heart is sad." Teacher thought he was referring to the imminent breakup of the household. She was sad, too, she replied, "and if ever I start housekeeping again, I'll send for you." "No," Ian said, "It isn't that. It's Miss Helen. Harry and I know." Harry Lamb was their

chauffeur. Ian proceeded to tell her that Fagan had been making love to Miss Helen and that the two were planning to elope.

Making love to Miss Helen! Oh my God . . . Shock waves must have reverberated throughout the household (as shockwaves rocked my own mind when I read that paragraph). Kate Keller confronted Helen immediately, with harsh anger and a firm conviction that this was a turn toward disaster. Unfortunately, instead of saying, "Back off, mother, this is my life," Helen denied the affair to (evidently) protect Peter. The affair, her thrilling relationship, her first love, unraveled from there.

Rosie Sultan wrote a well-received novel based on the Helen Keller romance called *Helen Keller in Love: A Novel* (2012). The novel is historical fiction so a few of the stories were made up or elaborated. Unfortunately, fictitious events have made their way onto the internet and false information has been molded into "fact." What we think happened is clouded by speculation and the repetition of "internet facts." We do not know what really transpired between the two lovers; except that it had a sad ending for both. I doubt that either Peter or Helen would have wished that their love for each other had never happened— better to have loved and lost than never to have loved and been loved.

Here is a paragraph from Kim Nielsen's book *The Radical Lives of Helen Keller* (2004) that is a nice summary of the affair with Peter Fagan:

. . . she [Helen Keller] and a finger-spelling fellow socialist, Peter Fagan, made secret plans to marry in November [1916] . . .

. . . Keller's biographer Dorothy Hermann argues that probable physical contact between the two occurred that went beyond hand-holding. Once learning of the secretly made plans to marry, Helen's extended family and Anne vigorously squashed the relationship with forced midnight train trips out of town, an angry gun-waving brother, and drama worthy of a bad novel. All felt adamantly that marriage and child-bearing were not options for a deaf-blind woman. With this pressure Helen apparently acquiesced . . . Peter Fagan disappeared from her life. Not only did her family and Anne hold eugenic fears about her possible reproduction and sexuality, but also many state laws prohibited women with disabilities from marriage and children.

Peter Fagan, the "fingerspelling socialist" was acting (in some versions of the story) as a temporary secretary for John Macy—others say that Fagan was hired to help Helen while Polly Thomson was away. Whatever the reason for Peter's presence at this moment in history, the result was a classic romance with a tragic Shakespearean ending.

The following was copied from an email exchange between movie director and actress Hillary Baack and Daniel Kish, which they have allowed me to share. Hillary had done more background research on the Keller-Fagan affair than I had; the relationship between Helen and Peter played a central role in her upcoming movie.

Hillary is explaining to Daniel how her movie project (called *Helen*) addressed the Keller-Fagan affair. Hillary is referring to a plan that Peter and Helen had hatched to meet up and then go off together—however, the rendezvous never happened:

> Everything leading up to the two missing each other was recorded, such as Kate [Helen's mother] taking Helen away from Peter on the train, while he took the boat, and including Warren, the brother-in-law, firing a gun at Peter. Horrifying, isn't it? I believe they also put an article in the paper about wanting to catch Peter if anyone saw him.
>
> Peter told his future daughters (he went on to marry and have four daughters) that he wrote Helen a letter that he would come wait for her in his car, and if he saw her on the porch, he would come get her. He was scared to go up to the door again, as he feared for his life. And he said that if she did not show up, he would assume she did not want to be with him, possibly understandable if he was going to be tearing her from her family.
>
> Helen said that she received a letter to meet him, and she went to wait for him on the porch with a packed bag, but Peter never came.
>
> They both thought the other one stood them up!

I had a mixture of emotions when the Fagan/Keller information unfolded for me. I read the above excerpt from Kim Nielsen's book and Hillary Baack's email with sadness. And I felt outrage that anyone should have interfered in a love affair between two sophisticated adults. Of course, it was 1916 and morality was a lot different then, as were attitudes and laws about disabilities, but Helen Keller was a brilliant and complex wunderkind. She would probably have birthed a brilliant poet-kid had she been allowed to procreate. The world would have lost the leadership of Helen Keller when she had to turn her attention to a husband (and maybe children), but it was her life, not ours. There is sadness in this story, sorrow, and bitterness.

I felt somewhat better when I read a comment in Anne Sullivan's biography that said Helen and Peter exchanged letters for a few months after the affair had been terminated; perhaps they had parted amiably and had sorted things out. As I said above, there are stories about this emotional drama that may have no basis in fact. Even what I reported here is questionable because several versions of the story exist, mixed with fictional accounts—we will never know for sure what happened; powerful emotions cloud the historical landscape.

∾

I was shocked when I read that American states had laws forbidding "handicapped" people from marrying and having kids. In a few decades after the Keller-Fagan affair, the Nazi regime in Germany would deliberately murder (in gas chambers, before firing squads, or using the guillotine) people who were not blue-eyed, blond-haired Nordic Aryans with perfect bodies. The Nazis murdered men, women, and children because these people were deaf, blind, physically impaired, emotionally impaired, alcoholic, or mentally ill. The same seeds of prejudice and hatefulness had taken root all over the world in the first half of the twentieth century—the Nazis were just the beasts who took the hatred to the nth degree. There is something nasty, unloving, spiritually unevolved and barren in the human being (especially, historically, the males); we have a lot of work to do as a species.

Walt Whitman, Henry David Thoreau, and Ralph Waldo Emerson

Midstream also contains a chapter about Helen's favorite authors. It becomes quickly clear that Helen Keller was extremely well read and that she met and had long dialogues with some of the best minds of her era. Her three favorite American authors were Walt Whitman, Henry

David Thoreau, and Ralph Waldo Emerson—Whitman was her favorite of the three. Of him, she wrote:

> The mystical predominates in him. That is why you get so near him. Many people miss him altogether because they lack that sense, you could set your net anywhere in Whitman and catch something worth taking home.

Helen comments that some people lack the mystical sense and so they miss what Whitman is about and misunderstand why he is revered. Not surprising, Whitman, Thoreau, and Emerson were influenced by Emanuel Swedenborg. This quote is from the Swedenborg House Online Blog:

> The leading American poet of the nineteenth century, Whitman was profoundly influenced by the work of Emerson. He was also influenced by Swedenborg who, he wrote, will probably 'make the deepest and broadest mark upon the religions of future ages here, of any man that ever walked the earth.' It has recently been argued that his [Whitman's] most famous work, *Leaves of Grass*, was deeply influenced by the doctrine of correspondences as expounded by Swedenborg.

The doctrine of correspondences is the first principle of esoterism—as above so below. As something manifests at one scale of space or time, so it also manifests at all other scales of space and time. The doctrine of correspondences is based on the physical reality of a spacetime fractal; everything is made of the same Lego bricks.

Thoreau is Helen's next favorite:

> When I read Thoreau, I am not conscious of him or the book or the words which flow under my fingertips, I am There. Through him Nature speaks without an interpreter. He puts his ear to her breast and hears her heartbeat; and she speaks to me in her own voice. I am part of the river, the lake, the field, the woods—I am spirit wild and free. I see everything for myself, no one interprets for me. I have the illusion of being free of my depravations—I live my life in my own way.

Here again we see that Helen Keller could sense and appreciate the outside world. She was at home in the woods and fields. She felt with her whole body what Thoreau was describing and she got the same emotional rush as any other sighted, hearing human being might. It is also important to note that Henry David Thoreau was in a reading group with Emerson in which they read Swedenborg, so Thoreau, too, was influenced by the esoteric musings of Emanuel Swedenborg.

Emerson is known as an American Transcendentalist, which is another way to say that he followed esoteric themes in his poems and essays. Transcendentalism was a reaction against the overly scientific enthusiasm of the Renaissance, which was turning science into a god (scientism) rather than a tool (a method, a process). Emerson, like Thoreau and Whitman, held true to esoteric principles, especially "as above so below" and "living nature," the universe as conscious. Emerson said of Swedenborg, he is "A colossal soul, he lies vast abroad on his times, comprehended by them, and requires a long focal distance to be seen." Emerson also wrote an essay called "Swedenborg, or the Mystic," which was published in his book *Representative Men* (1850).

Perhaps, Helen Keller ranked these three great Americans in the order in which they displayed their esoteric ideals. In her view, Whitman was the most mystical, most esoteric, most daring and challenging; he is found most often dancing on the edges of reality. Thoreau best exemplified a quiet esotericism, living close to the subtle vibrations that Helen knew so well. Emerson was, perhaps, the most pedantic and philosophical of the three; it is his esoteric intelligence (knowledge) that draws us to his great mind. Whitman's temperament was the most like Helen's; he mirrored her defiant, courageous essence—that was probably the major reason Whitman won her heart.

William James

An American who is somehow connected in my mind with Plato and Francis Bacon is Professor William James. When I was a little girl, he came to see Miss Sullivan and me at the Perkins Institution for the Blind in South Boston. He brought me a beautiful ostrich feather. "I thought," he said, "you would like the feather, it is soft and light and caressing." . . . He said then, and afterwards when I sent him a copy of *The World I*

Live In, that in our problems and processes of thought we do not greatly differ from one another. He was not surprised to find my world so much like that of everyone else, though he said he was "quite disconcerted, professionally speaking," by my account of myself before "my 'consciousness' was awakened by instruction."

Helen was a preteen when she first talked at length with Professor William James. From that first visit and from subsequent correspondance, she was able to give this analysis of the great man:

His thought was clear as crystal. His body, like his mind, was quick and alert. In argument his tongue was like a rapier, but he was always ready to listen to the other side, and always made me ashamed of my cocksureness about many things.

He was not a mystic—his mind could not thrive on air as mine does—but I think he was something of a poet as well as a philosopher.

That Helen Keller could so astutely read the aura of such a man as William James is astounding. She could read his greatness and his sharp intellect, just as she could see the essence of her friend Mark Twain. That James and Keller—two forces of nature—met and merged their souls is remarkable and wondrous. We wish we had the video replay of that first encounter—what a moment in history! There is also something symbolic and lovely in the gift of the ostrich feather.

I like best Helen's comment that "He was not a mystic—his mind could not thrive on air as mine does." Helen is very aware that she is a mystic, a woman who dwells in rarified air, a poet who knows another poet when she encounters one. Helen could perceive the poetic nature of William James vibrating beneath his enormous intellect.

James had come to meet Helen Keller not only because he was drawn to her essence, as so many others had been drawn to her, but James founded the field of psychology in the United States, his mission was to figure out how the human mind works. Helen Keller was an astounding opportunity, a living study for William James, a puzzle, a portal that could teach him about human cognition. James was on a quest to find a greater truth—something out there was waiting to be revealed, something hidden needed to be pulled from hiding.

In his quest for hidden knowledge, James became fascinated by paranormal activity; he was not afraid of esoteric speculations. James wondered what scientists and philosophers were missing—could there be energy systems which were not on the accepted list of senses or perceptions? When Helen said that she "thrived on air," she might have meant it literally. Perhaps, there is information in the atmosphere (in spaces, in space) that cannot normally be attained using vision and hearing. William James could almost smell this "something;" he was like a hound dog on a scent. Helen Keller, by her very existence, told humanity something critical about the human mind—but what was it? It must have been frustrating to be so close to a fundamental truth but not totally grasp it—or explain what was happening.

James corresponded with Carl Jung, the great esoteric psychoanalyst. Jung also wondered about energy that was below everyday consciousness. In 1925, Jung said of a dream, it "was the beginning of a conviction that the unconscious did not consist of inert material only, but that there was something living down there."

It is kind of creepy to sense/suppose that there might be a living entity thriving inside of us, slowly growing into a cosmically-supported consciousness. The German mystic and Goethe scholar Rudolf Steiner also envisioned consciousness as an outside energy system that attached itself to the human body during a lifetime. The American and European Transcendentalists held that the cosmos itself was alive—as I discussed in the section on esotericism in *The Esoteric Helen Keller*. There was a profound sense among some of the best minds of Helen Keller's generation that we were missing something fundamental in our effort to understand human cognition. In my opinion, *we are still* fumbling around some core truth.

James also defended Helen Keller's Faith-based worldview. His life was, in a broad way, a defense of Faith against the onslaught of materialism. William James knew that *Faith* (not traditional religion, not belief) was somehow critically important to human evolution and to everyday mental health. James also knew (he said as much) that his mind was somehow in tune with, and remarkably like Helen Keller's mind; in modern terms, the two great minds were surfing the same vibes. James could sense this sameness, but he could not explain it psychologically or scientifically. William James was obsessed with his quest to define "exceptional mental life." His mind was an example of "exceptionalness," and he could tell that Helen Keller's mind was also highly sophisticated and unusual.

Jung, another example of exceptionalness, said that unless duality was understood and embraced—he was speaking of conscious and unconscious—a human being was faced with mental illness. Whole cultures were also prone to mental illness when they did not have a grasp of the unconscious. Jung felt that wars, racial hatred, and all forms of brutality had their origin in the consciousness mind, which felt alone, without a sense of the unconscious. In my terminology, individuals who have no connection to the soul (to the Allocentric mind) are mentally unbalanced and prone to mental breakdowns. When a culture is filled with such soulless minds, then a whole culture can be hateful and destructive. I agree with Jung, as would Helen Keller if she were alive today. Helen was intimately in touch with her soul; she could "read" those who had yet to discover their souls within.

After their initial meeting, James and Keller exchanged letters until James' final illness and death in 1910. James also lectured at Radcliffe College, so he may have met Helen when she was a student there; they could have had further face-to-face discussions.

Below is a letter that William James sent to Helen in December of 1908, just two years before he died (age 68), and after her graduation. Radcliffe was associated with Harvard University, where James was a distinguished professor. Helen had evidently asked him about his views (edited for clarity):

> Dear Helen Keller, I thank you for answering my note. I have no explanation of the lack of emotional memory you speak of, and in general I am quite disconcerted, professionally speaking, by your account of yourself before your "consciousness" was awakened by instruction. But whatever you were or are, you're a blessing! It is no paradox that you live in a world so indistinguishable from ours . . . It makes no difference in what shape the content of our verbal material may come. In some it is more optical, in others more acoustical, in others more motor in nature. In you it is motor and tactile, but its functions are the same as ours; the relations meant by the words symbolizing the relations between the things.
>
> My wife sends back to you her love, and we both send you a Merry Christmas. Believe me Faithfully yours, Wm. James.

I had to edit this letter because there were several places where words or phrases were missing or unclear. However, there is enough insight in this short note to make it valuable. James had read Helen's books *The Story of my Life* and *The World I Live In*, so he was well versed in her circumstances. Helen had written that her earliest memories were entirely instinctual—she did not recall any emotions that were not completely associated with instinct.

James was disconcerted by Helen's description of her young self *as a phantom*; she held that without language she lacked something basic that defined humanity. James knew that human beings were a combination of instinct, emotion, intellect, and imagination; and he knew about embodiment (although he did not use that term): the elements of each mental ability are always embedded in a single body and within a domain. Helen may have felt like a phantom, especially on reflection, but James was telling her that her emotions were there, evolving alongside her other biological functions. In other words, just as her family had rebelled at her depicting herself as a phantom, so did William James disagree with her depiction; she was far more than just an instinctual animal, even as a young deaf-blind child.

In the above letter, James is also saying that there are innate abilities within Helen that are the same innate potentials inside all human beings. For example, Helen was hardwired at birth, like all of us, to eventually use language and to navigate through spaces. These innate potentials were not rendered mute by her loss of vision and hearing—she eventually developed sophisticated language and she could negotiate environments on her own through self-exploration and using spatial memory.

Descriptions of Helen Keller as a wild animal (before Anne Sullivan arrived) suggest that her instincts contained very primal *survival* emotions, especially the will to eat and to get her own way. Her basic needs—for food, shelter, clothing, cleanliness, protection, and companionship—were all being met by a loving and functional (healthy) family before Sullivan's arrival. Helen was born into privilege. She even had black servants to wait on her, to keep an eye on her wild-child movements and to clean up after one of her fits of rage.

However, before Anne Sullivan arrived, Helen's continually active, curious, starving-for-information mind was constantly bewildered and constantly searching for meaningful patterns—she was into everything like a modern two-year-old in a toy store. Helen's lack of discipline was the primary challenge for Sullivan after she arrived in Tuscumbia.

Sophisticated emotions develop over time and depend on the opportunity for experiences. Kate Keller's love for Helen, for example, was a sophisticated emotion, as was the love between teacher and pupil. Therefore, Helen was getting and receiving tenderness and firm guidance that would slowly shape her later ability to love, focus, and display empathy.

Human beings also have an innate "mirroring system" whereby the movements (behaviors) of others can be subconsciously copied. For example, children watch their parents and siblings and then mimic behaviors. Here is how psychologist Barbara Tversky put it in her book *Mind in Motion* (2019):

> Mirror neurons map other's bodies onto our own, allowing us
> to understand other bodies through our own and to coordinate
> our actions with others.

Emotions are also mirrored, including tone of voice, cadence, inflection, intensity, etc. In a way, we become the people we encounter as we are growing up. Only as adults do we begin to mold our own animation.

Helen's mirroring system was normal except that she had extraordinarily little to mirror—no voices and no visual image-patterns were available to her. However, this innate mirroring system was still functional in her biology. It is not clear how mirroring was accomplished without vision and hearing, but the mirroring system was not damaged after vision and hearing were lost—mirroring is as innate as the potential for language and navigation.

When I was researching the relationship between William James and Helen Keller, I came across a nice description of their relationship. Eugene Taylor had written an essay in 1981 in the Swedenborgian publication *Studia Swedenborgiana* (available online). Here are the first few paragraphs of that document:

> William James, philosopher-psychologist, psychical researcher,
> social activist, distinguished man of American letters; and
> Helen Adams Keller, deaf-blind author, lecturer, champion of
> the handicapped and oppressed, and emissary of world peace,
> met each other for the first time in the early 1890's at Perkins
> School for the Blind, when Helen was about eleven. Helen's
> "awakening" from the inner prison of a deaf-blind mute was

by then already well enough known that both she and her teacher, Anne Mansfield Sullivan, held the status of celebrities, rivaled only before that time by Samuel Gridley Howe's pupil, Laura Bridgman, whom Anne had known, conversed with, and studied before first meeting Helen. Helen and Anne's arrival in Boston was heralded by such greats as Oliver Wendell Holmes, John Greenleaf Whittier, Edward Everett Hale, and Phillips Brooks, all of whom quickly became Helen's friends.

James came to see Helen and her teacher at that same time, accompanied by W. E. B. DuBois, a fiery and rhetorical graduate student at Harvard who was soon to become a pioneer historian and sociologist of the Afro-American experience. A militant for Black equality and one of the founders of the NAACP, DuBois became a prominent early leader in the American civil rights movement. ~ "Studia Swedenborgiana," by Eugene Taylor, 1981.

The Helen Keller story has a new twist every other page, so it seems to this researcher. I had no idea Helen had met the remarkable William Edward DuBois. Nor did I know that DuBois was a student under William James. Years later DuBois would write these remarkable words:

When I was studying philosophy at Harvard under William James, we made an excursion one day out to Roxbury. We stopped at the Blind Asylum and saw a young girl who was blind and deaf and dumb, and yet who, by infinite pains and loving sympathy, had been made to speak without words and to understand without sounds. She was Helen Keller. Perhaps because she was blind to color differences in this world, I became intensely interested in her, and all through my life I have followed her career. Finally, there came the thing which I somehow sensed would come; Helen Keller was in her own state, Alabama, being feted and made much of by her fellow citizens. And yet courageously and frankly she spoke out on the iniquity and foolishness of the color line. It cost her something to speak. They wanted her to retract, but she sat serene in the consciousness of the truth that she had uttered. And so, it was proven, as I knew it would be, that this woman who sits in darkness has a spiritual insight clearer than that of many wide-eyed people who stare uncomprehendingly at this prejudiced world. ~ "Studia Swedenborgiana," by Eugene Taylor, 1981.

Helen Keller kept encountering one brilliant mind after another—before she was even a teenager. There are so many historical crosscurrents flowing through Helen Keller's life, it feels that only a well-written script could have conceived such a remarkable unfolding of synchronicities. I suppose it was a time in history when notoriety was rare enough that all the famous people in a culture could fit in the same small town.

The DuBois quote above is powerful, showing that Helen Keller impacted his important life. Maybe Helen contributed to the African American cause and DuBois' contributed to the cause of disability rights—I am stretching the point, of course, but these two remarkable people met and they both rocked American culture before they died. Great minds feed each other and who knows what can manifest from even short meetings.

William James went monthly (for many years) to a diner gathering where he would converse without obligation or pressure with close friends. Among those good friends were William Dean Howells and Oliver Wendell Holmes. Mark Twain was a part of this literary circle, as well. James had taken courses under Oliver Wendell Holmes and Holmes had presided over James's final oral examination. William James' father, Henry James Sr. was the premier American scholar on the life of Emanuel Swedenborg; this had a great influence on his remarkable children, including Henry James Jr. (the novelist), diarist Alice James, and Professor William James. In addition, both James and Keller were good friends with Alexander Graham Bell. Evidently, there was a soul-group swirling around Boston when Keller and James lived there. Meanwhile, James was also corresponding with Carl Jung about the nature of the human mind, and the human mind's curious duality.

Helen and Anne Sullivan also read books and articles by William James. They were especially impressed by his book *Talks to Teachers on Psychology* (1899), which Anne Sullivan read twice. James, like other older mentors (Alexander Graham Bell, John Hitz, Mark Twain) could see that Helen was a mysterious treasure—a "blessing" James called her. And given James' interest in the human mind, Helen Keller was a walking enigma that needed to be figured out. Probably because of Helen, James took an interest in deaf-blindness:

James, himself, remained profoundly attentive to the developments of Helen's career, both personally and professionally. In 1904, he published his article "Laura Bridgman" in the Atlantic Monthly, in which he devoted equal space to Helen Keller. Each age, he said, comes to see its own achievements as the epitome, or highest limit, of things possible; yet, that limit is always bested by some ensuing age. Such was the case of Laura Bridgman and Helen Keller, who followed her. Both were deprived of sight, hearing, and speech, while Laura lacked smell. Both learned to listen with all their other faculties, see through touch, and communicate not only their needs but also their ideas and feelings to the outside world. But, while Laura remained under institutional care, and moved about cautiously, as if a convalescent just arisen from a long stretch in bed, Helen traveled around the world twice, once when she was seventy. Laura spoke English by spelling with her fingers into an interpreter's hand. Helen learned French, German, Latin, Greek, and some Italian, in addition to English, and she not only learned to speak understandably, although deaf to her own sounds, but she also gave public lectures, performed on the Vaudeville circuit for a time, and occasionally sang. ~ "Studia Swedenborgiana," by Eugene Taylor, 1981.

Humm . . . so Helen Keller sang? I had not come across a reference to her singing until I saw this quote. There are references to a singing instructor, Charles White, working to improve her speech, and Helen had the opportunity to meet and "listen" to great singers. There is a YouTube clip showing Helen listening to Gladys Swarthout sing. William James might have been mistaken, although it would be like Helen to give singing a try. I have also seen references to Helen playing the piano and violin, followed soon after by references denying that she sang, played piano, or violin. Given Helen's try-anything-nature, I do not doubt she tried to sing, played a bit on the piano, and picked up a violin or felt one while someone played. Certainly, she did not sing often or play any instrument well enough to do repeat performances. I did come across one reference to her singing Auld Lang Syne on New Year's Eve.

James could see that Helen Keller not only had a "normal" mind; she also had a remarkably complex mind—not unlike his own genius cognition:

The processes of association and the richness of thought were the same in Helen as in any normal person, although her concentration more intense and her recall nearly total. Thus, "what clearer proof could we ask," he [William James] said, "of the fact that the relations among things, far more than the things themselves, are what is intellectually interesting, and that it makes little difference what terms we think in, so long as the relations maintain their character." ~ "Studia Swedenborgiana," by Eugene Taylor, 1981.

I was struck by James saying that Helen Keller's recall was nearly total. One mark of a prodigy is a prodigious memory. James also remarks in this quote on Helen's extraordinary ability to concentrate. Vision and hearing did not interfere with her innate attention system. What was it, we wonder, that was doing the concentrating? What was the sensory portal that Helen used to concentrate?

My own theory for the evolution of consciousness is very much in harmony with what William James is saying above. When I look at Helen's mind at work through the lens of her writing, I am struck by how normal she was on the surface, in everyday discourse. However, I am not at all surprised that her brain rewired itself to create a mind that went beyond merely "normal" to become mysteriously wonderful.

It was Helen Keller's mind that so amazed and puzzled the great William James. How can vision and hearing be totally wiped out and yet leave a normally operational mind? I like this quote below about James' fascination with "inner vision:"

James was, of course, referring to Helen's remarkable capacity for interior vision. While each of us interprets the external world by favoring different sensory modalities, it is clear that each one of us has a vast and unfathomable inner life. Exterior vision seems highly developed in most normal people, while *their potential for developing inner vision lies mostly dormant,* and may be awakened only under unusual circumstances, such as in Helen's case. ~ "Studia Swedenborgiana," by Eugene Taylor, 1981.

The italics above are mine. James makes an interesting suggestion: We all seem to use our exterior senses quite well, but our internal world (our inner vision) is often dormant, undeveloped, or unevolved. A powerful, disruptive calamity is often needed to turn on the inner light (jump-start the mind). James sounds like a modern developmental psychologist trying to explain levels of consciousness, suggesting why some people are more cognitively evolved than others and why trauma (shock) is often necessary to change worldviews.

John Macy

Helen also pays tribute in *Midstream* over several pages to her close friend John Macy, Anne Sullivan's husband:

> He was a great reader and an enthusiastic admirer of all that is beautiful in poetry and prose. Whenever in his own reading he found anything particularly interesting he read the passage to me.

John Macy introduced lengthy passages from William James' books as they were published. He read or had braille books made that allowed Helen to read Stevenson, Shakespeare, Shelley, H. G. Wells, Tolstoy, Hardy, Shaw, Anatole France, Karl Marx, and many others. Helen Keller might never have published so many beautifully written books had it not been for the expert and loving help of John Macy.

There was literary witchery, a magic that emerged during the years when Macy, Keller, and Sullivan collaborated. The articulate, astute writing style that we attribute to Helen Keller was deeply influenced by her contact with the unique, powerful writing styles of Anne Sullivan and John Macy.

John Macy was a brilliant student who became a brilliant professor at Harvard. He had been editor-in-chief of the *Harvard Advocate* and an editor of the *Harvard Lampoon*, showing that he had a refined sense of humor as well as a serious academic side. He was also chosen as class poet by his fellow students. Besides poetry, he wrote short stories, and he would go on to be an accomplished author of books. In historian Joseph Lash's book on Helen Keller (*Helen and Teacher*, 1980), Lash writes that John Macy "had won all sorts of prizes, for translations from the Latin and for an essay on Tolstoy's *Theory of Art* and had been elected to Phi Beta Kappa. He wrote well and knew the writer's craft."

In *Midstream*, Helen tried to capture her love and appreciation for John Macy. This quote is from Kim Nielsen's book *Beyond the Miracle Worker* (2009):

> Keller's introduction [to *Midstream*] expressed how keenly she still felt his [John Macy's] absence. "He was a friend, a brother, and an advisor all in one, and if this book is not what it should be, it is because I feel lonely and bewildered without his supporting hand." But his adulation went beyond the literary. She praised "his brotherly tenderness, his fine sensibilities, his keen sense of humor, and his curious combination of judicial severity, and smiling tolerance;" his "helpful kindnesses;" his "laughter that leaves the heart light and soothes the ruffled mind." "There are no words to tell," Keller wrote, "how dear he was to me or how much I loved him. Little incidents hardly noticed at the time but poignantly remembered afterwards crowd upon me as I write."

It is quite clear that Helen Keller loved and—we might cautiously suggest—was *in love* with John Macy. They were about the same age and fingerspelling meant that day-after-day they held each other's hands to enable communication. Powerful sensual, sexual, love-filled energies flow when two people hold hands. That kind of human contact—with all the attendant emotions—cannot he held in check. Emotions flow, there is no holding them back. Helen makes no excuses for her emotions; she says simply "I loved him." Helen Keller loved John Macy and he loved her. However, there is nothing in any record that suggests their affection went beyond handholding and genuine affection and respect.

But that is not the end of the emotional whirlwind. Helen Keller and Annie Sullivan loved each other for a lifetime. There were motherly, sisterly, teacher/student, sensual/sexual bonding energies swirling about as Helen and Anne held each other's hands every day for half a century. We have no facts to verify the extent of emotional bonding between the two legendary figures, but hand-to-hand bonding can become a special kind of relationship, especially if practiced every day for a lifetime.

Anne Sullivan also powerfully loved and was dedicated to her husband John Macy and he returned that love with equal intensity. They also frequently held hands, as lovers do, as husband and wife do. It is perfectly human to love more than one person—you just love them one at a time and with honest emotions (as honest as your character can muster).

It would be sweet to leave the reflection at this point—love swirling in a vortex around the threesome—but, unfortunately, the communal family experiment ended with irritation and bitterness. For reasons that will be forever obscure, the marriage between Macy and Sullivan slowly fell apart and finally ended, while the connection between Sullivan and Keller continued to flourish. John Macy's legacy is strongly tied to his politics and editorial skills—he was not just a friend and lover, not just an emotional force, he was also a brilliant thinker and a clear-headed writer.

John Macy was also a powerful guiding force in the development of Helen's early books. He was a fervent socialist and openly discussed his insights and passions. Helen makes it clear, however, that her own socialist views came about because of her own reading and her own values and not because of any influence from John Macy. Helen and John had lively discussions, they shared insights, they debated, and each influenced the other.

John Macy is often quoted as saying that he married an institution and that this eventually wore him down and caused the separation between he and Annie. Sullivan would not give him a divorce and held him dear for her entire lifetime. Despite John Macy's personal and interpersonal struggles, he loved both Annie and Helen deeply. Helen speaks kindly and affectionately of John in *Midstream*:

> I cannot enumerate the helpful kindness with which he smoothed our rugged paths of endeavor. Once, when my typewriter was out of order, he sat up all night, and typed forty pages of my manuscript, so that they might reach the press in time.
>
> Next to my teacher, he was the friend who discovered most ways to give me pleasure and gratify my intellectual curiosity. He kept me faithfully in touch with the chief happenings of the day, the discoveries of science, and the new trends in literature. If he was particularly pleased with a book, he would have Mr. John Hitz put it into Braille for me, or he would read it to me himself when he had time.

After his separation from Anne Sullivan, John Macy went on to be a successful writer. Just before he died in 1932 his book *About Women* was published. Anne and Helen got a copy of the book when they were in England and they both read it. Neither woman agreed with John's premise. Here is a paragraph from the book that suggests why the women reacted negatively:

> The discerning reader will perceive that the book is addressed to men. It is a slight prod to American men to bestir themselves and not allow the country, especially in its cultural and intellectual aspects, to be enfeebled by feminization.

John Macy was born into a male-dominated society where women had traditional places. Using levels of consciousness, we could say that John Macy was straddling the fence between the Traditional mind and the Modern mind. His book was very much his Traditional mind rebelling against the challenges of more Modern minds. In the Sullivan/Keller world, he stood face-to-face with extraordinarily strong female personalities. His wife Anne Sullivan was an independent powerhouse who, for a lifetime, defied male arrogance. Anne and John must have clashed repeatedly during the marriage years, especially if John had "old-fashioned" opinions about marriage and about the roles of husband and wife.

Essentially (and unfortunately), with his final book John Macy took his place in the patriarchy, lamenting how strong women have messed up the world. I like this summary sentence from Kim Nielsen's book *Beyond the Miracle Worker* (2009):

> In John's analysis, independent women destroyed marriage; in Annie's [analysis], marriage destroyed independent women.

Whatever side you wish to take, John Macy's last book hints at one reason why the marriage with Anne Sullivan could not last: he wanted to keep his male privileges while his two best friends were having none of that nonsense—he was living with two fiercely independent women who were in no way giving up their autonomy and convictions. John's views also suggest why Socialism and Communism turned out to be no better than the Capitalism he despised; all three economic theories still assumed that the male would stay on top of the hierarchy and run the show; these abstract theories were privileged old-white-boy isms.

I do not want to end this section about John Macy in a negative space. Let us remember that he was a highly skilled writer who impacted the writing styles of both Helen Keller and Anne Sullivan. He loved both these women as a friend, and he was one of the key individuals who helped shape the miracle and the miracle worker. Remember also that Helen was deaf-blind, and Anne was severely visually impaired; John Macy was living with two women who had extreme visual anomalies— he was constantly in the caregiver role. We do not know how much this wore him down over time. The household was also struggling financially during the years John lived with Helen and Anne. There were many forces that make the relationship complex and difficult to sustain. Whatever happened a century ago, let us remember John Macy as a sincere, complex, highly intelligent, and genuinely loving force in the lives of Helen Keller and Anne Sullivan.

Kate Adams Keller

My mother . . . succeeded in making me understand a great deal. I always knew when she wished me to bring her something, and I would run upstairs or anywhere else she indicated. Indeed, I owe to her loving wisdom all that was bright and good in my long night. ~ *The Story of my Life*, by Helen Keller, 1903.

As I read the available books about Helen Keller, it became clear to me that Kate Adams Keller, (1856–1921) Helen's mother, should have been buried alongside the three other heroes of this story. Helen Keller, Anne Sullivan, and Polly Thomson are buried side-by-side at the National Cathedral in Washington D.C.

As a teacher of blind students for three decades, I can say with complete conviction that the mothers of handicapped children are too often ignored by history, as well as in the everyday moments of a lifetime. It is almost inevitable that they are tragically under-appreciated, their sacrifices and sorrows sadly taken for granted. The toll on a mother's health is often extreme and her lifespan, because of the extreme stress of raising a child with severe impairments, can be shortened.

Kate Keller made Helen Keller possible. She birthed the prodigy; she lifted the deaf-blind toddler out of that near-death bed, and for the next four years she looked after Helen with love and devotion—all this before Anne Sullivan showed up. Kate did not give up on her child for a lifetime, and she was ultimately responsible for getting Anne Sullivan hired.

Every child with an impairment thrives or not depending on the support system of the family and community. It is not just the mother, of course, although mothers tend to be forced into the role as the center of organization and energy in a family. Yet, without the mother's love, constant attention, and heroic dedication and determination, there would be no famous children for us to be in awe about. Without Kate Keller's heroic determination, Helen Keller would have been put in an institution for the mentally impaired in Alabama and she would never have been heard from again. That is a truth that sends shivers of horror through the universe. And the screams that I hear from history are from all the poets and potential geniuses *who were locked away* (for a lifetime) in asylums, never to be appreciated or praised for their humanity and abilities.

In her biography of Anne Sullivan, Nella Braddy wrote the following about Kate Keller:

> The chances are that the mother of a deaf-blind child today would know what to do or would write to Helen Keller and find out, but in those days comparatively few people knew, especially people who lived in remote villages in the war-stricken South. The young woman [Kate Keller] saw no way out. Day after day she watched the child slipping from her, yet trying, even as she herself was trying, desperately, to hold on to the few strands of communication left them. What Mrs. Keller went through during those years is something the mind shrinks from contemplating.

I know from my association with *World Access for the Blind* that in the poorest regions of the world and in developing nations, services for any kind of disability are limited. And there is no Helen Keller or Anne Sullivan to contact. The more severe the impairment, the less chance there is for services to be available. Women, children, and especially women and children with disabilities are still in dire straits in the developing world as I write this. In many ways, the world is better than it was when Helen Keller lived, but the problems faced by disabled people are still unresolved in most places on the planet.

That Helen Keller did not end up in a mental institution is itself a miracle. Kate Keller's early decisions made all the difference for her little daughter:

Kate Keller was a voluminous reader, and she found in (Charles) Dickens' *American Notes* an account of his visit to deaf-blind Laura Bridgman. It had happened a long time before—forty years—and Dr. Howe and Laura Bridgman might even be dead, for all she knew. Kate asked a man from Boston who came through Tuscumbia selling harnesses if he had ever heard of a school called the Perkins Institution. He hadn't, but he promised to ask. ~ *Anne Sullivan Macy: The Story behind Helen Keller, by Nella Braddy, 1933.*

Kate Keller got the news that the Perkins School for the Blind was still open and that they were still training deaf-blind children. Remarkably, Laura Bridgeman was also still alive (Dr. Howe had passed), and she was still residing at Perkins. This good news resulted in Kate and her husband Arthur Keller looking in the direction of Boston for a solution to Helen's isolation. Arthur soon wrote to the Perkins Institute to inquire about Helen's education. "Before they wrote to the Perkins Institution, they went to an eminent oculist in Baltimore. He told them that Helen would never see or hear again and suggested that they ask Dr. Alexander Graham Bell about the best way to begin her education. Accordingly, they took Helen to Washington D.C. to see Dr. Bell."

At the age of six, through the efforts of Kate and Arthur Keller, Helen meet Alexander Graham Bell who was a champion for the rights of the deaf (his wife was deaf, and his inventions were at first meant for the deaf). Dr. Bell was instrumental in getting Helen Keller into Perkins. After a long process, Michael Anagnos, director of the Perkins School agreed to take on Helen's education. It was Anagnos who asked Anne Sullivan to travel to Alabama to begin the initial at-home training. In her book *The Radical Lives of Helen Keller*, Professor Kim Nielsen describes the beginning of Helen's educational journey:

Keller's first step toward our shared cultural memories came when Alexander Graham Bell first heard of the six-and-a-half-year-old child in 1886 . . . Responding to a letter from Helen's mother Kate, Bell already famous as an inventor of the telephone and as an educator of deaf people, met with Helen, her mother, and her father Captain Arthur H. Keller. He forwarded them to Boston's Perkins School for the Blind and its director Michael Anagnos. But Bell remained, in Keller's characterization, "a wise, affectionate, and understanding friend" until the end of his life. She vacationed with the Bell family and considered him a father figure. He always, she said, "considered me a capable human being, and not some sort of pitiable human ghost groping its way through the world."

When Bell first met Helen, he was stunned at the presence and grace of the little girl. He was so amazed and impressed that he took Helen under his wing and watched over her for the rest of his life. Kate Keller made this union happen. It was Kate Keller's resolve, her intentions, and her energy that opened the door for all that eventually happened in Helen Keller's life. Kate Keller set the miracle in motion and she pushed it along until momentum took over. It was also Kate Keller who met Anne Sullivan on the day Sullivan stepped off the train in Tuscumbia, Alabama.

After a dreadful train ride from Massachusetts to Alabama, Anne Sullivan arrived at the station in Tuscumbia to meet the Keller family. Her memories of that first meeting are preserved in records stored in the digital archives at the Perkins Institute and at the American Foundation for the Blind's Helen Keller Archives. Sullivan's amazing letters are also preserved in the book *The Story of My Life* (1903). Sullivan was "surprised to find Mrs. Keller so young looking"—not much older than herself . . ."When she [Kate Keller] spoke, a great weight rolled off my heart, there was so much sweetness and refinement in her voice."

Kate Keller and Anne Sullivan were remarkably young when they first met. Kate had been born in 1856 in Arkansas and Anne had been born in 1866 in Massachusetts—only ten years separated them. We can imagine their first encounter. They looked at each other at that train station and something magic happened, a bonding, a silent agreement was forged, an intention to do what must be done to save the soul of a little girl. From that first encounter, Anne and Kate forged a friendship that would endure for decades until death separated them (Kate died in 1921, Anne died in 1936). The bond between Sullivan and Kate Keller was unusual because Kate was suffering from a grief that would consume her for the rest of her life—the grief of caring for a damaged child who she deeply loved. Anne must have read this grief from their very first meeting, at that train station.

In the chapter about her mother in *Midstream*, Helen writes:

. . . when she was twenty-three came the illness, which left me deaf and blind, and after that life was never the same to her. It was as if a white winter had swept over the June of her youth . . . Her nature was not expansive or happy. She made few close friends, and wherever she sojourned, the sorrow and loneliness of her spirit persisted. The larger opportunities for enjoyment and intellectual enrichment which she gained on her journeys with us or her visits in our home at Wrentham did not erase from her heart the sense of tragedy and denial which my limitations kept always before her. That her suffering was crushed into silence did not lessen its intensity. But there was nothing selfish in her sorrow. What she had suffered broadened and deepened her sympathy for others.

That last sentence is a lovely sentiment and a tribute to her mother. Kate's grief did not destroy her spirit, it enabled a greater empathy for others. However, what is most remarkable about the above quote (for me) is that Helen Keller could read her mother's injured personality so finely. She must also, in her own way, have nurtured her mother from time to time. Mother and daughter nurtured each other as emotional tides ebbed and flowed. Also embedded in that quote is a child's awareness that her impairment impacted her mother. I suppose it is not unusual for any child to remember all the ways they have brought grief or conflict into the lives of their parents. However, when the child's disabilities are severe, the grief and conflict are often magnified. It takes a heroic effort, over decades, to forgive oneself, to forgive God, to forgive all those who doubted a tiny soul trying to emerge. Part of Helen Keller's mythology, the core of her hero's journey, is forgiveness, her unceasing dedication to love, and the use of service, a mission, to face grief and shame and, after all the struggles, to heroically live a quality (normal) life. Kate Keller set the stage for Helen's solid and steadfast personality to blossom.

Kate was quite a brilliant and articulate woman; this gift positively impacted Helen as she was growing up in Tuscumbia. Anne Sullivan left us glimpses of Kate's brilliance:

. . . Annie described Kate Keller as a "very tall, beautifully formed woman." Though she was "reticent" and "aloof," Sullivan admired her "delicate poise" and admitted that she "awkwardly tried to imitate" this woman . . . she admired the older woman's

"intellectual side" and remembered that "a discussion with
Mrs. Keller was a test of one's metal [sic]." Helen's mother read
widely and loved to discuss books. She shared Carlyle, Thomas
Hardy, and the poems of Byron . . . She loved politics, was "an
ardent suffragist," and had "to an unusual degree the gift of
swift rejoinder and vivid phrase." ~ *Anne Sullivan Macy: The
Story behind Helen Keller, by Nella Braddy, 1933.*

We can begin to see, from the above quote, why Helen Keller became
such an exquisite writer and thinker; her two most powerful female
influences were Kate Keller and Anne Sullivan, two brilliant and
articulate role models.

Fathers of handicapped children also suffer, of course, as do siblings,
grandparents, close friends, and relatives. No one thinks or even has the
inclination to write the biographies of these critically important people.
Although the bulk of exhausting daily demands and the overwhelming
emotional traumas that accompany childhood afflictions fall especially
on the mother, the father's pain should never be ignored—it seems
as if the story of paternal pain is more deeply hidden in history than
that of the mother's, at least, as in this case, the mother is occasionally
acknowledged and applauded.

Helen's father, Arthur Keller, was a lawyer and a newspaper editor.
He was called Captain Keller after his years of service in the Civil War.
From his first wife, he had two sons and with Kate he had two daughters
and a son, Helen, Mildred, and Phillips. In August 1896, Helen Keller's
father died and with him died all the emotions that he struggled with—
from the moment he realized that his little daughter was deaf and
blind to the arrival of the spitfire Anne Sullivan into his house. His
perspective is mostly lost to history. Anne Sullivan did write about the
Keller family and she left some reflections on Helen's father:

Captain Keller she considered a "good-natured man, fond of
fishing and hunting, a good shot, an agreeable companion" and
"one of the best story-tellers" she had ever heard. He was liked,
she believed, "for his neighborliness and geniality." He was
"hospitable rather than intellectual," and "thought everything
southern desirable, noble and eternal." Though she considered
his "ideas and abilities to be "ordinary," the family must have
enjoyed verbal repartee. During a household argument over

Tolstoy's *My Religion*, his wife once compared his logic to "playing leap-frog blindfolded." ~ *Anne Sullivan Macy: The Story behind Helen Keller, by Nella Braddy, 1933.*

I wonder if Helen's linguistic ability came partly from listening to her father's storytelling—or from a genetic predisposition to verbal prowess. It is also interesting that she named her own foray into religious writing *My Religion* (1927).

Helen was just 16 when her father died, so, unfortunately, Captain Keller did not get to share in her legendary rise to glory. However, he was instrumental through his correspondance in getting Helen accepted at the Perkins School for the Blind. Here is a letter to Captain Keller written on January 21, 1887 (available online through the Perkin's digital collection) in which the director of the Perkins School for the Blind (Michael Anagnos) introduces Anne Sullivan as a possible teacher for Helen:

My Dear Sir,

I can recommend to you a young lady as governess of your little daughter and without any reservation. Her name is Miss Annie M. Sullivan. She is one of the recent graduates of this school: but her sight has been for several years steadily improving, so that she is now able to read and write. She is exceedingly intelligent, strictly honest, industrious, lady-like in her manner and very amiable. Her moral character is all that can be desired. The valedictory address which she composed and delivered at the commencement exercises of this institution last June, and which you will find in the 125th page of our annual report, will give you some idea of her literary ability. She is familiar with Laura Bridgman's case and with the methods of teaching deaf-mute and blind children, and I assure you, that she will make an excellent instructress and most reliable guide for your young daughter. If you wish to employ the services of Miss Sullivan, please let me know the terms which you are disposed to offer and oblige.

Yours very sincerely,
M. Anagnos ~ Perkins School for the Blind Helen Keller Digital Archives.

This is an exceedingly kind and powerful endorsement of Anne Sullivan, although I laughed when I read Anagnos' comment that Anne Sullivan was lady-like! I suppose she knew how to behave as she was watched by others, but there was a fire in her that was powerfully not "lady-like." I have quoted from Sullivan's valedictory address in the Timeline for the date 1886.

Michael Anagnos made a brilliant decision to send Anne Sullivan to work with Helen Keller. After Sullivan had been in Tuscumbia for several months, Anagnos praised her work with Helen in a report to the Perkin's Board of Directors:

> What the little pupil has thus far accomplished is widely known, and her wonderful attainments command general admiration; but only those familiar with the particulars of the grand achievement know that the credit is largely due to the intelligence, wisdom, unremitting perseverance and unbending will of the instructress [Annie Sullivan], who rescued the child from the depths of everlasting night and stillness, and watched over the different phases of her mental and moral development with maternal solicitude and enthusiastic devotion. ~ Perkins School for the Blind Helen Keller Digital Archives.

There would later be a falling out between Anne Sullivan and Michael Anagnos, but history needs to be clear that it was his decision to select Anne Sullivan to be the miracle worker, and it was his enthusiasm and leadership that allowed the teacher full rein as she went about her seemingly impossible task of "rescuing the soul of a deaf-blind girl." Of course, Helen Keller had a sophisticated, healthy soul because her mother made that happen. Kate believed in her daughter and she helped Helen to blossom long before Sullivans arrival.

Mary Agnes (Polly) Thomson

Helen Keller and Anne Sullivan became so loved and admired that few people realize that Helen Keller lived 32 years after Annie Sullivan's death (Sullivan died October 20, 1936 in Forest Hills, New York). After Sullivan's passing, Helen traveled the world on behalf of the American Foundation for the Blind, advocating globally for the blind, meeting heads of state, and tirelessly fundraising. All the while, she continued to write in her eloquent prose, in books, magazines, and newspapers. All this would not have been possible without the dedication, hard work, and love of Polly Thomson, who picked up where Annie Sullivan left off. In her Journal (1938), Helen wrote of Polly:

> She is fearless, observant, eager to give me my share of educative, even hazardous experiences. ~ *Anne Sullivan Macy, The Story Behind Helen Keller*, by Nella Braddy, 1933

She wrote the above words on November 20th, 1938 in England on the day she and Polly went down a mine shaft into a coal mining operation. They each took a turn blowing up dynamite, "firing a shot" the miners called it.

In 1946, Helen and Polly began an around-the-world promotional tour sponsored by the American Foundation for the Blind's international division. They would travel seven times between 1946 and 1957, visiting 35 countries on five continents. Helen was 75 when she and Polly toured Asia.

Mary Agnes Thomson was born in Glasgow, Scotland and came to the United States in 1913. She was hired by Anne Sullivan Macy as a secretarial assistant and housekeeper in 1914. Polly was beside Helen Keller for the next 46 years. She translated for Helen and was her secretary and great friend for 24 years after Sullivan's death. Polly, Annie, and Helen were best friends, and they are buried side-by-side at the National Cathedral in Washington D. C. Anne Sullivan wrote about Polly in Sullivan's biography *Anne Sullivan Macy, The Story Behind Helen Keller*:

> [Polly] was a young woman from Scotland seeking a foothold in America. She had not heard of Helen and knew nothing of the manual alphabet or the needs of the blind and the deaf, but she was eager and quick to learn. She was as strong as the granite hills of her native country and had strength of character to match this splendid physique. She had deep emotional capacity with the emotions under steady control. She was not in any sense literary, no slight advantage in an already too literary household, but she could balance a bank account (no one at Wrentham had ever been able to do this) and she could read a

timetable without the help of a ticket agent. She could map out a vigorous cross-country schedule and keep it. She could manage a household, doing the cooking herself if it was necessary, and yet be the most gracious of hostesses. And she could stand a firm and uncompromising guard over a doorbell or a telephone, which was something else no one at Wrentham had ever been able to do. She learned to lead Helen and her teacher through the spasms of traffic without asking favors of policemen, learned to fit herself in with their plans and ambitions. When there was no money, she was willing to work without money. She came to the two women at a time when they needed her, and as the years have passed the need was deepened. She is today the right hand of the household; ears for Helen and eyes for both of them, an absolute necessity for their health and comfort and happiness. For more than forty years the friends of Mrs. Macy and Helen have wondered what they would do without each other. Now they wonder what either one of them would do without Polly Thomson.

That is quite a loving statement flowing from Sullivan's eloquent mind. You cannot help but bond with Polly Thomson after reading that tribute. A few things stand out in the above paragraph. That Polly would work for nothing means she was dedicated and resilient—her character was not deterred during the lean years. The paragraph also shows us that there were times when the money ran out for the three women. There were mentors, like Andrew Carnegie, Mark Twain, and Alexander Graham Bell who sent the women money, and publication funds trickled in when Helen sold an article, but the income was unsteady for the women until Helen and Anne went to work for the American Foundation for the Blind in 1924.

The three women were together in Scotland when Sullivan's health began to seriously decline (1930s). Polly's birth country, Scotland, became important a few years after that visit to Glasgow when Helen and Polly went there to grieve Sullivan's death (1936). Also, it is clear from the above quote that Polly was intensely caring for both Helen and Anne through periodic hard times. In a way, Polly Thomson was the center of organizational energy that allowed Helen and Anne to be creative, without their having to attend to the everyday challenges of life.

Helen and Polly never forgot the legacy of Anne Sullivan Macy. They carried her light from country to country, carrying on the work that Anne Sullivan had begun. Everywhere they went in the world, Sullivan was praised and eulogized, as this quote shows:

> . . . Polly and I spent an exquisite, tearful hour of joy at the Mexican Institute of Hearing and Speech. When we entered the hall, I touched the name "Anne Sullivan" carved on the wall. Then followed beautiful speeches about her work, and I felt my teacher very close indeed. With emotion that almost choked utterance I thanked the teachers for recognizing the source from which I had drawn my strength. Thus, it is that Teacher ever journeys with me to all places where new tests are laid upon me, and after all the years, still shares with me the joys "which mingled sense and spirit yield."

Given Helen's spiritual faith, she was probably quite serious when she says that Anne Sullivan journeyed with her and Polly on their adventures. When Helen says that she senses Sullivan's presence, we cannot dismiss this as wishful thinking. The more we discover about the power and strangeness of human consciousness, the more we become open and receptive to the esoteric universe.

From 1960 to 1968, after Polly Thomson had died, Winnie Corbally, a nurse, stepped in to care for Helen. Helen's health was failing over this period, she had a series of strokes, the first in 1961, and she was unable to continue her strenuous schedule. Winnie kept close contact with Helen's family, and she was the right person to be by Helen's side in the final years.

Nella Braddy Henney

I deeply appreciate Anne Sullivan's friend and biographer Nella Braddy. Braddy is articulate, fun to read, always filling in wonderful details that would have been lost to history had she not taken the time to record the lives of Keller and Sullivan. When Nella Braddy died, she left her records to the Perkins School for the Blind. These records have been digitized and are available online. The quote below was taken from the Perkins archives:

Nella Braddy Henney first met Anne Sullivan, Helen Keller, and Polly Thomson in 1924, when she came to the Sullivan-Keller-Thomson household to write Sullivan's biography *Anne Sullivan Macy: The Story Behind Helen Keller* (1933). Quickly mastering the manual finger language, she kept Keller in touch with the political, literary, and scientific world around her. She remained in Keller's life, as a friend, and also as Keller's power of attorney, acting agent for all Keller's literary matters, until 1963. She was married to Keith Henney, also a writer and editor, as well as a photographer who took many photographs of Helen Keller. Nella Braddy Henney died in 1973. ~ Perkins School for the Blind Helen Keller Digital Archives.

Keith Henney is also an important person in Helen Keller's history. He documented the life of Keller-Sullivan-Thomson in his photographs, many of which survive in the digital archives at Perkins and in the American Foundation for the Blind Helen Keller digital collection. Keith Henney has preserved for history pictorial treasures that become more valuable as each year passes.

In her biography *Anne Sullivan Macy, The Story Behind Helen Keller* (1933), Nella Braddy lists the people who helped with the book. This list is a remarkable rendering of the friends who surrounded and nurtured Helen, Annie, and Polly—it is worth a careful reading. Helen Keller can, of course, stand on her own with the force of her writing, speeches, and accomplishments, but she would never have become a planetary treasure had she not had the right family, the right teachers at Perkins and elsewhere, financial backing from the likes of Andrew Carnegie and Alexander Graham Bell, and lifelong friends like Nella Braddy herself.

As Sullivan's eyesight dwindled, there were times when she was unable to function as Helen's connection to the world. Helen wrote that "we were stymied, and a terrifying silence fell upon us." In *Teacher* (1955), she recounts how Nella Braddy came into their lives and rescued them from the "terrifying silence."

Fortunately, our gracious friend Mr. F. N. Doubleday came to our rescue and commissioned Nella Braddy . . . to serve as eyes for Teacher and me. From that memorable day to the present her rare, precious friendship had been as a benediction upon our lives.

As I read Nelly Braddy's words, I became aware of her remarkable writing skills. Braddy intimately knew Sullivan and Keller. As a result of this friendship, there is an emotional power to Sullivan's biography that highlights not only Anne Sullivan and Helen Keller, but also shows us how remarkable Nella Braddy was herself. Braddy's biography of Anne Sullivan is a precious work of art.

Deaf-Blind Friends: Laura Bridgman and Berthe Galeron

> Just one special "fact" existed to bridge the chasm between mankind and me—the education of Laura Bridgman, the first deaf-blind person ever to be taught to communicate with her fellow creatures. ~ *Teacher*, by Helen Keller, 1955.

Any report of the life of Helen Keller is lacking without honoring and marveling at the life of deaf-blind Laura Bridgman and her mentor and teacher Dr. Samuel Gridley Howe. Howe was the founder of the Perkins Institute and was the teacher who showed the world that deaf-blind people could develop language. Laura Bridgman and Samuel Gridley Howe built the foundation upon which Sullivan and Keller could stand in their battle against silence. Here is how William James, the Father of American Psychology put it:

> And if the ruddier pages which record Helen's exploits make the good Laura's image seem just a little anemic by contrast, we cannot forget that there never could have been a Helen Keller if there had not been a Laura Bridgman. ~ Laura Bridgman, Atlantic Monthly, Volume 93, 1904.

As the first deaf-blind person to reach the public eye in the United States, Laura Bridgman's own story is powerful and poignant. She was deeply religious and quite intelligent, even though, because she was first, her training did not unlock her full potential as it did later for Helen Keller. Laura's biographer Ernest Freeberg wrote of Bridgman's fame:

> The story of her accomplishment had been retold countless times, in newspapers, literary and theological journals, children's books, and most often in writings and speeches by Dr. Howe himself.

Fascinated by this state of intellectual resurrection, tourists flocked to the Perkins School to take a look for themselves. Each Saturday hundreds jammed into the school's exhibition hall to see Laura read, write, and talk with a manual alphabet. Many clamored for a souvenir—an autograph or a piece of knitting—made by Laura's own hand. By mid-century, Howe boasted that his student had become one of the most famous women in the world, second only to Queen Victoria. ~ *The Education of Laura Bridgman*, by Ernest Freeberg, 2001.

This sounds like the same rhetoric used to praise the life of Helen Keller, and no doubt it is well deserved. Laura Bridgman and Samuel Howe are the link between miracles past and miracles present. Helen and Laura were alike in many ways. They are among the rare few who have known total silence and total darkness; and they taught us about the experience. One characteristic stands out in both lives: From within their isolation, Helen and Laura shared a common hunger for spirituality, they wanted to know what was hidden from everyday humanity.

Like Helen Keller, Laura Bridgman struggled with religion at the same time as she embraced spirituality. For a deaf-blind child to suddenly get the message, slowly spelled into the hand, that there was a supreme almighty Father, who created everything and was in control of everything, was a puzzling shock. Both Helen and Laura asked simple, childlike questions. Whereas Helen wanted to know where Jesus went to school and who his teachers were, Laura asked:

"Why doesn't God want you in heaven now?"

"How do we know that God lives in heaven?"

"What is heaven made of? Wood or iron?"

"Does heaven have a door?"

"Does he know what you teach me?"

"Does he know what I think?"

"Why does he not love wrong people if they love him?"

"Why did God make troublesome mosquitoes?"

"Why did God make some people black?"

After a rain washed out an expedition that Laura had been looking forward to, she commented that "God was very unkind to make it rain, He knew we wanted to go."

I find these questions to be remarkable. And the answers are still awaiting a reply that is satisfying to the intellect. Laura might have found Swedenborg's spirituality helpful had she encountered his writing. However, the age difference was too great between Helen and Laura; we have no record of their communication about religion.

We do know that Helen Keller and Laura Bridgman were friends. *In Midstream*, Helen wrote:

> I remember Laura well. My interest in her began almost with my first word. My teacher knew her intimately. She had lived in the same cottage with her at Perkins Institution; and it was Laura who taught her the manual alphabet. Miss Sullivan has told me how excited Laura was when she learned her friend was going to Alabama to teach a blind deaf child. She had much advice to give as to my training. She admonished Miss Sullivan not to spoil me by letting me become disobedient. She made the clothes for a doll which the blind girls at the Institution sent me, and this doll was the subject selected for my first word. She wrote to Miss Sullivan in the early days of my education.

Looking at the emotions and intelligence of Laura Bridgman helps us put Helen Keller in better perspective. History tends to portray Helen as a miracle. Yet a quick review of deaf-blind individuals like Laura Bridgman and Oliver Caswell, two Perkin's alumni, reveals that intelligence and potential are recoverable in most cognitively normal deaf-blind people. Speaking of one young deaf-blind girl, Keller writes "Helen Schulz is another deaf-blind girl who proves that the spirit can sing in spite of limitations."

Helen Keller knew that this population was underserved and underappreciated. All through her career, Helen fought for the rights and needs of people like Laura and herself. In addition to the cause of the blind, the deaf, people with disabilities, and on behalf of those stuck in poverty and ignorance, it was the deaf-blind population that Helen understood best, and the public understood least. Helen Keller knew that deaf-blind people were in a desperate plight, and none had Anne Sullivan by their side.

In *Midstream*, Helen wrote about deaf-blindness:

> Perhaps it is impossible for one who sees and hears to realize what it means to be both deaf and dumb. Ours is not the stillness which soothes the weary senses; it is an inhuman silence which

severs and estranges. It is a silence not to be broken by a word of greeting, or the song of birds, or the sigh of a breeze. It is a silence which isolates cruelly, completely. Two hundred years ago there was not a ray of hope for us. In an indifferent world not one voice was lifted in our behalf.

Benevolent and determined voices eventually did stand up to help. Although history duly records how Helen Keller championed the cause of people who were blind, it is not as well known that Helen Keller, Anne Sullivan, and Polly Thomson were equally champions for the cause of the deaf and the deaf-blind. Work on behalf of the deaf was overshadowed in history because Keller, Sullivan, and Thomson were employed by the American Foundation for the Blind (AFB). From 1924 until her health declined in the 1960s, Keller traveled the globe on behalf of the American Foundation for the Blind; the Foundation was their livelihood, their major source of income. However, whenever they were sent on tours on behalf of the blind and AFB, they also crusaded on behalf of deaf people and deaf-blind people.

An entire chapter in *Midstream*, called "Muted Strings," is dedicated to the deaf-blind friends whom Helen Keller corresponded with during her lifetime. Thanks to this chapter on deaf-blindness, we get a much greater awareness of other remarkable deaf-blind individuals. For example, in France, deaf-blind Berthe Galeron wrote a book called *Dans ma Nuit (In my Night)*; numerous books and articles were written about Galeron in French. Berthe Galeron also wrote poetry and shared her poems with Helen. For over twenty years, Helen communicated with Berthe. Helen says of her that "of all the deaf-blind people I have known the one closest to me in temperament and sympathy of ideas is Madame Berthe Galeron. . . ." Berthe had read Helen's *The Story of My Life* and had contacted her soon after finishing the book. Speaking of their similarity, Helen wrote in *Midstream*:

We both find our chief delight and freedom in books. We both feel the impediment of deafness far more keenly than that of blindness. Both our lives have been made beautiful with affection and friendship. As my teacher is ever by my side, making the way straight before me, so has Monsieur Galeron watched over his wife for thirty years, guarding her against every hardship.

In the above quote, we find Helen Keller stating clearly that it is deafness that is the most difficult (emotional) disability, greater than the blindness that the media and public focus on. Isolation from the nuance and emotion of spoken language is devastating. Not being able to see images, especially faces, is harsh, but it does not have the sad impact of silence.

In Australia, there was another remarkable deaf-blind woman Alice Mary Betteridge Chapman (1901–1966), known as the first deaf-blind child to be educated in that country. Alice, like Helen, became blind around the age of two from suspected meningitis. She attended the Institution for the Deaf and Dumb and Blind from the age of seven (1904).

Alice had her own miracle worker, a teacher, Roberta Reid, who used fingerspelling to teach language to the young girl. A breakthrough, an Aha! Moment came when Reid spelled the word "shoe" while placing a shoe in Alice's hand. Just like Helen, Alice progressed quickly after the breakthrough, and soon began reading braille. Alice graduated in 1920 and remained at her school as a teacher for nine years. In 1939, Alice married Will Chapman, who was also deaf-blind. The couple lived together in Melbourne.

From these few examples, we can see that Helen Keller is not an isolated anomaly; many remarkable deaf-blind individuals were alive in her lifetime:

> Toward the end of her life, in the early 1930s, Anne Sullivan learned of a neglected deaf-blind baby born in Louisville, Kentucky. Something kindled in her heart and soul and she became determined to adopt the child and begin again to breathe life into a phantom.
>
> . . . the thought of imparting light and the music of joy to the little one went through her as if a flame of immortal youth had entered her tired body. It was only after many an unwilling argument that we who knew of her failing health induced her to give up the idea of adopting the baby. But her darkness throbbed with the hidden fire of that longing, and she would often remind me of the deaf-blind throughout the world waiting for deliverance. "Hold out your arms to them, forget yourself in them, and be faithful to their cause. That will be your true memorial to me, Helen. There may be a wall between

you and them, but hammer it down, stone by stone, even if you are broken by the effort, just as some of Florence Nightingale's nurses died of exhaustion." ~ *Teacher*, by Helen Keller, 1955.

In the quote above, we can see the emotional temperament of Keller and Sullivan interacting; here is their sentiment in the face of darkness and silence:

Hammer it down, stone by stone, even if you are broken by the effort.

We Bereaved (Peace at Eventide)

We Bereaved is a collection of short reflections on bereavement. It is meant to comfort those who suffer from loss. Here is the first comment from page one:

We bereaved are not alone. We belong to the largest company in all the world—the company of those who have known suffering. When it seems that our sorrow is too great to be borne, let us think of the great family of the heavy-hearted into which our grief has given us entrance, and, inevitably, we will feel about us their arms, their sympathy, their understanding.

The quote above is very Buddhist in nature: suffering is the lot of everyone born on earth. There is no escape from suffering unless a spiritual journey is undertaken. Helen found the same message within her Christian belief that Buddhists proclaimed in their teaching. Helen's religious beliefs and assumptions are the backbone of *We Bereaved*. We can also enjoy her wonderful, uplifting, and always positive writing style at work—here is an example:

In the first dark hours of our grief there is no comfort in all the world for us. The anxious efforts of our friends to console us seem an intrusion, "Leave us alone," we cry in our hearts; "leave us alone with our sorrow. That is the only precious thing left to us." But when our friends depart how quickly we change, how we creep to the side of some trusted loved one and reach out wistful hands for affection and understanding. Life is like that. Bereaved though we are, we are not ghosts, but living, breathing human beings, vibrant and eager for contact with our kind. And that is as it should be. God has taken away the beloved and left us here for some purpose. There is work to be done and people to be loved and helped. No normal human being can live with shadows.

Helen's advice is clear: Suffering, loss, death, and grief are inescapable during a human lifetime, yet if we breathe still, we must continue to take care of ourselves and others. We still have a purpose in life so long as our own life endures. There is always more work to be done. Helen would tell us to turn our attention to that necessary work and do our part to ensure that Love wins out over Hatred and Neglect.

Too often in a state of grief, we become closed down, unable to respond to help when it arrives. However, if we are patient, doors eventually open to new emotions and new opportunities:

When one door of happiness closes, another opens; but often we look so long at the closed door that we do not see the one which has opened for us.

It was her Faith that continually opened doors for Helen Keller. Rather than dwell on her limitations, Helen used her circumstances to help others. Her deep religious Faith gave her an emotional and spiritual foundation.

Helen could not have known that seven years after *We Bereaved* was published, Anne Sullivan would be dead. Helen fell into a deep grief after Sullivan died and that grief never fully left her. However, she took her own advice, she went on a global mission to improve the lives of people who were blind, deaf, and deaf-blind; she turned her grief into faith-based action.

On a personal note, I began writing after my wife Katherine died. The death of a soul-mate is devastating. The world goes dark and silent; a form of deaf-blindness envelops the soul. Shock, like a hard eggshell, surrounds the body to keep it from disintegrating. Time, if allowed to do its work, eventually stabilizes the body and soul, but the darkness and silence remain within for a lifetime, just behind the façade, just behind the personality. For me, the only way out of grief was a mission.

Even if spirituality had seemed like religious nonsense prior to a death, even if the scientific, materialistic mind had denigrated religion as unnecessary, even harmful, the only way forward was to courageously face the unknown, the hidden. The evolution of life and the furthering of loving kindness are worth fighting for. Within that insight is a mission that can get you up every morning and guide you sleepy-eyed to your chosen altar.

Sullivan encouraged Helen to write *Peace at Eventide* (the British title) to help those who were struggling. The household got many letters every day from people asking for Helen's and Annie's emotional and spiritual guidance. *Peace at Eventide* was meant for the many grieving individuals who had reached out to them over several decades.

1930: Travel to Great Britain

Helen, Polly, and Anne traveled abroad in 1930, eventually visiting Scotland, Ireland and England. They traveled abroad for over six months before returning to the United States.

What Else Happened in 1930?

Here are a few random events that happened in 1930: Helen Keller turned fifty this year. . . . Mao Zedong wrote "A Single Spark Can Start a Prairie Fire." . . . Clarence Birdseye was granted a patent for quick freezing food. . . . Noël Coward's "Private Lives" premiered in London. . . . Elijah Muhammad formed the Nation of Islam in Detroit.

1931: WORLD COUNCIL FOR THE BLIND

A collection of poems was published in 1931 called *Double Blossoms: Helen Keller Anthology*, complied by Edna Porter. 1931 is also an important year for the evolution of braille. Thanks to Helen Keller's leadership, English Braille was accepted as a global standard. Prior to 1931, blind individuals had to master (at least) New York Point, American Braille, English Braille, Moon Type, and Boston Line Letter. In 1931, Helen, Anne, and Polly participated in the first meeting of the World Council for the Blind in New York City. The World Council for the Blind was the institution that led the way toward unified action among blindness organizations.

The World Council for the Welfare of the Blind (WCWB) was an organization of agencies for the blind (visually impaired) established in 1949. It combined with the International Federation of the Blind in 1984 to create the *World Blind Union*, which is still a unifying force in our modern world.

What Else Happened in 1931?

Here are a few random events that happened in 1931: The *Star-Spangled Banner* was officially proclaimed the national anthem of the United States. . . . Nevada legalized gambling. . . . The first rocket-powered aircraft was patented by Robert Goddard. . . . Al Capone was indicted on 5,000 counts of prohibition and perjury. He was subsequently convicted of tax evasion and sent to prison. . . . Pope Pius XI published an encyclical saying, "We do not need fascism and Mussolini." . . . The Dick Tracy comic strip by Chester Gould debuted. . . . The Chinese People's Republic was proclaimed by Mao Zedong. . . . Jane Addams was the first U.S. woman to receive a Nobel Peace Prize.

1932: Honorary Doctor of Laws Degree

Helen Keller, Anne Sullivan, and Polly Thomson made another trip abroad in 1932, visiting Scotland and England. They sailed on April 1, 1932 for Plymouth, England on the S.S. President Roosevelt. Annie fiercely struggled against the decision to go abroad presumably because her health had deteriorated, and her vision loss had become severe. However, Helen thought it necessary for Annie's health to get her out of their Forest Hills home in New York City so that Annie could be refreshed and reinvigorated. Sullivan must have felt death nearing; she was in no state for an adventure—she was extremely sick the whole time they were away. The three women spent May in Cornwall and then visited Scotland in June. They returned to England in July and spent the remaining summer there.

After returning from the six-month journey abroad, Helen wrote a letter to her friend James Kerr Love that adds some nice details to the adventure:

> As for our news, I give it tremblingly. For I have a confession to make—a conspiracy of silence. Mrs. Macy, Miss Thomson (Polly), my secretary, and I sailed for England last April and spent six months wandering through Cornwall, Ireland, and Essex without breathing a word to any of our friends of our whereabouts. Only Polly's family and Miss Prince, the librarian of the National Institute for the Blind, London, knew that we were in England, and they kept our secret faithfully. Even my publishers did not know I had crossed the ocean.

Seriously, Dr. Love, it was a time of absolute quiet and relaxation for us three, and we did not attempt to do much sightseeing or meet people. My teacher had been ill a great deal as a result of overwork during many years, and a severe inflammation of the eyes had caused her acute suffering. Two operations on her eyes had failed to bring relief, and she was so nervous and depressed, we realized that something must be done at once if she was ever to get better. I begged her to go away with me for a long holiday. At first, she refused to leave the boat she had so faithfully steered—bless her heart! But once we found ourselves aboard the *President Roosevelt*, the change in her was gratifying. Her interest in life revived, her love of beauty in sea and sky asserted itself, and by the time we landed at Plymouth the "Wanderlust" was upon her. [49]

While in Scotland, on June 1, 1932, Helen was given an Honorary Degree of Doctor of Laws from the University of Glasgow. Conferring the degree W.W. McKechnie said:

It would be utterly inconsistent with one of the main lessons of Helen Keller's life if any of us today were to shrink from a task because it was difficult.

Helen's reaction to the ceremony began like this:

The assembly gave Teacher a splendid ovation. This pleased me more than the honor paid me.

There are a few other comments that caught my eye from McKechnie's celebration of Helen Keller:

How many imprisoned Ariels has the world lost for want of the culture and encouragement that were needed?
    We recall her warm friendships, her God-given sense of humor, her deep gratitude to all her teachers, her love of children, her pity for the poor, the weary, and the heavy-laden. We think of her indomitable courage and perseverance: [she says] "I slip back many times, I fall, I stand still, I run against the edge of hidden obstacles, I lose my temper and find it again

and keep it better, I trudge on, I gain a little, I feel encouraged, I get more eager and climb higher and begin to see the widening horizon. Every struggle is a victory."

[Helen tells us] "I love all writers whose minds, like Lowell's bubble up in the sunshine of optimism—fountains of joy and goodwill, with occasionally a slash of anger here and there, a healing spray of sympathy and pity."

As I was reviewing Helen Keller's life, I often had the sad feeling that many unknown and wonderful minds had perished leaving no trace in history—Helen narrowly survived this fate, but so many others did not survive and were unable to contribute to the evolution of humanity. As I looked over the war years, I was also sickened by the loss of so many brilliant minds, casualties of war. Humanity has wasted so many cognitive and spiritual souls—it is a wonder the species has survived.

I appreciated that W.W. McKechnie quoted Helen (above) in his tribute. He highlights her stubborn optimism. She loses her temper, she gets frustrated, she falls back, tries again, falls back again; but through it all she never gives up.

When Helen first heard about the desire of the faculty at the University of Glasgow to confer an honorary degree for her accomplishments, she wrote to her friend James Kerr Love to express her gratitude:

I have no words to express my astonishment when one morning, while I was at breakfast, the cablegram came from the University of Glasgow saying that the Faculty wished to confer an honorary degree upon me. In many ways I have gained a strong impression of the large-hearted generosity of Scotland. For eighteen years I have had a Scot by my side [Polly Thomson] whose loyal service has smoothed out many difficulties for me. Truly, I am proud to know my name will be included among those honored by a great Scottish university. The thought of you being there makes me all the happier.

I confess I tremble at the idea of facing you and those distinguished scholars with such a sense of my inadequacy. Nevertheless, I am most grateful. I feel encouraged also to think that this event may help to arouse more interest both in the blind and the deaf. I have always looked upon my limitations as a possible channel through which wider sympathy and service may flow toward the handicapped.

I love Helen's last sentence above. Her amazing mind decided, when she was just a preteen, to dedicate her existence on earth to cheerfully, steadfastly making the world a better experience for others. She looked beyond her own limitations. She forged a mission, forged intentions, and she made plan after plan to accomplish her intentions. She ended up helping all of humanity. Even after she has died, her soul continues its work.

During this trip to the British Isles, Anne Sullivan was quickly going blind—her sight was almost gone as the trip neared an end. She was reluctant to go anywhere and had little desire to meet strangers. On the other hand, there was one highlight that did momentarily rejuvenate Anne Sullivan.

In June 1932, the three women sailed on the ship *Bally Cotton* for Ireland. Anne wanted to research her Irish heritage, to see the land where her parents had been born and where a terrible famine had forced them to flee to the United States. It was a happy, invigorating time for Anne Sullivan, an event that probably made the whole difficult journey worth the struggle.

∾

John Albert Macy died in Pennsylvania on August 26, 1932. He had been born April 10, 1877 in Detroit, Michigan. He was just fifty-five when he had a stroke in the night and died from the complications. Annie and Helen got the news when they were in Scotland. Annie wrote these words after she heard the sad news:

> "Three thousand miles away his body, once so dear, lies cold and still," Annie wrote in her private memoir. "the dreadful drama is finished, the fierce struggle that won only despair is ended . . . I have been homesick for many a year for his arms. Perhaps it was wrong to look too deep within. Now he is dead." [50]

This is from the AFB Helen Keller Archives:

> Macy, John Albert was an author, critic, and poet from Detroit, Michigan, the son of Powell Macy and Janet Foster Patten, the

descendants of early New England settlers long associated with the whaling industry. His parents' occupations are unknown, although the family reportedly had meager resources. John Macy grew up in the Boston area and attended Malden High School in Malden, Massachusetts. Upon graduation in 1895, he enrolled at Harvard on a partial scholarship, majoring in English literature. [51]

This is from Ancestry.com:

> I am an independent researcher and scholar interested in finding the identity of the child of John Albert Macy (10 Apr. 1877–26 Aug. 1932). Macy was still married to Anne Sullivan when he had an affair with a deaf artist which produced a child. From what I understand, the woman died, and the child remained in Macy's care. I have searched far and wide and have been unable to locate the full name or the birth/death record of the child. I am hoping that someone with detailed information of the Macy family tree might be willing to help me locate the information of the child. Any help would be greatly appreciated.

I do not know if anyone was able to help answer this plea. I also pondered what might have become of John Macy's daughter. John died so suddenly and at such a young age that his daughter would have been thrown into a second trauma—losing a second parent at a young age. Here is a clue from Kim Nielsen's book:

> . . . she [Anne Sullivan] believed herself to have kept on loving John Albert Macy despite the failure of their relationship. His funeral services were held in Montclair, New Jersey, where his sister lived. He had left his five-hundred-dollar estate to his daughter, Margaret Briggs. Annie paid the burial costs, symbolically reclaiming him as her husband. [52]

So, the daughter's name was Margaret Briggs. I found no trace of Margaret on Ancestry.com. There is no record that John married Margaret's mother, who presumably also had *Briggs* as a surname. In Joseph Lash's *Helen and Teacher* (1980), Lash refers to John Macy's grandniece Susan Macy and her personal research into the relationship between John Macy, Anne Sullivan, and Helen Keller. I also found a reference that the mother's name was Myla.

In her book *Beyond the Miracle Worker* (2009), Kim Nielsen points out that John Macy—when he lived with Helen and Annie—began in the census records (for 1910) as *Head of Household*. Helen was listed as a boarder. At the next census (1920), Helen was listed as Head of Household and John Macy had disappeared from the household.

John Macy was instrumental in the editing and publication of several of Helen's early books and articles. Helen said of him: "I cannot enumerate the helpful kindnesses with which he smoothed my rugged paths of endeavor." John Macy is forever to be remembered and honored as an important part of the story of the Miracle and the Miracle Worker.

What Else Happened in 1932?

Here are a few random events that happened in 1932: Helen Keller was elected to AFB's board of trustees. . . . Hattie W. Caraway was elected the first U.S. woman Senator, as a Democrat from Arkansas. . . . George Burns and Gracie Allen debuted as regulars on the Guy Lombardo Show. . . . Amelia Earhart left Newfoundland to fly solo and nonstop across the Atlantic. . . . Gandhi began a hunger strike against the treatment of untouchables in India. . . . Wernher von Braun was named the head of the German liquid-fuel rocket program. . . . Groucho Marx performed on the radio for the first time. . . . Albert Einstein was granted a visa to enter America.

1933: Helen Keller in Scotland

Helen published a book about her trip to England and Scotland (in 1932) called *Helen Keller in Scotland: A Personal Record Written by Herself.* The book was edited by James Kerr Love (1858–1942), who Helen says was "my friend for a quarter of a century." James Kerr Love was one of the leading British otologists of the early 20th century, especially revered for his involvement with deaf children.

A common theme throughout *Helen Keller in Scotland* is, unfortunately, the comments about Anne Sullivan's health. Anne was often bedridden and exhausted from what was called a cold. In retrospect, Anne's health was declining from several ailments; she died less than three years after the three friends returned to the United States.

A main reason Helen, Annie, and Polly had gone to Scotland, as I wrote above, was because the University of Glasgow wished to confer an honorary doctorate on Helen. Weeks after the degree ceremony, Helen wrote to W. W. McKechnie of the Scottish Education Department (McKechnie had introduced Helen at the confirmation ceremony). In that letter is this lovely paragraph:

> The publicity given to the honorary degree conferred upon me by the University of Glasgow galvanized all kinds of institutions into a violent desire for me to visit them. It seemed ungracious not to gratify them as fast as humanly possible; so, for many weeks "The Three Musketeers" were kept on the run. We were sorely banged and bruised in the process of making everybody happy. We pushed on with indefatigable zeal to London, until

exhaustion outflanked us, and we surrendered to our nerves. But I must not dwell on those crowded days, they are in the realm of oblivion behind the moon, and already, as I look back on them, I see far more pleasure than pangs. [53]

I like that Helen, Polly, and Annie are referred to as "The Three Musketeers" in this letter. That fits with my image; they were certainly inseparable, bonded, and dedicated to a common mission throughout their lives. They also seemed unbeatable as champions of spiritual goodness.

What Else Happened in 1933?

Here are a few random events that happened in 1933: The Lone Ranger began a 21-year run on ABC radio. . . . President-elect Franklin D. Roosevelt survived an assassination attempt, but Chicago Mayor Anton Cermak was mortally wounded. . . . The Catholic newspaper *Germania* warned against the rise of both the Nazis and communists. . . . The first issue of *Newsweek* was published. . . . Mahatma Gandhi began a fast in protest to British oppression in India. . . . The Vatican state secretary Pacelli (Pius XII) signed an accord with Adolf Hitler. . . . The Nobel Prize for Physics was presented to Paul Dirac and Erwin Schrödinger. . . . Fox Films signed Shirley Temple, aged 5, to a studio contract. . . . The Great Depression was declared to be over as Roosevelt's New Deal was drafted in 1933.

~

1933 was also the year that the book *Anne Sullivan Macy: The Story Behind Helen Keller* was published. This was the only in-depth biography of Anne Sullivan until Kim Nielsen's book *Beyond the Miracle Worker: The Remarkable Life of Anne Sullivan Macy*, was published in 2009.

Anne Sullivan Macy: The Story Behind Helen Keller was written by a close friend of Helen and Annie, a professional editor by trade, Nella Braddy Henney. When Braddy's book came out, Helen was quoted as saying: "The book does not present Teacher to me as I know her." Therefore, Helen became determined to write her own version of history and eventually published *Teacher* in 1955.

Anne Sullivan Macy: The Story Behind Helen Keller

This book is an in-depth biography of Anne Sullivan. It was written by a close friend of Helen and Annie, a professional editor by trade, Nella Braddy Henney (described earlier in the timeline). Braddy was a member of the Heller-Sullivan-Thomson household on and off for many years. It took seven years for the Sullivan biography to be completed; research for the book was extensive and thorough and Braddy had to stay at the homestead for long periods while working on the book.

Becoming Sullivan's biographer was not easy for Nella Braddy. Anne Sullivan did not like the limelight and she did not always care for the opinions of the media, which put her either in a golden light or a black light, but never saw her as a down-to-earth normal teacher doing her best.

Sullivan also refused to be honored by those who understood the magnitude of her accomplishments. According to Sullivan, the hero's journey, the mythology, was about Helen Keller, not her. "A teacher is just doing her job," Sullivan said on more than one occasion. Sullivan felt she was only doing what any dedicated teacher would do. She refused the title of *miracle worker* because her efforts were no less miraculous than any other hardworking teacher.

I have met a few Anne-Sullivan-Souls during my teaching years, so I know Sullivan was not using hyperbole—dedicated teachers are at work every day all over the world, often with little recognition or even a drop of appreciation. However, my emotions are on the side of awe-struck humanity. In my opinion, Anne Sullivan really was a larger-than life miracle worker. She was an amazing, brilliant, wonderful human being. Whether she wanted to be loved and honored from now until eternity ends, or not, teachers like myself hold this woman to be Goddess-like. Braddy's biography reinforces this sense of awe many teachers feel about Anne Sullivan—the book does Sullivan due justice. I was delighted by this work of art—I have read it twice now.

Probably because she did not hold herself in high esteem, Anne Sullivan (tragically, I think) saw no need to keep records of her own life. Of course, she kept meticulous notes about Helen Keller's life, but she tossed out most of her own personal recollections, including burning her diary. Sullivan did attempt to write an autobiography (in novel form), but never pulled it together—fragments are still available through the AFB Helen Keller Digital Archives. As a friend, Nella Braddy could talk directly with Anne Sullivan and Helen Keller to get their personal recollections, but there were few documents to use to pull together the biography. Fortunately, Annie, Helen, and Polly Thomson had many close friends. Nella interviewed these friends and collected their documents and insights.

Nella Braddy was an excellent writer; her book flows along, engaging the reader on every page; it is carefully organized and crafted—one of the best books written about either Helen or Anne. The first few chapters are about Sullivan's youth, which was dreadfully sad and cruel. The reader sinks into the helplessness of so many Irish immigrants in the late 1800s in America. Annie's dreadful saga was repeated thousands of times by the impoverished Irish, her sadness seemed the norm for this group of Irish pioneers. Their babies rarely survived, they were constantly sick from tuberculosis or Scarlet Fever, they died from infections for which there was no cure. They were crammed into ghettos or almshouses and endured until death saved them from further torture. They were Roman Catholics in a land of Protestants; they were isolated and scorned. That Anne Sullivan escaped such poverty, disrespect, and neglect is a miracle all by itself. It seems, as we look back, that Anne Sullivan was emotionally groomed to be Helen Keller's miracle worker. A lesser person—who did not have Anne Sullivan's powerful character—would have abandoned the challenge; Anne Sullivan gave her life to the challenge and refused to ever take the spotlight off her student. This quote is from Dorothy Herrmann's biography called *Helen Keller, A Life* (1998):

> Whatever Anne Sullivan's motives, her experiment in breaking through to a deaf-blind mute was a brilliant success. In one of his letters Anagnos had referred to her as "a genius," a label that Annie demurely rejected. But Anagnos was right in calling her one. Her experiment in teaching Helen language was a superlative feat, combining intelligence, intuition, and stamina as well as devotion.

Although *Anne Sullivan Macy: The Story Behind Helen Keller* is a great book, Helen did not feel that it captured the teacher she knew so intimately for a half century. Therefore, in 1955, Helen published her own book about Anne Sullivan called *Teacher*. Wonderfully, the introduction to *Teacher* was written by Nella Braddy. Nella is the bridge between her own lovely portrait of Anne Sullivan and Helen Keller's tribute to Annie twenty years later.

318 | Helen Keller: A Timeline of Her Life

Helen Keller in Scotland: A Personal History

There are a few Helen Keller books that are rarely read (because they are unknown); this delightful book is one such gem. *Helen Keller in Scotland* takes place in the land where Polly Thomson was born. Polly's family welcomed Helen, Anne, and Polly, housing them on several occasions during their visits to Great Britain.

Helen was being recognized by the University of Glasgow on this trip in 1933, receiving an Honorary Degree of Doctor of Laws. Both Helen and Anne were later honored by the Educational Institute of Scotland; each of them receiving honorary fellowships. Here is Helen's opening comments in the Preface of the book:

> This collection of letters and speeches records chiefly experiences surrounding the Honorary Degree conferred upon me by the University of Glasgow. The material has been collected and edited by Dr. James Kerr Love, my friend of a quarter of a century.

The book begins with a lengthy and thorough introduction by Dr. Love and is then divided into three parts:

- My Pilgrimage; My Letters; and My Speeches. My Pilgrimage is a lengthy journal, recording the events of interest that occurred during the visit to Scotland and England.
- In Part Two of the book, James Love collected Helen's letters dating from 1910 to 1932, "including [commentary about] the greatest event of that period, the World War." After getting the honorary degree, Helen became a media star in Great Britain. She had to give speech after speech as she traveled about during her visit.
- Part Three ends the book with a collection of a few representative short speeches.

Dr. Love was a leading British otologist, a pioneer in the education of the deaf. He was a strong advocate for lip reading, maintaining that by this method a deaf person could lead a relatively normal life. He and Helen carried on a correspondence over many years before they met in person. It appears that it was through the efforts of Dr. Love that Helen Keller was honored by the University of Glasgow. Dr. Love arranged travel and lodging for Helen, Annie, and Polly, enabling them to come to Scotland, despite their shaky financial situation. Dr. and Mrs. Love initially hosted the trio when they arrived. Dr. Love carefully collected letters and speeches during the visit and then helped Helen publish this book.

It was hard for Helen to go anywhere in the world without being interviewed, photographed, invited to tea, urged to speak, and encouraged to visit tourist spots with enthusiastic local officials. On this trip to Scotland, Helen gave a speech at Queen Margaret's College (the Radcliffe of Glasgow), went sailing down the Clyde with hundreds of blind people and their guides, visited the Highlands with friends of Polly's family, motored to Loch Lomond, took a steamer to the Island of Arran, met the Duke and Duchess of Montrose, visited the home of Robert Burns in Ayrshire, and spoke at Bothwell Parish Church, where Polly's brother was the minister. After that whirlwind, they traveled to London for another frantic round of obligations.

When the three friends got to London, they secluded themselves in the Park Land Hotel for three days of rest. Helen says:

> The speed at which we went from one function to another during the next two weeks made this period a blur in my consciousness. I know I made three or four or five appearances every day; that I met many distinguished people; that I visited schools and made many speeches and examined the handicrafts of the blind and deaf; that I lunched with Captain Ian and Mrs. Fraser at St. Dunstan's, with Lord and Lady Astor, with Lady Paula Jones, and at the Royal Normal College for the Blind, at Leatherhead, Surrey, and at Swiss Cottage, institutions for the sightless; that I had tea with somebody or some group every day; that we dined with the Frasers in the House of Commons, and with Lady Fairhaven and her son Lord Fairhaven, and that we called on Sir Hilton Young, Minister of Health.

At Lady Astor's, Helen met the famous playwright George Bernard Shaw. In the quote below from *Helen Keller in Scotland*, Helen recounts her meeting with Shaw:

> Bernard Shaw was as bristling with egoism as a porcupine with quills. His handshape was quizzical and prickly, not unlike a

thistle. Lady Astor tried to interest him in me. 'You know, Mr. Shaw,' she said, that Miss Keller is deaf and blind.'

'Why of course!' he replied, 'All Americans are blind and deaf, and dumb.'

I asked him why he had never come to America.

'Why should I go to America,' he answered, 'when all America comes to me . . . '

In her journal, on December 16, 1936, Helen wrote more about her encounter with Shaw (GBS):

Teacher hesitated a few minutes before spelling his answer to me. From the silence that followed I knew something out of the common had happened. Then she repeated his words: "Why, of course, all Americans are deaf and blind!"

I was amused by this remark, which I thought levelled at me especially. I have since been told that he did not intend it for me at all; but whether he did or not, I was far from offended—I had become accustomed to his whimsical, incisive, in-and-out-of-season sayings.

At first, I had no idea of writing an article on the interview with Mr. Shaw; and after thinking it over, I decided that it could do no harm to repeat what he said, since he had taken every opportunity to censure or ridicule Americans. I never dreamed what harsh things would be said of him on my account, and I have regretted that article ever since.

My enthusiastic admiration for G.B.S. remains unquenched. Greatly has he wrought, mightiest among the Samsons tugging at the pillars of oppression and hypocrisy. The world is his debtor for the inhibiting fallacies he has destroyed, the idols he has broken, and the mute lips his fire has kindled into brave speech.

Helen had read and enjoyed many of Shaw's works, so she was not surprised to find him humorously sarcastic, like her good friend Mark Twain. Shaw was a leading dramatist in his generation; he was awarded the Nobel Prize in Literature in 1925. It is too bad Shaw and Helen did not hit it off at that first meeting, especially since George Bernard Shaw's plays, in part, are about the injustice of poverty and the need for women's rights—he was a sharp-tongued humanitarian, and like Helen Keller, he did not shy away from conflict and eloquence. In many ways, Shaw's worldview and emotional intelligence were parallel to Helen Keller's.

Helen implies that her visit with Shaw was abrupt and tense, but one wonders what was going on below the rhetoric; what emotional posturing was playing out, what misunderstandings arose during this social exchange at Lady Astor's mansion. It certainly sparked an enduring discussion. Here is an excerpt from the article Helen wrote about Shaw. I will leave it as the last word on the amusing conflict between the two geniuses:

> Frankly, I admire George Bernard Shaw. I admired him before I met him, and I still do. I think he is one of the greatest men now living; but since I have stood in his presence, I cannot think of him without a feeling of sorrow . . . Poor Bernard Shaw. He has fought himself free from so many of the enslaving chains of our existence, but from the prison of his own building he cannot escape. About himself, he has built a legend, which confines him more powerfully, more closely than any prison of stone and steel. Only Bernard Shaw could build a prison sufficiently strong to contain Bernard Shaw! ~ Helen Keller Digital Archives, American Foundation for the Blind.

It is not a good idea to tangle with a mind like Helen Keller's. She can read souls and she is not shy about making emotionally charged judgements. I have a feeling the two wordsmiths are still sparring in Heaven (with Mark Twain cheering them on).

After the interchange with Shaw had concluded, Helen, Polly, and Anne continued their rapid pace. It was too much, and the ladies crashed from exhaustion:

> After ten days of dashes, rushes, and flurries we three were utterly exhausted. Doing everything at top speed isn't the way to enjoy a holiday. Polly and I stayed in bed for two days. We were too weary to eat—I actually couldn't raise a strawberry to my lips!

Having recovered their stamina, the three travelers set out again, first to Canterbury and then to a series of engagements in the London area.

However, just before they were to head to London, they were invited to a Royal Garden party at Buckingham Palace. The American Embassy called to say that the Queen of England wished to meet them. All their current plans had to be canceled; if the Queen summons you, Helen says, that takes priority over all other obligations.

Helen describes meeting the King and Queen in lovely detail. The Three Musketeers (as she calls her trio) dashed off after saying goodbye to Royalty and arrived two hours late to a tea party. All the quests had gone by then, so they had a quick cup of tea and raced off again to meet American Foundation for the Blind officials at the Grosvenor Hotel. They missed the last train to Canterbury, where they were renting a cottage, and ended spending the night at the Park Land Hotel.

The next day, Helen spoke at a meeting of the British Medical Association. In the afternoon they visited the gardens at Hampton Court and then had tea "on a fascinating little island in the Thames." Their days proceeded at a frantic pace until Anne Sullivan got extremely ill. A doctor suggested they take a couple months, do nothing, and hang out breathing the oxygen rich air of the Scottish Highlands. Off they went.

The illness from which Anne Sullivan struggled has not been clarified, but it was severe and in a few years after this visit to Scotland, she would be dead. In a small way, this book is a chronical of Anne Sullivan's last adventure. I suggest that every Helen Keller library have a copy of this rare gem.

"Three Days to See," an article in The Atlantic Magazine

In January 1933, Helen published a fascinating article in *The Atlantic Magazine* called "Three Days to See." All the quotations below (except as indicated otherwise) were taken from the article. Helen was asked by the Atlantic staff to consider what she would do with the blessing of three magical days in which she had sight. Helen agreed to write the article, but before she launched into that imaginary world she reflected generally on life and the senses:

> Most of us take life for granted. We know that one day we must die, but usually we picture that day as far in the future. When we are in buoyant health, death is all but unimaginable. We

seldom think of it. The days stretch out in an endless vista. So, we go about our petty tasks, hardly aware of our listless attitude toward life.

The same lethargy, I am afraid, characterizes the use of all our faculties and senses. Only the deaf appreciate hearing, only the blind realize the manifold blessings that lie in sight. Particularly does this observation apply to those who have lost sight and hearing in adult life. But those who have never suffered impairment of sight or hearing seldom make the fullest use of these blessed faculties. Their eyes and ears take in all sights and sounds hazily, without concentration and with little appreciation. It is the same old story of not being grateful for what we have until we lose it, of not being conscious of health until we are ill.

The above quote reminds me of a line from a letter that the poet William Blake wrote, which has become well known:

The tree which moves some to tears of joy is in the eyes of others only a green thing which stands in the way . . . As a man is, so he sees. ~ Letters from William Blake to Dr. Trusler, August 1799.

Helen spends several paragraphs in *The Atlantic Magazine* article musing how the sighted seem to take their vision for granted. The sighted do not seem to gaze with admiration at the spectrum of colors; they do not pay attention to details; they do not feel awestruck by the gift of vision. Perhaps, she suggests, the reader should also do some imaging and suppose *that they* have only three more days of vision, after which they would never see again:

Perhaps I can best illustrate by imagining what I should most like to see if I were given the use of my eyes, say, for just three days. And while I am imagining, suppose you, too, set your mind to work on the problem of how you would use your own eyes if you had only three more days to see. If with the oncoming darkness of the third night you knew that the sun would never rise for you again, how would you spend those three precious intervening days? What would you most want to let your gaze rest upon?

> I, naturally, should want most to see the things which have become dear to me through my years of darkness. You, too, would want to let your eyes rest long on the things that have become dear to you so that you could take the memory of them with you into the night that loomed before you.

That last paragraph is immensely powerful. My first thought was that I would want to study the faces of everyone I loved, my children, grandchildren, my nieces and nephews, my sisters, all my relatives and friends. Helen says that she would divide her three days into three parts. The first part mirrors what I just wrote; Helen wants to see the faces of those she loves:

> On the first day, I should want to see the people whose kindness and gentleness and companionship have made my life worth living. First, I should like to gaze long upon the face of my dear teacher, Mrs. Anne Sullivan Macy, who came to me when I was a child and opened the outer world to me. I should want not merely to see the outline of her face, so that I could cherish it in my memory, but to study that face and find in it the living evidence of the sympathetic tenderness and patience with which she accomplished the difficult task of my education. I should like to see in her eyes that strength of character which has enabled her to stand firm in the face of difficulties, and that compassion for all humanity which she has revealed to me so often.

Helen has a list of things she would do on her first day. Besides looking at the faces of friends and strangers she would like to see her beloved dogs:

> And I should like to look into the loyal, trusting eyes of my dogs: the grave, canny little Scottie, Darkie, and the stalwart, understanding Great Dane, Helga, whose warm, tender, and playful friendships are so comforting to me.

On that first day, she would walk in nature; she would enjoy the fading light and the experience of twilight vision. And she would pray for "the glory of a colorful sunset." At night she would be unable to sleep as she awaited the sunrise:

The next day—the second day of sight—I should arise with the
dawn and see the thrilling miracle by which night is transformed
into day. I should behold with awe the magnificent panorama of
light with which the sun awakens the sleeping earth.

On that second day she wants to visit as many museums as possible
because she wants a pictorial history of mankind to remember:

I have longed to see with my eyes the condensed history of the
earth and its inhabitants displayed there—animals and the
races of men pictured in their native environment; gigantic
carcasses of dinosaurs and mastodons . . . realistic presentations
of the processes of evolution in animals, in man, and in the
implements which man has used to fashion for himself a secure
home on this planet; and a thousand and one other aspects of
natural history.

She would also go to the art museums on this second day:

I should try to probe into the soul of man through his art. . . . I
should look deep into the canvases of Raphael, Leonardo da Vinci,
Titian, Rembrandt. I should want to feast my eyes upon the warm
colors of Veronese, study the mysteries of El Greco, catch a new
vision of Nature from Corot. Oh, there is so much rich meaning
and beauty in the art of the ages for you who have eyes to see!

In the evening of the second day, she would go to the theater:

The evening of my second day of sight I should spend at a
theatre or at the movies. Even now I often attend theatrical
performances of all sorts, but the action of the play must be
spelled into my hand by a companion. But how I should like
to see with my own eyes the fascinating figure of Hamlet, or
the gusty Falstaff amid colorful Elizabethan trappings! How I
should like to follow each movement of the graceful Hamlet,
each strut of the hearty Falstaff!

If I could see only one play, I should know how to picture in
my mind the action of a hundred plays which I have read or had
transferred to me through the medium of the manual alphabet.

When she awakes on the third and last day of sight, Helen wants to watch the people of the earth go about their routines and responsibilities. New York City is close by and what better place to people watch could there be:

> Today I shall spend in the workaday world of the present, amid the haunts of men going about the business of life. And where can one find so many activities and conditions of men as in New York? So, the city becomes my destination.
>
> I look ahead, and before me rise the fantastic towers of New York, a city that seems to have stepped from the pages of a fairy story. What an awe-inspiring sight, these glittering spires, these vast banks of stone and steel—structures such as the gods might build for themselves! This animated picture is a part of the lives of millions of people every day.

What strikes me as I read this wonderful imaginary experience is that she wants to witness the rhythms of life, the animation of nature; it is *flow* that she longs to see. She wants to watch gestures and facial expressions change. She wants the challenge of reading emotions and personality in the body language of the people she encounters.

Helen also wants to get up high to perceive an overhead view of the world; she wants to grasp the biggest gestalt that she can find, a vast canvas, an animated map of humanity at work and play. And she longs to witness people as they work, and play, and interact with each other:

> From Fifth Avenue I make a tour of the city—to Park Avenue, to the slums, to factories, to parks where children play. I take a stay-at-home trip abroad by visiting the foreign quarters. Always my eyes are open wide to all the sights of both happiness and misery so that I may probe deep and add to my understanding of how people work and live.

She has only the evening of the last day left. Where will her wondrous mind take her? It is almost like your last day on earth—where to take a last long look around. I love her choice:

> My third day of sight is drawing to an end. Perhaps there are many serious pursuits to which I should devote the few

remaining hours, but I am afraid that on the evening of that last day I should again run away to the theatre, to a hilariously funny play, so that I might appreciate the overtones of comedy in the human spirit.

Oh yes, she wants to laugh on her last day. Not a lot has been written about Helen's sense of humor, but we can imagine that many of her days were spent laughing with (and at) her friends, the strange human conundrums that walk the earth beside us. If there is one thing that separates us from all the other sentient creatures it is this ability to laugh at ourselves and at each other.

Here is the last paragraph of this short but delightful article:

> I who am blind can give one hint to those who see—one admonition to those who would make full use of the gift of sight: Use your eyes as if tomorrow you would be stricken blind. And the same method can be applied to the other senses. Hear the music of voices, the song of a bird, the mighty strains of an orchestra, as if you would be stricken deaf tomorrow. Touch each object you want to touch as if tomorrow your tactile sense would fail. Smell the perfume of flowers, taste with relish each morsel, as if tomorrow you could never smell and taste again. Make the most of every sense; glory in all the facets of pleasure and beauty which the world reveals to you through the several means of contact which Nature provides. But of all the senses, I am sure that sight must be the most delightful.

When I reflect on this entire article, I am reminded of the books that I have read by (or about) the other Knights for the Blind in this book series, people like Jacques Lusseyran, Zoltan Torey, and Daniel Kish. They all used different language to say the same thing: The power of the eyes is rarely appreciated. Instead, the eyes take in superficial images, they pass over details, and they even allow themselves to be lied to. I am also thinking about Mark Twain telling Helen that "the world is full of unseeing eyes, vacant, staring, soulless eyes." Helen understands what Mark Twain is saying, but she also reminds us that standing among all the soulless, sleepy-eyed humans are the wide-awake eyes of poets, painters, dancers, musicians, empaths and saints, writers and vigilant caregivers. Humanity is slowly awakening. In the era in which she lived, deaf-blind Helen Keller could perceive deeper and wider than most of humanity.

I have one additional emotion to share before I leave this review. I am puzzled that we would set such an experiment, such musing before Helen Keller—"write about the loss of vision," we plead. But I wonder why no one asked Helen to write an article called "Three Days to Hear?" Strangely, we are not asked to reflect on what it would be like to have only three more days before we could no longer appreciate sounds. I know that I long to hear my wife Katherine's voice, but nowhere has it been preserved, even though I have a photographic record of her entire life. How I would love to hear my own voice as a child, as an adolescent, as a young college student, as a father. If you are inclined to answer Helen and to reflect on what you would choose to see if blindness were assured in three days, I ask that you also reflect on deafness and what you would choose to hear if only three more days remained of good hearing.

The Blind in School and Society

In 1933, The American Foundation for the Blind published a controversial book (for the time) by blind psychologist Dr. Thomas D. Cutsforth called *The Blind in School and Society: A Psychological Study*. Dr. Cutsforth was frank and outspoken in his criticism of current public practices and attitudes concerning the blind.

My colleague Daniel Kish has often said that he resents it when sighted people tell him how to be a blind man. Cutsforth says something similar, that blindness causes physiological and behavioral adaptations that essentially create a blind brain, which is significantly different from a brain crafted by vision. Therefore, it is misguided for a sighted person to educate or rehabilitate a blind man to behave like a sighted man.

Cutsforth says that his book was written to "acquaint the seeing with the blind and the blind with themselves." He is aware that not only is the sighted population ignorant of the behavioral adjustments that logically occur from blindness, but blind people themselves are not aware of what has happened to them. "The problems involved are many," Cutsforth says, as he begins the book. Blindness causes many physical challenges, that is well understood or assumed. But what Cutsforth sees is that personality, mental health, and a sense of well-being are seriously impacted by blindness and that neither the society nor the blind themselves have accepted this comprehensive picture.

The Blind in School and Society belongs in this timeline because Thomas Cutsforth is a rare critic of the teaching methods of Anne Sullivan. He also feels that the Helen Keller we have grown to respect and admire could have been more valuable to society had she not been so heavily molded in the image of sighted people—Anne Sullivan being the main culprit in the molding process. I do not sense that Cutsforth is blaming anyone for the circumstances of the time when Sullivan and Keller lived. He is trying to wake up his colleagues and fellow blind individuals to a greater perspective. Like Helen herself, Cutsforth was bold in his observations and opinions, and this boldness of expression was sometimes interpreted as disrespectful and unkind.

Cutsforth's strongest criticism was leveled at Helen's use of sensory language. Helen freely used colors and sounds to highlight her prose. Cutsforth found this disingenuous and misleading for the reader. He further suggests that this is Anne Sullivan's doing, the "making over" of a deaf-blind woman in the image of a seeing world. In his 1980 biography *Helen and Teacher*, Joseph Lash has a chapter called "The Dupe of Words" in which he recounts Cutsforth's perspective, and the counter arguments put forth to defend Helen and Annie. I will only add that neither Cutsforth nor Lash knew about synesthesia and the role brain-rewiring might have played in Helen's language development. I discussed synesthesia in *The Esoteric Helen Keller*.

Cutsforth says that blind children often develop what he calls *verbal unreality*, a disconnect between the name or description of an object and the reality of the object. For example, a blind child may be able to name different makes and styles of cars and discuss how automobiles are designed without ever examining a car. The words a blind child uses, even with eloquence are not attached to anything real in the physical universe. Cutsforth says that Helen had an extreme case of *verbal unreality*.

The Blind in School and Society is a sophisticated, complex work that has become a classic in the blindness field. Cutsforth made remarkable observations in the book that were shocking to the morality of the 1930s. He even dared to have a chapter on blindness and sexuality. Cutsforth writes with clarity and well-conceived logic; his book deserves a special place in this history of blindness studies.

1935: SOCIAL SECURITY ACT

Few people know that Helen Keller supported the Social Security Act of 1935. She allowed her name to be put on an amendment to expand vocational training for the blind. When you get your social security check in the mail, thank Helen Keller for helping to bring this act of socialism to the laws of the United States.

What Else Happened in 1935?

Here are a few randomly selected events that occurred in 1935: on January 11, Amelia Earhart flew non-stop from Honolulu to Oakland California. . . . On February 26, Adolf Hitler secretly authorized the formation of the Luftwaffe with Hermann Göring as commander-in-chief. . . . In June 30, the novel *Gone with the Wind*, by Margaret Mitchell was published in New York. . . . On August 14, President Franklin D. Roosevelt signed the Social Security Act into law. . . . On September 2, the strongest hurricane ever to strike the United States (up to that time) made landfall in the Florida Keys killing 423 people. . . . On November 3, President Roosevelt was re-elected for a second term in a landslide over Republican challenger Alfred Landon. Roosevelt received 60% of the popular vote and 98% of the Electoral College.

"How I Would Help the World"

"How I Would Help the World" is an essay by Helen Keller (published as a small book) about her spiritual devotion to the teaching of Emanuel Swedenborg. There is a modern introduction, about a third of the book, by Swedenborgian and Helen Keller scholar Ray Silverman, who also revised Helen's book *My Religion*.

The introduction is fascinating by itself and worth careful consideration. Professor Silverman makes two observations that are highly telling of Helen's worldview. First, Helen realizes that a key beauty of Swedenborg's philosophy is that the human mind can evolve—it can get smarter, wiser, and kinder throughout a lifetime. The human mind does not have to get stuck or stagnate at some mean (ignorant) level. Religion, at the mystical, esoteric core, is about the evolution of consciousness. For Helen, the evolution of the mind was the evolution of spirituality, which was the evolution of loving-kindness.

I discussed levels of consciousness in Chapter Three of *The Esoteric Helen Keller* and suggested that each level of cognition defined the same terminology differently; for example, the definition of *God* would naturally vary with the worldview of the individual. In "How I Would Help the World," Helen quotes Swedenborg's belief that God manifests at each level of consciousness in a guise appropriate for that level of consciousness:

> When the Lord appears to a person, he appears according to the quality of that person. This is because an individual receives the Divine not otherwise than according to the state of that person's consciousness. ~ *Secrets of Heaven*, by Emanuel Swedenborg, 1749.

The second observation (among many) that Silverman makes is that Helen felt education to be the key for moving consciousness (kindness) forward. Helen could see that education, as it existed around her, was almost completely rational, without artistic input. The very idea of seeing spirituality (Love) as a core and necessary part of the educational curriculum was considered ridiculous in the era when she lived. In my own terms, I would insist that education understands its role in teaching the Ego but has almost no appreciation or dedication to teaching the Self. This is primarily because there is no widespread understanding of dual-process theory.

To meld science with religion, in the third and last chapter of the essay, Helen says, "surely Christianity, rightly understood, is the science of love." Our educational system has found it inappropriate to discuss the development of the mind, especially in K-12 education. This is understandable because religious views vary widely and depend on levels of cognitive development. It is hard to find a teacher with an Integral Mind. Most teachers reflect the level of consciousness of their culture and so primarily have Ethnocentric, Traditional or Modern minds. Nevertheless, to leave the exploration of love, the exploration of mental evolution, outside the domain of public education is to teach only half a mind (especially regarding dual-process theory). It is scientifically unsupported to teach only the Ego while disregarding the science of Love (Soul).

Helen ends her essay by proclaiming that "Swedenborg's books are an inexhaustible wellspring of satisfaction to those who live the life of the mind." The final section of the book, an appendix called *The Three Essentials*, was written by Professor Silverman. This is a side-by-side comparison of Helen's words and Swedenborg's words concerning the three essentials of the Church: acknowledging the divinity of the lord, acknowledging the holiness of the Word, and "a life of useful service."

1936: The Death of Anne Sullivan

Anne Sullivan Macy died on October 21, 1936. She had been at Helen Kellers side for 49 years and now had passed, leaving a deep void in Helen's heart. Here are excerpts from the *New York Times* obituary:

> Mrs. Anne Mansfield Sullivan Macy, who for nearly fifty years was the kindly, patient and brilliant teacher of Miss Helen Keller, noted blind and deaf woman, died yesterday at their home, 71-11 Seminole Avenue, Forest Hills, Queens. She had been suffering from a heart ailment, which became acute early this Summer. Mrs. Macy was 70 years old.
>
> Mrs. Macy taught Miss Keller to read, speak and know the world about her by use of her fingertips. Their lifelong devotion to each other was internationally famous and one was seldom seen or heard of without the other. Blindness, which had shadowed the child Anne Sullivan's life and which she had conquered before she met Miss Keller, had returned to darken her last days, and Miss Keller had to become the teacher and Mrs. Macy the pupil.
>
> Miss Keller yesterday paid this tribute: "Teacher is free at least from pain and blindness. I pray for strength to endure the silent dark until she smiles upon me again."
>
> Miss Polly Thompson, Miss Keller's secretary, said yesterday that Miss Keller was "bearing up magnificently" under her loss. During the last week Miss Keller was almost constantly at Mrs. Macy's side. Mrs. Macy was in a coma from Thursday until

she died. On Wednesday she said: "Oh, Helen and Polly, my children, I pray God will unite us in His love."

Mrs. Macy, so long the link to light for Miss Keller, lost the sight of her own right eye in 1929, due partly to a cataract, for which an operation was performed. In May 1935, a cataract operation was done on her left eye, but thereafter she was able to distinguish only light and color with it. She could no longer read or guide her beloved Miss Keller, who, despite her own handicaps, devoted herself to her friend.

Born in Feeding Hills, near Springfield, Mass., on April 14, 1866, the daughter of Irish immigrants, John and Mary Mansfield Sullivan, Mrs. Macy suffered the loss of her mother when a young child. For a year or two she was supported by poor relatives, but at the age of 10 she was sent to the State Infirmary, Tewksbury, Mass.

She was already partially blind and at the infirmary two eye operations were performed, but her sight did not improve. She was led to believe that Frank B. Sanborn, chairman of the State Board of Charities, who sometimes visited the infirmary, might be able to aid her. She pleaded with him and he arranged for her entry into the Perkins Institution for the Blind in Boston, where lived Laura Bridgman, blind and deaf, who had been trained there.

Mrs. Macy entered the Perkins Institution in 1880 [the year Helen Keller was born], made there a brilliant scholastic record and learned to study with her fingers, and later, after two operations had restored her sight, to use her eyes. She learned the manual, or finger, alphabet, so as to be able to talk to Laura Bridgman. In 1886 she was graduated as valedictorian of her class.

Not long after her graduation Helen Keller's father wrote to the institution asking for help for her. Miss Sullivan was chosen to be her teacher and, after familiarizing herself with the details of her new work, went to Helen's home in Tuscumbia, Ala.

The two who were to mean so much to each other until Mrs. Macy's death yesterday met first on March 3, 1887, three months before Helen was 7 years old. Miss Keller said later that it was "the most important day I remember in all my life."

Teacher and pupil remained for a time at the Perkins Institution. Then, in 1894, Helen was enrolled in the Wright-

Humason Oral School for the Deaf in New York. Later Miss Sullivan took her to a school in Cambridge to prepare her for Radcliffe College and finally Helen passed triumphantly her entrance examinations, entered Radcliffe and in 1904 was graduated cum laude.

Throughout the college course Mrs. Macy was with Helen, spelling into her hands the words of the textbooks and the books of required reading. Miss Keller's career thereafter brought her more and more into the public eye. She became famous as an author, she raised huge sums for the blind, she traveled, she was everywhere acclaimed, and Mrs. Macy went everywhere with her.

"My own life," Mrs. Macy said once, "is so interwoven with my Helen's life that I can't separate myself from her."

In 1931 Mrs. Macy received the honorary degree of Doctor of Humane Letters from Temple University and the Order of St. Sava from the King of Yugoslavia. In 1932 she became an honorary fellow of the Educational Institute of Scotland. Mrs. Macy stayed in seclusion for several months in 1933 in Scotland while Miss Keller nursed her. Mrs. Macy's blindness grew more pronounced and on her return from Scotland she said:

"Helen is and always has been thoroughly well behaved in her blindness as well as her deafness, but I'm making a futile fight of it, like a bucking bronco. It's not the big things in life that one misses through loss of sight, but such little things as being able to read. And I have no patience, like Helen, for the Braille system, because I can't read fast enough."

Early this month the Roosevelt Memorial Association announced that Roosevelt medals "for a cooperative achievement of heroic character and far-reaching significance" would be presented to Miss Keller and Mrs. Macy. In a telegram of sympathy to Miss Keller yesterday Hermann Hagedorn, executive director of the association, said that presentation to Miss Keller would be postponed from Oct. 27 to next year.

Mrs. Macy was married to John Albert Macy, author and critic, in 1905. He died in 1932. There are no immediate survivors.

A funeral service will be conducted at 2 P.M. tomorrow at the Park Avenue Presbyterian Church, 1010 Park Avenue, by

the Rev. Dr. Harry Emerson Fosdick and the Rev. Edmund M.
Wylie, the pastor.

After the service, cremation will take place, in accord with
Mrs. Macy's wish, at the Fresh Pond Crematory, Queens.

The honorary pallbearers will be M.C. Migel, president of
the American Foundation for the Blind, which Miss Keller and
Mrs. Macy greatly aided; Robert Irwin, executive director of the
foundation; Harvey D. Gibson, Russell Doubleday, Dr. Conrad
Berens, Dr. Philip S. Smith, Dr. William F. Saybolt, Dr. John H.
Finley, Louis Bamberger, the Rev. Dr. Edward E. Allen, director
emeritus of the Perkins Institution; Dr. William Allan Neilson,
president of Smith College, and William Ziegler Jr.

I was struck by the comment Polly Thomson made after Anne Sullivan's
death, that Helen was "bearing up magnificently" under her loss. Why
would Helen have been so well-adjusted and accepting after the miracle
worker had passed from her life? I suggest that it was because Helen
Keller's faith was not just words uttered, but a life spent:

My faith never wavers that each dear friend I have "lost" is a
new link between this world and the happier land beyond the
morn. My soul is for the moment bowed down with grief when
I cease to feel the touch of their hands or hear a tender word
from them; but the light of faith never fades from my sky, and
I take heart again, glad that they are free. I cannot understand
why anyone should fear death.[54]

Toward the end of her travel journal, on April 3, 1937, Helen looked
back at the moments surrounding Sullivan's last days:

I cannot stop this onrush of sad memories. Teacher's last
attempt to throw off her illness at the little cottage by the sea
in Long island . . . the month in the hospital during which she
hung between life and death . . . her piteous eagerness to get
home. I ache all over as I remember how she grew thinner and
thinner.

I live over her last few minutes of her earth-life: the death-
raddle after an eight hours' struggle for breath—her darling
hand growing cold in mine—the smell of opiates heavy in the

room—sorrowing friends who drew me away so that her body might be prepared for the funeral—the Gethsemane [occasion of great spiritual suffering] I passed through an hour later when I touched not Teacher's blessed face, but fixed features from which expression had fled. I feel again the recoil, the cry that escaped me" "It is not Teacher, it is not Teacher!" . . . The next thing I knew I was sitting in the attic-study trying to efface that still, cold image—as final for me as the sound of the last shovelful thrown upon the coffin is for those who hear.[55]

Anne Sullivan wrote these words a few years before her death:

> I wait for death, not sad, not heroically, but just a bit tired. To love and succeed is a fine thing, to love and fail is the next best, and the best of all is to fail and yet keep on loving.

After Anne Sullivan died, Helen Keller and Polly Thomson traveled abroad again, setting out November 4, 1936, eventually visiting England, Scotland, and France. They continued traveling around the world after the European visit. All the while, Helen was writing in a journal, which was later published as simply *Helen Keller's Journal* (1938). That journal was a catharsis, a chance to slowly reflect and grieve the loss of Anne Sullivan.

Foolish Remarks of a Foolish Woman

It is not well known that Anne Sullivan was writing her own autobiography, a partly fictionalized account of her life called *Foolish Remarks of a Foolish Woman*. The surviving manuscript is available in the digital archives at the American Foundation for the Blind. Sullivan died before she was able to complete this work. For several reasons, it is difficult to read the manuscript as it was preserved. What follows is a heavily edited rendition of selected sections of the manuscript. What I decided to do was to highlight items that seemed relevant to Sullivan's personality.

This collection seems like random, often disconnected notes waiting for an editor. Sullivan was such an amazing writer it is a shame she never got around to organizing this string of musings. However, we are blessed that her rambling thoughts and confessions were preserved. Here are some random selections—how Sullivan saw herself:

- It was my privilege to be present at the birth of Helen Keller's mind, and to watch the first fluttering of its silken wings, the first rising and breath of *Thought* which I was to guide on the road to knowledge and happiness.
- By nature, I am as intolerant as Bismarck or Mussolini, and if I had not met Helen, I would probably have remained a human porcupine all my life.
- Only in Helen have I kept the fire of a purpose alive. Every other dream has been blown out by some interfering fool.
- I think there is not much to life, except to learn all one can about it, and the only way to learn is to experience much, to love, to hate, to flounder, to enjoy, and to suffer. My only personal regret is that I have idiotically let so many opportunities for learning about life slip by me.
- What exasperates me about my life is its lack of symmetry, composition. Long stretches of it are chaotic and a great deal of it is hideously barren. The thought of aging is repugnant to me. Only youth and life at full-tide are beautiful. There is nothing holier on earth than the unfolding of the child-mind.
- I do not take my opinions from others. I am not bound by traditions or dogmas and it seems to me that I have no reverence.
- Friends have always found it difficult to read my moods. Very few have known me intimately, but I have occasionally met people who understood me and whose hearts I reached without knowledge and without effort.
- In real life, I have not had many close friends. Those friends I like best are in biographies and autobiographies because there is less danger of disillusionment in book-friendships.
- Temperamentally, I am nervous and irritable. These faults are at the roots of my nature. They restrain my social activities, lessen my influence, and prevent me from doing anything remarkable.
- I think I am afraid of people in the flesh. Anyway, 1 am not particularly interested in the practical side of their lives.
- I am too driven to pay tribute to friendship. Some of us blunder into life through the back door.
- [I am fairly sure Sullivan is reflecting in this quote on her years

spent at the Tewksbury poor house]. The realization that life is much more horrible than I imagined grew and laid hold on me. I braced my back to sustain the shock. I must be brave, strong, self-sufficient. My heart hardened, my tongue became harsh and cruel. My spirit despaired because all the superfine things that I had been taught about life had turned to sand and ashes. There was no structure whatsoever to my existence because the foundations I built on were worm-eaten platitudes. The rough grain of truth was not in them, but, instead, some poor impermanent substitute. My soul would have withered unless I had found a new element in myself. The wise ones had nothing to tell me. I doubt if life, or eternity for that matter, is long enough to erase the errors and ugly blots scored upon my brain by those dismal years.

- An open mind is often a vacant mind. Ignorant minds are prisons, locked and bullet-proof.
- I am not spiteful, and I have never intentionally hurt anyone.
- I have never been a standard-bearer; I am too self-indulgent and changeable.
- I have a good memory for books and people who interest me, but I cannot remember dates, or names, or stories.
- After reading, which I enjoy most, I enjoy music and high politics.
- My chief foes are restlessness and moodiness. I dislike acquisitiveness, arrogance, and authority. Yet there are times when I appear to condone them. John Macy used to say to me, "You resemble the rich in the vulgarity of your tastes. You desire an extravagant house, the finest apparel, the fastest horse and automobile, expensive food, pedigreed dogs, and more things than I can enumerate."
- I never think about money until I haven't any.
- The extremes of wealth and poverty can have but one result. The great mass of humanity works unceasingly while a small group works not at all.
- After all, there is nothing to Heaven but our conception of it. I cannot conceive of God separate from nature. The idea of God as Father, Friend, or Consoler is unthinkable.
- I am not vain. I am sensitive and shy in society. I have endured much physical pain, and I can feel real pity for anyone who suffers. The misfortunes of the disinherited of the world rouse in me not only compassion but a fierce indignation.

- I hate all kinds of lying. It seems cowardly. I cannot imagine a courageous person deliberately deceiving anybody.
- I exhaust myself striving after perfection when circumstances make it unattainable. This desire of perfection renders it difficult for me to work with other people.
- I am painfully punctual and detest waiting for others.
- As we drove up in front of our farmhouse, we saw a gull close to the door. It lifted wide wings and flew away over the cornfields. As I entered, a telegram was put into my hand telling of John's death [her estranged husband, John Macy]. Now my heart is full of withered emotions. My eyes are blinded with unshed tears. Today only the dead seem to be travelling. I wish I was going his way. The House of Life is shattered with the wounds he inflicted; the broken walls are of his forgetting. Three thousand miles away his body, once so dear, lies cold and still. The dreadful drama is finished, the fierce struggle that won only despair is ended. I will not retell the things he did. I am not his historian. Deep in the grave, our dust will stir at what is written in our biographies.
- I have been homesick many a year for his arms. Perhaps it was wrong to look too deep within. Now he is dead.
- [Following are the last words Sullivan wrote before her sight failed]: Why did you not ask your questions before my heart was cold, my hair gray? What does it matter now who my father was? Or my mother? Or how my childhood was nurtured? Your need of praise or blame or sympathy or scorn cannot touch me now. I am as indifferent as a stone. Love has betrayed me; friendship is a broken reed. Life has pierced me in a thousand ways, but the wounds are all dry. I think I have forgotten how they used to bleed. You have been kept aloof, proud world, too long. The time for confidence is passed. The safest abode for my secret is where the darkness shelters all.

∾

Polly Thomson wrote down a few of Anne Sullivan's final words. These comments were copied from Joseph Lash's remarkable biography *Helen and Teacher* (1980):

- Goodbye John Macy, I'll soon be with you, goodbye, I loved you.

- I wanted to be loved. I was lonesome—then Helen came into my life. I wanted her to love me, and I loved her. Then later Polly came, and I loved Polly and we were always so happy together— my Polly, my Helen. Dear children, may we all meet together in harmony.
- My Jimmy, I'll lay these flowers by your face—don't take him away from me. I loved him so, he's all I've got. She took the bedclothes and threw the bucket of flowers out of there.
- Teacher was complimenting nurse and nurse said, Oh, you are playing to the gallery. Teacher threw her head back smiling and said, "I've play-acted all my life and I shall play act till I die!"
- Polly will take care of Helen. As the years go on her speeches won't be so brilliant as what people think [sic] but my guiding hand won't be there to take out what should be taken out.
- Thank God I gave up my life that Helen might live. God help her to live without me.

What Else Happened in 1936?

Here are a few randomly selected events that occurred in 1936: Adolf Hitler announced the construction of the Volkswagen Beetle (the People's Car). . . . Adolf Hitler violated the Treaty of Versailles by sending troops into the Rhineland. Nazi propaganda claimed that 99% of Germans voted for Nazi candidates. . . . Alan Turing submitted his paper "On Computable Numbers" for publication, in which he set out the theoretical basis for modern computers. . . . Margaret Mitchell's novel "Gone with the Wind" was published. . . . Spanish generals Francisco Franco and Emilio Mola lead a right-wing uprising, starting the Spanish Civil War. . . . The XI Summer Olympic Games were opened by Adolph Hitler in Berlin.

1937: JAPAN

In 1937, Helen and Polly visited Japan for the first time—she and Polly would return after the Second World War had ended. Helen Keller erected a strange humanitarian bridge between the savage ignorance that created World War Two and the exhausted quiet of the immediate post-war years. She was seen by both the Japanese and American governments as an unofficial goodwill ambassador.

During her visit to Japan in 1937, Helen was anxious to visit landmarks related to the Japanese blind scholar, the Buddhist Monk Hokiichi Hanawa.[56] According to Wikipedia "Hokiichi became blind when he was 5 years old. He learned history, literature, medical science and jurisprudence from several masters. Hokiichi compiled the "Gunsho Ruijū" (The Great Collection of Old Documents). This is from the Wiki article:

> In 1937, Helen Keller came to Japan and visited Hokiichi's memorial house. She expressed her impression as follows:
> "When I was a child, my mother told me that Mr. Hanawa should be my role model. To visit this place and touch his statue was the most significant event during this trip to Japan. The worn desk and the statue facing down earned more respect of him. I believe that his name would pass down from generation to generation like a stream of water.

I am struck by the statement that Kate Keller had introduced Helen to this Japanese blind scholar. Kate was far more sophisticated than history has recorded.

On this first trip, the Japanese government gave Helen a dog as a gift of their appreciation for her visit because they knew she loved dogs. The dog was a breed not found in the United States, an Akita, named Kamikaze-go.

This is a good time to list a few of Helen Keller's dogs. There is an article called "Helen Keller: A life with dogs," published in 2016 by Bill Winter. The article is available online at the Helen Keller Digital Archives at the Perkins School for the Blind. There are wonderful online pictures of Helen with the dogs listed below.

When she was about eight years old, the family had a Chesapeake Bay retriever named Jumbo. When she was a pre-teen the family had a dog named Belle. When Helen was an adolescent, the family had a bull mastiff named Lioness. In college, at Radcliffe, her classmates gave Helen a Boston bull terrier called Sir Thomas. When she was a young woman, after college, she had a French bull terrier called Kaiser. In middle age, she had a Great Dane called Sieglinde (who had numerous puppies). She had two Akita dogs. Presumably, there were more dogs than the ones listed in Bill Winter's article, since Helen often had more than one dog at a time.

Helen's interest in the Akita dog breed was made known and is the reason the Japanese gave her a dog from that famous lineage. Helen is credited with bringing the Akita breed to America. This was taken from the Akita Club of America (ACA) website:

> When Keller visited Akita Prefecture in Japan in July 1937, she inquired about Hachikō, the famed Akita dog that had died in 1935. She told a Japanese person that she would like to have an Akita dog; one was given to her within a month, with the name of Kamikaze-go. When he died of canine distemper, his older brother, Kenzan-go, was presented to her as an official gift from the Japanese government in July 1938. Keller is credited with having introduced the Akita to the United States through these two dogs. By 1939 a breed standard had been established and dog shows had been held, but such activities stopped after World War II began. Keller wrote in the Akita Journal:
>
> "If ever there was an angel in fur, it was Kamikaze. I know I shall never feel quite the same tenderness for any other pet. The Akita dog has all the qualities that appeal to me—he is gentle, companionable and trusty." [57]

Helen and Polly might have been doing important work for the United States government, but they were also grieving Anne Sullivan's death in 1937:

> At 7:30 PM Alexander Woollcott broadcast a moving tribute to Teacher—"a memorial to one of the great women of our time— or any time." His words, full of perceptive tenderness, caressed my fingers as Polly spelled them. She said he spoke beautifully with a throb of emotion in his voice. Tears welled up in my eyes as he told how fifty years ago tomorrow Anne Sullivan "started a work which has been recognized the world around as one of the heartening triumphs of the human spirit." I never felt prouder than when he said she "was made of the original stuff of creation." The sense of responsibility made me tremble as he spoke of the torch "handed on from Dr. Howe to Laura Bridgman, from Laura to Anne Sullivan, from Anne to Helen Keller, from Helen to . . ." We clasped hands as he ended with "this to Helen Keller and Polly Thomson as they start for the far east. Our prayers—and Anne Sullivan's too, maybe—the prayers of all of us go with you to Japan and back—now and always." [58]

We are thankful for people like Alexander Woollcott; he is on the spot in history, and he finds a way to speak for all of mankind. Such people say with deep honest emotion, and with articulate expression what we long to hear. Woollcott (1887–1943) was a commentator for *The New Yorker* magazine, an actor and playwright, and he was a well-known and respected radio personality.

Helen and Polly traveled for much of 1936 into 1937. Helen's comments about her grief and missing Anne Sullivan are recorded on many pages of her journal:

> Too well I know how often Teacher will seem to die again as I go from room to room, object to object, and find her not. I shall need every mental picture I have of Heaven, every beauty of God's word, all the high examples Teacher and I contemplated, to lift my soul to hers above such an immeasurable, down-dragging loneliness. [59]

I like Helen's comments in the following journal entry for March 11,

1937. She was being interviewed by Kathryn Cravens a reporter for Columbia Broadcasting:

> A very sweet woman, Kathryn Cravens of Columbia Broadcasting Co., interviewed me this afternoon . . . I knew we understood each other when I learned that we both love beauty, travel, and dogs . . . We both think life a wonderful game, and we are determined to play it to the finish; we believe that courage is a cure for every sorrow.

You must be at a high level of consciousness (spiritual evolution) to sense that *life is a wonderful game* to be courageously played until the very end. Helen Keller enjoyed her moments; she lived in a vivid state of presence.

On March 29, 1937, Helen wrote in her journal:

> En route from Kansas City to San Francisco, March 29th. At times, life seems nothing but a series of meetings and partings.

I put this quote here because Helen's journal is evidence of her overwhelming correspondence and her exceptionally busy schedule of speeches, meetings, and traveling to and from events. At each location friends and admirers were present, reporters and photographers pressed in around her. It is no wonder that she and Polly often felt exhausted and, at times, depressed by these intense and relentless experiences. After visiting Paris and then Japan, Helen and Polly returned to the states on February 9, 1937.

What Else Happened in 1937?

Here are a few randomly selected events that occurred in 1937: Spinach growers in Crystal City, Texas, erected a statue of Popeye. . . . New York City college students staged their 4th annual peace strike. . . . Neville Chamberlain became the Prime Minister of the United Kingdom. . . . Henry Ford initiated a 32-hour work week. . . . The Buchenwald Concentration Camp opened in Germany. . . . The Japanese attacked Marco Polo Bridge as they invaded China. . . . J. R. R. Tolkien's *The Hobbit* was published. . . . Adolf Hitler informed military leaders of his intention to go to war.

1938: Helen Keller's Journal is Published

Helen Keller's Journal (1938), a personal account of Helen's travels from 1936 through 1937 was published this year. Helen's journal begins on the ship S.S. Deutschland as the vessel slowly crossed the Atlantic Ocean. The first entry is "Midnight, November 4, 1936." There are many passages in the Journal that bemoan the loss of Anne Sullivan. The Journal is obviously an attempt at catharsis, a working out of grief and loss while trying to carry on with her mission and her many responsibilities. Here is a typical entry:

> The wrench of separation from a beloved, unique, life-long companion seemed to have torn away an essential part of me. Deaf-blind a second time, I find any effort to speak cheerfully, to resume interest in a changed world, to work along through substituted guides and minds different from Teacher's—all these I found as hampering as sharp pain-throbs. [60]

The Journal was helping her cope. On November 19, 1938 she wrote:

> This journal is Godsend. It is helping me to discipline my mind back to regular work ... Telling what I have enjoyed doubles my pleasure; writing of "blues," disappointments, and difficulties shrinks them to insignificance.

Regular work—getting back to necessary routines—involved answering a huge flood of daily mail. More letters arrived every day and Helen and

Polly did their best to give each letter a kind and content-filled response. Mostly, Helen said *thank you* repeatedly to all the people who invited her into their homes or invited her to give speeches. She reflects on this load of mail and the emotions that she felt as she read her correspondence. This was written November 20, 1939:

> Polly and I read more letters that opened up the wound in my soul. This multitude is a measure of the affection and honor in which Teacher was held; my suffering is a measure of her preciousness to me. But to be reminded every moment that the most cherished part of one's life is gone is intolerable.

In the book Notable American Women: The Modern Period: A Biographical Dictionary (1980), the authors comment that:

> *Helen Keller's Journal*, which appeared in 1938, was a revealing book and put to rest the question: "What will Helen Keller do without Teacher?"

This is also from the same book:

> Keller went abroad with Polly Thomson to adjust to a world without Macy. As a form of therapy and self-vindication she began a journal. "People will see that I have a personality, not gifted, but my own," she wrote.

As we look back on history, Helen Keller did not need to worry whether people would value her efforts; with or without Sullivan and Thomson, Helen is celebrated globally, long after her death. Helen's dedication and accomplishments stand without question. The work of Anne Sullivan is also rightfully praised and honored. The work of Polly Thomson seems not as well understood or honored, perhaps because Polly had to follow in the footsteps of the Miracle Worker. Thomson had a strong personality, and she played her role in history with great pride and determination. However, she often stood in the shadows as Keller and Sullivan were praised. Fortunately, the three strong women are buried side-by-side at the National Cathedral in Washington D.C.

What Else Happened in 1938?

Here are a few randomly selected events that occurred in 1938: Augustus Muir, who wrote the foreword to Helen Keller's Journal (1938), mentioned that "Helen Keller's beautifully typed examination papers have been preserved in the Harvard museum." . . . The March of Dimes was established to fight polio. . . . The Church of England accepted the theory of evolution as part of God's plan. . . . German troops entered Austria. . . . The Italian Air Force, in support of Francisco Franco, bombed Barcelona during the Spanish Civil War. . . . Just as they endorsed the Nazi regime, the Vatican recognized Franco's fascist Spain. . . . Japan formally declared war on China. . . . A radio broadcast by H. G. Wells called *The War of the Worlds*, narrated by Orson Welles, caused panic in some parts of the listening audience.

Helen Keller's Journal

This is from a New York Times book review:

> One notes without surprise that this journal from months of sorrow is not a sad book. It is before all else vital; and its quality of vitality is and continues to be amazing. In never-failing astonishment and in attentive response the reader follows this record of experience: the stay in Scotland, with its visits in several households, its descriptions of journeys, of houses, or gardens and people and dogs, the constant study of work for the blind, wherever Miss Keller is, and the glimpses of her own unending activities; and most of all, perhaps, the notes on acquaintances made and books read and plays and films enjoyed, and even music somehow "drifting in," as she says once, or sought in vibrations through hands and feet. This is the zest for life itself. And it seems it must be that her spirit is whole and free and untrammeled.

Helen Keller's Journal, complied between November 1936 and April 1937, begins only two weeks after Anne Sullivan died. *The Journal* was very much a catharsis, an attempt by Helen to re-establish her inner strength, to carry on her work with the blind while in a state of shock.

Death, war, and injustice came at Helen Keller in depressing waves during these pre-war years, but she did nor veer from her mission in life. Her optimism continued. Her work ethic survived. Her determination to do what she considered just was as strong as ever.

After Annie's death, Polly Thomson and Helen needed a dramatic change of scenery; they needed a fresh adventure that took them far from the months of pain and suffering which they had endured as Sullivan's health had slowly declined. A short time after Anne Sullivan's death, they boarded a ship and set sail to visit Polly's family at her ancestral home in the village of Bothwell in Scotland. The trip was a combination of work and recovery for Helen, part restful vacation and part fundraising and advocacy for the American Foundation for the Blind. Even in her grief, Helen continued to speak on behalf of blind individuals in every country she visited.

Helen Keller's Journal is a daily record of people, places, and emotional reflections. Helen muses about Anne Sullivan, about the dread of impending war in Europe, about the beauty of Scotland, and about encounters with dogs, children, and Royalty. Her next stop after Scotland was Japan so she spent many hours mentally preparing for that important visit. It was 1936 and the signs of another world war were evident. Germany, Italy, and Japan were rushing towards militarism.

Helen had been invited to Japan, and she would soon be embraced by the Japanese people. She wrote in her journal about the pending atmosphere of aggression that she could sense. She saw war as a human failing, a mirror that showed our species how extremely far we had to go to develop a spiritual global soul. Like so many other humanitarians, Helen Keller watched in horror as murder and atrocity were sanctioned in autocratic nations.

Helen Keller's Journal is another important work that should be in every Helen Heller collection; the book marks the end of the Anne Sullivan era. The next fifty years of Helen's life would show the world that Helen Keller was her own woman—whatever influence Anne Sullivan had over Helen was in the past. From the mid-1930s to the mid-1980s, Helen Keller tirelessly traveled around the world, giving speeches, raising funds, and laboring to change laws, old paradigms, and injustices.

1939: ARCAN RIDGE

Helen sold her home in Forest Hills and the household (Helen, Polly, and the dogs) moved to Arcan Ridge in Westport, Connecticut. Arcan Ridge is named after a location in Scotland that Helen and Polly loved.

What Else Happened in 1939?

Here are a few randomly selected events that occurred in 1939: The Spanish Civil War ended as Madrid fell to Francisco Franco. . . . Germany and Italy announced an alliance known as the Rome-Berlin Axis. . . . World War Two started when Germany invaded Poland. France, England Australia, New Zealand, South Africa, and Canada declared war on Germany. . . . Adolf Hitler announced plans to regulate the "Jewish problem." . . . The Irish Republican Army (IRA) began a bombing campaign in England. . . . The first nuclear fission experiment (splitting of a uranium atom) occurred in the U.S. . . . John Steinbeck published *The Grapes of Wrath*. . . . Frank Sinatra made his recording debut.

1940: LET US HAVE FAITH IS PUBLISHED

In 1940, Helen Keller published a small book called *Let Us Have Faith*. This book is not often read and analyzed by scholars, but I find the little book to be wonderful and important. Since I have already discussed dual-process theory (in *The Esoteric Helen Keller*) and made the point that human beings have two mutually exclusive minds, I can simply state that Helen Keller is talking in her book about the *Allocentric mind*, the *Self*, the *Soul*—I use all three of these terms as synonyms. If we confuse the Ego with the Self, there is no way that *Let Us Have Faith* can be understood or even entertained as a significant contribution.

The Egoic mind cannot truly comprehend a book like *Let Us Have Faith*, because, ironically, the Ego is deaf and blind to Faith. The Egocentric mind has an important role in evolution, but the Ego is not the seat of compassion. Helen captures this in the following quote (which reminds me of Goethe, who made a similar observation):

> Analysis is as destructive of emotion as of the flower which the botanist pulls to pieces. ~*Midstream,* by Helen Keller, 1929.

The Soul loves the whole flower without judgement or analyzation. The Soul loves the growth process; it does not dissect and freeze the world into ever finer fragments. The Allocentric mind is non-verbal, experiential, and wisdom-based. In contrast, the Ego is verbal, analytical, and intellectually-based. The Ego wants to define, categorize, compare, to be critical, to dissect, to judge, and to label. The Soul wants to be alive and aware, to feel, to merge, to go with the flow, to dance, to sing, but never to judge. Human beings can dwell in one mind or the other, but not in both minds at once. Of course, our two minds alternate very rapidly. How else could the Ego be employed to write down what the Soul wishes to express!

In *Let Us Have Faith*, Helen Keller is telling us about the Self/Soul and why it has so much power. She has witnessed two world wars and a global depression. She has seen the handiwork of the Egoic mind: the unevolved Ego can become a stupid and brutal beast. The unevolved Ego cannot comprehend Love because it *cannot feel* Love. The Ego can define Love, assign chemicals and biology as descriptors for Love, but the Ego is not designed to be compassionate—compassion and passion *are not* part of the Ego's biological mandate. Helen knew this even though the science that would validate her Faith did not arrive until after her death (i.e., dual-process theory is the validation).

If I start quoting from *Let Us Have Faith*, I will end up copying the whole thing. So, I will just record a few sentiments that leaped out at me as I read. It is chilling that Helen wrote this book in 1940 before the horrors of World War Two had fully unfolded. She had seen enough, however, to speak of the wreck of civilization. Here is the first paragraph of the book:

> For those of us who mourn the wrecking of half a civilization and the noble values it gave us to serve, it is hard to see good in the future. Blessings once sweet have turned to ashes because millions are in utter want of all things. But however dark the world may seem; we have a light at our command. It is faith, and it is ours to do with as we will. For faith is thought directed toward good, and like all thought-power it is infinite. ~ *Let us Have Faith*, by Helen Keller, 1940.

In this one paragraph, we see Helen Keller's optimism, her outrage, her spirituality, her morality, and her hopeful creed. Here is another quote from the book which I found important to share:

> Continents sink; empires disintegrate; but faith and the universe of heroic minds abides forever. ~ *Let us Have Faith*, by Helen Keller, 1940.

Helen Keller's heroic mind certainly seems to have impacted humanity. It seems she is as often quoted as Albert Einstein. We are not in any hurry to forget her life and the power of her faith. The quote below reminds me of the words of the Dalai Lama who made it abundantly clear that Karma implied action. Here is Helen saying the same thing in her own powerful language:

> Passive faith is no more a force than sight is in the eye that does not look or search out. Active faith knows no fear. It denies that God has betrayed His creatures and given the world over to darkness. It denies that men are to be judged after the appearance of race, color and opinion instead of according to the Law of Life. ~ *Let us Have Faith*, by Helen Keller, 1940.

Helen Keller does not back down in the face of evil. She refuses to give up on humanity. There is a light inside of human beings called *Faith* and it cannot be extinguished. Eyes that judge based on appearance are passive eyes, eyes without courage or wisdom, eyes disconnected from the inner light. How ironic that Helen Keller could see this inner light while so many modern human beings still cannot:

> [Faith] fires the imagination, and this is essential, for one must envision the higher life and behave as if it were a fact before it can unfold. ~ *Let us Have Faith*, by Helen Keller, 1940.

This insight is far more profound than it at first appears; it holds a very ancient secret. You cannot reach the higher realms of spirituality, the higher levels of consciousness, unless you first pass through a world of imagination. You must believe in magic before magic will happen to you. You must know that serendipity is real before serendipitous moments begin to unfold for you. You must accept that synchronicity is an actual phenomenon before synchronicities start happening in your life. You must have faith that faith is real before faith will manifest. . . . Oh my. The rational mind, mired in an Egoic world, finds this whole perspective to be superstitious and Pollyannaish nonsense—that's why Egoic levels of mind are so hard to pass beyond.

Helen knew that her accomplishments were built upon all the victories that came before. She stood on the shoulders of giants; she knew this, and she was deeply grateful:

> Just one special "fact" existed to bridge the chiasm between mankind and me—the education of Laura Bridgman, the first deaf-and-blind person ever to be taught communication with her fellow creatures. ~ Let us Have Faith, by Helen Keller, 1940.

Not only is Helen saying *thank you* to Samuel Gridley Howe and to Laura Bridgman, but she is also staring at an alternative future where her wonderful mind might have been locked in silent darkness for a lifetime, never knowing about Mark Twain, Jesus Christ, or Anne Sullivan. Just one event in time, shortly before she was born, was the difference between the glory of God and the abyss of never knowing greater realities, greater wonders. She knows that this gift come from faith-in-action, not in logical syllogisms:

> Proof is not my concern. Can anything really be proved— goodness, or beauty, or joy. You cannot define happiness any more than you can define health, but you know them when you feel them. What I want is to live. Not letting faith breathe in me would be death. ~ Let us Have Faith, by Helen Keller, 1940.

In the paragraph above, Helen is challenging the Ego to measure intangibles like goodness, truth, and beauty. She is challenging the Ego to measure and judge that which it cannot perceive or comprehend. Helen knows that the Ego is not up to the task. The Soul feels the body's animation; it just knows—the Soul is the mysterious location, the home, where Faith arises.

Here is another of her often-repeated sentiments: do not bring the little person to the table, she tells us; always bring the powerful, beautiful person to every event. We are not served by self-denigrating behaviors:

> We betray ourselves when we think the little choices of each day are trivial. Drama and risk are needed to vitalize every commonplace act or lesson or posture . . . Every day we should do a little more than is required . . . If to all we do we add a little more love, a bit more beauty, our interest will be too great to allow us to slip back into deaf, blind, and dumb routine. ~ Let us Have Faith, by Helen Keller, 1940.

How often do we dwell in deaf, dumb, and blind routines? How often do we feel numb, mildly depressed, joyless because we are detached from our Self, our Soul? Helen is telling is what modern gurus are saying to this very day: *Wake up*. There is more to you than an Ego.

What Else Happened in 1940?

Helen turned 60 in 1940. She told an interviewer from the *New York Times*, "I find life an exciting business." Her optimism and strong spirit still flowed as she approached her elder years.

Here are a few randomly selected events that occurred in 1940: Nazi Germany began the London blitzkrieg, also known as the Blitz. . . . Penicillin was first used. . . . The first synthetic rubber tires were manufactured. . . . Tiffany's in New York City became the first air-conditioned store. . . . The first commercial flights with pressurized cabins occurred. . . . The Jeep was manufactured for the U.S. Army. . . . M&Ms were first manufactured for the U.S. Army. . . . On February 6, 1940, Tom Brokaw, best-selling author of *The Greatest Generation* was born. . . . Walt Disney's animated movie "Pinocchio" was released. . . . Woody Guthrie wrote "This Land Is Your Land" (His original title was "God Bless America."). . . . Himmler ordered the building of the Auschwitz concentration camp. . . . The Pulitzer Prize was awarded to John Steinbeck for his book *Grapes of Wrath*.

1941: Pearl Harbor

On December 7, 1941, Japanese planes attacked the United States Naval Base at Pearl Harbor in Hawaii. More than 2,300 Americans were killed in the assault and much of the Pacific fleet was lost. President Franklin Roosevelt called December 7, 1941, "a date which will live in infamy." That date is still a symbol of Japanese tyranny and of the triumph of militarism and insane patriarchy in the unevolved minds of an entire culture. [61]

Helen Keller had developed genuine and respectful feelings for the people of Japan through her personal experiences as a representative of the American Foundation for the Blind. Prior to the attack on Pearl Harbor, many Japanese civilians had become Helen Keller's friends. In 1937, Helen was hailed as a Goodwill Ambassador to Japan during her pre-war visit there. So, we wonder: what was Helen Keller doing on that day, a Sunday morning in 1941, when the Japanese military attacked the United States of America?

In an indirect but still quite harsh way, the attack on Pearl Harbor was a personal slap to the face, a rudeness to Helen Keller that still reverberates as a side note in history. However, Helen Keller had a global humanitarian perspective; she was not about to blame every Japanese citizen for the madness of world leaders—most of the world's leaders were males steeped in an ancient and violent worldview. Joseph Lash (*Helen and Teacher*, 1980) makes it clear that it was a moderate, anti-war, humanitarian collective of Japanese citizens and leaders that invited Helen Keller to Japan. They were trying to send a message of peace and cooperation without antagonizing the young militants who were gaining power in their country. Like humanitarians everywhere, they were unable to stop the violent stupidity of authoritarian minds; the future played out as it did—millions of dead, millions more disabled, and a world in ruins.

In 1948, after the war had ended and Hiroshima and Nagasaki lay in ruins, Helen Keller was invited back to Japan:

> In October [1948], a private organization, the Nippon Lighthouse Foundation invited Helen Keller to visit Japan. The militant Socialist, suffragette and champion of the disabled toured the country, raising public awareness of the problems faced by the blind, deaf, and mute. By late 1848, these diverse currents had merged to form an irresistible movement for change. [62]

Here is a personal recollection by a Nagasaki survivor:

> The autumn of 1848, Helen Keller spoke with her own voice to the people of Hiroshima and Nagasaki. Touching the scars from the burns on people's faces both sickened Helen and filled her with indignation. The trip to Hiroshima and Nagasaki "scorched a deep scar" on her heart," Helen wrote later. "I felt sure that I smelt the dust from the burning of Nagasaki—the smoke of death." As Helen Keller left Japan, she resolved to fight "against the demons of atomic warfare . . . and for peace." Sachiko would not forget the day Helen Keller came to Nagasaki. [63]

I find it personally difficult to reconcile the contrast between the hatefulness of the Japanese military and the goodness of the everyday Japanese citizen. I suppose it is the same dilemma in any war—there is a belligerent patriarchal (fascist) class that has power and is aggressive, and then there are the citizens who look away or hide from the violence and cruelty—simple people without power are caught up in the madness. In her Journal, Helen reflected on the Japanese character. She was crossing the Pacific Ocean, on her way to Yokohama for her first visit to the country as she wrote these words aboard the Japanese vessel, the Asama-Maru:

> There are handsome, quiet Japanese aristocrats; there are brisk, shrewd businessmen. Others appear much interested in

athletics, and the deck sports are fascinating to watch. Others, like the captain, are thoughtful, troubled by the disorder and suffering in the world. But through these different types runs the same untranslatable race conjugation. I also perceive in them a conflict between an ancient civilization and modern times. Young and old alike seem pulled this way and that by opposing forces which they must try to comprehend quickly if they are to preserve their national life. Some are nervously self-conscious, as if trying to fit in with western ideals and methods that are changing the face of the earth. Unflinching loyalty to their emperor and intense patriotism are still a fundamental part of their mental equipment.[64]

Helen is not naïve as she reflects on the state of the world. Her innate optimism is struggling against a very evil everyday unfolding that she can read very clearly. She is cautiously examining the Japanese character as she gets ready for her visit. Her message of loving-kindness and service is trying to shine through, but a menacing shadow is descending over the earth, which she feels. She arrives in Japan just four years before patriarchal militarism wins out over loving-kindness in Japan.

An article published in 2014 by the *International Research Centre for Japanese Studies* looked at Helen Keller's diplomacy in Japan. Here is an abstract of that article:

This article analyzes Helen Keller's civil diplomacy in U.S.-Japan relations through her visits to Japan in 1937 and 1948. In 1937, Keller visited Japan and Manchukuo (Japan's puppet state in Manchuria) at the moment when the Marco Polo Bridge incident was poised to break out. Keller was welcomed in Japan by the Japanese emperor, the prime minister and other government officials. She delivered a letter from President Roosevelt that reconfirmed America's friendship with Japan. American ambassador to Japan, Joseph Grew, described Keller as one of the most successful American diplomats. Keller's trip was even extended to Korea and Manchukuo, which were under Japan's occupation at that time. Although the promotion of welfare was her purpose, Keller's trip to Manchukuo was enthusiastically supported by the Japanese government and by the Kwantung Army, eager to explain Japan's policy in northern China to the United States. In 1948, only three years after the Pacific War ended, Helen Keller was invited to Japan a second time. She toured over thirty cities across the nation, inspiring MacArthur to improve U.S.-Japan relations. As Keller toured ruined Hiroshima and Nagasaki, met Emperor Hirohito, shook hands with hundreds of thousands of Japanese citizens, mutual perceptions and public opinion in Japan and the United States started changing. Emperor Hirohito was portrayed as the benevolent leader of a new democratic Japan, a man who understood the significance of welfare for the disabled. Hiroshima and Nagasaki citizens interpreted Keller's trip to their cities as an America attempt at atonement. Keller's successful civil diplomacy in Japan made the U.S. State Department recognize her as their most effective symbol of America and so a valuable political asset. [65]

What Else Happened in 1941?

Here are a few randomly selected events that occurred in 1941: President Franklin Roosevelt made his famous Four Freedoms speech: freedom of speech, freedom of worship; freedom from want, freedom from fear. . . . Minister Winston Churchill warned Joseph Stalin that a German invasion was imminent. . . . British intelligence at Bletchley Park broke the German spy codes after capturing Enigma machines aboard the weather ship Muenchen. . . . Nazi Germany and its allies invaded the Soviet Union in the largest military operation in human history. . . . President Roosevelt approved an atomic program, the Manhattan Project. . . . Walt Disney's animated film "Dumbo" was released. . . . After the attack on Pearl Harbor, President Franklin D. Roosevelt delivered his Day of Infamy speech to the United States Congress.

1946: American Foundation for the Overseas Blind

Helen visited the blind, deaf, and disabled soldiers of World War Two in military hospitals around the country. She called this "the crowning experience of my life."

Helen and Polly make their first world tour for the American Foundation for the Overseas Blind (AFOB) in 1946, visiting London, Paris, Italy, Greece, and Scotland. In the next 11 years, Helen and Polly would visit 35 countries on five continents.

A fire destroyed Helen's home at Arcan Ridge on November 3, 1946 (while she and Polly were traveling internationally). Fire and smoke destroyed important historical letters and many of the gifts Helen and Annie had received from organizations and governments.

What Else Happened in 1946?

Here are a few randomly selected events that occurred in 1946: Mahatma Gandhi began a march for peace in East Bengal. . . . Earl Mountbatten was appointed as the last viceroy of India to oversee the move to an independent India. . . . Japan's post-war constitution went into effect, outlawing Japan's right to make war, granting universal suffrage, and stripping Emperor Hirohito of all but symbolic power. . . . Secretary of State George Marshall outlined the "Marshall Plan" to rebuild Western Europe. . . . Anne Frank's diary was published in The Netherlands. . . . India gained independence from Great Britain, remaining a dominion until 1950. . . . *You Bet Your Life* with Groucho Marx premiered on ABC radio.

1948: Arcan Ridge 2

After a fire destroyed their home, Helen and Polly settled into their new dwelling, which they called Arcan Ridge 2, an almost identical replica of the original Arcan Ridge house—friends had pitched in financially to rebuild their home. Helen and Polly did not spend much time at the new location at first because they were touring (fundraising) on behalf of the American Foundation for the Blind. In 1948, Helen and Polly visited Egypt, England, Syria, Lebanon, Jordan, Australia, New Zealand, Israel, and Japan as representatives of the American Foundation of the Overseas Blind (the international branch of AFB). When they reached Japan, Polly Thomson suffered her first stroke, and the remainder of the tour was canceled.

Helen visited Nagasaki on this trip and called the city a "black, silent hole." She used the occasion to speak out against nuclear war.

What Else Happened in 1948?

Here are a few randomly selected events that occurred in 1948: Mahatma Gandhi was assassinated by a Hindu extremist. Year by year, I traced Gandhi's activities as I pieced together this timeline. It is shocking to see such a dedicated humanitarian die suddenly at the hands of an agent of evil. Human beings like Mahatma Gandhi and Helen Keller are extraordinary; death does not end their influence. Such humanitarian souls become mythological role models championing the healthy evolution of cognition and empathy. When they die, their souls live on to remind us that Love and Service are our Earthly mandates.

The World Health Organization (W.H.O.) was formed by the United Nations (U.N.), which had been established on October 24, 1945, in San Francisco. . . . The U.N. Commission on Human Rights adopted the International Declaration of Human Rights. . . . J. D. Salinger's short story "A Perfect Day for Banana Fish" appeared in the New Yorker Magazine. . . . The Soviet Union began the West Berlin Blockade by stopping access to Berlin by road, rail and water. . . . President Harry Truman was re-elected in an upset victory over Republican Thomas E. Dewey. . . . American-born British poet T. S. Eliot won the Nobel Prize for literature.

1950 TO 1959: TRAVELING AND PUBLISHING

Helen turned 70 in 1950. She and Polly traveled to Paris in 1952 to celebrate the 100th anniversary of the death of Louis Braille. The blind of Paris marched in procession through the streets to gather for the tribute. Helen addressed the crowd in French saying that Louis Braille was the *Gutenberg for the Blind*. After the tribute, Helen was given the Legion of Honor metal by the French government. In June 1952, Helen's friend Van Brooks wrote in his diary:

> With members of Braille's family, [Helen] was present at the Pantheon when [Braille's] ashes were deposited there with those of the poets, philosophers and statesmen of France. She had paid tribute to him at the Sorbonne, thanking the authorities for recognizing "the spirit and efforts of all who refuse to succumb to limitations." She was made Chevalier of the Legion of Honor. "She spoke in heavily accented but faultlessly grammatical French," Florence Davidson writes after the ceremony. "Standing before the audience, she was radiant, and the applause was thunderous." [66]

Helen Keller was nominated for the Nobel Peace Prize in 1953 and again in 1954, but she did not win this honor. It would have been a tribute to the selection committee had they had the foresight to recognize Helen Keller's contributions to world culture. Leaving Helen Keller off the Nobel Prize list is like leaving Jesus off the list of religious leaders—a rather serious oversight.

Helen and Polly continued to travel the world in the 1950s, including Europe, South Africa, the Middle East, and Latin America. In Central and South America, they visited Brazil, Chile, Peru, Panama, and Mexico.

A documentary film of Helen's life, *The Unconquered* (later renamed *Helen Keller in Her Story*), was released in 1952.

In 1954, through the efforts of the Helen Keller Property Board of Tuscumbia and the State of Alabama, Helen's birthplace Ivy Green was made a permanent shrine and placed on the National Register of Historic Places. Ivy Green is located two miles off Highways 72 and 43 in Colbert County, Tuscumbia, Alabama. The grounds are lovely, the staff is delightful, Tuscumbia is a marvelous little town, flocks of birds sing for you when you arrive, and Helen's joyful soul hovers over the landscape.

In 1955, Helen and Polly embarked on a tour of the Far East, including India, Japan, Hong Kong, and the Philippines. In this same year, Helen Keller received an honorary degree from Harvard University, the first woman to be so honored. 1955 also saw the publication of *Teacher*, Helen's biography about Anne Sullivan Macy. *The Unconquered*, a documentary about Helen's life, won the Academy Award for best feature length documentary of 1955.

On November 15, 1956, Helen attended the dedication of the "deaf-blind building," *Keller-Macy Cottage* at the Perkins School for the Blind where both she and Anne Sullivan were students. The school was expanding deaf-blind services and the new building was the beginning of that endeavor. The Perkins School for the Blind Helen Keller Digital Archives contains press releases, seating lists, and a script of the dedication ceremony. The collection includes newspaper clippings about Helen Keller's role in the ceremony.

In 1957, Helen published *The Open Door: A Sense of Life; Selections from the Writings of Helen Keller. The Open Door* is about Helen's philosophy, her belief structure, her worldviews. The book is designed around daily reflections (meditations on an idea), each page contains a different pondering. In this year, Helen and Polly traveled to Canada, Iceland, Switzerland, Finland, Sweden, Norway, and Denmark.

In 1959, Tony-award winning playwright William Gibson wrote the script for the stage play *The Miracle Worker*. Gibson said that most of the credit for his work belongs to the biography of Annie Sullivan, written by Nella Braddy. Gibson also used letters written by Anne Sullivan and Helen Keller as well as autobiographical material to craft the script.

Gibson first attempted to write *The Miracle Worker* as a dance piece but later rewrote it as a television play for the series *Playhouse 90*; it aired on CBS on February 7, 1957. Gibson soon received offers to adapt the TV production for stage and film. He decided to write it for the stage so that he could have artistic control over the production.

William Gibson was born in the Bronx, New York, on November 13, 1914. He spent his childhood in New York City and attended the City College of New York from 1930 until 1932. After graduation, Gibson moved to Kansas. In Topeka, Kansas, Gibson produced his first plays, most of which were comedies. Gibson's first major critical success came in New York City years later. His first successful play was called *Two for The Seesaw*, which opened on Broadway in 1958. However, it was Gibson's second Broadway production, *The Miracle Worker*, for which he is best known.

After the success of the stage play, *The Miracle Worker* was adapted as a feature-length black and white film starring Anne Bancroft as Annie and Patty Duke as Helen. In 1962, the story was again produced for television, and then in 1979 the story was for a third time portrayed on television, this time with Patty Duke playing the role of Annie and Melissa Gilbert as Helen.

Gibson returned to the New York stage in the 1980s where he wrote the script for *The Monday after the Miracle*, a sequel to *The Miracle Worker*. *The Monday after the Miracle* opened on Broadway on December 14, 1982, at the Eugene O'Neill Theatre. However, this adaptation was a much darker piece than its predecessor and it got poor reviews and few people came to see the play. It closed after a short run. Despite that unfortunate ending to Gibson's remarkable career, his reputation rests on the glory and success of his great work of art, *The Miracle Worker*— his play continues to thrill audiences across the globe, as does the black and white movie classic.

1955: Teacher

Helen began writing *Teacher* in her home in Westport, Connecticut (Arcan Ridge) where she lived with Polly Thomson and their handyman Herbert Haas. Haas is another of those unsung players who have a supporting role in the nurturing of a miracle. He deserves to be remembered. In *Helen and Teacher*, Joseph Lash says of Herbert:

In the early thirties, while they were still living in Forest Hills, a youthful Herbert Haas had attached himself to the three women. He was quiet, considerate and good-humored, and so helpful that the women made little effort to check his antecedents, especially as he was willing to take care of an ailing Teacher during Helen's and Polly's absences on Foundation business. Teacher grew so fond of him that before she died, she said to him, "I leave Helen and Polly in your hands." He was a conscientious manager of the household, could repair Helen's typewriter and Braille machine as well as the car, tended their roses lovingly and was always ready for a game of checkers with Helen.

Haas made himself a welcome addition to a busy household. He could fingerspell and read braille and he often drove the women to and from obligations. Because of Herbert and Polly, Helen was able to turn her full attention to writing the book she had waited a lifetime to complete.

In the introduction to *Teacher*, Nella Braddy wrote:

To begin with, she had Braille notes, some of them nearly thirty years old, she had all the letters that Teacher had ever written her and intimate letters from her mother and sister and her foster father, Mr. John Hitz, who was Dr. Bell's secretary, and many other friends. She lost them all, she lost everything, in the fire that burned her house in 1946. A paralyzing disaster, but friends rebuilt and refurbished the house and after a time Helen began again—no author ever more alone. The book was in her heart.

No disaster was going to stop Helen Keller from completing this work, no set back would be final. She knew how to write books, she was confident in her skills, she knew she was listened to and valued by people all over the planet, and she also knew that she had to leave something valuable to future generations. This book was one last attempt to validate and celebrate her soul-friend (and everyone else's *Miracle Worker*). The miracle we call Helen Keller had a few final words to impart about her best friend. Helen knew this was the last book about Anne Sullivan by someone who knew her intimately.

Helen and Polly were in Rome when they got the news that their home had been burned in a fire. In *Teacher* she tells of the moment she first heard the terrible news:

We were at the Excelsior Hotel when we received a cable that our house at Arcan Ridge in Connecticut had been terribly damaged by fire—a frame house, all wood. We feared the worst and Polly and I fell into each other's arms stunned. It seemed incredible that everything had gone from us in a moment—the home where we and Herbert, our faithful man Friday, had thought to spend the rest of our days—Polly's and my irreplaceable treasures from Japan and tokens of our friends' affection, my library with all its books and papers, the letters I had cherished from Mother, Teacher, and indeed from people all over the world. With anguish I thought of the "Teacher" manuscript, three-fourths written, on which I had worked in spare moments during twenty years.

Helen's response to this disaster should not surprise us. She was homeless, but her spiritual home, she says, was intact, as strong and defiant as ever. Her core was courageous and optimistic; she knew that nothing could destroy spirituality—love endures even as the material world burns to the ground. Helen had no intention of abandoning this critical book. She would begin again, using her magnificent memory and amazing mind to craft the book anew.

At some point, during her period of anguish and regret, Helen realized that something positive had come from the fire that had destroyed twenty years of work on her book about Anne Sullivan. It seems that Annie had been watching, looking over Helen's shoulder as the initial manuscript was being created. Now Anne Sullivan was dead, no longer guiding Helen's thoughts:

> For a long time, the burning of my first manuscript on her life seemed to me an irreparable draining away of my powers, but a day came when I realized that the book over which I had grieved was not, after all, the kind I wanted to write about her. I had begun the manuscript under her dictatorial supervision. Very seldom did she give me free rein in describing her trials and illnesses and she never let me refer to the frequent indifference towards her as my guide to the treasures of light and beauty. My affection for her has not changed, but I am free as I write this to speak of our two separate souls, minds, hearts, and strengths. I picture her, who lent her humanity to create mine,

as fulfilling her destiny on earth and following a happy path of life in another world, from which in critical moments she sends down a smile of approval to me or a gesture of warning.

Those of us who write about Helen Keller also feel, from time to time, that Helen and Annie send both smiles and warnings down from above as we mix our personalities with their souls. When the Allocentric mind is flowing, when we are in a flow-zone, we sometimes sense feelings of support or despair. Intuitively, we sense that we are getting help from some divine space. As I have said in other contexts, I am not being naïve, not losing my grip on everyday reality—I am simply talking about sensing intuitive energy. It does not matter to me what the source is for this energy; what I feel is gratitude.

There is also the feeling that fate sometimes helps by destroying what we thought was "our art." I recall a time decades ago—when computer word processors were new—when I accidently hit the delete key after absentmindedly selecting "all" and then watched in horror as a novel I had worked on for years was erased—forever, all three hundred pages. I can smile now, looking back, knowing the "novel" was not ready to be shared; it was the work of an immature writer still struggling to find a voice.

∽

Helen writes at the beginning of the book that she was just a phantom, a shadow-being when Sullivan first arrived. The phantom child responded only to instincts, in the moment. As a child, Helen had no sense of past and future, no awareness of death, no understanding of knowledge, reason, or intuition. She had no awareness of infinity and eternity. She was a hollow sphere, unknowing, all potential. Helen even writes of herself in the third person in the book, because as a child she had no Ego, no sense of "I am." In another context, Helen referred to her younger self as "an incorrigible imp," and remembers repeatedly, every chance she got, pinching her grandmother, who she did not like at the time.

I wrote earlier how Helen had rushed from room to room in her house (Sullivan's observation) and I pondered how a deaf-blind kid could do that without colliding with everything in her path. In *Teacher*, I found one explanation—Helen *did* collide with everything in her path. Here is Helen using third person narrative to explain her movements:

> It was weeks before Teacher could break the child's habit of
> pushing aside lamps or other objects which she bumped. Without
> damping Helen's joy in perpetual motion, Teacher showed her
> how to handle everything gently—a canary, a kitten's fur, a rose
> on its stem with a chain of dew drops hanging from its leaves,
> her year-old sister Mildred in the swing. The importance of a
> delicate touch was shown by the death of a baby pigeon which,
> it grieves me to remember, Helen overfed. And Teacher caught
> Helen heartlessly poking a captured grasshopper around in a
> box without air, trying to make it "sing."

Evidently, Helen's method of locomotion was to push aside any offending
obstacle, be it a lit oil lamp or her baby sister. This reminded me of one
of my young students who refused to use a cane; I stood in amazement
as he crashed his way down a hallway filled with boxes, red wagons,
tricycles, and other school children—not a pretty sight (but a valuable
learning experience for the young lad).

It soon becomes obvious as you read this book that Helen is trying to
set some things straight, to poke some holes in the mythology, to weaken
the legend that she and Sullivan had become. First and foremost, Helen
wanted readers to be truly clear how difficult was the task of educating
a phantom wild child. There were great physical battles, pushing,
crashing, pinching, fists flying and wild kicking. Helen was a young
colt that needed training but refused all direction and discipline. Every
day, Sullivan had to muster strength and monumental resolve—which,
remarkably, she did. The spirit of the colt was never broken, but Helen
learned discipline and gentleness.

Most people focus on the tragedy of Helen being deaf and blind—
the focus was always on Helen, rarely on her teacher. But Helen was
adamant that the reader know how unbelievably bad Sullivan's eyesight
was from day one until her sight was totally gone on the day Annie
died. Sullivan would often have to go to bed with severe headaches and
nausea because the pain in her eyes was so bad. She had to hold reading
material an inch from her best eye to read. Her eyes did not focus well,
and the two eyes did not have equal acuity, which probably destroyed
her ability to see in depth. She probably did not have binocularity—the
ability to consistently use both eyes at once. Sullivan was also at the
mercy of lighting conditions, able to function in the delicate morning
sun, but incapacitated by the bright light of the noon day sun, which

caused severe pain. Dim light made it extremely hard for Annie to see. The light had to be optimal for Sullivan to perceive her surroundings.

Anne Sullivan would have been labeled *legally blind* by today's standards. I used to say, as a teacher, that totally blind kids could learn to function much easier and faster than the kids who were severely visually impaired, like Sullivan was. The reason for this is because visually impaired kids have highly fluctuating vision, never dependable, and always changing as lighting conditions vary.

Helen says that her adult life was heavily influenced by Anne's health issues. We know that Sullivan was (perhaps) misdiagnosed as having tuberculosis—that is why she ended up in Puerto Rico for several months. She had numerous operations on her feet and eyes and once she fell down steps after a lecture and broke her arm and dislocated her collarbone. Toward the end of her life, it was clear that she had a serious heart condition. Sullivan also got the flu when the Spanish Pandemic was petering out—we do not know what kind of flu Sullivan had, but it was serious enough to deeply frighten Helen—the flu often caused damage to vital organs.

The making of the movie *Deliverance* was a result of Helen's desire to provide income for Anne Sullivan if Helen was unable to support the household. Helen became concerned that Annie have a way to survive should she herself die or become incapacitated.

~

Not much was ever said about Sullivan's personality, so Helen was intent on correcting this oversight. From Helen's perspective, Sullivan's emotions and her personality were forever affected by early experiences, by Annie's childhood poverty, her abandonment by her father after her mother had died young, her severe visual impairment, the death of her little brother, and the loss of her sister (who was adopted). As a preteen, Sullivan found herself totally alone, living in an Almshouse, without family, friends, or hope. She had not been taught to read or write, and it seemed she had no chance for any kind of decent future. The very fact that she got herself out the almshouse and eventually became a student at the Perkins School for the Blind shows her remarkable will to survive and her determination to guide her own destiny.

Helen Keller gave Annie Sullivan a reason to endure, to hope, a mission in life. But Annie was emotionally scarred by her awful past and she would emotionally struggle over a lifetime with fearful memories and deep sadness; she struggled with the idea that anyone could love her.

Helen assures us, however, that Anne Sullivan was fiercely determined. Sullivan was a perfectionist, driven by the best in people, the best in art, by sophisticated behavior. She valued eloquent conversation and was bored by simpleminded discourse. Annie was also restless, always seeking adventure:

> She was forever seeking an outlet for her restlessness. She believed in going somewhere often and seeing something new. By that I do not mean to imply a trivial craving for amusement, but a need of self-renewal.

Sullivan put her own hopes into Helen. The two women evolved together; and they became brilliant together. But Sullivan could periodically crash and burn when her emotions, her over-drive, and her exhaustion overwhelmed her. She could be moody and lash out. She struggled with depression. She fought her own demons all the while that she was determined to give life to Helen. As Sullivan got older, her health began to gradually decline. Helen writes:

> With sorrow I noted that Teacher's robust health was beginning to weaken. That was due partly to her periods of nervous tenseness, the never ceasing torment of her eyes, her enormous disappointment in not having a baby. Other physical distresses piled upon her—a major operation before we set out on our lecture tours, frequent severe colds on the road, and an accident in which she fell down the steps breaking her arm and dislocating her collarbone.

There is little in the literature that suggests why John Macy and Anne Sullivan's marriage slowly deteriorated. Perhaps the issue of having a child together was a factor.

There was also an artistic quality to Anne Sullivan. She loved the written word, in poetry and in everyday discourse. I have no doubt that Helen Keller's fiery prose, choice of words and phrases in her powerful articles, letters, and speeches evolved as Sullivan communicated with her. Sullivan's articulate and passionate character helped shape the adult Helen Keller.

We know enough about Sullivan's personality to surmise her response to media attention. She knew that she was just another human being, not anyone gifted, or mythological, or miraculous. Overblown accolades came from the press and from people who were ignorant of the day to day lives of Sullivan and Keller. Sullivan would also insist that her poverty, ignorance, and emotional pain arising from her early years were not unusual at that time in history, especially within the population of Irish immigrants. She was lucky that her life unfolded in a way that gave her a mission in life, love, friends, an adopted family, and, most of all, Helen. I will add that Sullivan eventually became a role model and a legendary historical figure because people need positive role models and larger-than-life heroes. As she grew older, Sullivan adapted to this uncomfortable role, but she would still never let herself be unduly praised while she lived.

Sullivan probably fought against feelings of inferiority—as many of us do. She projected her desire to be special and talented onto her student, onto Helen. Sullivan would not accept the early critical judgment that Helen was extraordinary, a miracle, and was, therefore, "not normal." Sullivan knew that Helen had a normal soul inside her deaf-blind body.

Sullivan insisted that Helen become competent and sophisticated, but it was exhausting work. The wild child fought back emotionally and physically. Two powerful wills clashed, and alchemical magic was the result—beneficial for both females. Just know, Helen says, that Anne Sullivan was beset by emotional storms that brought Sullivan down from time to time. But then, because her internal strength was so remarkable, Annie got right back up from whatever emotional or physical state had felled her and she started over again—with laser focus and loving intention. There would be no long-enduring failures on her watch.

It is well understood that the two women did not agree about religion (or spirituality). As I read the various comments on this difference, I could not help but see that the two women were not as far apart as observers surmised. Both women had Love and Service at their core— that is the key connection. How you carry out your service and who helps you spiritually evolve is a personal matter. Annie had been told by Michael Anagnos to avoid religion if possible, to not indoctrinate Helen's maturing mind, and Sullivan did her best. But a time came when the two mature women stood toe-to-toe and "had it out" about spirituality:

During those young days so full of stimulating discovery and mental gymnastics to foster my spiritual growth, I sometimes discussed religious subjects with Teacher. She had waited on time and the growth of my individuality to talk with me as frankly as she did with others. Like Robert Ingersoll, she had little use for the various creeds and dogmas whose jarring "noise" echoes through the pulpits of the world. "Religion," she would say, is a way of living and not of believing only. Bear witness to what appears true to you in deeds rather than words. Through the ages people have torn each other to pieces over religious beliefs, and what good has that done?

There is a delightful imaginary exchange in the book between Helen and Anne as they debate religion and spirituality. Both women come off splendidly. Sullivan ends the exchange by saying:

Let us agree to disagree and to the best of our ability live up to our ideals. Yes, dear, I am your mother in heart and mind, but I do not own you. I want you to form your views independently. Only keep yourself clear of competitive sects and creeds, and do not get involved in any fanaticism. Always be just and generous to those with whom you differ.

You do not often read that Sullivan saw herself as a "mother figure" for Helen, but it does make sense. Their relationship was complex: teacher, sister, mother, fellow student, soul-mate, life-long friend—all the roles overlap and ebb and flow.

Another point Helen makes clear is that it was her ability to speak—as poor as it was in her judgement—that made her feel whole. Her Ego seems to have been solidified as she became more and more able to fluidly speak. When I first studied Helen Keller, I had assumed that it was fingerspelling that developed her communication skills, but I now realize that she spoke often and preferred to speak. She worked on her articulation and tonal control her whole adult life. She also seems to have developed an internal voice—she could talk to herself like the rest of us do. Our internal voice is a powerful force that gives us the illusion of being independent from the world around. Sullivan felt that the task of learning to speak was too immense for a deaf-blind individual, but Helen insisted. Sullivan put aside her own reservations and threw her usual intense energy into the training.

Anne Sullivan was remarkably smart and articulate. She was a good match as she went toe-to-toe with the spiritually infused Helen Keller. When she was recovering from a physical illness in Puerto Rico and feeling healthier each day, Annie wrote to Helen often. Here is a typical reflection from the eloquent pen of Anne Sullivan:

> If I had a grain of the sense of the humming-birds that are circling around the banana tree like a string of fire-opals, I shouldn't have wasted so much time and so many punches on reflections about war. Aren't we foolish to fill our minds with the deviltries of men instead of with the beauties of nature? But we must try to keep sane, all the more if we believe the world has gone mad.

I have a sense that every generation feels that the world has gone mad—I certainly feel that way (in 2021) as I survey the global problems of our planet and the too-slowly evolving cognition of the human species. But Helen and Annie are role models for us—they did not stop being courageous and determined. There is an affirmation of life, an optimism in their combined souls—we can draw goodness and strength from their example.

For me, there is one overarching and recurrent theme in Helen's tribute to her teacher. Helen is *always grateful* for the dedication, sacrifice, and character of Anne Sullivan. Helen *never disparages* Anne Sullivan, never doubts Annie's soul. Helen *never stops appreciating* the blessing that flowed through Anne Sullivan and saved Helen's life. This book is a statement of love and friendship and it is a fitting summation of a miracle that still inspires the best in human beings.

∼

Anne Sullivan received an honorary Doctorate of Humane Letters from Temple University in 1931 for her rare achievements in pedagogy, for her work with Helen Keller, and for her contributions to the deaf-blind community. Temple University honored both Annie and Helen with degrees. Prior to this well-deserved tribute, Annie and Helen had both been named *Fellows of the Educational Institute of Scotland.* This was a powerful statement from fellow teachers celebrating excellence in their field.

All her adult life, Helen felt that people did not realize that it was Anne Sullivan they should have been reaching out to. Here was a master teacher who had learned through raw experience what worked and what did not work. Helen felt that it was a great historical sadness that Anne Sullivan was not more often interviewed and consulted—always it was the miracle Helen Keller that people rushed toward with tears in their eyes. Sullivan stood in the shadows and approved of what people were doing—she was okay with being ignored. Anne Sullivan never felt herself worthy of more praise than any other hardworking, dedicated teacher. However, Helen Keller did not agree with Annie—Helen knew the physical and emotional toll of Sullivan's sacrifice and she knew how extraordinary Annie was. That is why Helen was so determined that this book be preserved and widely read as the decades unfolded.

Toward the end of the book, Helen recalls Annie resting in an armchair with Helen, Polly, and Herbert by her side. Helen wrote of these last moments:

> My last memory of Teacher as I knew her was an October evening when she was fully awake, sitting in an armchair with us around her. She was laughing while Herbert told her about the rodeo he had just seen. She spelled to me all he said, and how tenderly she fondled my hand! Her dearness was without limit, and it was almost intolerable. Beautiful was her touch— the creative flame from which sprang the joy of communication, the power of love binding me to my kind, and the intelligence that quickened new senses within my limitations. Afterwards she drifted into a coma from which she never awoke on earth.

Anne Sullivan had watched while the media and well-intentioned people turned Laura Bridgman into a scientific specimen for study and a curiosity, like an animal in a circus. This drained Laura's humanity; her soul was ignored as she was probed and "dissected." Knowing this, Sullivan became an emotional fortress around Helen Keller; in no way was she going to let science reduce her student and soul-mate to something less. Helen's humanity, her beautiful soul, was to be protected and preserved at all costs. Helen soon came to understand this devotion—her understanding comes across clearly in this lovely book; this is a powerful tribute to a deeply loved teacher. I will leave this review with the last sentences in the book:

There was such virtue and such power of communication in Teacher's personality that after her death they nerved me to endure and preserve. I was gripped by the might of destiny she had mapped out for me, it lifted me out of myself to wage God's war against darkness. Of course, there is always a choice between two courses, and, shocked out of all security, I might have let go any further activity, but Teacher believed in me, and I resolved not to betray her faith. Conscious of her being alive within me, I have sought new ways to give life and yet more life to men and women whom darkness, silence, sickness, or sorrow are wearing away. And at times it seems that God is using her, who touched my night to flame, to kindle other fires of good. Advancing in years and knowing that I shall be glad to get rid of my worn-out body, I yet experience new birth and youth in the soul of Teacher. The certainty that her creative intelligence and truly human quality of mind do not perish, but continue their vivifying work, sweetens my loneliness and is like the warm spring air in my heart.

Helen Keller: Sketch for a Portrait

This Book-of-the Month Club selection was written by Helen and Annie's friend Van Wyck Brooks. There is a charming flow to the book; Brooks is a talented writer with strong convictions—his insights add to the mythology of Keller and Sullivan in ways not found in other books. Brooks also has a knack for reframing the often-told stories. Here he discusses Sullivan's opinion about pity:

Anne was bent on teaching Helen how to protect herself against the hostile elements of nature and the world, and she always treated Helen as if she were a seeing and hearing child whom no one was ever allowed to pity. For she knew how destructive was this element of pity, along with the over-protectiveness that led to so many tragedies for the blind. As Helen wrote in later years, "A person who is severely impaired never knows his hidden sources of strength until he is treated like a normal human being and encouraged to shape his own life." She called pity "the chief stumbling block to the sightless," and she remembered that Anne had never permitted anyone to praise anything she did that was not done well.

This is a very modern worldview. A teacher needs to see and relate to the soul of a student and not to superficial appearances or circumstances. To overlay pity onto a blind individual is harmful, it dismisses, overlooks, and ignores the normality and humanness of that person's essence.

Chapter Two of *Sketch for a Portrait* is called "Prodigy," which seems relevant and reaffirming after my anguish over the term in Chapter Five in *The Esoteric Helen Keller*. Obviously, Helen Keller was strikingly expressive to the extent that people were startled by her eloquence and animation. The director of the Perkin's Institute, Michael Anagnos, crisscrossed through Europe proclaiming to Kings, Queens, and the media that Helen Keller was an "intellectual prodigy." Anagnos was not alone in his amazement. Brooks suggests (as did I) that it is proficiency with language that demonstrates Helen's prodigy status:

> At no age at all she was deep into German, soon to be followed by Latin and Greek, and at ten, without assistance, she wrote to Anagnos, who was in Greece, a long idiomatic letter in French . . . Asked, at twelve, what book she would like to take on a long train journey, she replied "Paradise Lost," which she read on the train; and at thirteen, busy translating Latin, she tried to master French pronunciation. At the time she was reading *Wilhelm Tell*, Racine and La Fontaine and chuckling at the comic situations of Molieres *Le Medecin Malgre Lui*, as her fingers moved slowly over the raised-print lines.

Brooks says that Helen was so good with languages because "she had, as everyone observed, a power of concentration that ordinary people never knew." Helen knew she had a powerful mind. That mind could be extraordinary even without vision and hearing. Brooks writes:

> [Helen stated that] "Deafness and blindness were of no real account. They were to be relegated to the outer circles of my life." In time, in college, she was to find . . . the phrase of Descartes . . ."I think, therefore, I am" . . . this enabled her to feel that since deafness and blindness were not part of her mind, they were not an essential part of her existence.

I believe a better word than "concentration" would be "memory." Prodigies are astounding because they have prodigious memories and rapid recall. As I argued in Chapter Four of *The Esoteric Helen Keller*, Helen's mind became extraordinary to compensate for deaf-blindness. Deafness and blindness do not impair the ability to reason, emote, imagine, or to make a difference in the lives of individuals or cultures; sensory loss does not deny a person the ability to contribute to history.

Van Brooks kept a notebook of encounters with Helen. His observations are delightful and important. Here he remembers friends quizzing Helen about her abilities:

> Someone asked her how she knows the difference between day and night. "Oh," she said, "in the day the air is lighter, odors are lighter, and there is more motion and more vibration in the atmosphere. In the evening quiet there are fewer vibrations. The air is dense, and one feels less motion in things.

In July of 1946, Van Brooks was at dinner with Helen and Polly and recorded these words in his notebook:

> She was up at five, as usual this summer, clipping the borders [of her garden]. Then, after making her bed, she always runs down the ramp from her door and goes out for her walk. She follows the handrail that Polly calls "Helen's walk," and that twists its way through the woods and curves back to the house.

Helen loved gardening and she knew her way around the plants. She pulled out weeds, planted her flowers and vegetables, and harvested in the fall, as part of her daily routine.

On the back-cover jacket of this book is a commentary by Clifford Fadiman of the *Book-of-the Month Club News*. Fadiman and his wife were guests at a party in which Helen Keller was a member. This last quote is a fitting final statement for Van Brook's loving remembrance of Helen:

> I was given the pleasure of meeting one of the most interesting persons in the world. At first one marveled at Helen Keller, at the astounding technical performance. Here was a woman blind, deaf and semi-mute, playing her proper part in a reasonably

complex conversation that lasted over three hours, exchanging ideas and impressions with a group, at least two of whom she had not previously met. But the real marvel lay in the fact that within a short time one ceased to marvel. One began to enjoy Helen Keller, not as a prodigy, but as a person exceptionally endowed with the power to enhance life. I was prepared, of course, to encounter high intelligence and rare sensitivity, but they were not the impressions that dominated. What my wife and I carried away with us was above all a sense of joy. Compared with Helen Keller, most of us in the room seemed somehow handicapped.

The Open Door

This book is billed as "philosophical reflections" from the mind of Helen Keller. The offerings are one to two-page sentiments taken from Helen's previous books—she dedicated the work to Anne Sullivan. The reflections were collected by Helen's friend Katharine Cornell. The title is taken from one of Helen's comments:

> When one door of happiness closes, another opens; but often we look so long at the closed door that we do not see the one which has been opened for us.

Here are a few random sentences from the book that jumped out at me:

- Be happy, talk happiness. Happiness calls out responsive gladness in others. *There is enough sadness in the world without yours.*
- He who does not see that joy is an important force in the world misses the essence of life.
- . . . in spirit, I am one of those who walk the morning.
- What is science but faith staking everything on imaginative hypotheses so that it may retrieve larger hopes . . .
- Character cannot be developed in ease and quiet.
- Our destiny is our responsibility, and without faith we cannot meet it competently.
- Liberty not joined to faith is already half dead.
- So long as the memory of certain beloved friends lives in my

heart, I shall say that life is good.

- I trust, and nothing that happens disturbs my trust . . . this is my religion of optimism.
- Even more amazing than the wonders of nature are the powers of the spirit.
- We betray ourselves into smallness when we think the little choices of each day are trivial.
- My friends create my world anew each day.
- Knowledge—broad, deep knowledge—is to know true ends from false, and lofty things from low.
- The mortally wounded [she speaks of herself here, as well as others] must strive to live out their days cheerfully for the sake of others. That is what religion is for—to keep hearts brave to fight out to the end with a smiling face.

The Miracle Worker

The Miracle Worker, a 3-part stage play first performed on October 19, 1959, was made into a TV drama and then into a classic black and white movie. When I re-watched the movie, after reading the books reviewed here, I was amazed how accurate and powerful the play still is. *The Miracle Worker* was written by William Gibson. It was based on Helen Keller's autobiography *The Story of My Life* and on Anne Sullivan's biography.

The play premiered at the Playhouse Theatre on October 19, 1959 and closed on July 1, 1961, after 719 performances. The play was directed by Arthur Penn with costumes by Ruth Morley and staging and lighting by George Jenkins. The cast starred Anne Bancroft as Anne Sullivan, Patty Duke as Helen Keller, Torin Thatcher as Captain Keller, Patricia Neal as Kate Keller, and Michael Constantine as Anagnos.

What Else Happened in 1950 to 1959?

Here are a few randomly selected events that occurred in the 50's decade: Senator Joseph McCarthy alleged there were communists in U.S. Government . . . The first business computer Univac was built . . . Dwight David Eisenhower was elected the 34th President of the United

States . . . The DNA double helix was discovered . . . The Montgomery Bus Boycott began in Alabama . . . The Russian satellite Sputnik was Launched.

1960 TO 1968: THE DEATH OF POLLY THOMSON AND HELEN KELLER

On March 21, 1960, Helen's longtime companion Polly Thomson died. Here is one of the obituaries written about Polly:

Helen Keller's Companion Miss Mary Agnes (Polly) Thomson, 75, of Arcan Ridge, Easton [Connecticut], who as Helen Keller's companion for nearly half a century, helped her to communicate with the World despite blindness and deafness, died at 10:30 last night in Bridgeport hospital where she was admitted Dec. 1 for medical treatment.

Private services will be conducted Wednesday at 2 p.m. from the Mullins and Redgate funeral home, 1297 Park Avenue. Cremation will be in the Mountain Grove crematory. A member of the Keller household since 1914, Miss Thomson served first as housekeeper and manager and later became Miss Keller's inseparable companion after the death in 1936 of Mrs. Anne Sullivan Macy, the woman who first taught Miss Keller to speak and read. Miss Thomson came to the United States from her native Scotland in 1913 to visit an uncle in Swampscott, Mass. In October of the following year, she was brought to the attention of Mrs. Macy who hired her at their first meeting. A few months later both Mrs. Macy and Miss Thomson set out with Miss Keller on a tour of the continent.

In 1921, in Toronto, Canada, when Mrs. Macy became ill, Miss Thomson made her first appearance on the lecture platform with Miss Keller. From that time on it was she rather than Mrs. Macy who stood beside Miss Keller and interpreted her friend's broken speech to audiences. They traveled widely together.

In 1937 they sailed on a 4,000-mile trip to the Orient on behalf of the handicapped and in 1950 they made a 40,000-mile plane trip around the world. Miss Keller, who will celebrate her 80th birthday this June, was consultant to the American Foundation for Overseas Blind at that time.

Born in 1885 in Glasgow, Miss Thomson became a naturalized citizen of the United States in 1937 with Miss Keller at her side as a character witness. After her trip to the Orient, Miss Keller received invitations from governments and organizations throughout the world. Miss Thomson and Miss Keller toured the Far East and Australia, New Zealand, India and the Middle East, South Africa, South and Central America, Europe, Scandinavia and Iceland . . . Two years were spent visiting war-blinded veterans in Army and Navy hospitals throughout this country in addition to countless appearances before legislatures, committees and other groups.

Miss Thomson's father was a draftsman in an engineering firm in Glasgow and her mother, Isabella Fraser Thomson, was a member of the Fraser clan. She is survived by a brother, Robert Thomson, a retired minister in the Church of Scotland how living in Glasgow and a sister, Margaret Thomson, also living in Scotland.

Describing how she interpreted to Miss Keller, Miss Thomson once explained: "Miss Keller holds my right hand loosely with her right hand and I form letters with my fingers. Sometimes, of course, she reads with her fingers on my lips."

They frequently attended the theater together. Miss Thomson was able to interpret at the rate of 85 words a minute, giving essentials of the dialogue and describing the stage settings and movements of the players. Reading the morning newspaper was a three-way proposition when Mrs. Macy's sight was failing. Miss Thomson propped the newspaper in front of her at the breakfast table and read from it. Mrs. Macy listened and passed on the news to Miss Keller with her fingertips.

Helen Keller may not require a replacement for Polly Thomson, it was reported today. M. R. Barnett, executive director of the American Association for the Blind, said this morning Miss Keller, regardless of her age, is "quite capable." "It would be a misconception," he continued, "to think of Miss Keller as needing constant care." According to Mr. Barnett, the Keller household retains a housekeeper and several assistants capable of seeing to Miss Keller's needs. In addition, she has in her employ a full-time secretary, Mrs. Evelyn Davidson Seide, who attends to all administrative details although she does not reside in Miss Keller's Easton home.

Miss Keller once said that death never removed her friends. "My relationship is spiritual," she said. "I never see my friends. When death strikes, they're gone physically but spiritually they are always close to me."

Since Miss Thomson's illness in December, Miss Keller has made no public appearances, preferring to remain with her companion. And it is not expected that she will undertake any strenuous tours from now on because of her age although Mr. Barnett reported her to be in excellent health. Miss Keller learned of Miss Thomson's death this morning at the breakfast table. A member of the household said the news was withheld from her until this morning on the advice of her physician. Mrs. Seide said the news was somewhat of a shock, but that Miss Keller had known her ailing companion "could not get better." She added, "I believe she is taking it beautifully." [67]

Helen suffered her first stroke in 1961 and retired from public life. She lived seven more years under the care of a nursing staff:

After [Polly] Thomson died in 1960, Keller carried on. Her nurse, Winifred Corbally, and a Secretary, Evelyn Seide, served as her interpreters. Interviewed on her 80th birthday about her plans for the future, she replied: I will always—as long as I have breath—work for the handicapped. [68]

In 1964, President Lyndon Johnson conferred the Presidential Medal of Freedom, the nation's highest civilian honor, upon Helen. She was unable to attend the ceremony and sent a niece to accept the honor. President Johnson said:

> [Helen Keller is] an example of courage to all mankind, she has devoted her life to illuminating the dark world of the blind and the handicapped.

In 1965, Helen was elected to the Women's Hall of Fame at the New York World's Fair.

Helen Keller died in her sleep at Arcan Ridge in Connecticut on Saturday afternoon, June 1, 1968; she was close to 88 years old. Funeral services were held at the National Cathedral in Washington DC, and her ashes were placed next to those of Anne Sullivan and Polly Thomson. Over 1,200 mourners attended the funeral at the National Cathedral.

After her death, the American Foundation for the Blind issued a tribute written by Alden Whitman called "Triumph Out of Tragedy." Alden Whitman was an American journalist who wrote personalized obituaries for The New York Times. Below are some excerpts from Mr. Whitman's tribute.

> For the first 18 months of her life Helen Keller was a normal infant who cooed and cried, learned to recognize the voices of her father and mother and took joy in looking at their faces and at objects about her home. "Then" as she recalled later, "came the illness which closed my eyes and ears and plunged me into the unconsciousness of a newborn baby."
>
> Her life thereafter, as a girl and as a woman, became a triumph over crushing adversity and shattering affliction. In time, Miss Keller learned to circumvent her blindness, deafness and muteness; she could "see" and "hear" with exceptional acuity; she even learned to talk passably and to dance in time to a fox trot or a waltz. Her remarkable mind unfolded, and she was in and of the world, a full and happy participant in life. . . . she graduated from Radcliffe; she became an artful and subtle writer; she led a vigorous life; she developed into a crusading humanitarian who espoused Socialism; and she energized movements that revolutionized help for the blind and the deaf.
>
> Miss Keller's life was so long and so crowded with improbable feats—from riding horseback to learning Greek—and she was so serene yet so determined in her advocacy of beneficent causes that she became a great legend. She always seemed to be standing before the world as an example of unquenchable will.

Many who observed her—and to some she was a curiosity and a publicity-seeker—found it difficult to believe that a person so handicapped could acquire the profound knowledge and the sensitive perception and writing talent that she exhibited when she was mature. Yet no substantial proof was ever adduced that Miss Keller was anything less than she appeared—a person whose character impelled her to perform the seemingly impossible. With the years, the skepticism, once overt, dwindled as her stature as a heroic woman increased.

Tall, handsome, gracious, poised, Miss Keller had a sparkling humor and a warm handclasp that won her friends easily. She exuded vitality and optimism. "My life has been happy because I have had wonderful friends and plenty of interesting work to do," she once remarked, adding: "I seldom think about my limitations, and they never make me sad. Perhaps there is just a touch of yearning at times, but it is vague, like a breeze among flowers. The wind passes, and the flowers are content."

A tireless traveler, Miss Keller toured the world with Miss Sullivan and Miss Thomson in the years before World War II. Everywhere she went she lectured on behalf of the blind and the deaf; and, inevitably, she met every one of consequence. She also found time for writing: *My Religion* in 1927; *Midstream— My Later Life* in 1929; *Peace at Eventide* in 1932; *Helen Keller's Journal* in 1938; and *Teacher* in 1955.

The Journal, one of her most luminous books, discloses the acuity and range of Miss Keller's mind in the thirties. In her comments on political, social and literary matters, she condemned Hitlerism, cheered the sit-down strikes of John L. Lewis's Committee for Industrial Organization and criticized Margaret Mitchell's *Gone with the Wind* as overlooking the brutalities of Southern slavery.

Despite the celebrity that accrued to her and the air of awesomeness with which she was surrounded in her later years, Miss Keller retained an unaffected personality and a certainty that her optimistic attitude toward life was justified.

"I believe that all through these dark and silent years, God has been using my life for a purpose I do not know," she said recently, adding: "But one day I shall understand and then I will be satisfied." [69]

This is from a newspaper article written June 2nd, 1968:

"She died gently, with a smile on her face," said Miss Keller's physician, Dr. Forris Chick. [70]

That is exactly how I choose to remember the last moments of Helen Keller, smiling to the very end, gently exiting the corporeal realm, still full of Faith, still optimistic.

The Three Lives of Helen Keller

The Three Lives of Helen Keller was co-authored by Richard Harrity and Ralph G. Martin in 1962. The book does not have a table of contents or an index, and it is not divided into chapters, so it is difficult to navigate. However, the book is still a treasure trove of pictures, many of which are now rarely seen.

It was not clear as I read the book what the three lives of Helen Keller were. I imagine that the first life was the seven years before Anne Sullivan arrived, the second life featured Helen's studies with Sullivan, and the third life her time with Polly Thomson after Sullivan's death. With Thomson, Helen traveled the globe in the role of spokesperson for the blind, deaf, and deaf-blind. Here is a quote that I found powerful in the book, having not seen this summary in other works:

Helen Keller's third life is the most important and the dearest to her heart . . . She visited every state in the Union time after time, covered every continent and nearly every country during six grueling world tours, and raised vast sums to provide better care and education for those afflicted as she is.

I found in this book references that I had not encountered before (although I believe much of the text was taken from Joseph Lash's in-depth biography *Helen and Teacher*). There is a detailed look at a time when Helen was studying for her entrance exams for Radcliffe College. A controversy erupted wherein the director of the Cambridge School for Young Ladies, Arthur Gilman, tried to separate Annie from Helen. The result was that the inseparable pair left Mr. Gilman's school. History should hold no doubt, however, that Arthur Gilman appreciated, praised, and supported Anne Sullivan. He clearly saw the miracle and miracle worker up close, and he knew he was witnessing a remarkable phenomenon. That he eventually felt that the two women were overly dependent on each other is no surprise, because they were, indeed, inseparable. Apparently, his personality and Sullivan's were not compatible.

We will never know all the emotions and Egoic positioning that happened between Sullivan and Gilman, nor will we ever have an entirely clear idea of all the personalities involved (many people weighed in on the conflict). I prefer to leave people in history unscathed by my own viewpoint except to think the best of everyone involved in inevitable human conflicts.

Arthur Gilman should be remembered for his humanitarian and insightful leadership. He was no lightweight in the academic world. He believed that woman should be educated at a time in history when that view was not popular. Because of his leadership, Harvard established Radcliffe College when Gilman was a member of the College's governing body. He was an author and an extraordinary schoolmaster. Soon after Helen arrived at the Cambridge School for Young Ladies, Gilman administered a set of old Harvard entrance examinations to provide a baseline for Helen's abilities. Much to everyone's shock, *Helen passed all the examinations* before she took a single class at the Cambridge School. She passed the exams in German, French, English, and in Greek and Roman history. It did not take long for Gilman to become one of Helen's most fervent supporters.

There is a short section in this book about Helen's and Annie's exploration of Love. I found this discussion exceedingly important given Helen's unfolding future in which Love and Service to others were to become her creed. There must have been a defining moment when the concept of Love first appeared in Helen's mind. The authors explore the idea that Helen, like any woman, was entitled to know sensual and sexual love—that she was entitled to consider marriage and family life.

From the above thread, the author's explore Helens only loving (physical) encounter with a young man, Peter Fagan. Several pages are allotted to this "affair."

In summary, it is the photographs that make this book an important addition to Helen's life story. The issues raised in the text are best explored in Helen Keller's two in-depth biographies.

Helen Keller, Her Socialist Years

Helen Keller, Her Socialist Years, is another look at Helen's radical position on the attitudes of her generation. Edited by Dr. Philip S. Foner, an American labor historian, the book contains Socialist selections from Helen's articles, speeches, and books. Helen was (during her midyears, especially) an anti-war, anti-capitalist, feminist firebrand; she was a major supporter of the United States labor movement during the early 1900s.

There are rare selections in the book that are not found in her other biographies. Below, for example, is a quote from a speech Helen gave at the Labor Forum at Washington Irving High School in New York City on December 19, 1915:

> The burden of war always falls heaviest on the toilers. They are taught that their masters can do no wrong and go out in vast numbers to be killed on the battlefield. And what is their reward? If they escape death, they come back to face heavy taxation and have their burden of poverty doubled. Through all the ages they have been robbed of the just rewards of their patriotism as they have been of the just reward of their labor.
>
> The only moral virtue of war is that it compels the capitalist system to look at itself in the face and admit it is a fraud. It compels the present society to admit that it has no morals it will not sacrifice for gain. During the war, the sanctity of a home, and even private property is destroyed. Governments do what it is said the "crazy Socialists" would do if in power.

Helen wanted men to be more intellectually sophisticated and compassionate than they were. Unfortunately, she was addressing a low level of consciousness, a collection of (mostly) males in power who had rigid worldviews. These worldviews were not about to change. It took two global wars to even begin to shake this collective mind awake. Words matter, so the opinions and passions of humanitarians had to be denigrated and suppressed by the forces that were hellbent on fighting—determined to reinforce their cognitive and spiritual shallowness. The generations that fought two world wars died out, but Helen Keller's words and convictions still reverberate. *Helen Keller, Her Socialist Years* is an important little book, one which belongs in every Helen Keller collection.

There are so many rich quotes in this collection that need to be remembered. Here is one, out of the multitude, that I feel best expresses Helen' emotions:

> I have come to loathe traditions and institutions that take away
> the rights of the poor and protect the wicked against judgment.

History, as it is laid out in various forms of media, has served to hold a mirror to past events. The bad actors, the cruel, the greedy, the narcissistic, the power hungry, all those who have done damage to the spiritual evolution of the species, have been exposed by all manner of artists—writers, poets, playwrights, painters, historians, etc. History has been watching and judging. Helen said that "Men vanish from the earth leaving behind them the furrows they have ploughed." So have women like Helen Keller ploughed some deep furrows, which have become pathways for future generations to follow.

I would be remiss if I did not point out, from a historical perspective, that Helen's views were at times naïve or shortsighted. She was sure about Love and she was sure that Love was not being served or protected in her lifetime. However, her insistence on Socialism or Communism as benevolent forms of governance and economics, and her vilification of Capitalism were undermined by the same low levels of consciousness that she opposed. Socialist and Communist experiments often failed because they were still run by males with low levels of cognition and unevolved spirituality. Democratic Socialism, a major exception to this criticism, has a positive foothold in our century and there is hope that the best features of all economic systems can be blended for the common good.

What Else Happened in 1968?

Here are some random events that occurred in the last year (1968) of Helen Keller's life: Martin Luther King Jr. was assassinated . . . The first Big Mac went on sale for the first time . . . Dr. Christian Barnard performed the first successful heart transplant . . . the Boeing 747 made its maiden flight . . . Emergency 911 service started in the U.S.A. . . . The Dow Jones Industrial Average ended the year at 943 . . . The average cost of a new home was $14,950.00.

1973: THE DEATH OF NELLA BRADDY

Nella Braddy Henney died in 1973. Her notes and correspondance are available for viewing online at the Perkins School for the Blind Helen Keller Digital Archives. Nella was a close friend, an expert editor, and a trusted confidant for Helen and Annie. Nella Braddy belongs on the same list of key friends surrounding Helen Keller, including Anne Sullivan, John Macy, Alexander Graham Bell, Michael Anagnos, Mark Twain, John Hitz, and Sophia Hopkins. Joseph Lash [71] does an admirable and in-depth review of Nella's relationship with Helen, Polly, and Anne. Like all close friendships there were times of joy and times of regret— Nelly had the full range of emotions during her long companionship with Helen.

What Else Happened in 1968?

Here are a few random events that occurred in 1973: In Roe v. Wade, The U.S. Supreme Court overturned state bans on abortion . . . Former President Lyndon B. Johnson died at his Johnson City, Texas ranch . . . President Nixon announced that a peace accord had been reached in Vietnam.

On January 27, 1973, the Vietnam War ended with the signing of the Paris Peace Accords . . . The first handheld cellular phone call was made in New York City . . . Secretariat won the Kentucky Derby . . . The United States Congress passed the Education of the Handicapped Act (EHA) mandating Special Education. The Endangered Species Act was passed in the United States.

1980: Helen and Teacher is Published

Helen and Teacher, The Story of Helen Keller and Anne Sullivan Macy, written by Joseph Lash, was the first in-depth biography of Helen Keller and Anne Sullivan. This is the work of a master historian. The thick book (786 pages in my edition) flows like a novel; it is a masterpiece. Before he took on the task of recording Helen and Annie's story, Lash had won both the Pulitzer Prize (1972) and the National Book Award for his two-part biography about Eleanor and Franklin Roosevelt, simply called *Eleanor and Franklin.* Helen Keller scholars are lucky that such a capable and articulate writer took on the complex task of analyzing the history of Helen Keller and Anne Sullivan. Lash knew that the story he was telling was about two equally magnificent females who became soulmates; that is why the title honors both Helen Keller and Anne Sullivan. Lash was a wonderfully articulate professional historian; he was the right person to preserve the story for posterity.

Joseph P. Lash (1909–1987) has been described as an American political activist, a journalist, and an author. He was born in 1909, in New York City, the son of Jewish immigrants from Russia. In 1930, when Helen was fifty and Sullivan was sixty-four, Lash (age 21) joined the Socialist Party of America (he resigned in 1937). There is much in the personality and actions of Joseph Lash that mirrors the life of Helen Keller.

Joseph Lash and Helen Keller were both prolific authors, each enjoyed the craft of writing and are remembered for their eloquence. Both were humanitarians and (for a while in their youth) both were socialists. Lash and Keller could also see that horrible regimes had taken hold of the minds of people in Germany, Italy, and Japan. These awful events had to be faced and put down; pacifism had to pause— militarism and authoritarianism were arising across the globe; war was coming regardless of an individual's idealism or morality. Like Helen Keller, Lash never lessened his humanitarian ideals. We can sense his integrity and human spirit as we read the pages of this wonderful book.

As I read *Helen and Teacher*, I was struck by how often I mumbled to myself "I didn't know that. Where did Lash get that information?" Obviously, this was a thoroughly researched work that took Lash years to assemble. For example, Lash tells us about Anne Sullivan's teachers at Perkins. As a teacher myself for thirty years, I know that moments of kindness or carefully crafted honesty (as we review a student's work, for example) can impact a child for a lifetime. Teachers form critically important bonds with their students; they have a unique emotional and moral obligation in every culture. Lash singles out two of Sullivan's teachers, Miss Newton and Miss Mary C. Moore. Miss Newton says of Annie:

> [She was] a wholesome, vigorously active, impulsive, self-assertive, generally happy girl, inclined to be impatient and combative towards any opinion not in agreement with her own. She evidenced much executive ability and initiative.

Anne Sullivan says of Miss Moore:

> Miss Moore exerted a salutary influence over me. I respected her mind, and I fancied she did not think I was quite such a dyed-in-the-wool black sheep as the others did. When I was deliberately rude or expressed opinions, which betrayed the meagerness of my information, she often pretended not to notice it. She changed the subject so adroitly that I was not sure she had really noticed it. Sometimes I had the uncomfortable feeling that she was getting me under her thumb, which made me uneasy and suspicious. The mind was willing and docile, but the spirit carried a chip on its shoulder. I now wonder at her good will towards me. I might easily have collapsed before a student so intractable as I was. Little by little she disciplined my unorderly mind.

When Annie would fall into depressive funks as a schoolgirl it was often Miss Moore who helped her work through her depression:

> "Health-minded people, especially young people, are not pessimistic," she would counsel Annie. "If you look about you, Annie, you cannot help seeing that a lot of things in the world are fine. A lot of people are kind and generous. The sun shines most of the time. The air we breathe is plentiful. Some of the books we read are delightful. Make up your mind to see the pleasant side of life and you will be happier.

Perkins was, perhaps, the most famous school for the blind in the world—certainly, it was the premier school for the blind in the United States when Anne Sullivan was a student there. But new buildings do not make a school an excellent place; it is the teachers and staff who make a school world-class and admired. Perkins, no doubt, had carefully selected extraordinary teachers like Miss Moore and Miss Newton, and administrators like Michael Anagnos. That Anne Sullivan would become the valedictorian of her class speaks as much to the skills, dedication, and stubborn kindness of her teachers, as it does to her innate abilities.

Lash was able to piece together the individuals behind the scenes who supported Helen and Annie through all the ups and downs of their extraordinary lives; he helps us understand that friendships and family were always present, always ready to help. When Helen decided that she wanted to get a college degree, for example, which was an expensive undertaking, many wealthy friends came forward to make sure that the miracle and the miracle worker were able to do their important work rather than be overcome by poverty. And Helen and Annie were always one step removed from poverty, two severely impaired young women trying to financially survive month to month without a reliable income.

It appears to have primarily been the wives of famous males who worked behind the scenes to convince their husbands to be financially supportive. I am sure I will miss many but here are some important benefactors that Lash discovered: Mark Twain, Dean Howells, William Randolph Hearst, Charles Dudley Warner, Bishop Greer, Edwin King, Hampton Robb, Andrew Carnegie, George Goodhue, John Spaulding, Alexander Graham Bell, John Hitz, William Wade, Sophia Hopkins, Annie Pratt, Lucy Derby, Henry H. Rodgers, and Laurence and Eleanor

Hutton. It was Eleanor Hutton who took charge and slowly gathered the financial team together—they would eventually finance Helen's education as well as pay the monthly expenses of Sullivan and Keller for decades.

Lash divided his book into seven parts. In part one, he tells the story of Annie Sullivan as a young girl, her harsh childhood followed by her struggles and triumphs at the Perkins School for the Blind.

In part two, Sullivan meets Helen, and the legend begins. This section follows the two women from Tuscumbia Alabama, to Boston, to New York, as Helen's education intensifies.

In part three, Helen goes to Radcliffe College to study for a university degree. While at Radcliffe, she begins writing two of her books, *Optimism* and *The Story of My Life* (both published in 1903). She graduates with honors in 1904.

Part four tells the story of the marriage between Anne Sullivan and Harvard professor John Macy—the newlyweds lived together with Helen to form what Lash calls the "extraordinary triangle." The marriage ends with Macy saying that he feels like he married an institution. Helen's socialist views begin to solidify after her university experience, and she publishes more books with the editorial support of John Macy and Anne Sullivan.

Part five tells the story of the years when Sullivan, Keller, and newly arrived Polly Thomson live and work together—the three traveled often and formed a remarkable bond. This section ends with the death of Anne Sullivan and the beginning of the decades when Polly Thomson and Helen Keller crisscrossed the globe working for the American Foundation for the Blind.

Part six is about the Thomson-Keller years, four decades of friendship and hard work during which Helen Keller solidified her legend—she became loved and admired everywhere on the planet.

Part seven is about the final years of Helen's life. Polly Thomson dies, and Helen is left alone to fight her final battles. The book ends with an epilogue about Helen's religion. She is optimistic to the very end.

I see from reading most of the books about Helen Keller that authors have relied heavily on the research and perspective of Joseph Lash—he is often quoted and the stories he told have been repeated in books and articles for decades. If you read just one book, make it *Helen and Teacher*. I am in awe of this man's accomplishment; his thoroughness and gentle eloquence are deeply inspiring.

What Else Happened in 1980?

Here are some random events that occurred in 1980: John Lennon was shot and killed in New York . . . Post-It Notes went on sale for the first time . . . the Pac-Man arcade game was released . . . War broke out between Iraq and Iran . . . Mount St. Helens erupted in Oregon . . . the year end close of the Dow Jones Industrial Average was 963 . . . The Rubik's Cube debuted . . . the average cost of a new house was $68,700 . . . CNN (Cable News Network) began broadcasting on June 1st . . . the average income per year was $19,500.00 . . . The United States Olympic ice hockey team made history at the 1980 Lake Placid Winter Olympics in what was later called the "Miracle on Ice." . . . the cost of a gallon of gas was $1.19 . . . the average cost of a new car was $7,200.00.

1987: THE CAPE COD CAMPUS

When I was doing research for this book, at the Perkins School for the Blind in Watertown, Massachusetts, sitting in their famous library, I came across an article called "The Cape Cod Campus." This was a serendipitous moment that happened when I was just starting out on the journey to write my two books about Helen Keller.

"The Cape Cod Campus" is a short piece—rarely seen by causal readers—about Anne Sullivan's lifelong friend Sophia Hopkins. The "Campus" was Mrs. Hopkin's seaside home facing the Atlantic Ocean, a place of rest and friendship for Annie and Helen; they would stay with Sophia for weeks at a time, bathing in the frigid Atlantic, laying in the warm sand, walking the beach together.

Many letters were exchanged between Sullivan, Keller, and Hopkins during the critical years when Sullivan and Keller were still young. These letters are now a national historic treasure. The surviving letters are available online in the Helen Keller Digital Archives at both the Perkins Institute and at the American Foundation for the Blind.

Sophia Hopkins is a member of the small group of key individuals who molded the characters of both Helen and Annie. Sophia deserves to be remembered and revered for her significant contributions to the Sullivan-Keller legacy. She was behind the scenes throughout the most important moments in the young adult lives of Keller and Sullivan; her home was a Campus where the three women shared their emotions and talked about their remarkable lives.

What Else Happened in 1987?

Here are some random events that occurred in 1987: The Simpsons first episode aired . . . the first criminal was convicted using DNA evidence . . . The U.S. stock market dropped 22.6% in one day in October . . . United States President Ronald Reagan delivered a speech at the Berlin Wall on June 12th . . . The average cost of a new home was $92,000 . . . The average price of a new car was $10,3055.00 . . . A gallon of gas cost 89 cents . . . a dozen eggs cost 65 cents.

1994: LIGHT IN MY DARKNESS IS PUBLISHED

Light in My Darkness, originally published in 1927 as *My Religion,* by Helen Keller, was a tribute to Emanuel Swedenborg. The original publication of *My Religion* was hastily printed by Doubleday, Page & Company, but it was considered by critics to be an unpolished and hurried book. In 1994, Ray Silverman, a Swedenborgian minister and literary scholar, revised and edited *My Religion.* Silverman added new information and reorganized the chapters. He also made grammatical and spelling changes and he corrected some historical inaccuracies. Silverman emphasized that his revisions did not alter Helen Keller's passion or intent. Swedenborgians treasure Helen's dedication to the works of Emanuel Swedenborg; Dr. Silverman's retouching of *My Religion* is a gift to those who understand and appreciate Swedenborg's monumental contributions to the evolution of human spirituality.

Light in my Darkness

Light in my Darkness is a re-edited version of Helen's book *My Religion.* Professor emeritus Dr. Raymond Silverman, a Swedenborgian scholar and expert on Helen Keller, made many important organizational improvements to Helen's original work. Helen Keller's biographer Dorothy Herrmann wrote the introduction to *Light in my Darkness* and Norman Vincent Peale wrote the Foreword.

Swedenborgianism is the religion that Helen Keller selected after being exposed to several other Christian theologies. She was influenced (guided) by her close friend John Hitz, who gave Helen braille editions of Emanuel Swedenborg's books. Helen was drawn to Swedenborg because the man was an accepted intellectual genius, a Renaissance Man dedicated to science, knowledge, and spiritual truth. He had all these splendid attributes long before he turned his attention to religion. Swedenborg insisted that Love and Service was at the core of Christianity. And it was this core that appealed to Helen Keller. Helen defined *Service* as "Love made visible." She spent her lifetime making her love visible, touching lives to this very day.

Helen trusted Swedenborg, so when he described going into trance states and "traveling" to Heaven and Hell, she believed him. Helen knew that Swedenborg used metaphor and symbolism in his writing, so she does not have to believe he traveled to actual locations—he is simply and honestly describing what happened to him during a trance state. Others, of course, including Anne Sullivan, thought it mad that anyone could believe that they had visited Heaven and Hell, for real *or* telepathically. Helen's mind, unencumbered by vision and hearing, sensing only the vibrational world, could detect a truth in Swedenborg that was beyond surface appearances—she was not so quick, not so sure, to be critical of his methods or observations.

It was not just his visits to Heaven and Hell that intrigued Helen, she was mostly taken by the messages that Swedenborg brought back from his trance-induced adventures. It did not matter to Helen whether Swedenborg's adventures were derived from *The Kingdom Within* or from actual discussions with angels. It was his clear and loving words that drew her to the man. He was explaining a religion and a set of beliefs that Helen could understand and support:

> Since my seventeenth year, I have tried to live according to the teachings of Emanuel Swedenborg. By "church," he did not mean an ecclesiastical organization, but a spiritual fellowship of thoughtful men and women who spent their lives for a service to mankind that outlasts them. He called it a civilization that was to be born of a healthy universal religion—good-will, mutual understanding, service from each to all, regardless of dogma or ritual.

Helen Keller was surrounded by friendships, by sophisticated individuals who understood what a "a spiritual fellowship of thoughtful men and women" looked like. She was part of a universal church whose members were dedicated to love and service. She met like-minded spiritual souls in all corners of the world as she travelled.

Helen reviews the usual impressive list of artists, poets, and humanitarians who also had gathered Swedenborg to their hearts—she was not alone, and she knew it. Other empaths, other sensitive and highly evolved souls could feel the deep truths previously hidden in the Bible, but Swedenborg had carefully *explained* these hidden truths. He told Christians to stop taking the Bible literally, to see the real purpose of the Bible, which was to show the spiritual and cognitive evolution of the human species—the Bible used parables, analogies, and stories written over a vast historical time frame to demonstrate the evolution of spiritual cognition. For Swedenborg and Helen Keller, the Bible is a history of the evolution of human consciousness—that is why it has such enduring power. Helen calls the Bible "the most important record of the groping of the human spirit that mankind possesses."

Swedenborg addressed the journey of the soul and spirit as—decade by decade—humanity became ever more loving, tolerant, and active in the service of kindness. The Old Testament reflects the "good old days," when the spirit and soul were dormant, in the dark, and unmanifest. The Book of Genesis is the birth of consciousness, from material to immaterial—aware-life arising from the clay of the earth. Swedenborg's message, that religions came from our shared need to historically document the rise of cognition and spirituality, goes beyond Christianity and allows other faith-based groups to appreciate and learn from Swedenborg, despite his deeply Christian perspective. All religious texts, Helen tells us, are efforts to create more sophisticated and loving adherents. Swedenborg, Helen says, "Gave the world a spiritual philosophy, overthrowing ecclesiastical despotism."

Swedenborg also said that he was writing for the future. He clearly saw that the level of most minds in his era would not allow his fellows to grasp his insights. Indeed, humanity has clung—for centuries—to the literal interpretations of the sages who crafted world religions. Only now, as the Modern, Post-Modern and Integral Levels of consciousness have become more widespread, is there an audience for Swedenborg's insights. His message was clear and simple: Love, and Service (Love Manifest). That was Helen's adopted insight; her life was guided throughout by this simply-stated calling:

No matter from what angle Jesus started, he came back to this fact, that he entrusted the reconstruction of the world, not to wealth or caste or power or learning, but to the better instincts of the human race—to love, which is the mover of the will and the dynamic force of action. He turned his words every conceivable way and did every possible work to convince doubters that love—good or evil—is the life of their life, the fuel of their thoughts, the breath of their nostrils, their heaven or their deconstruction. There is no exception or modification whatever in his holy, awesome, supreme Gospel of Love.

Knowing that there is a supreme Gospel of Love gives us a foundation upon which to judge behaviors—of individuals, of tribes, of nations, of a planet. Evil stands out (to put it crudely) like a festering boil on a lovely face. The supreme Gospel of Love is a pure countenance, filled with health, goodness, and radiance. The supreme Gospel of Love was Helen's foundation.

Swedenborg followed esoteric principles, most notably the *Law of Correspondences*—as above so below. Therefore, he held that biblical statements had to be translated. Certain words and phrases were used repeatedly in the Bible and they held a significance beyond their appearances. The Bible was an esoteric document with profound messages for human souls on a spiritual path.

In a heading called *The Source of the Mystic Sense*, Helen explains her connection to the spiritual world:

Possibly my own partial isolation from the world of light and sound gives me insight into Swedenborg's extraordinary experience. I do not know if it is the "mystic" sense I possess; but certainly, it is perceptive. It is the faculty that brings distant objects within the cognizance of the blind so that even the stars seem to be at our very door. This sense relates me to the spiritual world. I gain from an imperfect touch-world that presents it to my mind for spiritualization. This sense reveals the divine to the human in me; it forms a bond between earth and the great beyond, between now and eternity, between God and humanity. It is speculative, intuitive, and reminiscent.

There is not only an objective physical world but also an objective spiritual world. The spiritual has an outside as well as an inside, just as the physical has an inside and an outside. Each has its own level of reality. There is no antagonism between these two planes of life, except when the material is used without regard to the spiritual that lies within and above it.

This logic follows the law of correspondence: as above so below; as on this side (physical reality), so also on that side (spiritual reality)—they are mirror images of each other. Swedenborg said that the physical world was perceived by physical senses, while the spiritual world could only be perceived by spiritual senses. Mysticism makes no sense to a mind that only knows the world through the physical senses. Only when we learn to uses the spiritual senses do we begin to perceive spiritually. I do not want to detract too much from this lovely image, but I will point out that the Egocentric mind perceives using the external senses and the Allocentric mind perceives using the internal senses—there may be a physiological reason for Swedenborg's and Keller's perspectives.

The more I read this little book, the more I felt as if the Bible was a hermetic text complied by multiple voices over several centuries. As each sage wrote their piece, they inadvertently exposed (revealed) the culture from which they had evolved. The New Testament was a new mind emerging from an old mind. The Bible is a chronology of the evolution of Love:

> Swedenborg interpreted the whole world of human experience in terms of love—the states of love; the activities, powers, and functions of love; the constructive, protective, and courage-stirring dictates of love.

But it is not enough just to be filled with love or to join the chorus of those in praise of love. It is necessary to have a mission in life. A purpose is needed, which spreads love and transforms human minds into vessels of love. Here, Helen talks about the purpose of life:

> Sick or well, blind or seeing, bound or free, we are here for a purpose, and however we are situated, we please God better with useful deeds than with prayers or pious resignation.

To become skilled at finding and sharing love, it is necessary to work on the refinement of the soul. In other words, human consciousness must evolve to become ever more tolerant, ever more loving, and ever more dedicated to service.

What Else Happened in 1994?

Here are some random events that occurred in 1994: The Channel Tunnel opened on May 6, 1994 between England and France . . . The first genetically engineered tomatoes were approved in the United States . . . The Irish Republican Army announced a cessation of military operations . . . The Java programming language was released by Sun Microsystems . . . The Winter Olympic Games were held in Lillehammer, Norway . . . The cost of a gallon of Gas was $1.09 . . . The average cost of a new car was $12,350.00 . . . a loaf of Bread was $1.59 and a dozen Eggs was 86 cents.

1998: Helen Keller, A Life is Published

This is the second comprehensive biography of Helen Keller. Like Joseph Lash's 1980 work *Helen and Teacher*, this biography is also a masterpiece of clear writing and comprehensive authorship. Written by Dorothy Herrmann two decades later, this version covers the same stories Lash explored, but with (so I sensed as I read Herrmann's prose) more of the author's soul mixed with Helen's. My own approach resonates with Herrmann's; I sense that it is okay to have emotional and (perhaps) judgmental comments mixed with the history. Mary Loeffelholz, writing in the *Boston Sunday Globe*, called the book "fully embodied and unflinchingly candid."

Dorothy Herrmann was an experienced biographer when she took on the task of surveying the life of Helen Keller. Herrmann had written two highly acclaimed biographies, *S. J. Perelman*, in 1986, and *Anne Morrow Lindbergh*, in 1992, before taking on Helen Keller and Anne Sullivan. It is noteworthy that a female biographer took on this role—I could feel a more intuitive and emotional force as I read the book than I felt when reading Lash's remarkable work. Both biographers have combined to give us a perspective that neither could have accomplished singly. I recommend reading both biographies. Following are a few comments from reviews of Dorothy Herrmann's biography.

Dinitia Smith, in a *New York Times* review, wrote that Herrmann's book was, perhaps, the most intimate biography published about Helen Keller. Smith writes that the book gives Helen Keller back "her sexuality and imbues her with a true humanity." "*Helen Keller: A Life*," Smith believes, "has some of the texture and the dramatic arc of a good novel."

Ron Charles, in a review for the *Christian Science Monitor*, called the book "fascinating" and added that it "stripped away decades of well-meaning sentimentality."

"We meet an entirely unexpected Helen Keller," writes Joan Mellen, in her review for the *Philadelphia Inquirer*. Mellen, reflecting on the ambience of Herrmann's biography, calls Helen "a woman with deep if concealed ambivalence toward her self-sacrificing teacher."

Dennis Drabelle, in his review for the *Cleveland Plain Dealer*, calls the book a "well-proportioned biography of the deaf and blind girl who became a great American crusader." Drabelle says the biography "rescues its subject from the shackles of sainthood without destroying her as an American hero." It is exceedingly difficult (I confess) to separate the desire to confer sainthood from the responsibility to relate factual events. Dorothy Herrmann has given history an "unflinchingly candid" portrait of Helen Keller without sailing off into the esoteric realms—this is an important and enduring contribution to the Keller/Sullivan mythology.

What Else Happened in 1998?

Here are some random events that occurred in 1998: Google was incorporated in Menlo Park, California by Larry Page and Sergey Brin . . . the International Space Station began operating in December, 1998 . . . the United States announced the first budget surplus in 30 years . . . The Belfast Agreement was signed between the Irish and British governments and most Northern Ireland political parties thus ending terrorist activity in Northern Ireland and mainland Britain . . . Europeans agreed on a single currency called the Euro . . . Exxon and Mobil merged to create the world's largest petroleum company . . . 19 European nations agreed to forbid human cloning . . . India and Pakistan tested nuclear weapons.

2000: DISNEY'S THE MIRACLE WORKER

On November 12, 2000 Walt Disney debuted their version of William Gibson's the *Miracle Worker.* Disney called their production *The Miracle Worker: The Contemporary Version of an American Classic!* I had not intended to watch this movie because I had saturated myself in Helen and Annie's story for two years and felt that I knew every slice of their fascinating lives. However, I started watching the movie out of a sense of obligation, but I was soon completely hooked.

Disney Studios did a wonderful job with this rendition, staying close to actual events—it is a historically accurate version. As I got more and more engrossed in the film, I started to feel that this was the version teachers should show to their students, especially if the kids are being introduced to the Helen Keller story for the first time.

The little girl who plays Helen, Hallie Kate Eisenberg, is the most delightful and lovely Helen Keller ever portrayed—I was totally smitten by this little actress. I am happy to report that Hallie is still acting in 2021, with an impressive resume. True to Disney movies, the rest of the cast members were lovely, talented people. Alison Eliot is a brilliant and beautiful actress—we feel that she *is* Anne Sullivan. Kate Greenhouse as Kate Keller, David Strathairn as Captain Keller, and Lucus Black as James Keller are polished and believable characters. Disney has made another Helen Keller classic.

What Else Happened in 2000?

Here are some random events that occurred in 2000: The State of Vermont passed HB847, legalizing civil unions for same-sex couples . . . the average income per year was $40,343.00 . . . Concorde Air France Flight 4590 crashed after takeoff from Paris killing all 109 aboard and 5 on the ground . . . the cost of a gallon of Gas was $1.26 . . . Divers discovered the ancient port of Alexandria the home of Cleopatra and Mark Anthony . . . the average cost of a new car was $24,750.00 . . . The first crew to live on the International Space Station (ISS) arrived at their new home . . . a U.S. Postage Stamp cost 33 cents . . . In December, the U.S. Supreme Court ruled to give the presidency to George W. Bush . . . a loaf of bread cost $1.72 . . . The average lifespan in the U. S. was 77.5 years . . . a dozen eggs cost 89 cents . . . The DotCom Bubble Burst and many high-tech companies went bankrupt.

2003: National Women's Hall of Fame

In 2003, Anne Sullivan Macy was inducted into the National Women's Hall of Fame. The American Foundation for the Blind received a commemorative medal in Sullivan's honor. This is a significant milestone. Helen Keller (through no fault of her own) stole the spotlight from all those who stood near her. Anne Sullivan understood this, even insisted upon it—Sullivan did not like the spotlight, it hurt her eyes figuratively and literally. However, as I have stated in several places in my books, our failure to honor Anne Sullivan as fervently as we celebrate Helen Keller is most unfortunate. Sullivan deserved a degree from Radcliffe, she deserved honorary doctorates from major universities, and she deserved a statue of her own in the United States Capital, next to Helen's.

At her birthplace, Feeding Hills, Massachusetts, there is a statue of Helen and Anne in a Memorial Park honoring Anne Sullivan. The statue of Helen and Anne sitting together on the ground was created by Romanian-American sculptor Mico Kaufman; it captures the moment Anne Sullivan taught Helen Keller that words can be used to communicate. The statue was dedicated on June 28, 1992. It is my hope that people travel to this shrine as well as to Ivy Green. It is time that we elevated Anne Sullivan in the eyes of the world—miracles do not occur without miracle workers.

What Else Happened in 2003?

Here are some random events that occurred in 2003: The Human Genome Project was completed. Scientists successfully sequenced about 99% of the human genome . . . The Space Shuttle Columbia disaster happened on February 1, 2003 . . . The United States Department of Homeland Security began operations . . . China launched Shenzhou 5, its first manned space mission carrying China's first astronaut Yang Liwei . . . The biggest blackout in history in North America affected about 50 million people . . . The Concorde made its last commercial flight, bringing the era of supersonic travel to a (temporary) close.

2004: THE RADICAL LIVES OF HELEN KELLER IS PUBLISHED

The Radical Lives of Helen Keller takes a hard look at Helen Keller's passion for social justice. The author, Dr. Kim Nielsen is a political historian with a specialty in women's studies. She is focused on the lives and contributions of the most influential women of the twentieth century. Because of her books about Helen Keller, Nielsen has become a well-known and highly regarded Helen Keller scholar.

Dr. Nielsen says of her book:

> The selection of speeches, essays and articles in this book, largely written by Keller herself, reveal a woman of fierce intellect, driven by the strength of her political convictions to champion the most radical of causes at a time when to be a left radical was to risk vilification and imprisonment.

Dr. Nielsen adds that her book is a starting point for those interested in Helen Keller as a deep thinker and a political activist. The book is divided into four sections: Disability and Class; Socialism; Women; and War. Under each heading, Dr. Nielsen provides examples from Helen's articles.

As a historian, Professor Nielsen can see the bigger picture taking place during Helen's lifetime. Helen was intellectually and emotionally moved by those around her and by the circumstances of her life; she became a global spokesperson for people with blindness, deafness, and deaf-blindness. Nielsen feels that Helen Keller, despite her spiritually-driven contributions, missed a great opportunity to holistically support the *disability movements* occurring during her lifetime:

> Aided and encouraged by Anne Sullivan and the leadership of the AFB, Keller avoided contact with other people with disabilities throughout most of her life. She repeatedly turned down requests to speak to groups of self-organized disabled people . . . she insisted on learning about and taking action regarding female suffrage, radical politics, oral speech, and the Christian teachings of Emanuel Swedenborg, all against Sullivan's wishes. But she seems to have made no inquiries about disabled professionals, disabled trades-people, or other adults with disabilities living on their own.

People with disabilities, on a global scale, have had to stand together because cultural worldviews have perpetuated cruelty, ignorance, and a demeaning lack of expectation. The plight of disability groups is still endangered; political action groups have had to continually fight against societal failures right up to this moment. Helen could have been a spokesperson for all disability groups, but history took her attention elsewhere. For Professor Nielsen, this oversight is unfortunate.

Dr. Nielsen is the Professor and Chair of Disability Studies (History of Women's and Gender Studies) at the University of Toledo, in Ohio. She is the author (or co-author) of six books:

1. *Un-American Womanhood: Antiradicalism, Antifeminism and the First Red Scare*, Ohio State University Press, 2001.
2. *The Radical Lives of Helen Keller*, New York University Press, 2004 (paperback 2009).
3. *Helen Keller: Selected Writings*, New York University Press, 2005.
4. *Beyond the Miracle Worker: The Remarkable Life of Anne Sullivan Macy and Her Extraordinary Friendship with Helen Keller*, Boston: Beacon Press, 2009.
5. *A Disability History of the United States*, Boston: Beacon Press, 2012.
6. *The Oxford Handbook of Disability History*, New York: Oxford University Press. With Michael Rembis and Catherine J. Kudlick, 2018.

What Else Happened in 2004?

Here are some random events that occurred in 2004: The Olympic Games were held in Athens, Greece . . . The Cassini-Huygens space probe entered Saturn's orbit and took the first close-up photos of Saturn's rings . . . The CIA admitted that there was no imminent threat from weapons of mass destruction before the 2003 invasion of Iraq . . . The Boston Red Sox won the World Series for the first time since 1918 . . . *Facebook* was launched as a social networking site serving students from Harvard University . . . Filmmaker Michael Moore's *Fahrenheit 9/11* opened in movie theaters.

2005: Helen Keller: Rebel Lives is Published

Rebel Lives is a book series featuring writings about people "who played significant roles in humanity's ongoing fight for a better world." The book series highlights the political views of well-known figures who were not customarily considered famous rebels. Helen Keller fits this mold nicely; she is primarily remembered for overcoming sensory depravations, but not usually for her political views, a circumstance which greatly frustrated her.

Like the *Radical Lives of Helen Keller,* this small book by historian John Davis is a vivid look at Helen's social activism. These two books, the first by Kim Nielsen and the second by Davis, together explain Helen's political passions; the two books reveal Helen Keller in a more complete and complex manner. Davis collected Helen's politically salient articles, speeches, and letters and presented them in an organized way.

Helen Keller: Selected Writings

In Helen Keller: Selected Writings, Professor Kim Nielsen has compiled a comprehensive collection of "letters, articles, speeches, and book excerpts written during all periods of Helen Keller's life." The book divides Helen's life into four sections: 1889 to 1900 (ages eleven to twenty); 1900 to 1924 (college years and first work with AFB); 1924 to 1945 (years given to activism for the blind); and 1946 to 1968, the international years when she and Polly Thomson traveled the world for AFB. I enjoyed the way this book is divided into 80 easy to read and short sections—it makes the book a nice (much enjoyed) bedside companion. It is also a valuable resource for Helen Keller scholars.

What Else Happened in 2005?

Here are some random events that occurred in 2005: Hurricane Katrina hit Louisiana, Mississippi and Alabama coasts . . . *YouTube* was founded . . . Pope John Paul II died . . . Cardinal Joseph Ratzinger was elected as the new Pope, taking the name Pope Benedict XVI . . . Four Robotic vehicles successfully crossed a 240km stretch of Nevada's Mojave Desert . . . the United States Supreme Court ruled that people who use Medicinal Marijuana can be prosecuted for violating federal drug laws . . . Steve Fossett broke the world record by flying the Virgin Atlantic Global-Flyer around the world, non-stop, and without refueling . . . The Airbus A380 made its first flight . . . Microsoft released the Xbox 360 gaming console.

2006: Connecticut Women's Hall of Fame

Helen Keller was inducted into the Connecticut Women's Hall of Fame in 2006. She and her friends Anne Sullivan and Polly Thomson lived in Connecticut during their most productive years. Here is an excerpt from the induction presentation:

"I am not dumb now." These are the five words that Helen Keller vocally exclaimed to the public in 1930. Deaf and blind since she was 19 months old, the then 50-year-old Keller was also considered by many to be mute. When she first told her teacher, Anne Sullivan, that she wanted to be able to speak using her mouth and not just her hands, Sullivan considered the challenge insurmountable. With the resolve so characteristic of her life, Keller was determined to prove the world wrong. She was not dumb, not in any sense of the word. It was with this same tenacity that Keller fought for others' rights and made a name for herself as one of the world's most respected and tireless champions of civil liberties. Keller made Easton, Connecticut her home for the last three decades of her life.

Keller was also very politically aware, and many of her views brought her under public scrutiny. She wholeheartedly believed in the suffragist movement, was a proponent of birth control, publicly expressed distaste for the war during World War I and considered herself a socialist. Throughout her life, Keller wrote many books and essays, but her book *Out of the Dark* highlighted her socialist views and was burned by the Nazis.

She responded to this book-burning in a letter, in which she spoke out against the atrocities of Nazism.

Keller committed her entire adult life to the battle for civil liberties and received numerous honors for her work. She was presented the Presidential Medal of Freedom by President Lyndon Johnson in 1964, was the first woman to receive an honorary Doctorate from Harvard and was named one of the 100 most influential people of the 20th Century by Time Magazine. Keller moved to Connecticut in 1936 and lived in Easton until her death in 1968. [72]

Blind Rage: Letters to Helen Keller

For me, one of the most fascinating books for peering into Helen Keller's everyday life is Professor Georgina Kleege's *Blind Rage: Letters to Helen Keller*. Kleege immersed herself in Helen Keller's life, even traveling to the Keller homestead in Alabama and to the Wrentham, Massachusetts house where Helen lived with Sullivan and Annie's husband John Macy. What Kleege did as a novelist, which no historian would dare do, is speculate, muse, and daydream about the everyday moments in Helen's life. Kleege dares to challenge the saintliness of Helen Keller and Anne Sullivan, and she asks questions too delicate for historians even to ponder. In this quote, Kleege talks directly to Helen:

> What am I up to Helen? I know you've probably grown tired of asking yourself this question. It's bad enough that I've read every word you ever published, and every biography ever written about you, and that I bore all my friends with tidbits of Helen Keller trivia. But now, I find myself spending endless hours speculating about the truth behind the facts of your life, wondering what really happened. I extrapolate, I read between the lines, I out-and-out fictionalize.

Kleege is like Sherlock Holmes, picking up on obvious clues that others overlooked or suppressed. For example, when she examines the years that Keller, Sullivan, and John Macy lived together at the house in Wrentham, Massachusetts, years that Helen called among the happiest of her life, the reader starts to get a little uneasy:

The man mattered to you. You can't deny it. And those nine or ten years with him at your house at Wrentham were, if not the happiest of your life, at least the most central, most formative. You were living a dream, a dream someone might even have today. The literary-political commune, the non-traditional family—I don't know what name to give it because it's not a dream I have. But you lived it, the three of you, sharing affection, labor, and aspirations. And even while there was turmoil, it was never boring while he was there.

Kleege suggests that there had to be loving energy between John Macy—Anne Sullivan's husband—and Helen Keller; something beyond genuine friendship. Kleege ponders how you can live for ten years in the same house with a handsome, brilliant man who is your age—who fingerspells in your hand every day—without intimacy developing, and then sparks would fly, and then, well, maybe emotional fires broke out from time to time. Maybe John Macy was badly torn between his desire to be morally good, a faithful husband, and feelings for Helen. The emotional conflict could drive a man to drink, and John Macy certainly drank heavily if we are to believe the accounts.

Kleege is fearless with her pen and musings; she goes even further, suggesting that ten years in a household with two women and a "new-age" man would naturally lead to powerful, confusing, and at times thrilling emotions. If we were uncomfortable with the previous quote, this one leaves us stunned:

> What I am saying is this. Did the three of you decide that since the world was not ready to accept a marriage between a Normal man like him and a disabled woman like you, to avoid scandal, he should marry Teacher instead? Or did the two of you, Macy and you, keep your relationship, attraction—whatever you want to call it—secret from Teacher? Or did you and Teacher share him? Or did he shuttle from her bed to yours, concealing the truth from both of you? Or what, Helen?

If the reader was not uncomfortable at the beginning of Kleege's book, this paragraph certainly takes care of that—you do not find this kind of musing in any other book about Helen Keller. On the other hand, one does wonder why Anne Sullivan burned her diaries and letters. There was something in those diaries that was none of the world's business. The public *did not* have a right to know all the details of a person's life, even if that person was famous. Anne Sullivan loved her husband, and the marriage meant the world to her; Sullivan said so herself and biographers have commented on this bond.

There is a very normal energy that flows between people who are conversing one-on-one; a bubble forms around the two people as their emotions are silently exchanged; that is the way human beings work. Emotions happen, all kinds of confusing emotions swirl about when two people are face-to-face, exchanging ideas and emotions. And that is okay. We are constantly fiddling with *appropriate boundaries.*

Kleege does not stop with just the suggestion that John Macy and Helen Keller might have been lovers; she even ponders out loud whether the two women, Sullivan and Keller had an intimacy that went beyond teacher and pupil:

> . . . how can one person be so close to another human being, day in and day out and not develop complex bonds that go beyond what the culture is comfortable discussing, or even entertaining? How can you teach a deaf-blind child about history, science, and art, and not also address the passions, needs, and embarrassments of the body?
>
> So, the inevitable question is this: Did he [John Macy] have to find out about it once he'd been married to her for a while, or were you open about it from the start? Was the Macy marriage a sham to conceal another truth? He was a modern man, a man of the world. He valued the both of you enough to want to protect you. It was one thing when you were a child or a girl in school. Then, your close intimacy with Teacher could be perceived as, well, a teacher-pupil relationship, raising no eyebrows. But once you were out in the world, two unmarried women living together—even in 1905 people would have to wonder. There were plenty of people, even friends of yours, who wondered why Teacher stayed with you after you graduated from Radcliffe, why she didn't become the teacher of some other deaf-blind marriage. In private notes and letters, he sometimes called Teacher Bill and you Billy. Why male nicknames? What am I to make of that?

As I had read letters written by Helen up until Sullivans death, I saw that Helen always referred to Anne as *Teacher* (she capitalized the word). That notion of teacher and pupil must have been hugely important for Helen—that her life was blessed with a constant, trustworthy teacher, a life-long mentor. It is hard to envision that this trust-based relationship could have been over-powered by sexual energy—maybe sexual energy appeared at times, but there are emotions in the life of these two women that are incredibly complex and mixed, extremely hard to interpret . . . and, I suppose, none of our business.

If it turned out that Helen Keller was, indeed, a silent spokesperson for the right to love another woman, and for the right to be respected and protected for that choice, it would be in line with her other views on human and civil rights. If she lived in our time, and if there was a lesbian relationship between her and Anne Sullivan, Helen would have been out of the closet and campaigning on the streets for the right to be herself. The intimacies and love that we give and share with others, across the table or under the sheets, is between two people at certain moments of eternity; let us be respectful of such moments. Here is Kleege's forceful summary of the delicate business:

> Face it Helen, what your biographers find so threatening about the idea of your sexuality comes from the fear that you might have been a lesbian. Personally, it makes no difference to me. I have no stake in preserving the notion of you as heterosexual virgin. I would like to believe that you had sex with someone: him, her, it doesn't matter. What seems most significant is that you and Teacher lived together for almost fifty years. Whether or not you would define it as such, there may have been some sexual aspect to your relationship with Teacher. Whether or not you ever acted on it is something I will never know, because you sure as hell aren't going to tell me. And it hardly matters.

The notion of a lesbian relationship is certainly a possibility in Helen's life. However, as a little girl, according to her family, Helen was happier in the company of men. Many of her closest friendships were with males, interesting and charming men like John Hitz and Mark Twain. The one time in her life when she tried to elope was with Macy's personal assistant Peter Fagan. Little is known about this affair, and the small bits of information we have are reviewed in every one of the biographies written about Helen. This is Professor Kleege musing again as we look on, somewhat in shock:

> She and Fagan took out a marriage license, and Helen later stood on the porch of her sister's home is Alabama most of the night waiting for her lover to steal her away. Perhaps he did try to retrieve her from that porch—and oh, how history would have changed if the elopement had been successful— but he was driven away by her sister's gun-toting husband (as some suggest), or perhaps he was not able to get there for other reasons. Whatever happened, it's a sad image: a deaf-blind girl standing motionless in the cricket-filled darkness, ever more anxious and grief-filled as the hours passed and no lover came.

Kleege goes deeper into the Fagan-Keller relationship, probing like Sherlock Holmes in a modern novel into the moments of the crisis when her mother and Sullivan confronted her. It was not until the local newspaper reported the marriage license that family and friends found out about Helen's intentions; they were emotionally broadsided, stunned. Kleege even muses that perhaps Helen had gotten pregnant, and a long emotional crisis ensued. Right after the Fagan fiasco, Helen went back to Alabama to be with her sister Mildred, while Sullivan and Polly Thomson went to upstate New York and later went to Puerto Rico. "Why were they gone from Helen's life for months," Kleege asks. "How many months?"

Helen wrote a letter to her Scottish friend James Kerr Love while she was in Alabama with her sister—while Anne and Polly were in Puerto Rico. That letter is preserved in Helen's Book (compiled by Kerr) *Helen Keller in Scotland* (1933). Below is a paragraph from the letter that fills in some details for that time period. Helen does not share her grief over the Fagan affair in the letter, although this was written shortly after her failed attempt to elope. It was probably the shock of that incident that sent everyone into a tailspin:

> I have been spending the winter here in Montgomery, Alabama, with my sister [Mildred] and two lovely little nieces, and they have been an inexpressible comfort to me . . . I wish I could give you news as pleasant as yours. But life has been hard for my Teacher and me the last year. We worked more than usual lecturing, and when we returned from our tour last summer

she was quite worn out. Then she became ill, and her physician ordered her to go away for a complete rest. She was in Puerto Rico all winter. She has enjoyed her stay there immensely . . . She is now on her way back to Wrentham, and mother and I are leaving today to join her. This is the longest time I have been separated from her, and I can scarcely wait until I see her and find out what I can do to help her get well as quickly as possible.

It is important to understand that Anne Sullivan was quite sick at this time (1916); she had been initially diagnosed with tuberculous and had gone off to a sanatorium in the Adirondacks, taking Polly Thomson along to help (and, unintentionally, leaving Helen free to interact with Peter Fagan). In retrospect, it is not clear whether the TB diagnosis was correct. The symptoms apparently cleared up after months of rest and sun, although there are hints that—whatever the ailment—it came and went and might have been a factor in Sullivan's eventual death two decades later. Sullivan had many ailments going on for much of her adult life, including bouts of depression and exhaustion from overwork. Her eyes were a constant source of pain—too often, the pain was excruciating and debilitating.

Sullivan hated the winter in the Adirondack sanatorium and headed to Puerto Rico and warmer weather with Polly. After many months in Puerto Rico, Sullivan felt much better and was able to come home to Helen with an uplifted spirit. Sullivan would live for 20 more years, dying in 1936. During this entire time, she struggled with unstable and painful vision, which ended in total blindness her final year of life. If she did have TB (or some chronic bug), the intensity of her symptoms, her misery, must have increased over those last 20 years—there was no cure for TB at the time, no antibiotics until after 1940. Faced with suffering and death and with worry about Helen's future, the Peter Fagan affair did not hold the spotlight long.

Even so, Helen was deeply affected by the Fagan affair; it was her only chance at a domestic life. She might not have mentioned it in her letters, but she was still musing about it as late as the 1950s. In her book *The Open Door* (1957), Helen reflects on the fate that denied her a normal life:

What Earthly consolation is there for one like me, whom fate has denied a husband and the joy of motherhood? At the moment, my loneliness seems a void that will always be immense.

Fortunately, I have much work to do—more than ever before, in fact—and while doing it I shall have confidence as always that my unfulfilled longings will be gloriously satisfied in a world where eyes never grow dim nor ears dull.

Helen is optimistic, as usual, and she is positive about the future; that is her innate personality speaking. However, we can feel her pain; she wanted to be a wife and a mother, but the universe had other plans.

We must remember that Helen Keller was in her mid-thirties when the Fagan affair happened; Sullivan was fifty. This was not an innocent schoolgirl discovering sex and all the complications of intimacy. Keller was a graduate of Radcliffe College, a published author, a world-famous adult woman with a mind of her own. Whatever happened, it was adults confronting adults. But what Professor Kleege does so well is bring small moments home for close viewing. Kleege is not afraid to go too far with her speculations, which I find refreshing as well as unnerving. Here she creates a fictional exchange between Helen and Anne, after Annie has discovered the Fagan affair. I am not sure that Sullivan ever spoke this way to Helen, but Kleege's musing is plausible. Speaking to Helen, Kleege writes:

> But you know where this argument is heading. You've argued enough with this woman over the years to know that sooner or later, she will resort to her secret weapon, the one statement you have no answer for and no defense against. And sure enough, here it comes. She straightens her spine as if assuming the throne, and her hand in yours is not so much forming the words as transmitting the message like a jolt of electricity. "I sacrificed my life for you, and this is how you repay me?"
>
> She's said this so many times and in so many different contexts, you'd think you'd be inured to it. But the words shut down all avenues of response. The words sacrifice and repay are especially brutal. They slice deep grooves into your palm, making the tender nerves throb.
>
> She says it again. "I sacrificed my life for you. Everything. Where would you be without me?"

Professor Kleege is hard on Anne Sullivan. The miracle worker is reduced to mere fallible human, but that is always what Anne Sullivan insisted upon anyway—she would not have it any other way. Sullivan did burn her diary, page by page; and who knows what else she burned. Clearly, Sullivan did not want strangers like Kleege and me dredging up titillating dirt in the name of history.

An interesting insight (for me) is that Kleege and Sullivan were both severely visually impaired. Although they lived in different eras, both remarkable women had to face cultural judgement based on their disabilities. Sullivan struggled mightily with her issues, keeping them hidden from public scrutiny; she could also hide behind Helen's deaf-blindness, where most observer's interests were directed. Kleege worked out her angst and resentment through her writing. I am sure *Blind Rage* (2006), and *Sight Unseen* (1999), were cathartic books for Georgina; these books now serve as helpful guides to others who struggle against the consequences of visual disabilities.

The global culture has only recently been able to look at such notions as out-of-body journeys, out-of-wedlock pregnancy, extramarital affairs, lesbianism, and non-binary identity, without undue shock and derision. These were taboo subjects (or were unknown) in the Keller/Sullivan era.

Kleege also suggests, as she fearlessly charges forward with her speculations, that Anne Sullivan made some decisions that Helen was not aware of, maybe she even inadvertently or subtly coxed history in a particular direction:

> Anyway, I raise an ugly possibility here. Yes, it is possible that Teacher deceived you, altered people's words to you, distorted facts, left things out on purpose. But it was a possibility you willed yourself to ignore. You trusted Teacher. You trusted Teacher because you had always trusted Teacher. You took her word for everything, because if you started questioning her accuracy, much less her motives, there would be no end to questions. That's why they call it blind faith.

Sullivan was clocked—fingerspelling in Helen's hand—at a hundred words a minute; she was so fast that as speakers talked, she could transcribe what they said instantaneously. But as she finger-spelled, she had to quickly decide what was relevant, what was appropriate, and what needed editing. She also had to translate Helen's words and feed this back to the listeners in real-time. Sullivan's own views must have occasionally found their way into the mix.

If we fast forward a decade or two, the table has turned. Anne Sullivan is frail and nearing blindness when the two became advocates for the American Foundation for the Blind. Now Anne Sullivan's correspondance had to go through Helen Keller: Sullivan would fingerspell her intentions to Helen who then typed Sullivan's words. Ironically, Helen, the student, had to become Anne Sullivans advocate and voice, not unlike an adult having to care for an aging parent. Here is Professor Kim Nielsen on the issue:

> Publicly Helen Keller was the disabled one. Indeed, the deaf-blind woman was a public figure because of her disability. Privately, however, by the mid-1920s Annie experienced her body as far more debilitating than Helen's had ever seemed to be, weighed down by the ever-changing multiple disabilities of fluctuating eyesight, chronic pain, and depression. Helen Keller, the world's most famous disabled person, had become Annie's personal assistant.

Sullivan could not proofread what Helen had interpreted, she had to trust Helen. The word-witchery that both writers possessed must have mixed as it always had done, but this time it was Helen who was doing the interpreting and editing.

I personally do not care what chemistry happened when the two teamed up to communicate. I believe they were true to each other and as honest as they could be moment-to-moment—that is my own optimism and my trusting-nature leaning on history.

All the players in the Sullivan-Keller saga were fallible human beings living at a time in history that now looks rather primitive (although most of Helen's and Annie's reflections seem timeless and precious, worthy of mythology). Let us forgive them their human failings, whatever they were, and remember their inspiration and bravery. I am personally not willing to cast any negative fog over their wonderful story, but I do admire and support Georgina Kleege's courage to muse and speculate, to reveal emotions that had been previously hidden beneath scholarly discourse. Kleege, of course, had personal reasons for confronting Helen Keller and Anne Sullivan. Kleege spoke for those, like her, who find themselves dismayed rather than inspired by Helen Keller's life:

> Since I was a child, I have heard [Helen Keller's] name invoked as a reminder that I should be grateful for how lucky I was. I resented her for this, and suspected that her life, especially versions that appeared in my schoolbooks and in popular entertainments like the Miracle Worker, were too good to be true.

Further along, Kleege states in an imaginary letter to Helen Keller:

> Like you, I am [legally] blind, though not deaf. But the most important thing you need to know about me, and the reason for my letter, is that I grew up hating you. Sorry to be so blunt, especially on such a short acquaintance, but one of the advantages of writing to a dead person is there's no need to stand on ceremony. And you should know the truth from the start. I hated you because you were always held up to me as a role model, and one who set such an impossibly high standard of cheerfulness in the face of adversity.

Kleege is not alone in her anguish. In *Anne Sullivan Macy: The Story Behind Helen Keller* (1933), biographer Nella Braddy wrote:

> . . . with all her superb abilities and all the endless service, Helen has not . . . been entirely a blessing to the blind. Through no fault of her own, she has sometimes worked havoc with them. This is true of all eminently successful blind persons . . . Many a little blind girl of mediocre ability or of even greater natural ability than Helen Keller has been twisted out of her proper course of development in an effort to make her another Helen Keller. The fingers of a dozen hands would not be sufficient to count the blind girls who, since about 1890, have been hailed as second Helen Kellers.

Of course, this negative response to Helen Keller came about without any ill-intention from Helen; she was just being herself. Helen was born with a cheerful disposition; she grew up to be an emotionally steady individual, especially if we are to believe what virtually everyone who knew her has recorded. She also developed, from early adolescence, her exceptionally strong, faith-based spirituality that allowed her a deep acceptance of her fate. However, that Mona Lisa frozen smile on her face probably was complex, displaying a deep religious peace but also masking normal human angst and grief.

What Else Happened in 2006?

Here are a few randomly selected events that occurred in 2006: *Google* purchased *YouTube* for $1.65 billion . . . NASA launched the New Horizons mission to Pluto January of 2006 . . . Saddam Hussein was found guilty of crimes against humanity and sentenced to death by hanging . . . President Bush acknowledged there were secret CIA prisons around the world outside of U.S. legal jurisdiction . . . The European Space Agency's Venus Express Orbiter arrived at Venus in April of 2006 . . . Pluto was downgraded from a Planet to a dwarf planet.

2009: A Statue Honoring Helen Keller

Thanks to the efforts of the people of Alabama, Helen Keller was immortalized by the United States government in 2009:

> A statue honoring Helen Keller was unveiled at the U.S. Capitol in Washington, D.C. The bronze statue depicts Keller as a seven-year-old child by a water pump where she first learned to communicate by sign language. It was donated by the state of Alabama. [73]

Small replicas of the statue are available at the Helen Keller gift shop at the Ivy Green family homestead in Tuscumbia, Alabama. Mine sits on my desk and smiles down on me as I write.

Beyond the Miracle Worker: The Remarkable Life of Anne Sullivan Macy

> The wonderful feat of drawing Helen Keller out of her hopeless darkness was only accomplished by sacrificing for it another woman's whole life. ~ New York Sun

Beyond the Miracle Worker: The Remarkable Life of Anne Sullivan Macy, by Professor Kim Nielsen, is the second book to explore the life of Anne Sullivan. Dr. Nielsen is an academic scholar who became an expert on the lives of Helen Keller and Anne Sullivan. Not since Nella Braddy's book

Anne Sullivan Macy: The Story Behind Helen Keller, published in 1933, has such an in-depth biography appeared. Unlike Nella Braddy, Nielsen had access to the research archives at the Perkins School for the Blind and at the American Foundation for the Blind (both archives are now digitalized). Nielsen is a great writer; her prose reads like a novel as we follow the fascinating and historic life of Anne Sullivan from birth to death.

The book begins with a fresh look at Sullivan's first ten years of life (1866 to 1876), from her birth in Feeding Hills Massachusetts—to starkly poor Irish parents, struggling to survive in a new nation—to the eventual loss of her mother, father, and siblings. In Chapter Two, Nielsen recounts Sullivan's painful stay at the Tewksbury Almshouse from 1876 until 1880. These were devastating years for Sullivan; the memories of this sad place stayed buried in Sullivan's subconscious for most of her life. Only when Helen was 50 years old (and Sullivan was nearing death) were the Tewksbury stories told to Helen. Helen writes that many things in Annie's personality only became clear after she heard about Sullivans dreadful preteen years.

From 1880 to 1886 (age 14 to 20), Sullivan was a student at the Perkins School for the Blind. Dr. Nielsen covers these instrumental years in Chapters Three and Four. The experience at Perkins changed Annie's life; we could even say that being admitted to Perkins *saved* her life. Sullivan met sophisticated and nurturing teachers within a loving academic environment. She also found challenges and hope at the school—it was one of the best schools for the blind in the United States, and perhaps, in all the world. Being admitted to Perkins was a most fortunate turn of luck for the fiery, streetwise teenager. She graduated as the school valedictorian.

Dr. Nielsen tells of Sullivans growing relationships (at Perkins) with Sophia Hopkins and Michael Anagnos; these two role models and eventual friends helped Sullivan grow from a rebellious teenager to a sophisticated and well-educated young adult. Hopkins and Anagnos would continue to influence Anne Sullivan for as long as the two lived.

In 1887, Sullivan took advantage of an offer to travel to Tuscumbia, Alabama to teach Helen Keller. Sullivan was not trained as a teacher and she had never been out of Massachusetts; the task she took on was far beyond her skill set, but the challenge was not beyond her determination, courage, and intellectual brilliance.

In Chapters Five and Six, Dr. Nielsen introduces the reader to the Keller family, especially Helen's parents and to the "Jim Crow south."

Anne Sullivan was a fiery-tongued anti-slave Northerner entering a land devastated physically and morally by the Civil War. Helen was a wild child with no language and little discipline. There were many circumstances that might have caused Sullivan's plans to fail, but the result—after years of fierce struggle—was a woman, Helen Keller, who became a champion for Love, kindness, and service to others. Sullivan found a home and a life mission in Alabama, and the Keller family found a dedicated and passionate teacher for their deaf-blind child.

Chapter Five tells the story of how Sullivan abandoned her pedagogical outline soon after her arrival and went with her intuition as she guided Helen's transition from wild child to enthusiastic learner. It is an interesting circumstance that Anne Sullivan's beloved younger brother Jimmy had died when he was just six years old, the same age that Helen was when Sullivan first laid eyes on her. There was probably a deep longing in Sullivan to save this little girl after she had understandably been unable to save her tubercular little brother.

Chapter Six (1888–1891) tells the story of Sullivan's early efforts to discipline and educate Helen. Helen was six years and eight months old when Sullivan met her for the first time on the porch at the Keller farmstead. These are the miracle years—Helen eventually discovered language and Sullivan found her life's mission. The bulk of this chapter concerns Anne Sullivan's relationship with Michael Anagnos, the director of the Perkins School. What soon becomes obvious is that Anagnos could sense history unfolding; he knew that Helen Keller was a phenomenon, and he knew that Anne Sullivan was performing miracles. Whether he was deliberately using Helen and Annie to promote the Perkins school, or if he was bringing the unique story to a wider public, the result was that Helen and Annie began to gain recognition and fame as Anagnos published glowing reports of Helen's progress.

Chapter's Seven and Eight are called *The Battle for Helen* (Round One and Round Two). There was a behind the scenes battle going on between the deaf community—led by Alexander Graham Bell—and the blind community, led by Michael Anagnos, to claim Helen for their own purposes. The eventual winner was the Keller-Sullivan mythology. Anagnos sought to feature the Perkins School using Helen as an example. Bell wanted Helen to champion the deaf community; he was an advocate for oral speaking over sign language. Helen did justice to the ambitions of both men, but she also transcended their parochial wishes. Chapter Seven tells the story of Helen and Perkins, with Anagnos at the center. Chapter

Eight tells the story of Bell's influence. Both powerplays essentially ended when Helen was accepted at Radcliffe College and began asserting herself as an intellectual and spiritual power of her own making.

This decade (1890 to 1900) was also when the infamous debacle called the Frost King plagiarism scandal unfolded. In the final analysis Helen was found not guilty of plagiarism, but a pall was cast over Sullivan's credibility—Anagnos never quite forgave Annie for presumably influencing Helen. It was obvious that Sullivan was driven and determined; she pressured Helen toward perfection. Observers thought at the time that Sullivan's zeal was excessive and harmful (Sullivan strongly disagreed). Anagnos had lavished extravagant praise on Sullivan for her teaching methods when she began helping Helen, but he soured on this view as time went on and as he saw the power that Sullivan had over Helen's emerging worldview.

Helen's thirst for knowledge and her hunger for communication exploded in these years, from 1890 to 1900. These are the years when people (especially Anne Sullivan) began to see that Helen Keller was no ordinary human being—she had a remarkable personality and a prodigious memory; she was a phenomenon.

From 1900 to 1904 (Chapter Nine), Helen attended Radcliffe College. In retrospect, it was Anne Sullivan who was at the center of this great accomplishment. Helen learned the academic material and passed all the tests with honors, but Sullivan had to interpret all the lectures, all the textbooks, all the assignments—under incredibly stressful conditions. When Helen emerged with her degree in 1904, she had essentially become her own person; she moved beyond Anne Sullivan, beyond Alexander Graham Bell, beyond Michael Anagnos—this painful transition was emotionally hard on everyone, but these three were Helen's friends and long-time champions; they were pleased—if somewhat befuddled—to see her blossom so quickly.

Helen's writing career began in college and her worldview was altered by her college experience. She was now a socialist, a strong-willed suffragette, and a fervent Swedenborgian, much to everyone's bewilderment. John Macy also came into her life in this eventful decade—Helen's life in the household with John Macy and Annie Sullivan was, she wrote, one of the happiest times in her life.

Chapter Ten tells the story of the John Macy decade (1904–1914) when Sullivan fell in love and got married to the handsome and brilliant Harvard Professor. This was an up and down marriage that faded as the two eventually drifted apart. Sullivan never divorced John Macy and she kept his last name—the two had love and respect for each other the rest of their lives apart. There are many speculations that can be made about why they fell in and then out of marriage, but neither John nor Annie left written material to explain. Powerful personalities in troubling times can clash and long-term damage can result. This decade was significant in the Keller-Sullivan saga; the marriage between John Macy and Anne Sullivan changed the lives of the three friends and molded how each of them went on to impact history.

Chapter Eleven begins with the sorrow and stunned grief Annie felt after her marriage failed. Chronic ocular pain, dreadful childhood memories, and the emotional loss of John's love and support caused melancholy, depression, and a sense of hopelessness. Suffering from exhaustion after a lecture tour, Sullivan was diagnosed (perhaps incorrectly) with tuberculosis and told to rest. Sullivan took Polly Thomson along to help, first to a sanitorium in Lake Placid and then to Puerto Rico.

While Sullivan and Polly Thomson were away at Lake Placid, Helen met and fell in love with Peter Fagan and that whole unfortunate ordeal played out.

The next decade in Sullivan's life (1914 to 1924) tells the story of the roller coaster ride that happened to Sullivan and Keller as they tried to earn a living together and to satisfy the demands of history. They went on the Vaudeville Circuit together performing an "act" that Helen loved, and Annie did not. They also went to Hollywood to shoot a silent movie that unfortunately was a commercial flop. This extraordinarily rich chapter (Eleven) addresses some of the most eventful years in the lives of Annie, John, Helen, Polly, and Peter Fagan. In 1917, their wonderful friend Sophia Hopkins died.

From 1924 to the early 1930s (Chapter Twelve), Helen traveled with Annie and with Polly Thomson around the United States and then overseas on behalf of the American Foundation for the Blind. Employment with the American Foundation for the Blind gave the women a stable livelihood and a life full of adventure and travel. Unfortunately, Anne Sullivan's health was deteriorating over these years and she died October 20, 1936 with Helen and Polly by her side. Chapter Thirteen tells the story of Anne Sullivan's final years.

This book is a treasure; it was carefully crafted by a professor of disability and women's studies—I cannot think of a better background from which to survey and highlight the life of one of America's greatest teachers, Anne Sullivan. This is a must read for all those who wish to understand the complexity of the rich, loving lives of soulmates Helen Keller and Annie Sullivan.

What Else Happened in 2009?

Here are a few randomly selected events that occurred in 2009: Barack Obama was inaugurated as the 44th President of the United States of America, becoming the first African-American president . . . the first cases of the pandemic H1N1 swine flu occurred in the United States . . . Nasa repaired the Hubble Space Telescope . . . American icon Michael Jackson died . . . The Icelandic banking system collapsed causing the collapse of the Icelandic government and resignation of Prime Minister Geir Haarde . . . Albania and Croatia joined the North Atlantic Treaty Organization . . . NASA launched the Lunar Reconnaissance Orbiter probe, announcing in November 2009 that water had been discovered near the Moon's south pole.

2011: WORLD TRADE CENTER

An important archive of historical treasures pertaining to Helen Keller was lost in the September 11th attack on the World Trade Center in New York City. The offices of *Helen Keller International*, located a block from the World Trade Center, were destroyed. Among the items lost were first editions of Helen Keller's books, correspondence between Helen and the executive director of the Royal National Institute for the Blind in England, and a lifetime of photographs, including images of Helen Keller beside every living president who served during her lifetime.

Some of the items in the archive were spared because *Helen Keller International* had shared documents with the *American Foundation for the Blind*, also based in New York City, on West 31st Street, a safe distance from the disaster area.

What Else Happened in 2011?

Here are a few randomly selected events that occurred in 2011: U.S. Congresswoman Gabrielle Giffords and twelve others were shot while Giffords was making a public appearance in Tucson, Arizona. . . . In Japan, an underwater earthquake caused a tsunami, which triggered a nuclear disaster at the Fukushima Daiichi Nuclear Power Plant. . . . NASA launched the Juno spacecraft on a mission to study Jupiter. . . . U.S. special forces killed al-Qaida leader, Osama bin Laden, in a raid on a house in Abbottabad, Pakistan.

2012: Helen Keller in Love is Published

Helen Keller in Love is a fictional story about the love affair between Helen Keller and Peter Fagan. It is an important work because it is Allocentric, storytelling. Most books about Keller and Sullivan are fact-based Egocentric perspectives where emotions are kept at arm's length while "truth" is revealed. As I explained in my textbooks, we need to come at our challenges using both of our minds, each of which has a different expressive style, and each of which serves a different purpose. Each style is half the story, half the truth.

Rosie Sultan has humanized Helen with this story. We see in Helen Keller a vulnerable young woman who has a philosophy of love, a creed of loving-service, but who has never stood inside another person's intimate space and felt the power of feminine energy and masculine energy confronting each other. Intense sensual/sexual love would never have been known by Helen had she not met Peter Fagan. This fictionalized account has an underlying reality to it that goes beyond, and yet complements the legendary Helen Keller.

What Else Happened in 2012?

Here are a few randomly selected events that occurred in 2012: The U.S. Consulate in Benghazi, Libya was attacked. . . . China's Communist Party named billionaire businessman's Xi Jinping the country's next president. . . . After 246 years, the Encyclopedia Britannica discontinued its print edition. . . . Vladimir Putin was elected President of Russia. . . .

a Middle East respiratory syndrome coronavirus outbreak occurred. . . . The Mars Science Rover Curiosity successfully landed on Mars. . . . Barack Obama was reelected President of the United States. . . . A shooting at the Sandy Hook Elementary School killed twenty-eight people (mostly small children)—the United States Congress, controlled by Republicans, voted *to do nothing* in response to the tragedy.

2016: Helen Keller's Forgotten Oscar

In 2016, Bill Winter wrote an article called "Helen Keller's forgotten Oscar." The article is available online at the Helen Keller Digital archives hosted by the Perkins School for the Blind. Here are excerpts from that article:

> She is best known as an activist and author, but the deaf-blind icon also had a moment in the Hollywood spotlight. Helen Keller . . . accepted the award for "Helen Keller in Her Story," a 1955 documentary film about her life.
>
> Written and directed by Nancy Hamilton, the film used archival newsreel clips and photos to trace Keller's early years. Newer film footage showed Keller during an ordinary day later in her life—going for a walk, reading a braille Bible, answering correspondence and meeting friends for tea. The film, originally released as "The Unconquered," was narrated by actress Katharine Cornell.
>
> No ingénue, Keller received the Oscar at age 75. Photos from that evening show her holding the statuette, a broad smile on her face.
>
> Seven years later, 16-year-old Patty Duke won an Academy Award for best supporting actress for her portrayal of a much younger Keller in "The Miracle Worker," the story of how teacher Anne Sullivan helped Keller break though the barriers of deaf-blindness and learn to communicate. Anne Bancroft, who played Sullivan, won the Oscar for best actress.

That brings up another Academy Award trivia question: Who is the only actress to win an Oscar for a role in which she says only one word?

Answer: Patty Duke. In the most famous scene in the movie, Sullivan signs letters into Keller's hand, trying to help the youngster understand there is a word for the liquid gushing from a pump. When Keller finally makes the connection, her face lights up and she says, "Water!" It is the only word Duke speaks in "The Miracle Worker." [74]

What Else Happened in 2016?

Here are some random events that occurred in the (leap) year 2016: Great Britain voted to leave the European Union . . . the Soviet Union interfered with the U.S. Presidential Election, actively working to elect Republicans . . . Donald Trump won the Presidency of the United States without winning the popular vote . . . Rodrigo Duterte became President of the Philippines . . . Brazil and South Korea impeached their Presidents . . . Gravitational waves, faint ripples in the fabric of the cosmos, were detected for the first time . . . Launched in August 2011, NASA's Juno spacecraft became the first human-made object to orbit Jupiter. . . . NASA and NOAA confirmed that 2015 was the hottest year on record globally, shattering the previous record by the largest margin ever seen.

BEYOND

Helen Keller was the miracle that Anne Sullivan, the miracle worker, released from social and sensory isolation. It is wonderful and ironic that this miracle woman then went forth and affected so many lives—across the whole of our planet.

Amazingly, Helen Keller is still affecting lives, decades after her death. There is every reason to suggest that her positive impact will continue as history is kept alive by human beings who repeat her story and reflect on her philosophy of Love and Service.

When I look at Helen's life, I see that *the miracle became a miracle worker herself*; Helen Keller wrought miracle after miracle in the hearts and souls of the people who came to know her—she touched my life as a teacher and as a writer, and now she has touched your life. Helen Keller's loving-kindness, her never-yielding courage, and her unshakable faith still nurtures and heals the souls of those who come to know her. We pray that Helen Keller will continue to touch and transform new generations decades and centuries from now. Helen Keller has blessed these pages and for that I thank her with my whole heart.

∾

As I said at the beginning of *The Esoteric Helen Keller*, each new generation of artists who discover the Helen Keller story will reinterpret the miracle to fit "modern" times. As I am finishing this book, I know that the Digital Archives at the American Foundation for the Blind and at the Perkins School for the Blind will continue to expand and become more sophisticated in the years ahead. These archives will tell the Keller-Sullivan story in ever more detail. I am also sure that more documentaries will be done, more movies, more podcasts; Helen Keller websites and YouTube channels will come and go as the decades roll forward.

I know of two projects in-progress as I record these final observations. Deaf actress and writer-director Hillary Baack has written a script (simply called *Helen*) for a new rendition of the Keller-Sullivan story. Hillary's perspective will provide a fresh and needed statement from the deaf community—a perspective that has been lacking until now. I had a brief, enjoyable three-way email exchange with Hillary Baack and with Daniel Kish in 2020; Daniel is now a consultant for Hillary's pending movie.

Filmmaker Laurie Block is working on a documentary for PBS ("American Masters" series) called *Becoming Helen Keller*. Block is producing, directing, and co-writing the film, which highlights Keller's political and social perspectives.

What Else Happened in 2020 and 2021?

Here are some random events that occurred in 2020 (the year from hell) and 2021 (the year of renewed hope): The Covid-19 pandemic shocked the entire planet—economies sagged, the rich got richer, the poor got poorer, and over three million people died from the virus (at the time when I recorded this) . . . The Dow Jones Industrial Average suffered its worst single-day point drop in history on March 9, 2020 (but later soared to record heights even as the pandemic raged) . . . Science quickly rose to the occasion. In record time, companies Pfizer, Moderna, and Johnson & Johnson (and others) created vaccines to protect humanity . . . Donald Trump lost the Presidential election and Joe Biden took the helm of government . . . Trump was impeached and acquitted twice . . . Kamala Harris broke the glass ceiling, becoming the first woman, first African American, and first Asian American to be elected Vice President . . . Black lives Matter protests broke out all over the United States . . . radical Trump supporters overwhelmed police and wandered the halls of Congress in an attempt to overturn the results of the 2020 elections . . . Ruth Bader Ginsburg died and was replaced on the U.S. Supreme Court by Amy Coney Barrett . . . 2020 was the hottest year ever recorded . . . climate change continued to endanger all life on the planet.

Important Pathfinders of the Twenty-First Century (2000 to 2100)

Technology, Philosophy, Freedom, War

Rather than select outstanding individuals to venerate—a hopeless task since there are so many deserving people—I will instead list categories or teams of people who I think will impact the entire twenty-first century. I am using my visionary powers to peer into the unknown—I say this with self-effacing good humor since my futurist credentials keep expiring. In Helen Keller's honor, I am going to err on the side of optimism, trust, reckless abandon (smile), and loving-kindness.

There are hard predictions, calculated by simply looking at present trends and projecting them forward, and there are soft trends that may play out depending on the decisions made by governing bodies and global corporations across the globe. There is also the advent of surprising breakthroughs (like the internet, stem cells, and 3-D printers were) that nobody saw coming but which rocked the foundations of science and society—we are never sure when such destructive events might occur. I will play it safe in this short discussion; I will stick with the hard trends.

Here are four observations you will find (in one form or another) in the predictions of most modern futurists:

1. Our technologies will get smaller (trending toward the invisible), faster, smarter, cheaper, and ever more networked. Take computers

or cellphones as examples of faster, smarter, smaller trends. Better yet, take the components (parts) of phones and computers—the microcircuits that enable shrinkage. These components have gotten faster, smarter, smaller, cheaper, and more networked at a predictable pace.

2. The second most common thing futurists tell us is that the speed with which things are getting smaller, faster, smarter (etc.) is exponential. The pace of change is picking up speed.

3. The third observation is that the human brain is not evolving fast enough to keep up with technology. Unevolved minds are becoming increasingly dangerous as technologies become more powerful and cheaper.

4. Technologies will merge with our biology; the immaterial will blend with the material. Human beings will take over the responsibility of evolving their own minds and bodies—we will merge with our inventions to become a new species, which some have called *Robosapiens*.

Below is a list of technological (hard trends) that seem destined to appear sometime in the twenty-first century (2000 to 2100)—predicated, of course, on the assumption that we do not annihilate all life forms on the planet. These trends will come about because of networked teams of professionals instantly sharing their research:

- Human beings will make significant breakthroughs toward the ability to live forever. All diseases (cancer, heart disease, diabetes, etc.) will be cured or managed. Already, as I write this in 2021, we are starting to print body organs that are compatible with our individual molecular and genetic biology. We are editing genes and fixing our genetic code. We are discovering ways to lengthen telomeres.

- Human beings will be living on planetary bodies outside the earth before 2050. Moon colonization will rapidly occur in the next ten years, followed by colonies on Mars and on the moons of Jupiter and Saturn. Artificial space villages will proliferate as waystations between these planetary colonies.

- Humanoid robots that are indistinguishable from flesh and blood humans will be operating among us before the end of the twenty-first century. Perhaps, more feasibly, *we will become* these new creatures, having been replaced piece by piece as we are "repaired" and "updated." Robosapiens will have the same rights as (rapidly disappearing) natural humanity.

- Quantum computers and fusion energy will be commonplace by 2050. These technologies will follow well-established patterns, getting smaller, faster, cheaper, smarter, and more connected at regular intervals. Energy will become unlimited and free.

- We will turn the earth green again—rivers and oceans will be unpolluted, the air will be pure and fresh, the climate crisis will stabilize and become manageable—and we will manage the weather. We will also learn how to terraform the moon and other extra-earth locations.

- Nation states will disappear as a world government forms. Armies will disappear, replaced by a global peace-keeping force. Freedom will be granted and protected for all living creatures.

- Human beings will embrace their duality and work to enhance both their minds; their Egocentric mind and their Allocentric mind will evolve as part of unnatural selection. Robosapiens (the new "us") will become integral creatures, creative, kind, tolerant, scientifically brilliant, compassionately networked souls.

- The ability to alter the human brain and nervous system will accelerate as the decades of the 21st century unfold. There will evolve a legislative body within the planetary government that will debate what a human mind ought to become (Oh God, maybe this is George Orwell's *Ministry of Truth*). We will alter (experiment with) the worldviews of humanity using psychedelic drugs ("medicines" that alter cognition), as well as through quantum/molecular/genetic manipulation. We will also evolve toward ever more connectivity until we arrive at a fluidly evolving global hive-brain.

- Helen Keller will take her place alongside the Venerated Pioneers of the 19th and 20th centuries (Albert Einstein, Mark Twain, William James, Carl Jung, as examples) who set the foundation for a compassionate, peace-loving, optimistic, trusting, and never-yielding future for our species. We must keep the fairies and magic wands close to our hearts as we race into this frightening, exhilarating future.

NOTES

1. *Midstream*, by Helen Keller, 1929.
2. Orthodox History; the Society for Orthodox Christian History in the Americas: https://orthodoxhistory.org/2010/09/06/michael-anagnos-who-made-the-sightless-see/.
3. *Beyond the Miracle Worker* by Kim Nielsen, 2009.
4. *Women in American History: A Social, Political, and Cultural Encyclopedia,* by Peg A. Lamphier, Rosanne Welch, 2017.
5. *The Story of My Life: The Restored Edition*, by Helen Keller, 2003.
6. *Mansfield* sounded sophisticated and aristocratic, so Sullivan took the name when she was young. As far as we know, there is no ancestral reason for the name addition.
7. *The Story of My Life: The Restored Edition*, by Helen Keller, 2003.
8. "Laura's World: What a deaf-blind girl taught the nineteenth century;" by Louis Menand, *The New Yorker Magazine*, June 25, 2001.
9. *American Notes*, by Charles Dickens,1842.
10. "Laura's World: What a deaf-blind girl taught the nineteenth century;" by Louis Menand, *The New Yorker Magazine*, June 25, 2001.
11. *The Story of My Life: The Restored Edition*, by Helen Keller, 2003.
12. Helen Keller Digital Archives, American Foundation for the Blind.
13. "A Modern Wonder: Helen Keller, The Phenomenal Blind and Deaf Mute," the *Lincoln Evening Call* (Lincoln, Nebraska), March 25, 1892.
14. *Beyond the Miracle Worker* by Kim Nielsen, 2009.

15. *The World I Live In*, by Helen Keller, 1908.
16. The Wrentham Lions Club website: http://wrenthamlions.org/.
17. *Beyond the Miracle Worker* by Kim Nielsen, 2009.
18. *Helen and Teacher* by Joseph Lash, 1980.
19. *Helen and Teacher* by Joseph Lash, 1980.
20. "Helen Keller begins attending Radcliffe College of Harvard at age 20." Ashville, *North Carolina Citizens-Times*, October 19, 1900.
21. *Out of the Dark: Essays, Lectures, and Addresses on Physical and Social Vision*, by Helen Heller, 1913.
22. *The Story of My Life: The Restored Edition*, by Helen Keller, 2003.
23. "I Must Speak: A Plea to the American Woman," by Helen Keller, *Ladies Home Journal.*
24. *The Story of My Life: The Restored Edition*, by Helen Keller, 2003.
25. Copied from the AFB Helen Keller Archives and edited for clarity.
26. *Beyond the Miracle Worker* by Kim Nielsen, 2009.
27. The Wrentham Lions Club website: http://wrenthamlions.org/
28. Helen Keller Digital Archives, American Foundation for the Blind.
29. *Helen Keller in Scotland: A Personal History*, by Helen Keller, 1933.
30. "Helen Keller: Brief life of a woman who found her own way: 1880–1968," *Harvard Magazine,* by Roger Shattuck, July/August edition, 2004.
31. Spartacus Educational: https://spartacus-educational.com/USAkeller.htm
32. International Socialist Review: https://isreview.org/issue/96/politics-helen-keller.
33. *Teacher,* by Helen Keller, 1955.
34. "On Behalf of the I.W.W.: Helen Keller's Involvement in the Labor Movement," by Mary M. Fleming and William H. Ross, Ph.D. Department of Management University of Wisconsin La Crosse; https://core.ac.uk/download/pdf/211325563.pdf
35. *The Radical lives of Helen Keller*, Kim Nielsen, 2004.
36. *Women in American History: A Social, Political, and Cultural Encyclopedia*, Peg A. Lamphier, Rosanne Welch, 2017.
37. *Beyond the Miracle Worker* by Kim Nielsen, 2009.
38. Helen Keller International: https://www.hki.org/
39. Letter to the NAACP endorsing their work, February 13, 1916.
40. *Beyond the Miracle Worker* by Kim Nielsen, 2009.
41. This could quite possibly have been the Spanish flu that killed millions. We cannot know for sure, of course, but it was described

as severe and Helen was deeply worried about Annie's health, especially because Sullivan had other health issues.

42. The flu can cause lingering and severe side effects, as scientists discovered during the Covid pandemic. Through the 1920s until her death in 1936, Sullivan reportedly had numerous ill-defined ailments. From our perspective, a hundred years later, it seems that Sullivan had overlapping reasons for her declining health, including possible tubercular-related ailments, chronic inflammation of her eyes that might have had systemic affects, and (less likely, but possible) lingering effects from severe flu.

43. *Helen Keller: Sketch for a Portrait*, by Van Wyck Brooks, 1956.

44. "Oppose All Injustice, Helen Kellers Creed," *The Minneapolis Star* (Minneapolis, Minnesota), August 31, 1921.

45. *Helen Keller in Scotland: A Personal History*, by Helen Keller, 1933.

46. *Beyond the Miracle Worker* by Kim Nielsen, 2009.

47. I know from many years working alongside the members of Lions International that it is individuals who make all the difference. All over the planet, members of Lions Clubs have raised funds for blind kids, responded to the needs of the elderly blind, given away long canes to blind people, and answered the prayers of community members who approached them. I also know that women became Lions Club members and worked alongside the men to relieve the suffering of community members. Lions Clubs also never restricted their charity to the blind; they helped disabled people in their communities regardless of whether they were sighted or blind. This book was an opportunity to thank these generous people, each and every one.

48. Helen Keller Kids Museum online; a blog post for August 2008.

49. *Helen Keller in Scotland: A Personal History*, by Helen Keller, 1933

50. *Beyond the Miracle Worker* by Kim Nielsen, 2009.

51. Helen Keller Digital Archives, American Foundation for the Blind.

52. *Beyond the Miracle Worker* by Kim Nielsen, 2009.

53. *Helen Keller in Scotland: A Personal History*, by Helen Keller, 1933

54. *The Open Door*, by Helen Keller, 1957.

55. *Helen Keller's Journal*, by Helen Keller, published in 1938.

56. This is from an article called "Helen Keller's Civil Diplomacy in Japan in 1937 and 1948." *Japan Review*; No. 27, 2014.

57. Akita Club of America (ACA), https://www.akitaclub.org/

58. This refers to a radio address given by their friend Alexander

Woollcott: from *Helen Keller's Journal*, March 2, 1937.

59. *Helen Keller's Journal*, by Helen Keller, journal entry for January 27, 1937, published in 1938.

60. *Helen Keller's Journal*, by Helen Keller, entry for November 18, 1936, published in 1938.

61. The modern nations of Japan, Germany, and Italy have come to terms with their past and are now Democratic nations full of citizens with only a memory of past wars. There are probably few nations without a record of historic cruelties carried out in the name of nationalism. As the world becomes global, let us hope that war becomes an anachronism.

62. Helen Keller Digital Archives, American Foundation for the Blind.

63. *Sachiko: A Nagasaki Bomb Survivor's Story*, by Caren Stelson, Lerner Publishing Group, 2016.

64. *Helen Keller's Journal*, by Helen Keller, journal entry for April 5, 1937, published in 1938.

65. "Helen Keller's Civil Diplomacy in Japan in 1937 and 1948;" Japan Review; No. 27 (2014); Published by: International Research Centre for Japanese Studies, National Institute for the Humanities.

66. *Helen Keller: Sketch for a Portrait*, by Van Wyck Brooks, 1956.

67. Helen Keller Digital Archives, American Foundation for the Blind.

68. *Notable American Women: The Modern Period: A Biographical Dictionary*, 1980.

69. Helen Keller Digital Archives, American Foundation for the Blind.

70. *Greenville News* (South Carolina) published June 2nd, 1968.

71. *Helen and Teacher* by Joseph Lash, 1980.

72. Connecticut Women's Hall of Fame website: https://www.cwhf.org/.

73. *Matilda Ziegler Magazine for the Blind* published October 26, 2009.

74. Perkins School for the Blind Helen Keller Digital Archives.

BIBLIOGRAPHY

More than at any other time, when I hold a beloved book in my hand my limitations fall from me, my spirit is free. ~ *Midstream*, 1929.

Adamson, Glenn, Fewer, Better Things: The Hidden Wisdom of Objects, Bloomsbury Publishing, 2018.

Armstrong, David, Stokoe, William, Wilcox, Sherman, *Gesture and the Nature of Language*, 1995.

Ball, Philip, "Quantum Darwinism, an Idea to Explain Objective Reality, Passes First Tests;" Quanta Magazine (online), 2019.

Battro Antonio M., Stanislas Dehaene Wolf J. Singer (editors), The Proceedings of the Working Group on Human Neuroplasticity and Education, October 2010.

Blatt, Burton, "Friendly Letters on the Correspondence of Helen Keller, Anne Sullivan, and Alexander Graham Bell;" *Exceptional Children*: Volume 51 issue: 5, page(s): 405–409, February 1, 1985.

Blaxall, Arthur William, *Helen Keller Under the Southern Cross*, January 1, 1952.

Blesser, Barry and Linda-Ruth Salter, *Spaces Speak, are you Listening? Experiencing Aural Architecture*, 2007.

Borglum, John Gutzon de la Mothe, "Eyes of the Soul," available on the American Foundation for the Blind Helen Keller Digital Archives.

Brooks, Van Wyck, *Helen Keller: Sketch for a Portrait*, 1965.

Chesterton, G. K., *What's Wrong with the World*, 1910.

Cromwell, John, *Hitler's Pope*, 1999.

Cutsforth, Thomas D., *The Blind in School and Society, A Psychological Study*, 1933.

Dickens, Charles, *American Notes*, 1842.

Easton, Steward C., *Man and World in the Light of Anthroposophy*, by Steward C. Easton, 1975.

Emerson, Ralph Waldo, "Swedenborg, or the Mystic," published in his book *Representative Men*, 1850.

Evans, Jonathan,
- In Two Minds: Dual Processes and Beyond, 2009.
- Thinking twice: Two Minds in one Brain, 2010.
- Thinking and Reasoning: A Very Short Introduction, 2017.
- "The Duality of Mind: Historical Perspective," an online summary of dual-process theory, with Keith Frankish.

Frankish, Keith, Mind and Supermind, 2007.

Freeberg, Ernest, *The Education of Laura Bridgman* 2001.

Hawkins, Jeff, *A Thousand Brains: A New Theory of Intelligence*, 2021.

Huth, John Edward, The Lost Art of Finding Our Way, 2013.

Garrett, Leslie, *Helen Keller: A Photographic Story of a Life*, 2004.

Genechten, Désirée Martina van, A Psychobiographical Study of Helen Keller, Faculty of Health Sciences, Nelson Mandela Metropolitan University, November 2009.

Gitter, Elisabeth, *The Imprisoned Guest: Samuel Howe and Laura Bridgman, the Original Deaf-Blind Girl*, 2001.

Goodrick-Clarke, Nicholas, *The Western Esoteric Traditions: A Historical Introduction*, 2008.

Haldane, J.B.S., *Fact and Faith*, 1934.

Hanegraaff Wouter J., *Western Esotericism: A Guide for the Perplexed*, 2013.

Harrity, Richard and Ralph G. Martin, *The Three Lives of Helen Keller*, 1962.

Harry, Gerard, *Man's Miracle: The Story of Helen Keller and her European Sisters*, 1913.

Henney, Nella Braddy, *Anne Sullivan Macy: The Story Behind Helen Keller*, 1933.

Hong, Howard V. and Hong, Edna H., *The Essential Kierkegaard*, 1997.

Humphrey, Nicholas,
- "Consciousness Regained:" Chapters in the Development of Mind, Oxford University Press, 1983.

- *In a Dark Time*, (ed. with R. J. Lifton), Harvard University Press, 1984.
- *Leaps of Faith: Science, Miracles, and the Search for Supernatural Consolation*, 1996.
- *The Inner Eye: Social Intelligence in Evolution*, Faber & Faber, 1986; Oxford University Press 2002,
- *A History of the Mind*, Chatto & Windus 1992, Simon & Schuster, 1992.
- *Soul Searching: Human Nature and Supernatural Belief*, 1995.
- "How to Solve the Mind-Body Problem," Imprint Academic, 2000.
- *The Mind Made Flesh: Essays from the Frontiers of Evolution and Psychology*, Oxford University Press, 2002.
- *Seeing Red: A Study in Consciousness*, Belknap Press/Harvard University Press, 2006.
- *Soul Dust: The Magic of Consciousness*, Quercus Publishing, 2011, Princeton University Press, 2011

International Research Centre for Japanese Studies, "Helen Keller's Civil Diplomacy in Japan in 1937 and 1948." Japan Review; No. 27, pp. 201–220. National Institute for the Humanities, 2014.

James, Henry (senior), *Substance and Shadow, the Secret Life of Swedenborg*, 1863.

James, William,
- The Principles of Psychology, 1890.
- The Will to Believe, 1896.
- Talks to Teachers on Psychology, 1899.
- The Varieties of Religious Experience, 1902.
- "Laura Bridgman," Atlantic Monthly, Volume 93, 1904.
- The Letters of William James, Volumes one and two, 1920.

Keller, Helen
- **1901:** "I Must Speak: A Plea to the American Woman," is published in January 1901 in the *Ladies Home Journal*. Helen was 21 when this article appeared, a second-year student at Radcliffe.
- **1903:** *The Story of My Life* is Helen's autobiography (up to age 22). There is an abridged version credited to Helen, only 75 pages, and there is an unabridged version co-authored by John Macy, Anne Sullivan, and Helen that contains letters written by Sullivan, and a section about Helen's education—this collection was started by Sullivan and John Macy in 1901.

- **1903:** *Optimism*, Helen's second book, was written when she was in her last year at Radcliffe College, with the encouragement of her English professor Charles Copeland.
- **1905:** Essay "A Chat About the Hand," by Helen Keller, printed in Century Magazine.
- **1908:** *The World That I Live In* was written by Helen. Into this book (she says) she poured "everything that interested me at one of the happiest periods of my life."
- **1909:** "I must speak: A plea to the American woman," Ladies Home Journal, Volume 26, January 1909.
- **1910:** *The Song of the Stone Wall* is a long poem published as a book. I found this fascinating because for me it is a reflection on the vibrational universe that Helen lived within.
- **1911:** "Social Causes of Blindness;" published in the socialist daily *The New York Call*, February 15, 1911.
- **1911:** "The Unemployed;" published in the *Zeigler Magazine for the Blind*, 1911.
- **1912:** "The Hand of the World," an article for *American Magazine*, December 1912.
- **1912:** "How I Became a Socialist," published in the socialist daily paper *The New York Call*.
- **1913:** *Out of the Dark: Essays, Lectures, and Addresses on Physical and Social Vision*. This is a collection of early articles and speeches written by Keller. It was reissued in 1920.
- **1919:** *Deliverance* is a silent motion picture about Helen's life. It is a convoluted, over-the-top symbol-heavy dramatization of Helen's mythical life. It was a flop at the box office and somewhat of an embarrassment for Helen, yet she never regretted her enjoyable experience in Hollywood.
- **1927:** *My Religion* is Helen Keller's attempt to explain her religion, Swedenborgianism.
- **1928:** "A Vision of Service." An address delivered May 14, 1928 at the Church of the Holy City, Washington, D.C. Available as a pamphlet in the Swedenborg School of Religion Library, in Newton, Massachusetts.
- **1929:** *Midstream, my later Life*, was written by Helen with a lot of help from Professor John Macy. The book is a look back at the first half of Helen's remarkable life.
- **1929:** *We Bereaved* is a short set of inspirational comments by

Helen. *Peace at Eventide* is the same book printed in Great Britain; there are very minor differences.

- **1931**: *Double Blossoms: Helen Keller Anthology*, complied by Edna Porter.
- **1931**: The Underprivileged, published
- **1932**: "Put Your Husband in the Kitchen," August 1932 article in The Atlantic.
- **1933**: *Anne Sullivan Macy: The Story Behind Helen Keller*. This is the only in-depth biography of Anne Sullivan. It was written by a close friend of Helen and Annie, a professional editor by trade, Nella Braddy Henney.
- **1933**: *Helen Keller in Scotland: A Personal History Written by Herself*, as recorded by James Kerr Love.
- **1933**: "Three Days to See," an article in The Atlantic, January 1933.
- **1935**: "The World I Would Help," a long essay by Helen Keller about her spiritual process as influenced by Emanuel Swedenborg. With a modern introduction by Helen Keller scholar Ray Silverman.
- **1938**: *Helen Keller's Journal*, foreword by Augustus Muir. Helen wrote this after the death of Anne Sullivan.
- **1940**: *Let Us Have Faith*, by Helen Keller.
- **1944**: Comments to the U.S. House of Representatives Committee on Labor.
- **1951**: *Ladies Home Journal*, March 1951, "The World Through Three Senses."
- **1955**: *Teacher* is Helen Keller's personal reflection on her education and her relationship with the demanding and loving Anne Sullivan.
- **1957**: *The Open Door*, by Helen Keller.
- **1957**: *The Miracle Worker* was a 3-part stage play that was later made into a TV drama, and classic movie. When I watched this after reading all of the books listed here, I was amazed how accurate and powerful this play still is. The Miracle Worker is a play by William Gibson. It was based on Helen Keller's autobiography *The Story of My Life*.
- **1962**: *The Three Lives of Helen Keller* by Richard Harrity and Ralph Martin.
- **1967**: *Helen Keller, Her Socialist Years,* is another look at Helen's radical position on the attitudes of her generation; edited by Philip S. Foner.

- **1980:** *Helen and Teacher* by Joseph Lash was the first in-depth biography of Helen Keller. It is very beautifully written and enjoyable.
- *1987:* An article called the *Cape Cod Campus*. This is a short article about Anne Sullivan's lifelong friend Sophia Hopkins. Many letters were exchanged between Sullivan, Keller, and Hopkins that are now a national historic treasure. *The Cape Cod Campus, Summer-Fall 1987.*
- **1994:** *Light in my Darkness* is a re-edited version of Helen's book *My Religion*. Ray Silverman, a Swedenborg scholar and expert on Helen Keller re-interpreted *Light in my Darkness.*
- **1998:** *Helen Keller, A Life*, by Dorothy Herrmann.
- **2000:** *To Love This Life: Quotations by Helen Keller*, AFB Press, American Foundation for the Blind.
- **2004:** *The Radical Lives of Helen Keller*, written by Professor Kim Nielsen takes a hard look at Helen's lifelong passion for social justice. Nielsen is a Helen Keller scholar.
- **2005:** *Helen Keller: Rebel Lives*, by John Davis. Like *the Radical Lives of Helen Keller* this small book is a vivid look at Helen's social activism.
- **2006:** *Blind Rage: Letters to Helen Keller* is a form of novel, written as a series of letters to Helen Keller after she had died. The author is Georgina Kleege, a Berkeley professor of English who is blind herself. This is a feisty, fun book written by a woman who became a Helen Keller scholar.
- **2009:** *Beyond the Miracle Worker: The Remarkable Life of Anne Sullivan Macy*, by Kim Nielsen.
- **2016:** "Helen Keller: A life with dogs; From scrappy Scotties to dignified Great Danes to a famous Akita."
- There is a YouTube channel dedicated to Helen Keller. This is a wonderful archive of old photos and film clips.
- There are many children's books written about Helen Keller, but I did not use them in this narrative.
- Alabama History Notebook: A collection of Alabama symbols, maps, and photographs for students; Alabama Department of Archives and History, 624 Washington Avenue, Montgomery, AL 36130; www.archives.alabama.gov.

Kish, Daniel with Jo Hook, *Echolocation and FlashSonar*; American Printing House for the Blind, 2016.

Kleege. Georgina,
- Home for the Summer, 1989.
- Sight Unseen, 1999.
- Blind Rage, 2006.
- More Than Meets the Eye, 2018.

Kurzweil, Ray,
- The Age of Intelligent Machines, 1992.
- The Age of Spiritual Machines When Computers Exceed Human Intelligence, 2000.
- The Singularity Is Near: When Humans Transcend Biology, 2006.
- How to Create a Mind? The Secret of Human Thought Revealed, 2013.

Lamphier, Peg A. and Welch, Rosanne, *Women in American History: A Social, Political, and Cultural Encyclopedia*, 2017.

Lash, Joseph, *Helen and Teacher, 1980*. This was the first in-depth biography of Helen Keller.

La Mettrie, Julien Offray de, *Man a Machine* (French: *L'homme Machine*), 1747.

Leiber, Justin, "Helen Keller as Cognitive Scientist," Philosophical Psychology, Volume 9, Issue 4, 1996.

Lusseyran, Jacques,
- Against the Pollution of the I: Selected Writings of Jacques Lusseyran, 2006.
- And There Was Light, 1963

Macy, John Albert
- The Story of My Life (1887–1901) and a supplementary account of her education, including passages from the reports and letters of her teacher Anne Sullivan, by John Macy, Helen Keller, and Anne Sullivan, 1903.
- Edgar Allan Poe, 1907.
- Child's Guide to Reading, 1909.
- A Guide to Reading for Young and Old, 1910.
- The Spirit of American Literature, 1912.
- Socialism in America, 1916
- Walter James Dodd: A Biographical Sketch, 1918.
- The Critical Game, 1922.
- Story of the World's Literature, 1925.
- Do You Know English Literature? A Book of Questions and Answers for Students and General Readers, 1930.

- American Writers on American Literature, 1931.
- About Women, 1932.

McDermott, Robert A., *The Essential Steiner: Basic Writings of Rudolf Steiner*, edited and introduced by Robert A. McDermott, 1984.

Menand, Louis, "Laura's World: What a deaf-blind girl taught the nineteenth century;" by Louis Menand in *The New Yorker Magazine*, June 25, 2001.

Nielsen, Kim, E.,
- The Radical Lives of Helen Keller, 2004.
- Helen Keller: Selected Writings, 2005.
- "Was Helen Keller Deaf? Blindness, Deafness, and Multiple Identities," Double Visions: Multidisciplinary Approaches to Women and Deafness, edited by Susan Burch and Brenda Brueggemann, 2006.
- "The Southern Ties of Helen Keller," Journal of Southern History, 2007.
- Beyond the Miracle Worker: The Remarkable Life of Anne Sullivan Macy, 2009.

Neumann, Erich, *The Origins and History of Consciousness*, by Erick Neumann, 1954.

O'Connor, M. R., *Wayfinding: The Science and Mystery of How Humans Navigate the World*, 2019.

Pike, Kenneth, *Language as Particle, Wave, and Field*, 1959.

Porter, Edna, *Double Blossoms: Helen Keller Anthology*, 1931.

Rajneesh, Bhagwan Shree (Osho),
- The Mustard Seed: A Living Explanation of Jesus from the Gospel According to Thomas, 1975.
- Philosophia Ultima, 1983.

Rose, Jonathan S., *Swedenborg's Garden of Theology: An Introduction to Emanuel Swedenborg's Published Theological Works*, 2010.

Saxe, John Godfrey, The poems of John Godfrey Saxe, 1872.

Shattuck, Roger,
- "Two Hearts that Beat as One," *New York Magazine* review of Joseph P Lash's book *The Story of Helen Keller and Anne Sullivan Macy*, June 30, 1980, with George V. Higgins.
- Restored Classic: *The Story of my Life*, edited by Roger Shattuck, with Dorothy Herrmann, 2003.

Sicherman, Barbara and Green, Carol Hurd, *Notable American Women: The Modern Period: A Biographical Dictionary*, 1980.

Sperry, Reverend Paul Andrew, "New Church History Fun Facts: Helen Keller Letter about Swedenborg." New Church history website: http://www.newchurchhistory.org/funfacts/index6ca3.html?p=534#more-534.

Steiner, Rudolf,
- *How to Know Higher Worlds*, by Rudolf Steiner, 1994.
- *Intuitive Thinking as a Spiritual Path: A Philosophy of Freedom*, by Rudolf Steiner, 1995.
- *Becoming the Archangel Michael's Companions: Rudolf Steiner's Challenge to the Younger Generation*, from the Collected works of Rudolf Steiner, 2007.

Stelson, Caren, *Sachiko: A Nagasaki Bomb Survivor's Story*, Lerner Publishing Group, 2016.

Strassman, Rick, *DMT: The Spirit Molecule: A Doctor's Revolutionary Research into the Biology of Near-Death and Mystical Experiences*, December 2000.

Sullivan, Anne, Teacher Whimsically Sketches Her Life and Philosophy, Calling Them 'Foolish Remarks of a Foolish Woman.' Available on the American Foundation for the Blind Helen Keller Digital Archives.

Sultan, Rosie, *Helen Keller in Love: A Novel*, 2012.

Swedenborg, Emanuel,
- Heaven and Hell, 1758.
- Arcana Cœlestia, 1756.

Takemae, Eiji, Ricketts Robert, and Swann, Sebastian, *Allied Occupation of Japan*, 2003.

Taylor, Eugene, Studia Swedenborgiana: "William James and Helen Keller;" Vol. 4, January 1981.

Tversky, Barbara, *Mind in Motion*, 2019.

Thomson, Jeanie, *The Myth of Water: Poems from the Life of Helen Keller*, 2016.

Versluis, Arthur, *Magic and Mysticism: An Introduction to Western Esotericism*, 2007.

Wehr, Gerhard, *Jung and Steiner: The Birth of a New Psychology*, 2002.

Wells, H. G., *New Worlds for Old*, Global Classics, 2019.

Werner, Marta L., "Helen Keller and Anne Sullivan: Writing Otherwise," an online article at: http://labos.ulg.ac.be/cipa/wp-content/uploads/sites/22/2015/07/86_werner.pdf

Wilson, Frank, *The Hand: How its Use Shapes the Brain*, 1988.

Winter, Bill, Helen Keller: A life with dogs; From scrappy Scotties to dignified Great Danes to a famous Akita, dogs always brought joy to Helen Keller, June 24, 2016. Available online at http://www.perkins. org/stories/helen-keller-a-life-with-dogs

Whitman, Walt, *Leaves of Grass*, 1855.

Woods, Katherine, *Helen Keller's Journal*, a book review from the New York Times, June 5, 1938.

Zajonc, Arthur, *Catching the Light: The Entwined History of Light and Mind*, 1993.

Zeldin, Theodore, *An Intimate History of Humanity*, 1994.

The American Foundation for the Blind and Perkins School for the Blind have extensive online archival material about Helen Keller (see below), which they continue to compile and clarify. I took advantage of both archives and was helped by librarians and staff at these two wonderful institutions.

American Foundation for the Blind Helen Keller Archives

(Copied from the AFB webpage)

The Helen Keller Archive at the American Foundation for the Blind (AFB) is the world's largest repository of materials about and by Helen Keller. Materials include correspondence, speeches, press clippings, scrapbooks, photographs, photograph albums, architectural drawings, audio recordings, audio-visual materials and artifacts.

The collection contains detailed biographical information about Helen Keller (1880–1968), as well as a fascinating record of over 80 years of social and political change worldwide. Keller was a feminist, a suffragist, a social activist, and a pacifist, as well as a prolific writer and published author.

Her impact reached far beyond the United States. She traveled to 39 countries as an advocate and global goodwill ambassador and met and corresponded with many of the leading figures of her time, including nine U.S. presidents, and prominent social activists, philanthropists, industrialists, writers, artists, and actors. The collection contains information on all these subjects and individuals as well as the countless ordinary men, women, and children who corresponded with her.

Thanks to the enormous generosity of the National Endowment for the Humanities, this digital archive is being made accessible to blind, deaf, deafblind, sighted, and hearing audiences alike. Please note that additional accessibility features are being constantly added.

This collection contains 58,733 items comprising 186,820 images.

Perkins School for the Blind Nella Braddy Henney Archives
(Copied from the Perkins webpage)

The Nella Braddy Henney Collection is comprised of correspondence, notes, photographs, articles, clippings, publications, and other materials related to Helen Keller, Anne Sullivan Macy, Polly Thomson, and Nella Braddy Henney. The correspondence spans the years of 1927 to 1969, and is to and from Helen Keller, Anne Sullivan Macy, Polly Thomson, and Nella Braddy Henney between themselves and others.

The notes, photographs, articles, clippings, publications and other materials relate to the lives of Helen Keller, Anne Sullivan Macy, Polly Thomson and Nella Braddy Henney, and are interspersed throughout the collection, as well as within their respective series.

The extensive correspondence collection contains letters, memos, and notes in relation to Braddy Henney's work for Helen Keller during Keller's lifetime, and on research for Braddy Henney's book, Anne Sullivan Macy: The story behind Helen Keller (1933). Keller's correspondence includes letters with others, such as Samuel Clemens (Mark Twain; copies), Perkins Directors Edward E. Allen and Gabriel Farrell, Charles F. F. Campbell, actress Katherine Cornell, and other notable people. These letters were forwarded to Nella Braddy Henney for use while working on her book.

Nella Braddy Henney's personal journal entries are included in this collection and supplement the correspondence. These journal entries span the years of 1938 and 1962.

The photograph collection includes portraits, publicity photographs with prominent individuals, materials related to film projects in Hollywood, advocacy for blinded veterans, many casual images from visits to Helen Keller's Arcan Ridge and Forest Hills homes, and trips to Martha's Vineyard with Eleanor Roosevelt. Many of the photographical items can be attributed to the work of Keith Henney.

The American Antiquarian Society in Worcester, Massachusetts also has retained materials about Helen Keller and Anne Sullivan. The Perkins School has collaborated with The American Antiquarian Society to digitally combine their materials.

Newspaper Articles

There are thousands of newspaper (media) reports about Helen Keller. I used a subscription to Newspapers.com, a genealogical resource, to track a few of these. The American Foundation for the Blind Helen Keller Digital Archives also contain an extensive list of newspaper links. I will list what I found below. I did not read all the references because there is considerable redundancy. If I did find a gem, I hand-typed what I found and included the quote in the book. I organized this section by publication date.

1887: "A Deaf-Mute Evolution: How a body may get on with only one sense." Published in *The Sun*, New York, New York, July 11, 1887 . . . a story about Laura Bridgman with comments about Helen Keller, age 7.

1888: "The Most Wonderful Child of the Age," published in *The Montgomery Advertiser* (Montgomery, Alabama) March 2, 1888. Observations of Job Williams while visiting Helen when she was learning to speak.

1888: "Helen Adams Keller; She is Blind, Deaf and Dumb and Rivals Laura Bridgeman," published in *The Burlington Weekly Free Press* (Burlington, Vermont), May 4, 1888.

1890: "A Blind, Deaf Mute Talks," published in *The Charlotte Democrat* (Charlotte, NC), June 6, 1890.

1891: "A Wonderful Child," published in the *Hartford Courant*, February 20, 1891.

1892: "A Modern Wonder: Helen Keller, The Phenomenal Blind and Deaf Mute," published in the *Lincoln Evening Call* (Lincoln, Nebraska), March 25, 1892.

1896: "Miss Helen Keller Admitted to Harvard," published in *The Kansas City Journal* (Kansas City, MO), October 25, 1896.

1900: "Helen Keller a Radcliffe Pupil: Blind, Deaf, and Dumb Girl Now Studying There," published in the *Asheville Citizen-Times* (Asheville, North Carolina), October 19, 1900. Original from the *New York Sun*.

1900: "Helen Keller begins attending Radcliffe College of Harvard at age 20." Published in the *Ashville, North Carolina Citizens-Times*, October 19, 1900.

1900: "Helen Keller Talks," published in *The Evening Star* (Washington, DC), December 17, 1900.

1902: "How Helen Keller Writes," published in *The Free Press* (Southern Pines, NC), March 14, 1902.

1903: "A Human Document: Helen Keller's Story of Her Life," published by *The Inter Ocean* (Chicago, Illinois), March 23, 1903.

1904: "Helen Keller, Most Wonderful of Girls, Graduates from College Next Week," published in The Evening World (New York, NY), June 25, 1904.

1904: "Wonders of the Fair "Seen" and Described by Miss Helen Keller," published in *The St. Louis Republic* (St. Louis, MO), October 23, 1904.

1912: "Helen Keller, Deaf-Blind Wonder Would Like to be Socialist Orator," published in *The Farmer and Mechanic* (Raleigh, NC), June 25, 1912.

1913: "Helen Keller's Glowing Speech: Opens Her Novel Lecture Tour at Tremont Temple," published in *The Boston Globe* (Boston, Massachusetts), March 23, 1913.

1913: "Thinks Drinking Is A Result of Poverty," published in *The South Bend News-Times* (South Bend, IN), December 22, 1913.

1914: "Helen Keller, Blind, Sees Great Light That Will Purify the World," published in *The Day Book* (Chicago, IL), March 18, 1914.

1915: "At Home with Helen Keller," published in *The Arizona Republican* (Phoenix, AZ), March 7, 1915.

1916: "Helen Keller Would Be I.W.W.'s Joan of Arc," published in *The*

New-York Tribune (New York, NY), January 16, 1916.

1916: "Wonderful Helen Keller Lectures in Greenwood," published in *The Commonwealth* (Greenwood, MS), March 24, 1916.

1916: "Did Helen Keller Really Hear Caruso?" published in *The Richmond Times-Dispatch* (Richmond, VA), May 14, 1916.

1916: "Helen Keller Gives Interview to Newspaperwoman," published in the Quad-City Times (Davenport, Iowa), January 12, 1916.

1920: "Launch New Organization to Protect Civil Rights," published in *The Richmond Times-Dispatch* (Richmond, VA), January 20, 1920.

1921: "Oppose All Injustice Helen Kellers Creed," published in *The Minneapolis Star* (Minneapolis, Minnesota), August 31, 1921. Speaking out after World war One:

1926: Into the Light, by Helen Keller: "More of Anne Sullivan." *Boston Daily Globe* (September 29, 1926).

1930: "Helen Keller, at Fifty, Looks Forward to Years of Further Good Deeds," published in the *Star-Gazette* (Elmira, New York), June 27, 1930. This article celebrates Helen's 50th birthday.

1932: "Helen Keller's Tutor Gets Degree." *New York Times* (February 16, 1932).

1933: "The Liberator of Helen Keller," by Wilson, P.A. *New York Times* (October 1, 1933).

1933: "Great Teacher, Great Pupil: How Anne Sullivan, Herself Almost Blind, Opened Up the World for Helen Keller," by Ross, M. *New York Herald Tribune.* (October 1, 1933).

1933: "The Other Self of Helen Keller: An Irish Immigrant's Daughter Who Taught a Blind Girl to *See*," by Copinger, Irene May, published in *The Baltimore Sun*, November 19, 1933.

1936: "Mrs. Macy is Dead," published in *The New York Times* on October 21, 1936.

1937: "U.S. Celebrates Helen Keller's *Tribute Year*: Period Until March 3 Marks the 50th Anniversary of Her Meeting with Teacher." Published in the *New York Herald Tribune* October 18, 1937.

1938: "Schools, Churches Honor Helen Keller." Published in *The Chicago Defender (National Edition)* March 12, 1938.

1938: "The Blind See: The Dumb Speak," published in *The Age* (Melbourne, Victoria, Australia), March 5, 1938.

1938: "The Beauty I have Seen," by Helen Keller, published in the *Weekly Magazine of The Sunday Star*, Washington, D.C. April 10, 1938.

1955: "Helen Keller In Her Life," by Cornell, K., published in *Newsday*

June 24, 1955.

1955: "Helen Keller, America's First Lady of Courage, Marks 75th Birthday," by Grover Brinkman, published in the *Palladium* (Richmond, Indiana), June 27, 1955.

1966: "Awards to Honor Helen Keller's Teacher." Published in *The Washington Post, Times Herald* March 16, 1966.

1968: The September 1968 issue of *The New Outlook for the Blind* was devoted to Helen Keller; it contains a biographical sketch by M. Robert Barnett.

1968: "Helen Keller Dies at Country Estate," published in *The Greenville News* (Greenville, South Carolina), June 2, 1968.

1980: "How Much of 'Helen Keller was Anne Sullivan." by Whitman, A. published in *Newsday* May 25, 1980.

1980: "How the Miracle Worked: Helen and Teacher," by Evans, W. K. E. published in *The Washington Post* June 15, 1980.

1987: "Making Pilgrimage to Helen Keller's Alabama Home," published in the *St. Louis Post-Dispatch* (St. Louis, Missouri), June 7, 1987.

2003: "How Helen Keller Learned to Write," by Cynthia Ozick, published in *The New Yorker Magazine*, June 16/23.

2004: "Helen Keller: Brief life of a woman who found her own way: 1880–1968," published in Harvard Magazine by Roger Shattuck. In the July/August edition.

Index

Author Bio

Doug Baldwin is a retired special education teacher from Michigan. He has a doctoral degree in Optometry and a master's degree in Blind Rehabilitation. He is also the founder of two non-profit agencies established to help children in special education, *The Special Needs Vision Clinic*, and *The Institute for Innovative Blind Navigation*. Dr. Baldwin is the author of four previous books about the evolution of human consciousness. His ideas are based on dual-process theory, the concept that evolution engineered duality into the anatomy and physiology of bilateral creatures. Dr. Baldwin worked as an Orientation and Mobility teacher for thirty years for the Saginaw Public School system in Michigan before retirement in 2010. He continues to write and is now working on a multi-volume set of biographies called *Knights for the Blind in the Battle against Darkness*.

∿

The artist who created the front and back covers for this book series, Terry LeBarr, enjoys drawing what she calls Personalized Typography Art. She created the typography design for the cover of *Helen Keller: A Timeline of Her Life*, and she did this image for my author pages. Digital publishing does not allow for color, so this is a black and white version of the original artwork. Here is Terry's explanation of my personalized typography:

The D
DOUG: You love bread, soups, and cheese. Music is also a big part of your soul, so I put your guitar and Bodhran next to your favorite foods.

You enjoy duality and write about this in your books, so I drew opposites like rain and sun, Tortoise and Hare, Yin and Yang. The Tibetan bell represents your interest in Eastern religious ideas, especially Buddhism. The entire D represents Winter, which you love (or why would you live in Michigan!) Each letter in your name represents a different season. At the base of the staff, part of the D, is a partial view of a woman's face. She is Scottish as is your ethnicity; she is showing you an eye by lowering her sunglasses. The eye and sunglasses symbolize your profession.

The O

As you move onto the O, you come across ants, which refer to your first book *Bugs, Blindness and the Pursuit of Happiness*. If you look behind the ants, you see a shovel and a plant coming up from the pile of dirt (I was told you love plants). Notice that the O is black and white (duality again). I mixed in green, representing new growth. The tulips and rain are symbolic of Spring. The tortoise (representing the evolution of consciousness) is creeping along while the Rabbit (representing technology) is still hanging out at the D.

The U

U is the heart of your name, representing Summer, sunshine, and water. The purple in the top of the U represents the loyalty you have towards the sight-impaired and special education. The dolphin is symbolic of wisdom; its playfulness reminds us to enjoy living in the moment with friends and family. The staff of the letter says *family*; family adventure has been instilled in your kids and grandkids. Next to the word family is a Luckenbooth, a Scottish symbol of romance. It has two hearts entwined and a crown above representing love and loyalty.

The G

At the base of the G, you see a suitcase and backpack, representing your love of travel and adventure. The images are meant to bring back memories of when you and Kathy traveled around the world as young hippies, and later, when you traveled with your kids. G depicts Fall and all the glorious colors that trigger poignant thoughts of days gone by. G holds a refreshing chill, meant to be deeply breathed in and savored. And there are clear night skies filled with stars. You will find the books you wrote at the base of the G. You will see the thoughts still hanging around them every time you notice them. Maddie [from *A Martyr for Mandelbrot*] is there, camera in hand. She is wearing her blond wig this time (she felt it was the best choice with the hat). Last, but not least is your cat Napoleon (Nappy), a treasured gift left by your daughter Anna when she went off on her own youthful adventures.

Other Books by Doug Baldwin
Bugs, Blindness, and the Pursuit of Happiness, 2016
Consciousness: A New Slant on an Old Conundrum, 2017
The Confusion Caused by Being Your Own Twin, 2018
A Martyr for Mandelbrot; Inside the Minds of God, 2019

Made in the USA
Monee, IL
15 October 2021